Introduction to Electric Generation Systems

AUTHORS

Dr. Lalit Chandra Saikia
Associate Professor
National Institute of Technology
Silchar, Assam

Dr. Nalin Behari Deb Choudhary
Professor
National Institute of Technology
Silchar, Assam

REVIEWER

Dr. Sandip Hazra
Assistant Professor/Lecturer
The New Horizons Institute of Technology,
Durgapur, West Bengal

KHANNA BOOK PUBLISHING CO. (P) Ltd.
4C/4344, Ansari Road, Darya Ganj,
New Delhi, India

All India Council for Technical Education
Nelson Mandela Marg, Vasant Kunj,
New Delhi, India

Dear Readers,

To prevent the piracy, this book is secured with HIGH SECURITY HOLOGRAM on the front title cover. In case you don't find the hologram on the front cover title, please write us to at contact@khannabooks.com or whatsapp us at +91-99109 09320 and avail special gift voucher for yourself.

Specimen of Hologram on front Cover title:

Moreover, there is a SPECIAL DISCOUNT COUPON for you with EVERY HOLOGRAM.

How to avail this SPECIAL DISCOUNT:

Step 1: Scratch the hologram
Step 2: Under the scratch area, your "coupon code" is available
Step 3: Logon to www.khannabooks.com
Step 4: Use your "coupon code" in the shopping cart and get your copy at a special discount
Step 5: Enjoy your reading!

ISBN: 978-93-5538-656-4
Book Code: DIP443EN

Introduction to Electric Generation Systems

by Dr. Lalit Chandra Saikia and
Dr. Nalin Behari Deb Choudhary

First Edition: 2025
Reprint: 2026

Originally Published by:
All India Council for Technical Education, Ministry of Education, GOI

Exclusively Published & Distributed by: **Khanna Book Publishing Co. (P) Ltd.**
4C/4344, Ansari Road, Daryaganj,
New Delhi (INDIA)

Visit us at: **www.khannabooks.com**
Write us at: **contact@khannabooks.com**

To view complete list of books,
Please scan the QR Code:

Printed in Bharat.

प्रो. टी. जी. सीताराम
अध्यक्ष
Prof. T. G. Sitharam
Chairman

अखिल भारतीय तकनीकी शिक्षा परिषद्
(भारत सरकार का एक सांविधिक निकाय)
(शिक्षा मंत्रालय, भारत सरकार)
नेल्सन मंडेला मार्ग, वसंत कुंज, नई दिल्ली–110070
दूरभाष : 011–26131498
ई–मेल : chairman@aicte-india.org

ALL INDIA COUNCIL FOR TECHNICAL EDUCATION
(A STATUTORY BODY OF THE GOVT. OF INDIA)
(Ministry of Education, Govt. of India)
Nelson Mandela Marg, Vasant Kunj, New Delhi-110070
Phone : 011-26131498
E-mail : chairman@aicte-india.org

FOREWORD

Engineers are the backbone of any modern society. They are the ones responsible for the marvels as well as the improved quality of life across the world. Engineers have driven humanity towards greater heights in a more evolved and unprecedented manner.

The All India Council for Technical Education (AICTE), have spared no efforts towards the strengthening of the technical education in the country. AICTE is always committed towards promoting quality Technical Education to make India a modern developed nation emphasizing on the overall welfare of mankind.

An array of initiatives has been taken by AICTE in last decade which have been accelerated now by the National Education Policy (NEP) 2020. The implementation of NEP under the visionary leadership of Hon'ble Prime Minister of India envisages the provision for education in regional languages to all, thereby ensuring that every graduate becomes competent enough and is in a position to contribute towards the national growth and development through innovation & entrepreneurship.

One of the spheres where AICTE had been relentlessly working since past couple of years is providing high quality original technical contents at Under Graduate & Diploma level prepared and translated by eminent educators in various Indian languages to its aspirants. For students pursuing 2nd year of their Engineering education, AICTE has identified 87 books, which shall be translated into 12 Indian languages - Hindi, Tamil, Gujarati, Odia, Bengali, Kannada, Urdu, Punjabi, Telugu, Marathi, Assamese & Malayalam. In addition to the English medium, books in different Indian Languages are going to support the students to understand the concepts in their respective mother tongue.

On behalf of AICTE, I express sincere gratitude to all distinguished authors, reviewers and translators from the renowned institutions of high repute for their admirable contribution in a record span of time.

AICTE is confident that these outcomes based original contents shall help aspirants to master the subject with comprehension and greater ease.

T.G. Sitharam

(Prof. T. G. Sitharam)

ACKNOWLEDGEMENT

The authors are grateful to the authorities of AICTE, particularly Prof. T. G. Sitharam, Chairman; Prof. M. P. Poonia, Vice-Chairman; Prof. Rajive Kumar, Member-Secretary and Dr Amit Kumar Srivastava, Director, Faculty Development Cell for their planning to publish the books on Introduction to Electric Generation Systems. We sincerely acknowledge the valuable contributions of the reviewer of the book, Dr. Sandeep Hazra, Assistant Professor, Dept. of Electrical Engineering (EE), New Horizons Institute of Technology, Gandhi More, Durgapur -713208, West Bengal for making it students' friendly and giving a better shape in an artistic manner. We also offer our sincere thanks to Ph.D. scholars Mr. Satish Kumar Ramoji, Mr. Biswanath Dekaraja, and Mr. Sanjeev Kumar Bhagat, Electrical Engineering Department, National Institute of Technology Silchar for their help in preparing some topics and figures for this book. At last, it is wise to thank Mrs. Krishna Dutta Saikia for her all-around support during the writing of this book.

This book is an outcome of various suggestions of AICTE members, experts, and authors who shared their opinion and thought to further develop engineering education in our country. Acknowledgments are due to the contributors and different workers in this field whose published books, review articles, papers, photographs, footnotes, references, and other valuable information enriched us at the time of writing the book. All-around

Dr. Lalit Chandra Saikia,

Dr. Nalin Behari Deb Choudhury

PREFACE

The book titled "Introduction to Electric Generation Systems" is an outcome of the rich experience of our teaching of power system-related basic courses in electrical engineering. The initiation of writing this book is to expose the fundamentals of electrical power generation systems to electrical engineering students. The basics of power plant economics and interconnected power system are also presented. Efforts have been taken to enable the students to get an insight into the subject.

Keeping in mind, the purpose of wide coverage as well as to provide essential supplementary information, we have included the topics recommended by AICTE, in a very systematic and orderly manner throughout the book. Efforts have been taken to explain the fundamental concepts of the subject in the simplest possible way.

During the process of preparation of the manuscript, we have considered the various standard textbooks, and accordingly, we have developed sections like critical questions, solved and supplementary problems, etc. While preparing the different sections emphasis has also been laid on definitions and principles of energy conversion and also on comprehensive synopsis of formulae for a quick revision of the basic principles. The book covers all types of medium and advanced-level problems and these have been presented in a very logical and systematic manner. The gradations of those problems have been tested over many years of teaching to a wide variety of students.

Apart from illustrations and examples as required, we have enriched the book with numerous solved problems in every unit for a proper understanding of the related topics. Except for unit 5, laboratory practicals as recommended by AICTE are included in the units.

In addition, besides some essential information for the users under the heading "Know More" we have clarified some essential basic information in the appendix and annexure section.

This book is concerned with the basics of electrical power generation using thermal plants, hydro plants, solar power plants, wind power plants, and biomass plants. All are grouped in separate units. The power plant economics, interconnected power system, and issues like blackouts and brownouts at national and international levels are discussed in the last unit.

We sincerely hope that the book will inspire electrical engineering students to learn and discuss the ideas behind electrical power generation from various sources and will surely contribute to the development of a solid foundation for the subject. We would be thankful for all beneficial comments and suggestions which will contribute to the improvement of future editions of the book. It gives us immense pleasure to place this book in the hands of the teachers and students. It was indeed a big pleasure to work on different aspects covered in the book.

Dr. Lalit Chandra Saikia,
Dr. Nalin Behari Deb Choudhury

OUTCOME BASED EDUCATION

For the implementation of an outcome-based education the first requirement is to develop an outcome based curriculum and incorporate an outcome based assessment in the education system. By going through outcome-based assessments, evaluators will be able to evaluate whether the students have achieved the outlined standard, specific and measurable outcomes. With the proper incorporation of outcome based education there will be a definite commitment to achieve a minimum standard for all learners without giving up at any level. At the end of the programme running with the aid of outcome-based education, a student will be able to arrive at the following outcomes:

Programme Outcomes (POs) are statements that describe what students are expected to know and be able to do upon graduating from the program. These relate to the skills, knowledge, analytical ability attitude and behaviour that students acquire through the program. The POs essentially indicate what the students can do from subject-wise knowledge acquired by them during the program. As such, POs define the professional profile of an engineering diploma graduate.

National Board of Accreditation (NBA) has defined the following seven POs for an Engineering diploma graduate:

PO1. Basic and Discipline specific knowledge: Apply knowledge of basic mathematics, science and engineering fundamentals and engineering specialization to solve the engineering problems.

PO2. Problem analysis: Identify and analyses well-defined engineering problems using codified standard methods.

PO3. Design/ development of solutions: Design solutions for well-defined technical problems and assist with the design of systems components or processes to meet specified needs.

PO4. Engineering Tools, Experimentation and Testing: Apply modern engineering tools and appropriate technique to conduct standard tests and measurements.

PO5. Engineering practices for society, sustainability and environment: Apply appropriate technology in context of society, sustainability, environment and ethical practices.

PO6. Project Management: Use engineering management principles individually, as a team member or a leader to manage projects and effectively communicate about well-defined engineering activities.

PO7. Life-long learning: Ability to analyse individual needs and engage in updating in the context of technological changes.

COURSE OUTCOMES (CO)

By the end of the course, the students will be able to:

CO-1: Identify the parts of all the power plants.

CO-2: Explain the working of various power plants and combine operation of power plants

CO-3: Classify power plants and their components.

CO-4: Illustrate various terms and faults related to power plants and the economics of power generation

CO-5: Analyse various problems associated with electrical power generation and power plant economics.

Course Outcomes	EXPECTED MAPPING WITH PROGRAMME OUTCOMES (1- Weak Correlation; 2- Medium correlation; 3- Strong Correlation)											
	PO-1	PO-2	PO-3	PO-4	PO-5	PO-6	PO-7	PO-8	PO-9	PO-10	PO-11	PO-12
CO-1	3	1	3	3	-	-	-	-	-	-	-	-
CO-2	3	3	3	3	-	-	-	-	-	-	-	-
CO-3	3	1	3	1	-	-	-	-	-	-	-	-
CO-4	3	2	3	1	1	-	-	-	-	-	-	-
CO-5	3	3	2	3	1	-	-	-	-	-	-	-

GUIDELINES FOR TEACHERS

To implement Outcome Based Education (OBE) knowledge level and skill set of the students should be enhanced. Teachers should take a major responsibility for the proper implementation of OBE. Some of the responsibilities (not limited to) for the teachers in OBE system may be as follows:

- Within reasonable constraint, they should manoeuvre time to the best advantage of all students.
- They should assess the students only upon certain defined criterion without considering any other potential ineligibility to discriminate them.
- They should try to grow the learning abilities of the students to a certain level before they leave the institute.
- They should try to ensure that all the students are equipped with the quality knowledge as well as competence after they finish their education.
- They should always encourage the students to develop their ultimate performance capabilities.
- They should facilitate and encourage group work and team work to consolidate newer approach.
- They should follow Blooms taxonomy in every part of the assessment.

Bloom's Taxonomy

Level	Teacher should Check	Student should be able to	Possible Mode of Assessment
Creating	Students ability to create	Design or Create	Mini project
Evaluating	Students ability to Justify	Argue or Defend	Assignment
Analysing	Students ability to distinguish	Differentiate or Distinguish	Project/Lab Methodology
Applying	Students ability to use information	Operate or Demonstrate	Technical Presentation/ Demonstration
Understanding	Students ability to explain the ideas	Explain or Classify	Presentation/Seminar
Remembering	Students ability to recall (or remember)	Define or Recall	Quiz

GUIDELINES FOR STUDENTS

Students should take equal responsibility for implementing the Outcome Based Education (OBE). Some of the responsibilities (not limited to) for the students in OBE system are as follows:

- Students should be well aware of each Unit Outcome (UO) before the start of a unit in each and every course.
- Students should be well aware of each Course Outcome (CO) before the start of the course.
- Students should be well aware of each Program Outcome (PO) before the start of the program.
- Students should think critically and reasonably with proper reflection and action.
- Learning of the students should be connected and integrated with practical and real life consequences.
- Students should be well aware of their competency at every level of OBE.

ABBREVIATIONS AND SYMBOLS

List of Abbreviations

General Terms			
Abbreviations	**Full form**	**Abbreviations**	**Full form**
RCC	Reinforced concrete cement	DC	Direct current
MKS	Meter kilogram second	W	Watt
C.H.U	Centigrade heat unit	kWh	Kilowatt hour
kWp	Kilowatt peak	TI	Turbulence index
RSC	Rotor side converter	Fig	Figure
B.Th.U	British thermal unit	kV	Kilovolt
kVA	Kilo volt ampere	MVA	Mega volt ampere
VAWT	Vertical-axis wind turbines	p.f	Power factor
WPP	Wind turbine power plant	AC	Alternating current
BWR	Boiling water reactor	UK	United kingdom
MeV	Million electron volts	V	Volt
SCIG	Squirrel-cage induction generator	PO	Programme outcome
WRSG	Wound rotor synchronous generator	WPD	Wind power density
		RPM	Revolution per minute
WPD	Wind power density	TSR	Tip speed ratio
MD	peak load or maximum demand	PV	photovoltaic
SAFE	Solar automated feature extraction	IG	Induction motor
		IM	Induction motor
DFIG	Doubly fed induction generator	PMSG	Permanent magnet synchronous generator
SG	Synchronous generator		
PMSG	Permanent magnet synchronous generators	MW	Megawatt
		CO	Course outcome
HAWT	Horizontal-axis wind turbines	kcal	Kilo calorie
LWT	Large wind turbine	LC	load curve
SWT	Small wind turbine	LF	load factor
PWR	Pressurized water reactor		
LDC	load duration curve		
Cal	Calorie		

List of Units and Symbols

Symbols	Description	Symbols	Description
m	Meter	kg	kilogram
e	Efficiency	%	Percentage
D°	Degree centigrade	λ	decay constant/Tip speed ratio
σ	Solidity	ρ	The air density factor
Pw	wind power	N_s	Synchronous speed
Cp	Power coefficient	s	slip
f	frequency	R_b	Beam radiation
R_d	Diffuse radiation	R_r	Reflected radiation from ground and surroundings

LIST OF FIGURES

LIST OF TABLES

CONTENTS

1 Thermal Power Plants: Coal, Gas/ Diesel, and Nuclear-based

UNIT SPECIFICS

Through this unit we have discussed the following aspects:

- Introduction to thermal power plants;
- A brief introduction to parts of coal-based power plant;
- Diesel-based power plant and its components;
- Gas turbine power plants and their components;
- Nuclear power physics - Fusion and fission;
- Nuclear power plants- descriptions and types;
- Practical experiments on coal-based, diesel-based, gas turbine, and nuclear power plants.

The concept of thermal power generation and its advantages and disadvantages over others and practical applications of the topics are discussed for generating further curiosity and creativity as well as improving problem-solving capacity with some numerical problems.

Besides giving a large number of multiple-choice questions as well as questions of short and long answer types marked in two categories following lower and higher order of Bloom's taxonomy, assignments through several numerical problems, a list of references, and suggested readings are given in the unit so that one can go through them for practice.

Some practical experiments related to the courses covered in Unit-1 are also appended at the end of this unit to make the students aware of the hands-on on these topics. For the thermal and nuclear power plant, some specific videos on different parts of the power plant and some videos on routine maintenance are added.

After the related practical on the topic, based on the content, there is a "Know More" section appended. This section has been designed to supplement additional information and higher learning skills on the topic.

RATIONALE

This fundamental unit on thermal power generation helps students to get a primary idea about the conversion of thermal energy to electrical energy and different types of power plants. Thermal power plants are mainly coal-based, gas-based, nuclear, and diesel plants. Coal-based and gas-based plants use turbines and different types of turbines are also discussed. The physics behind nuclear power generation and the use of various types of nuclear reactors are also discussed at length to develop the basic idea about power plants. Furthermore, safe practice and use of thermal power plants in the modern day and its pros and cons also give up-to-date knowledge on the topic.

Some related problems are pointed out after each section with their solutions which can help further for getting a clear idea of the concern topics on thermal power generation. Conversion of energy from one form to another and its relationship will certainly help students with numerical problem-solving.

As a student in the field of electrical engineering, this unit on thermal power generation helps students to grasp the basic knowledge of various types of energy generation.

PRE-REQUISITES

Fundamentals of Electrical & Electronics Engineering (ES104)

UNIT OUTCOMES

After completion of Unit-1 students will be able to:

U1-O1: Describe the working of thermal power plants and their components

U1-O2: Explain the nuclear physics and nuclear power generation

U1-O3: Explain the working principle of working various types of boilers

U1-O4: Realize the importance of safe practices in power generation

U1-O5: Identify the routine maintenance parts of various thermal plants

Unit-1 Outcome	EXPECTED MAPPING WITH COURSE OUTCOMES (1 - Weak Correlation; 2 - Medium Correlation; 3 - Strong Correlation)				
	CO-1	CO-2	CO-3	CO-4	CO-5
U1-O1	3	3	3	1	2
U1-O2	3	3	2	2	2
U1-O3	3	2	2	1	-
U1-O4	3	2	-	2	-
U1-O5	3	2	-	-	-

1.1 INTRODUCTION

Electrical energy is the superior form of energy. It is because of its cleanliness, cheapness, flexibility, efficient transmission, and easy control. This form of energy is obtained from natural sources like the kinetic energy of wind, solar energy, pressure head of water, the chemical energy of fuel, and atomic. There are mainly two methods of power generation. They are

(a) Conventional.

(b) Non-conventional.

Prime movers are used in the conventional method. On the other hand, no prime movers are used in the non-conventional method. The prime mover converts natural sources into mechanical energy. An electrical machine called a generator converts mechanical energy into electrical energy. Electrical energy is generated in power plants. The power plant includes energy conversion equipment such as a prime mover, generator, transformer, and related control gears.

1.2 CLASSIFICATION OF THERMAL PLANTS

There are two ways of classifying thermal plants. They are based on the fuel and prime mover used in the plant.

As per fuel used, they are classified as

(a) Fossil fuel-based thermal power plants: This type of plant uses either coal or natural gas or liquid fossil fuel (Diesel) as fuel to produce steam. A prime mover called a steam turbine is used to convert steam energy into mechanical energy.

(b) Nuclear power plant: This type of power plant uses nuclear material as fuel. The heat is produced due to nuclear fission. The fission takes place in the reactor. The heat is utilized to produce steam to run the steam turbines.

(c) Renewable energy plants or Biomass fueled power plants: This type of plant uses waste material as fuel to produce heat. The heat is utilized for the production of electrical energy.

As per the Prime mover used

(a) Steam turbine power station or steam power plant: This type of power station uses a steam turbine as the prime mover

(b) Gas turbine-based power plant: This plant uses a gas turbine.

(c) Combined cycle power plant: In this type of plant both gas and steam turbines are used.

(d) Diesel power plant: In this plant diesel engine is the prime mover.

Various thermal plants such as Coal - based, Gas-based, Diesel based, and Nuclear based will be discussed in this unit.

1.3 COAL-BASED THERMAL POWER PLANT

1.3.1 Introduction

The generating station or power plant that converts heat energy obtained by burning coal into electrical energy is called a Coal - based (or coal-fired) thermal plant. The plant operates on the Rankine cycle. The water is converted into steam in the steam generating plant. The boiler is the heart of the steam generating plant. The steam is expanded in the turbine and runs it. As a result, mechanical energy is developed at the shaft of the turbine. The exhaust steam is sent to the condenser. Finally, after condensation, it is fed into the boiler again.

1.3.2 Fuel and Its Properties

Coal: Coal is a solid fuel. It is used in Coal - based power plants. Coal is composed of elements like are carbon, hydrogen, introgen, sulfur, moisture, and ash. Followings are the properties of coal.

(a) Energy content or heating value.

(b) Sulphur contents.

(c) Burning Characteristics.

(d) Grindability.

(e) Weatherability.

(f) Ash softening temperature.

Good coal should have:

(a) Low ash content and high calorific value.
(b) Small percentage of Sulphur.
(c) Good burning characteristics.
(d) High grindability index.
(e) High weatherability.

1.3.3 Working of A Typical Coal-Based Thermal Plant

Fig.1.1 shows a simplified schematic of a coal-based thermal plant. The working of the thermal plant can be explained by dividing the whole plant into four circuits as follows.

(a) Coal and ash circuit
(b) Air and gas circuit
(c) Feed water and steam circuit
(d) Cooling water circuit
(e) Electrical circuit

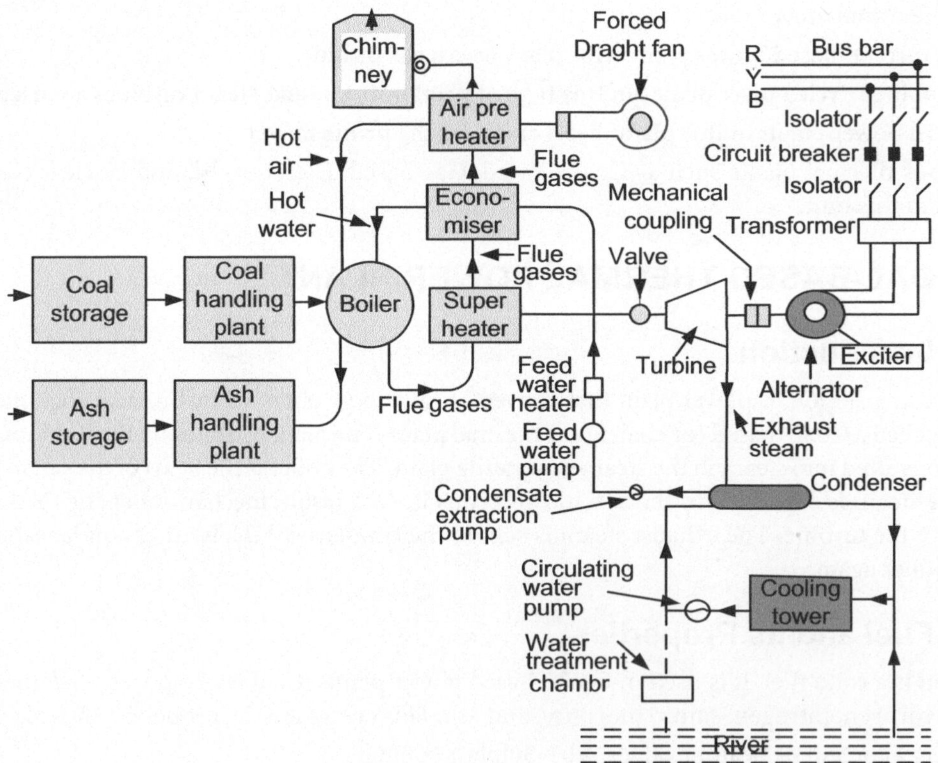

Fig.1.1 A schematic of Coal - based thermal plant

(a) **Fuel and ash circuit:** The fuel used in Coal - based thermal plants is coal. The coal is carried to the plant and stored in a coal storage plant. The stored coal in the storage plant is transferred to a plant called the coal handling plant. In this plant, the coal is crushed into small pieces for easy burning. The crushed coal is burnt in the boiler and heat is produced. When coal is completely burnt ash is produced. The ash is removed from the boiler and shifted to the ash handling plant and finally, it is stored in the ash storage for disposal.

(b) **Air and Gas circuit:** The boiler has a combustion chamber where crushed coal is burnt. The atmospheric air is supplied to this chamber with help of a forced draught fan. Before entering the boiler, the air is heated in the air preheater. The air preheater utilizes the heat of flue gas leaving the boiler. The flue gas then passes through the superheater. After that, it goes through the economizer and air preheater. Finally, the flue gases are exhausted into the atmosphere via a chimney. The air and gas circuit is shown in Fig. 1.2

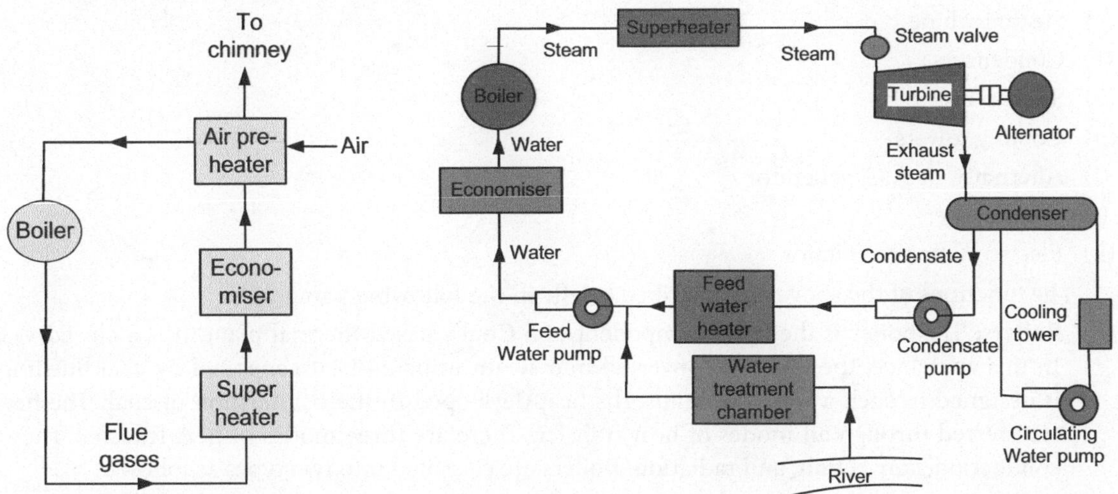

Fig. 1.2: Air and gas circuit

Fig. 1.3: Feed water, steam flow, and cooling water circuit

(c) **Feed water and steam circuit:** The steam is expanded in the turbine and exhausted to the condenser through the lowest pressure extraction point of the turbine. After condensation in the condenser, the same is fed to the boiler again. Before entering the boiler, the water is passed through the feed water heater and economizer. The economizer uses the heat from flue gases to heat the water feeding to the boiler. A small percentage (about 1%) of water and steam passes through different components lost. Thus, water is added to the feed water system as make-up water. This is done by the feed water pump. In the boiler, the water is heated by burning coal to produce steam. The steam is then passed to the turbine via the superheater and steam valve. The circuit is shown in Fig.1.3.

(d) **Cooling water circuit:** The heart of the cooling system is the condenser. It condenses the exhaust steam from the turbine. The condenser maintains a low pressure at the exhaust. This permits the expansion of steam in the turbine. This improves the efficiency of the thermal plant. After condensation, the water is circulated via the feed water pump and the economizer to the plant. A condenser requires a huge amount of water to condensate the steam. The required water for cooling water is taken from a nearby river or lake. A large source of water may not be available near a thermal plant. In this situation, most of the plants use a cooling water system. A cooling pond or cooling tower is used in this cooling system. In the cooling tower or pond, the warm water losses its heat to the atmosphere and are reused again. The circuit is shown in Fig. 1.3

(e) **Electrical circuit:** The steam turbine is coupled mechanically with the alternator. The alternator converts mechanical energy to electrical energy. The electrical output of the alternator is stepped up with the help of a transformer. The electrical bus bar is supplied from the secondary of the transformer via the circuit breaker and isolating switches.

1.3.4 The Constituents of a Thermal Plant

The followings are the main and auxiliary equipment in a thermal plant.

(a) Boilers
(b) Economizers
(c) Air preheaters
(d) Superheater and reheater
(e) Steam turbine
(f) Condensers
(g) Spray pond
(h) Cooling towers
(i) Alternator or A.C. generator
(j) Transformer
(k) Electro static precipitator

The functions of the above are described briefly in the following paragraphs.

(a) **Boilers:** The boiler is the main component of a Coal - based thermal plant. It is a closed vessel. In this appliance, the water is converted into steam utilizing heat generated by coal burning. It is designed in such a way that it absorbs heat developed in the combustion of coal. The heat is transferred through all modes of heat transfer. There are three modes of heat transfer. They are conduction, convection, and radiation. Boilers are classified into two types as follows.

1. Fire tube   2. Water tube

Fire tube boiler: In this type, the products from the combustion of coal pass through the tubes. The tubes are surrounded by water. The tubes may be placed horizontally or vertically. If the tubes are vertical the boiler is called a vertical tube boiler and if the tubes are horizontal, the boiler is called a horizontal tube boiler. The tube may be internally fed or externally fed. The pictures of fire tube boilers are shown in Fig. 1.4 (a) and Fig. 1.4(b)

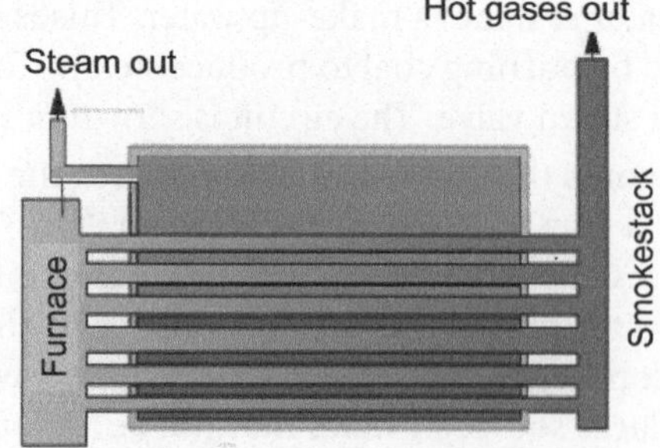

Fig. 1.4 (a): Horizontal type fire tube boiler

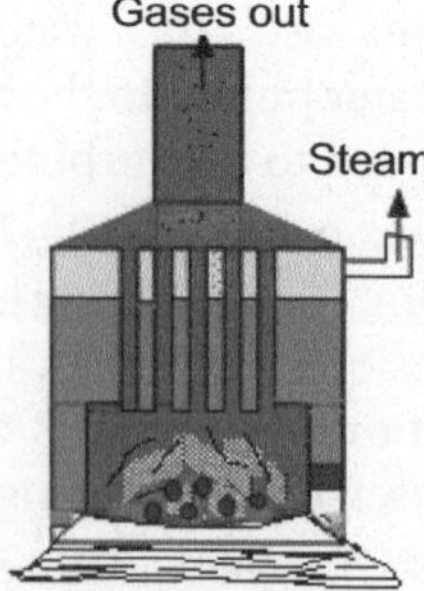

Fig. 1.4 (b): Vertical type fire tube boiler

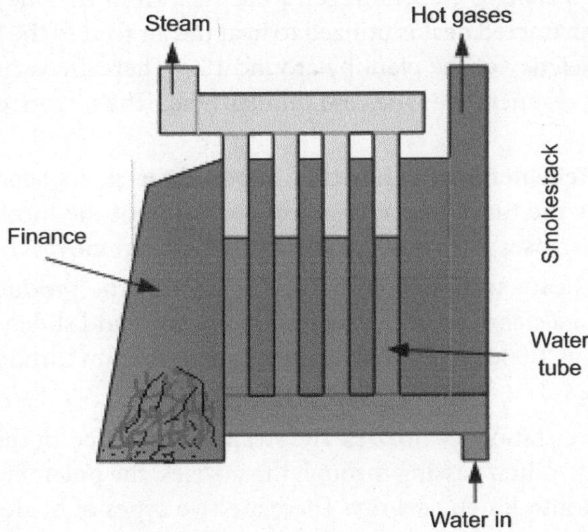

Fig. 1.5: Water tube boiler

Water tube boiler: In this type of boiler, water circulates inside the tubes and hot gases are outside the tubes. The tubes are connected to a water channel. The water tube boilers are of three types, they are vertical type, horizontal type, and inclined type. The water is circulated through the tube via a water channel by natural or forced circulation. Fig. 1.5 shows a vertical-type water tube boiler.

(b) Economizers: The flue gases carry heat energy. A part of this heat is extracted by the economizer. The economizer transfers the heat to the water feeding the turbine. In an economizer, there is a large number of tubes and two headers. The tubes are placed between the headers. The diameter of the tubes is small with the thickness being thin. The water enters through one header and leaves through another header. A picture of an economizer is shown in Fig. 1.6

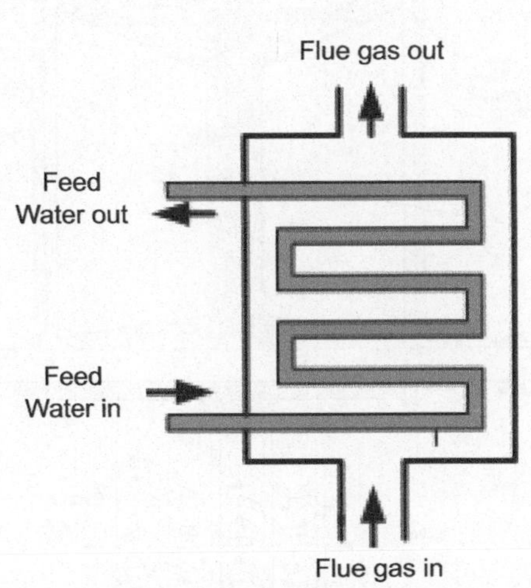

Fig. 1.6: Economiser

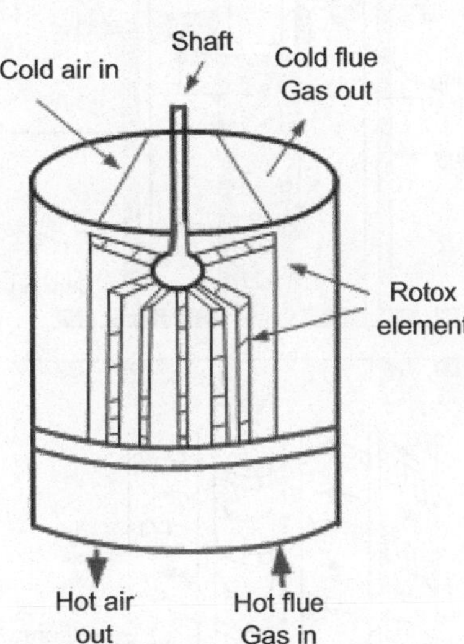

Fig. 1.7: Air preheater

(c) **Air-Preheater:** After leaving the economizer, some heat from the flue gases is extracted by using an air preheater. The extracted heat is utilized to heat the air feed to the boiler for combustion. This process raises the efficiency of the plant by around 1%. There are various types of air preheaters. Examples: Plate type, regenerative type, and tubular type. The picture of an air preheater is shown in Fig. 1.7

(d) **Superheaters and Reheaters:** The function superheater is to superheat steam. The use of superheated steam by the turbine results in less corrosion of the turbine blades. Also, the use of superheated steam increases the overall efficiency. Reheater removes the moisture from the steam.

(e) **Steam turbine:** The steam turbine converts the energy of the produced steam by the boiler to mechanical energy. In a steam turbine, there are no pistons and slide valves. A steam turbine can be built in large sizes as 1,000 MW. There are two types of steam turbines. They are

1. Impulse turbine
2. Reaction turbine

Impulse turbines have stationary nozzles The steam is expanded in the nozzles. Expanded steam acquired high velocity. When passing through the nozzles, the potential energy of the steam under pressure is converted into kinetic energy. There are two types of blades. Some are stationary and some are moving.

The reaction turbine is nozzle-less. There are two types of blades. Some are stationary and some are moving. A partial drop of pressure is used to allow the steam into the moving blades. Figs.1.8 and Fig.1.9 show impulse and reaction turbines respectively.

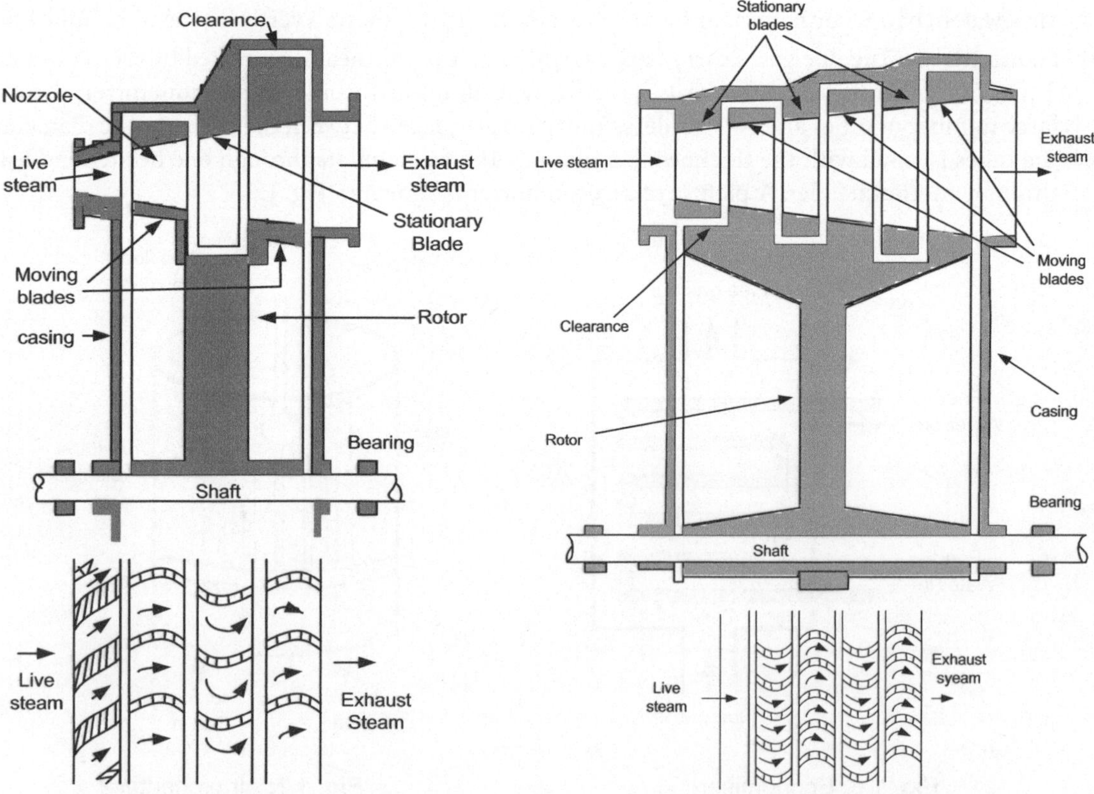

Fig. 1.8: Impulse turbine

Fig. 1.9: Reaction turbine

(f) **Condensers:** This device condenses the exhaust steam. It has two purposes.

1. It creates low pressure at the exhaust of the turbine. Hence, the condenser allows the expansion of steam in the turbine.
2. The condensate steam can be used as feed water to the boiler.

Thus, there is a considerable saving in water. It also removes the air and non-condensable gases from the steam.

(g) **Spray Ponds:** It consists of a tank. In this tank, the water is cooled and distributed by pipes. The water is sprayed through nozzles. Water is sprayed over the pond and has a considerable surface of contact

(h) **Cooling Towers:** The quantity of cooling water requirement is high in thermal plants. Hence, a source of water is required for a continuous water supply. The river or lake situated nearby is a good source. If such a facility is not available cooling towers are the alternative source. Generally, cooling towers are available in each plant. Cooling towers cool the warm water discharged from the condenser and the cooled water is fed to the condenser. In a cooling tower, water is divided into smaller quantities (drops). These water drops fail from a height of 8 to 10 meters to the bottom of the cooling tower. The height of the cooling tower and its water handling capacity is suitably designed for particular cases. The splitting of water into small droplets, and the large evaporating surface help to cool water very quickly. Water from the cooling tower is pumped to the condenser. The cycle is repeated. There are two types of cooling towers. They are wet type add dry type. Fig.1.10 and Fig.1.11 show the schematic diagram of the same.

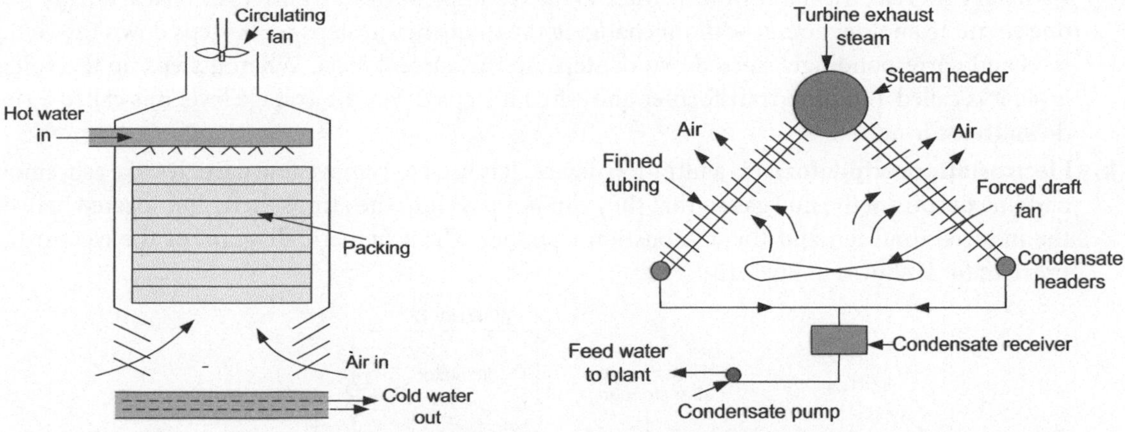

Fig.1.10: Schematic of a wet cooling tower

Fig.1.11: Schematic of a dry cooling tower

(i) **Alternator or A.C. generator or synchronous generator:** The alternator is an A.C. electrical machine. It is also called a synchronous generator. It converts mechanical energy into electrical energy. It has two parts called a stator and a rotor. The stator is stationary and it comprises of armature core and armature winding. The armature winding is a three-phase winding and it is connected either in the star or in the delta. The rotor has field poles and field winding. The field winding is excited with D.C to create magnetic poles. The shaft of the alternator is mechanically coupled with the shaft of the turbine. When the turbine rotates, the rotor of the alternator also rotates, and the conductor of the armature winding links with changing magnetic flux. Thus, as per Faraday's law of electromagnetic induction e.m.f is induced in the armature winding. The schematic diagram of an alternator is shown in Fig.1.12 (a) and Fig.1.12 (b).

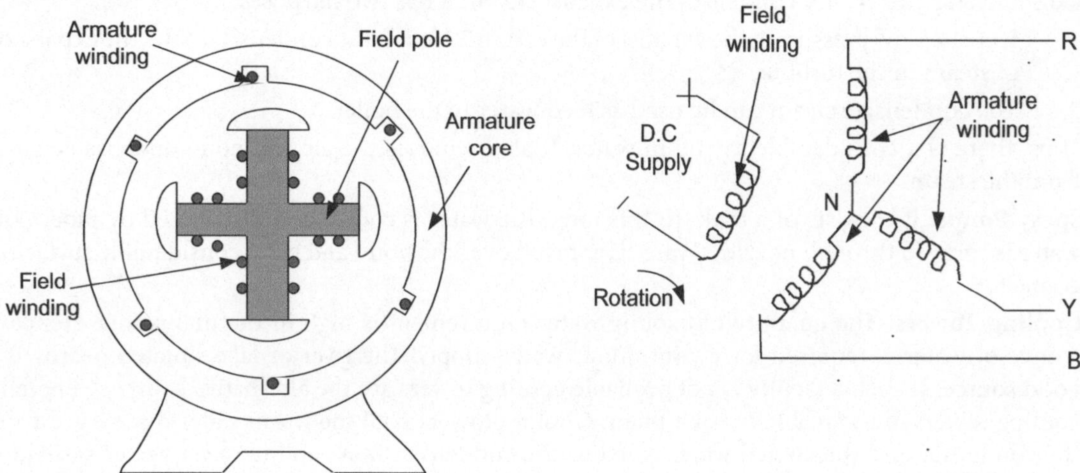

Fig.1.12 (a): Cross-sectional view of the alternator

Fig.1.12 (b): Alternator showing field and armature winding

(j) **Transformer:** The generated electrical power is transmitted to the load centre via a transmission system. The voltage level at the generator terminal is generally low and it is transformed into transmission level voltage (high voltage) using a step-up transformer. The transformer is a stationary A.C electrical machine i.e there are no rotating parts. It transfers electrical energy from one circuit to another circuit without changing the frequency. It steps up or steps down the voltage level and correspondingly steps down or steps up the current level. When it steps up the voltage level, it is called a step-up transformer and when it steps down the voltage level it is called a step-down transformer.

(k) **Electrostatic precipitator:** It is a filtration device. It is used to remove fine particles like ash, smoke, and fine dust from the flue gas so that they can not pass into the atmosphere. It is located between the induced draft fan and the combustion chamber. The schematic diagram of the electrostatic precipitator is shown in Fig.1.13

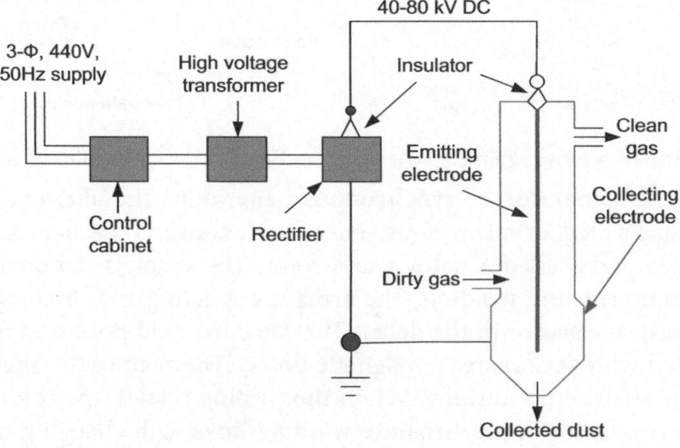

Fig.1.13: Schematic of Electrostatic precipitator

1.3.5 The Layout of Coal - Based Power Plant

The site layout should be optimum so that it leads to the minimum overall cost, easy operation, and good appearance. Fig.1.14 shows a simple layout of a Coal - based thermal power plant. This diagram is not drawn for a specific plant capacity. While planning for the construction of a Coal - based power plant, the following points must be taken care of.

1. The main connections between different items like circulating water systems, main steam and pipe feeding, coal conveyors, flue gas circuit components, and electrical connections.
2. Arrangement of turbine and generator.
3. The placement of the boiler should be such that the water treatment plant is nearer to it.
4. Clearance must be maintained so that maintenance is easy.
5. Adequate transportation facility to the site.
6. Cooling towers may be grouped. Usually, one or two.
7. Water treatment plant may be compact.
8. A Sufficient area of land is required. The land must be optimally utilized for appliances, offices, and workshops.
9. Provisions for future scope for expansion of the plant must be kept.

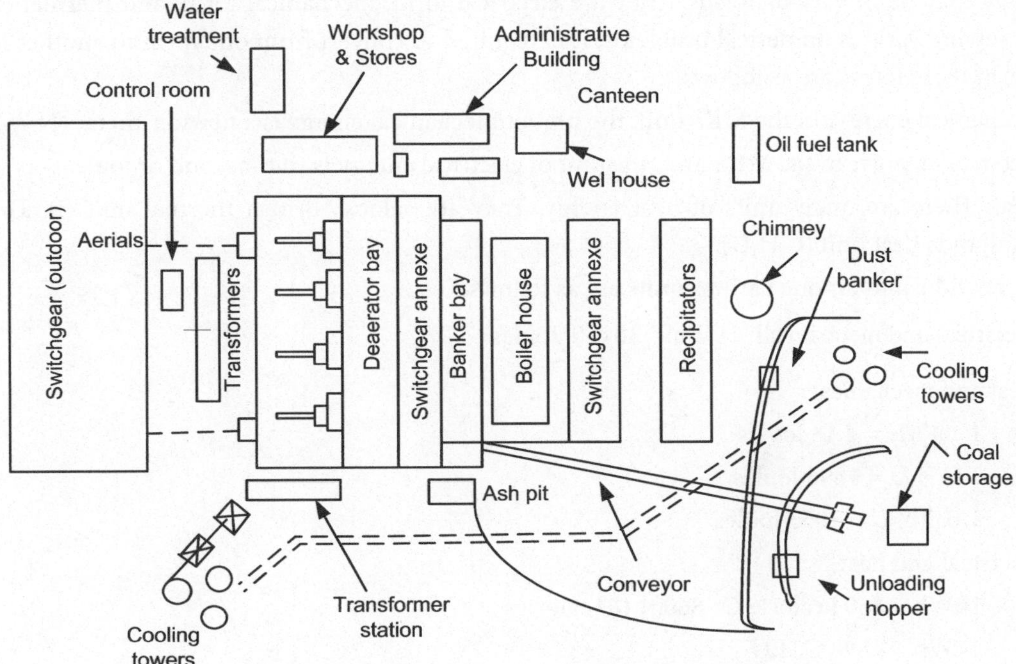

Fig.1.14 The layout of Coal - based thermal plant

1.3.6 Safe Practices of Coal-Based Thermal Plants

The followings are the safe practices of coal-based thermal plants.

1. Dust: The dust generated must be less as possible since it may create health hazards.

2. Air emission: The diesel plant emits several gases. The emission of these gases must be controlled since they may create health hazards. In this case, care must be taken in the selection of coal. The coal should have a high heat content as well as low ash and sulfur content
3. Heat: The boilers and pipelines carrying steam should be insulated to prevent heat loss and maintain safe working conditions.
4. Noise: Noise generated by the machinery and auxiliaries must be at a safe level.
5. Vibration: It is generated by tools and machinery and should be at a safe level.
6. Radiations: Radiated hazards particularly from fly ash should be minimum.
7. Care must be taken for electrical hazards like an electrical shock, or burns from energized equipment.
8. Fire and exposure: Necessary firefighting measures must be provided.
9. Chemical hazards: Necessary precautions must be provided in the plant for chemical hazards generated in the plant.

1.3.7 Units of Energy

The energy may be in various forms. They are electrical form, mechanical form, and thermal (heat) form. In solving various numerical problems, it is required to convert from one form to another form. The units of these forms are as follows.

1. Mechanical energy: In the MKS unit, the unit of mechanical energy is a newton-meter (N-m).
2. Electrical energy: In the MKS unit, the unit of electrical energy is watt-second or joule.
3. Heat: There are many units of heat energy. They are calorie, British thermal unit (B. Th. U), centigrade heat unit (C.H.U).

The relationships among various units are as follows.

1. Electrical and mechanical: $1\text{kWh} = 36\text{x}10^5\text{Joules}$
2. Heat and mechanical
    - 1 calorie = 4.18 Joules
    - 1 C.H.U = 1896 Joules
    - 1 B. Th. U = 1053 Joules
3. Electrical and heat
    - 1kWh = 860 kcalorie Or 860×10^3 calories
    - 1kWh = 1898 C.H.U
    - 1kWh = 3418 B. Th. U =$3\,6 \times 10^5$ Joule

1.3.8 Efficiency of Thermal Power Plant

The efficiency of a plant, equipment, etc. is the ratio of output to input. In the case of electrical power generation, the input and output may be power or energy. The efficiency is generally denoted by η (eta).

1.3.8.1 Boiler Efficiency

The ratio between boiler output the boiler input is called boiler efficiency. Generally, both the input and output of the boiler are expressed in heat units of energy. The input heat energy is the heat energy obtained from burning coal. The boiler efficiency is expressed as equation (1.1).

$$\eta_{Boiler} = \frac{\text{Boiler output (equivalent)}}{\text{Boiler input (heat equivalent)}} \tag{1.1}$$

1.3.8.2 Turbine Efficiency

The ratio between turbine output and turbine input is called turbine efficiency. Generally, the input and output of the turbine are expressed in the heat units of energy. Input to the turbine is the steam energy (boiler output) and output is the mechanical energy obtained at the shaft. The turbine efficiency is expressed as equation (1.2).

$$\eta_{Turbine} = \frac{\text{Mechanical power transmitted to the shaft (heat equivalent)}}{\text{Heat equivalent of turbine input or boiler output}} \tag{1.2}$$

1.3.8.3 Thermal Efficiency

The ratio between turbine output and boiler input is called thermal efficiency. Generally, input to the boiler and output of the turbine is expressed in the heating unit of energy. The input heat energy to the boiler is the heat energy obtained from burning coal. Turbine output is the mechanical energy transmitted to the shaft. Thermal efficiency (η Thermal) is also called mechanical efficiency (η Mechanical). The thermal efficiency is given by equation (1.3) or (1.4).

$$\eta_{Thermal} \; Or \; \eta_{Mechanical} = \frac{\text{Mechanical power transmitted to the shaft of tubine (heat equivalent)}}{\text{Boiler input (heat euivalent)}} \tag{1.3}$$

$$or \quad \eta_{Thermal} = \eta_{Boiler} \text{ x } \eta_{Turbine} \tag{1.4}$$

1.3.8.4 Electrical Efficiency

The ratio between electrical output (heat equivalent) to the mechanical power input to the alternator (heat equivalent). Mathematically, it is given by equation (1.5).

$$\eta_{Electrical} = \frac{\text{Electrical output of the alternator (heat equivalent)}}{\text{Mechanical power transmitted to the shaft (heat equivalent)}} \tag{1.5}$$

1.3.8.5 Overall efficiency

The ratio between the electrical output of the alternator (in heat equivalent) to input to the boiler (heat equivalent). It is given by equation (1.6).

$$\eta_{Overall} = \frac{\text{Electrical output of alternator (heat equivalent)}}{\text{Input to the boiler (heat equivalent)}} \tag{1.6}$$

From the above equations, it is seen that the overall efficiency is the product of mechanical and electrical efficiency. Mathematically, it is expressed as equation (1.7).

$$\eta_{Overall} = \eta_{Mechanical} \; x \; \eta_{Electrical} \tag{1.7}$$

1.3.9 Calorific Value

It is the amount of heat produced by the combustion of 1 unit of weight of fuel. When the calorific value of a fuel is more, the fuel is more able to produce heat. For solid fuels like coal and liquid fuel, it is in general expressed as kilocalorie (or kcal)/kg or calorie (or cal)/g. In the case of gaseous fuel, it is kcal/m^3 or cal/m^3.

1.4 DIESEL-BASED POWER PLANT

1.4.1 Introduction

In a diesel-based power plant, the diesel engine is used as the prime mover to generate electrical energy. Though the diesel power plant was familiar, nowadays due to the high cost of generation, it is used for emergency power generation or mobile plants. Diesel oil is used in the diesel engine.

1.4.2 Fuel for Diesel Power Plant and Its Properties

Diesel oil: Diesel oil is a petroleum product. Petrol and diesel are the refined forms of the crude coil. The diesel oil is used in the diesel engine of the diesel power plant.

Properties of liquid fuels

(a) Specific gravity
(b) Flashpoint
(c) Fire point
(d) Volatility
(e) Pour point
(f) Carbon residue
(g) Viscosity
(h) Octane number
(i) Cetane number
(j) Ash content
(k) Corrosive property
(l) Gum content
(m) Heating value
(n) Sulphur content

The requisite properties vary from device to device which uses the fuel to generate power. In general liquid fuels should have the following properties.

(a) Low ash content
(b) High heating value
(c) Low gum content
(d) Less corrosive tendency
(e) Low sulfur content
(f) Low pour point.

1.4.3 Application of Diesel Power Plant

The diesel power plant is small in size. The cost of power generation is very high because of high fuel and maintenance costs. Hence, this plant is used as

(a) Emergency plants for many industries, hospitals, schools, and colleges.
(b) Use as an auxiliary plant for starting the auxiliaries of the large Coal - based power plant.
(c) Mobile plant
(d) Peak load plant
(e) Standby plant

1.4.4 Advantages of Diesel Power Plants

(a) Simple design
(b) Layout, design, and construction of foundations and buildings are simple and cheap.
(c) Can be started quickly.
(d) Require less fuel storage space.
(e) Free from ash handling
(f) Can be located near the load center
(g) Low capital cost

1.4.5 Disadvantages of Diesel Power Plants

(a) High cost of fuel
(b) Short useful life
(c) High repair and maintenance cost
(d) Develop pollution
(e) Small overload capacity

1.4.6 Schematic Diagram and Working of Diesel Power Plant

Fig.1.15 shows the schematic diagram of a diesel engine power plant. The diesel engine and the alternator are the major equipment in the diesel power plant. Besides these, there are many auxiliaries such as fuel system, air intake system, exhaust system, cooling system, lubrication system, engine starting systems, instrumentation, and switchgear and control equipment. A brief description of each is given below.

(a) **Diesel Engine:** It is an internal combustion engine. It may be either a four-stroke or two-stroke engine. In a four-stroke engine, the cycle of operations is completed in four strokes or two revolutions. The four strokes are suction, compression, working, and exhaust. In the two-stroke engines, all four operations are completed in two strokes or one revolution. Two-stroke engines develop more power than four-stroke engines with the same speed, same piston displacement, and cost. However, the efficiency of the four-stroke engine is more than the two-stroke engine. It is because of lower specific fuel consumption and an effective lubricating system. The ignition of the fuel may be through compression ignition or spark ignition. In a compression-type ignition engine, the combustion starts by spontaneous ignition of fuel and air because of the high temperature developed by the compression of the air. On the other hand, a spark ignition engine uses a spark plug to ignite the fuel-air mixture. The former is the most common type of ignition.

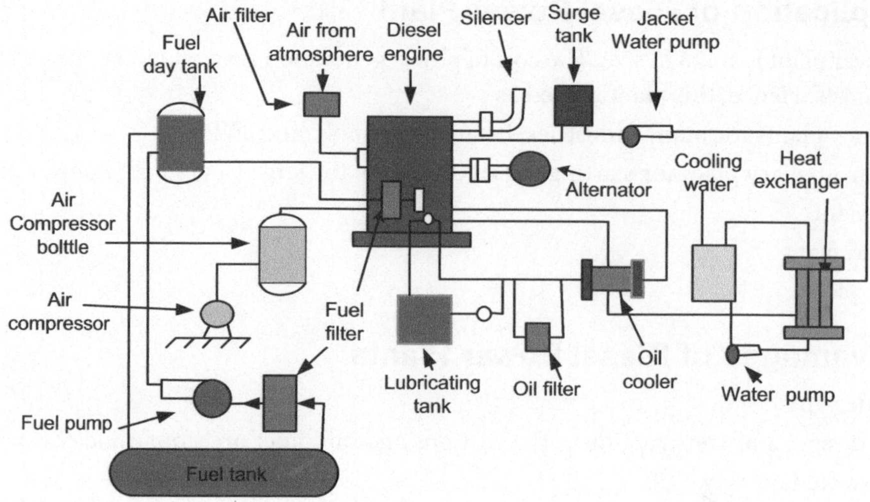

Fig.1.15: Schematic diagram of the diesel engine plant

(b) Alternator: The shaft of the engine is mechanically coupled with the alternator. An alternator is an electrical machine that converts the mechanical output of a diesel engine into electrical energy. The alternator for this plant has a rotating field salient pole structure. The number of poles of the machine may vary from 6 to 28. The capacity of the alternator ranges from 25 to 500 kVA at 0.8 power factor lagging. The voltage rating for a small machine is of the order of 440V and it may be of the order of 2.2kV for bigger machines. The alternator is provided with an automatic voltage regulator to keep the terminal voltage at a specified limit. The details of the alternator are provided in section 1.3.

(c) Fuel system: It consists of the storage tank, strainers, fuel transfer pump, and all-day fuel tank. The storage tank is located outdoors for safety. A transfer pump is used for transferring diesel into the all-day tank daily or at suitable intervals through the strainer and meters. Strainers are used to remove impurities. Clean oil is pumped into the engine through the fuel injection pump. The fuel system of the diesel power plant is shown in Fig.1.16

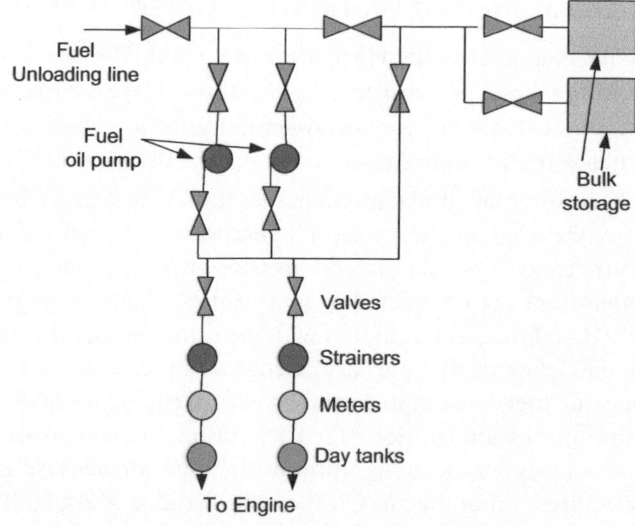

Fig.1.16: Fuel system for a diesel power plant

(d) **Air intake system:** This system is used to supply necessary air to the engine for the combustion of fuel. It consists of pipes to supply fresh air from the atmosphere and filters are used to remove dust particles from the air.

(e) **Exhaust System:** This system discharges the engine exhaust gas into the atmosphere. A good exhaust system should keep the noise at a low level, reduce pollution, and reduce vibrations. A silencer is usually incorporated into the system to reduce the noise level.

(f) **Cooling system:** To keep the temperature of the parts of the engine within a safe limit cooling system is used. It consists of a water source, pump, and cooling towers. The cold water is sent to the engine cylinder jacket using a pump. The takes away the heat from the engine and becomes hot. The hot water is cooled by cooling towers. The closed loop cooling system is shown in Fig.1.17

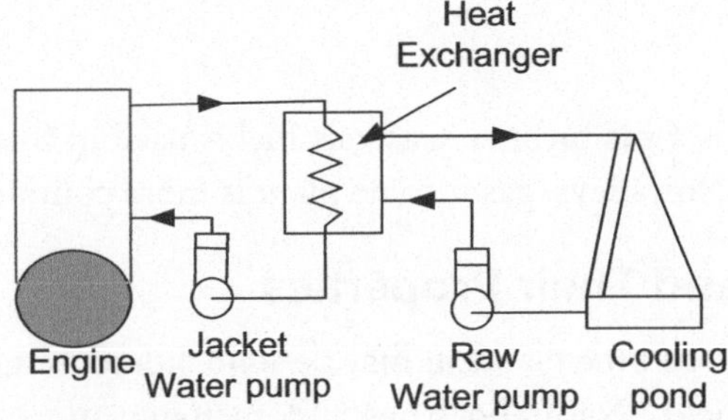

Fig.1.17: Closed circuit cooling system of diesel engine power plant

(g) **Lubricating system:** The lubricating system minimizes the wear of the rubbing surfaces of the engine. This system comprises the lubricating oil tank, pump, filter, and oil cooler. The lubricating oil is drawn from the tank using the pump. The oil is passed through the filter to remove the impurities present in the oil. The oil cooler keeps the temperature of the oil low.

(h) **Engine starting system:** The engine cannot be started by hand cranking because of high compression pressure. A compressed air system is commonly used for starting. Compressed air from the air tank, at about 20 times atmospheric pressure is admitted to a few of the engine cylinders making them work like a reciprocating air motor to turn the engine shaft. A motor-driven compressor is used to supply air to the compressed air tank.

(i) **Instrumentation:** Several instruments are used to ensure satisfactory operation. The instruments such as thermometers (or pyrometers) for measuring the temperature of the exhaust, jacket water, lubricating oil, fuel oil, air compressor; wattmeter, voltmeters, and ammeters, and synchronizing equipment; visible and audible alarms are used in the diesel engine plant.

(j) **Switchgear and control equipment:** It includes bus bars, station transformers, circuit breakers, overcurrent and under voltage relays, etc. The switchgear is grouped in the form of a switch board. It is placed in the engine hall in the alternator. The engine governors can be controlled from the switchboard to enable easy synchronizing of the alternator.

1.4.7 Safe Practices of Diesel-Based Power Plant

The followings are the safe practices of diesel-based thermal plants.

1. Air emission: The diesel plant emits several gases and greenhouse gases like carbon dioxide (CO_2). The emission of these gases must be controlled since they may create health hazards. In this case, care must be taken in the selection of the grade of oil.

2. Heat: The exhaust pipelines should be insulated to maintain safe working conditions.
3. Noise: Noise generated by the machinery and auxiliaries must be at a safe level.
4. Vibration: It is generated by tools and machinery and should be at a safe level.
5. Care must be taken for electrical hazards like electrical shock, or burns from energized equipment.
6. Fire and exposure: Necessary firefighting measures must be provided.
7. Chemical hazards: Necessary precautions must be provided in the plant for chemical hazards generated in the plant.

1.5 GAS TURBINE POWER PLANTS

1.5.1 Introduction

The prime mover of this plant is a gas turbine. Gaseous fuel is used in this plant. In the past, this plant was used as a peak load plant. Nowadays, gas turbine plant is more common for power generation.

1.5.2 Gaseous Fuel and Their Properties

A variety of fuels are used in gas turbine plants. It may be solid, liquid, or gas. Natural gas is widely used as fuel in plants near the gas field. Natural gas has 80% methane and small fractions of other gases. Liquid fuels like kerosene, diesel oil gas oil, and residual oil can be used but are generally costly.

Natural gas: The main constituents of natural gas are methane (CH_4) and ethane (C_2H_6). It has a calorific value of nearly 21000 kJ/m^3. Natural gas is used alternately or simultaneously with oil for internal combustion engines.

Properties of Gaseous fuel

(a) Heating value or calorific value
(b) Viscosity
(c) Specific gravity
(d) Density
(e) Diffusibility

1.5.3 Application of Gas Turbine Plants

Followings are the application of gas turbine plants

1. The gas turbine plant can be started quickly and hence can be used as a peak load plant.
2. Gas turbine plant has a high operating cost. Hence is rarely used as a base load plant. If natural gas is available at the location, it can be used for base load.
3. This plant can be used for supplying auxiliaries of Coal - based plants. Small-size gas turbine plants (about 25MW) are used in Coal - based power plants for starting the auxiliaries. It is installed in the main building or a separate building of a Coal - based plant.
4. Standby power plant in Coal-based thermal power plant: It is also sometimes used as a standby plant in Coal-based thermal plants.

1.5.4 Working of Gas Turbine Plants

This plant consists of a compressor, gas turbine, combustion chamber, alternator, and other auxiliaries like starting devices, fuel system, duct system, and lubricating system.

1.5.4.1 Working Principle

The compressor takes atmospheric air and compresses it. The compressor may be mounted on the same shaft of the turbine or coupled to the turbine. It supplies compressed air to the combustion chamber. The fuel is injected into the combustion chamber and burnt in the stream of air supplied by the compressor. The temperature of air raises and increases its volume under constant pressure. The hot pressurized gas expands in the turbine and produces mechanical power and runs the turbine rotor. The alternator connected to the shaft of the turbine converts mechanical energy into electrical energy. The turbine output exceeds the input to the compressor due to the high temperature produced in the process of combustion. Thus, the turbine drives the compressor and surplus power drives the alternator. Hence, the gas turbine has to drive the compressor as well as the alternator. A variable speed synchronous motor is used as a starting motor to balance the torque in the turbine shaft and the alternator. The starting motor receives the signal for unbalanced torque from the turbine. There are two types of gas turbine plants namely open-loop gas turbine plants and closed-loop gas turbine plants which are discussed in the subsequent section.

1.5.4.2 Open Loop Gas Turbine Plants

The products of combustion i.e burnt high-temperature gases, after expansion through the turbine, are finally exhausted into the atmosphere. At the exhaust, the temperature may be 475^0-550^0C. Such plants are known as open-cycle gas turbine plants. Fig. 1.18 shows the open cycle gas turbine plant with one turbine.

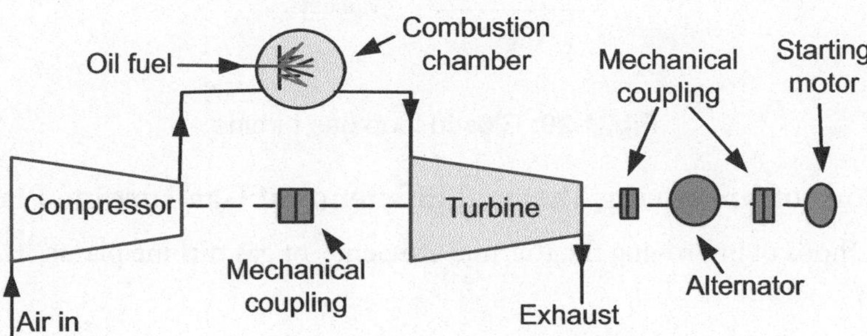

Fig. 1.18: Open cycle gas turbine plant

Sometimes two gas turbines are used. One is a high-pressure turbine and the other is a low-pressure turbine, The high-pressure turbine drives the compressor and the low-pressure turbine drives the alternator. Fig. 1.19 shows the arrangement with two turbines.

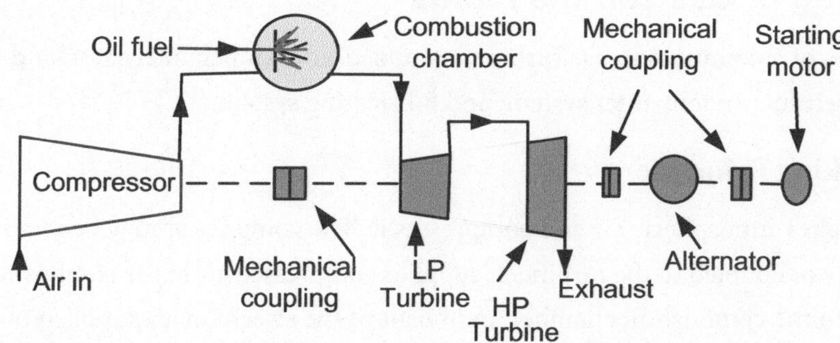

Fig. 1.19: Open cycle gas turbine plant with HP and LP turbines

1.5.4.3 Closed Cycle Gas Turbine Plants

In the case of an open-cycle gas turbine plant, the product of combustion is exhausted into the atmosphere. When the product of combustion is not exhausted into the atmosphere but the same is used, again and again, the plant is called a closed cycle gas turbine plant. Fig. 1.20 shows the closed cycle gas turbine plant.

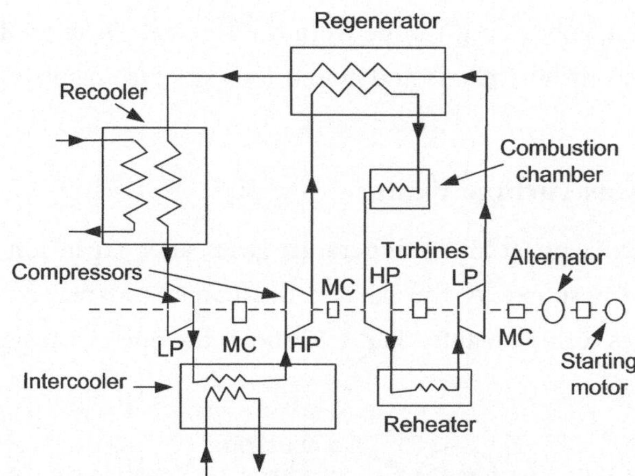

Fig. 1.20: Closed loop gas turbine

1.5.4.4 Methods of Improving Thermal Efficiency of Gas Turbine Plant

There are three methods of improving the thermal efficiency of gas turbine plants. They are

1. Regeneration
2. Intercooling
3. Reheating

Regeneration: The process of transferring the heat energy of the exhaust gas of the turbine to the air coming out from the compressor is called regeneration.

Intercooling: This requires two stages of compression namely low pressure and high pressure. Intercooling means the removal of heat from the compressed air between different stages of compression.

Reheating: The gases after partial expansion in the turbine may be reheated so that they can be expanded further and produce additional work. This process requires a compounding of the turbine.

The arrangement of all the above methods is shown in Fig. 1.20

1.5.5 Combined Cycle Gas Turbine Plant

In this plant, the heat content of the exhaust is not used for regeneration instead it is used as a source for the steam plant cycle. In many countries, such plants are successfully utilized for power generation. In, Fig. 1.21, a combined cycle gas and steam plant. Here gas turbine exhaust passes through a heat exchanger to heat feed water to the boiler. On the other hand, a combined cycle plant in which exhaust is used to preheat air for the boiler is shown in Fig. 1.22.

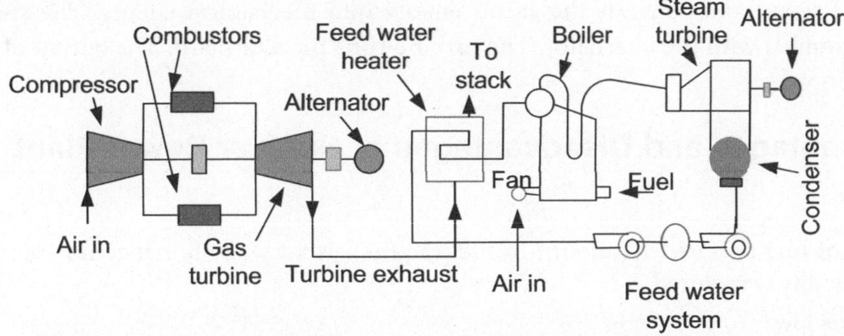

Fig. 1.21: Combined gas and steam plant

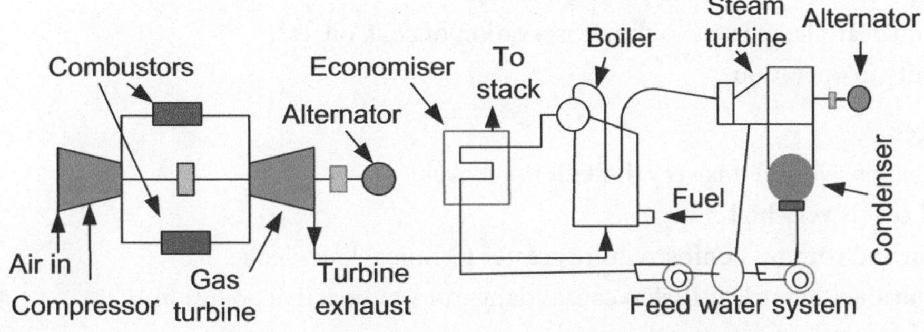

Fig. 1.22: Combined gas and steam plant

1.5.6 Safe Practices of Gas Turbine Plant

The followings are the safe practices of gas turbine plants.

1. Heat: The exhaust pipelines should be insulated to maintain safe working conditions.
2. Noise: Noise generated by the machinery and auxiliaries must be at a safe level.
3. Vibration: It is generated by tools and machinery and should be at a safe level.
4. Care must be taken for electrical hazards like an electrical shock, or burns from energized equipment.
5. Fire and exposure: Necessary firefighting measures must be provided.

6. Chemical hazards: Necessary precautions must be provided in the plant for chemical hazards generated in the plant.

1.6 NUCLEAR POWER PLANT

1.6.1 Introduction

In nuclear power plant nuclear energy is converted into electrical energy. In this plant, heavy elements like Uranium (U^{235}) or thorium (Th^{232}) are subjected to nuclear fission in a special apparatus. This apparatus is known as a nuclear reactor. Heat energy is released in nuclear fission. The heat is utilized to convert water into steam. The steam thus produced is at high temperatures and pressure. The steam turbine utilized steam and converts the steam energy into mechanical energy. The steam turbine is mechanically coupled with the alternator. The turbine runs the alternator. The output of the alternator is electrical energy.

1.6.2 Advantages and Disadvantages of Nuclear Power Plant

Advantages

1. Amount of fuel required isAmount of fuel required is very small, hence no transportation and storage facility is required.
2. Fuel cost is low.
3. Require less area than other conventional plant.
4. It is very economical for bulk power production
5. Use of nuclear plants leads to the conservation of coal, oil, etc.
6. Reliability in operation

Disadvantages

1. Fuel is expensive and it is very difficult to recover.
2. Capital cost is very high.
3. Erection and commissioning require greater technical knowledge.
4. The byproduct of nuclear fission causes dangerous radioactive pollution.
5. High maintenance cost.
6. It can be used for base load only.
7. Disposal of byproducts of nuclear fission is a big problem.

1.6.3 Selection of Location/Site of Nuclear Power Plant

The location/location of the nuclear power plant is selected based on the following points

1. **Water availability:** The cooling process required a huge amount of water. The plant site should be such that sufficient water is available at that location. It is better to select a location near the river or sea.
2. **Waste Disposal:** Nuclear fission developed radioactive waste products. This must be disposed of to avoid health hazards. It must either be buried in a deep trench or disposed of in the sea at a sufficient distance from the sea shore.

3. **Distance from the populated area:** It should be situated away from the populated area since it is dangerous due to the presence of radioactivity.
4. **Transportation facility:** There must be an adequate transportation facility to transport heavy equipment to the plant.
5. **Meteorology:** Metrological calculations are used to find the maximum dose received at a specified distance in a specified metrological situation. It is an important factor to be considered while selecting a site for nuclear power plant. Wind and atmospheric stability are two main meteorological factors. These factors are involved in atmospheric transport and dilution of airborne contamination.
6. **Seismology:** The seismic history of a site and surrounding region must be known before the selection of the site of the nuclear power plant. Accordingly, the design of the plant building and foundation of the machinery, etc. are designed.

1.6.4 Nuclear Fuel and Nuclear Physics

In the nuclear power plant, nuclear energy released from heavy material like Uranium or Thorium is subjected to nuclear fission. The properties of these nuclear materials should be such that it is capable of undergoing nuclear fission and maintaining chain reaction.

Nuclear physics

1. **Structure of atom:** The matter is composed of atoms. The atom consists of the nucleus at the Centre. Each atom has three particles namely proton, neutron, and electrons. Protons are positively charged. The electrons are negatively charged. Neutron has no charge. The electrons are revolving around the nucleus in a specified orbit. The mass of the atom is concentrated in the nucleus. The number of electrons is equal to the number of protons and this number is called the atomic number. The sum of the number of protons and neutrons is called mass numbers. An atom is identified by its mass number and its symbol.
2. **Isotopes:** Atoms that have the same atomic numbers but different mass numbers are called isotopes.
3. **Radioactivity:** This is the process of breakdown of the nucleus of unstable isotopes. Isotopes of some elements like radium, uranium, and thorium are unstable. The nucleus decay occurs in one or more states. Radioactivity may be natural or artificial. Artificial radioactivity is often produced by neutron bombardment. In the process of radioactivity few radiations are emitted. They are α particles, β particles, and γ rays and neutrons. The α particles are nuclei of a helium atom ($_2He^4$), β particles are electrons, and γ rays are similar to x-rays.

   The α particles are heavy particles of positive charge and travel at around one-tenth of the velocity of light. When α particles are emitted due to radioactivity, the nucleus of the isotope changes to the nucleus of other atoms. Some examples are as follows.

$$_{92}U^{238} \rightarrow {}_2He^4 + {}_{90}Th^{234} \tag{1.7}$$

$$_{94}Pu^{239} \rightarrow {}_2He^4 + {}_{92}Th^{235} \tag{1.8}$$

   In equation (1), the isotope of uranium ($_{92}U^{238}$) is subjected to radioactivity, and two isotopes namely helium ($_2He^4$) and thorium ($_{90}Th^{234}$) are produced. In equation (2), the isotope of plutonium ($_{94}Pu^{239}$) is subjected to radioactivity and two isotopes namely helium ($_2He^4$) and thorium ($_{92}Th^{235}$) are produced.

When a β particle is emitted, the nucleus gains a unit of positive charge, and hence, it becomes an element one unit higher in the periodic table.

The γ rays are produced when α or β particles are emitted due to radioactivity. The produced smaller nucleus is in an excited state and emits excess energy as γ rays.

4. **Radioactive decay, half-life, and average lifetime:** The process of radioactive decay is random. The activity or rate of decay or decay rate is proportional to the number of atoms at any instant. The decay rate is expressed in terms of the decay constant (λ) and the number of nuclei (N). The decay constant is the probability of decay per unit of time. Thus, the decay rate or activity can be expressed as (1.8). The minus sign is the representation of the decay of the nucleus.

$$\text{Activity} = \text{decay rate} = \frac{-dN}{dt} = \lambda N \tag{1.8}$$

Integrating equation (1.8), we will get equation (1.9), in which N_0= Number of nuclei at t = 0

$$N = N_0 e^{-\lambda t} \tag{1.9}$$

A very useful term called half-life is generally used to measure the time up to which the delay process takes place. Half-life is the time in which half the nuclei are present at any instant. In equation (4) above, $N = \frac{N_0}{2}$ at t = half-life., Thus half-life can be expressed as equation (1.10)

$$\text{Half life} = 0.693 / \lambda \tag{1.10}$$

The average lifetime of an isotope is given by equation (1.11).

$$T_{AV} = \frac{1}{\lambda} = \frac{\text{Half life}}{0.693} \tag{1.11}$$

5. **Energy mass relationship:** According to Einstein's theory of relativity, mass and energy are interchangeable. If the mass is destroyed energy is produced, and if energy is spent mass is produced. Mathematically, the relation is given by (1.12), where Energy is in joules, m = mass in Kg, and c = velocity of light (3×10^8 m/second).

$$\text{Energy} = mc^2 \tag{1.12}$$

Nuclear energy is produced by destructing mass.

6. **Nuclear fission and fusion:** There are two ways of getting nuclear energy. They are fission and fusion. In the case of fission, heavier elements are splits and in the case of fusion, lighter elements are fused. In both cases, a huge amount of energy is released. The nuclear fission process is used in nuclear power plants. The fission of heavy elements is initiated by bombarding the element with a slow-moving neutron. The fission of uranium nuclei in nuclear power plants releases huge energy and neutron. This neutron is called fission neutron. These fission neutrons cause further fission, and short while, an enormous amount of energy develops. This process is called a chain reaction. Fig. 1.23 shows nuclear fission.

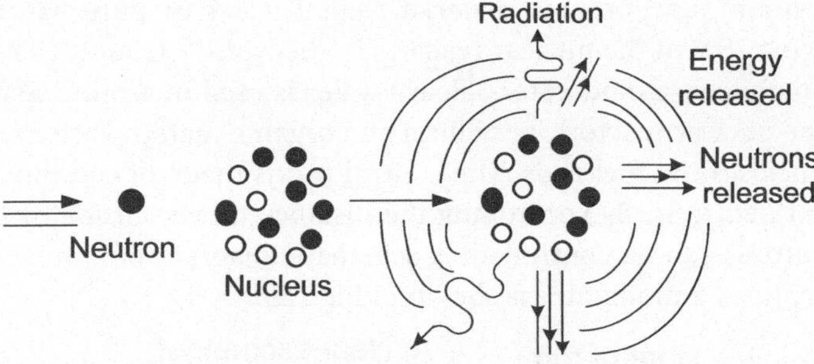

Fig. 1.23: Nuclear fission

1.6.5 Basic Layout and Working of Nuclear Power Plants

The plant is similar to a Coal - based thermal plant except that the nuclear reactor and heat exchanger replace the boiler. Some of the auxiliaries are similar to a Coal - based thermal plant. The basic layout diagram of the nuclear plant showing the main parts is shown in Fig.1.24

The followings are the main equipment of the nuclear power plant

(a) Nuclear reactor.
(b) Heat exchanger.
(c) Steam turbine.
(d) Alternator.
(e) Condenser.

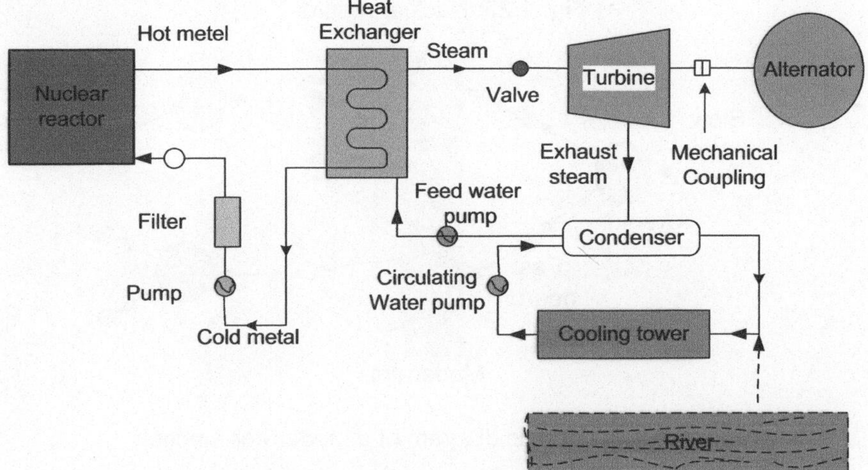

Fig. 1.24: Basic layout showing the main parts of the nuclear power plant

(a) **Nuclear reactor:** The reactor is an apparatus in which the fission of nuclear fuel takes place. It controls the chain reaction. It is a cylindrical vessel. It houses the fuel rods, moderator, and control rods. The fuel may be natural uranium, enriched uranium, and plutonium. The fuel rod is the fuel material. The function of the moderator is to slow down the neutrons before bombardment. There are various materials used as a moderator. They are light water or pure natural water, graphite, heavy water, beryllium, and organic material. Light water or pure natural water is used as a moderator in almost 75% of the nuclear reactors in the world. Around 20% of nuclear reactors in the world used graphite as a moderator. Heavy water is used in around 5% of nuclear reactors in the world. In some nuclear reactors, beryllium and organic material are also used as a moderator. The moderator encloses the fuel rods. The control rod is made of cadmium. Cadmium is a very strong absorber of neutrons. By controlling the distance moved inside by the cadmium rod, the absorption of neutrons can be controlled. A schematic diagram of a nuclear reactor is shown in Fig.1.25. A schematic of a moderator is shown in Fig.1.26.

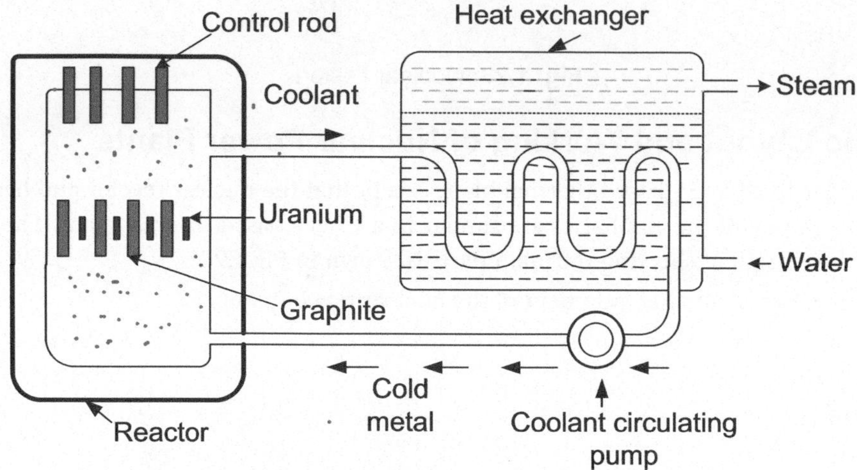

Fig. 1.25: Nuclear reactor

Fig. 1.26: Schematic diagram of a moderator function

(b) **Heat exchanger:** The coolant carries the heat and the heat is utilized to convert the water into heat in the heat exchanger. The coolant is again circulated into the reactor from the heat exchanger through the coolant circulating pump.

(c) **Steam turbine:** The steam produced in the heat exchanger is fed to the steam turbine via the steam valve. The turbine utilized the steam energy to produce mechanical energy at the shaft.

(d) **Alternator:** It is mechanically coupled with the turbine. It converts mechanical energy into electrical energy.

(e) **Condenser:** It condenses the hot exhausted steam from the steam turbine. The condenser creates a very low pressure at the steam outlet of the turbine. This low pressure facilitates the expansion of steam in the turbine. Also, the condensate of the condenser can be used for the boiler again.

1.6.6 Types of Nuclear Reactor

Nuclear reactors are classified in many ways. The classification is given below.

1. Based on fission
   - Slow
   - Intermediate
   - Fast
2. Based on fuel used
   - Natural uranium
   - Enriched uranium
   - Plutonium
3. Based on the state of fuel
   - Solid type
   - Liquid type
4. Based on the fuel cycle
   - Burner type
   - Converter type
   - Breeder type
5. Based on the arrangement of fossil and fertile material
   - One region
   - Two regions
6. Based on the arrangement of moderator and fuel
   - Homogeneous
   - Heterogeneous
7. Based on moderator material
   - Heavy water
   - Graphite
   - Ordinary water
   - Beryllium
   - Organic
8. Based on the cooling system
   - Direct cooling
   - Indirect cooling
9. Based on coolant
   - Gas
   - Water

- Heavy water
- Liquid metal

10. Based on the purpose
    - Research and development
    - Production
    - Power

Though nuclear reactors are classified as above, one reactor may belong to another type.

In the case of the heterogeneous type of reactor, there are a large number of fuel rods with coolant circulating around them and carrying away the heat released by nuclear fission. In the case of the homogeneous type of reactor, the fuel and the moderator are mixed, e.g a fissionable salt of uranium like uranium sulphate (or nitrate) dissolved in the moderator like H_2O or D_2O. But due to difficulties like component maintenance, induced radioactivity, erosion, and corrosion, a homogeneous class of reactors is not commonly used. Nowadays nuclear reactors are of a heterogeneous class.

In countries like UK, Franc, and Germany, high-temperature gas-cooled reactors have been used. A fast nuclear reactor uses high-energy neutrons for fission and requires no moderator. The fast nuclear reactor utilizes a liquid metal as a coolant and either plutonium or a plutonium–uranium mixture for fuel. A breeder reactor produces more fissionable isotopes than what it consumes. The details of light water-cooled reactors and the corresponding power plants are presented below.

1.6.6.1 Light Water-Cooled Reactors

Light water-cooled and moderator reactors (LWR) using slightly enriched uranium fuel are the most commonly used reactors in power production. These reactors are further classified into two types.

(a) Pressurized water reactor (PWR)
(b) Boiling water reactor (BWR)

Pressurized water reactor (PWR)

The schematic diagram of a pressurized water reactor is shown in Fig.1.27(a). Due to the excellent properties of water as a coolant and as a moderator, it is the natural choice for power reactors. Fig.1.27(b) shows a PWR power plant. It is composed of two loops in series. They are the coolant loop also called the primary loop and water – steam loop also called the working fluid loop. The coolant picks up heat in the reactor and transfers it to the working fluid in the steam generator. The steam is then used in a Rankine-type cycle to produce electricity. The fuel in PWRs is slightly enriched uranium in the form of thin rods or plates. Stainless steel or zircaloy is used for cladding. The steel pressure vessel must be 20-30 cm thick. A typical PWR contains about 200 fuel assemblies. Each assembly is an array of rods. In practical fuel assembly, there are 264 fuel rods and 24 guide tubes for control rods.

Boiling water reactor (BWR)

The schematic diagram of a boiling water reactor (BWR) is shown in Fig.1.28(a) and the power plant using BWR is shown in Fig.1.28(b). In BWR the steam is produced directly in the reactor core. The steam is separated and dried with the help of a mechanical device situated in the upper part of the pressure vessel assembly. The dried steam is sent directly to the high-pressure turbine and runs the same. Thus, it eliminates the need for a steam generator. The coolant thus serves the triple function of coolant, moderator, and working fluid.

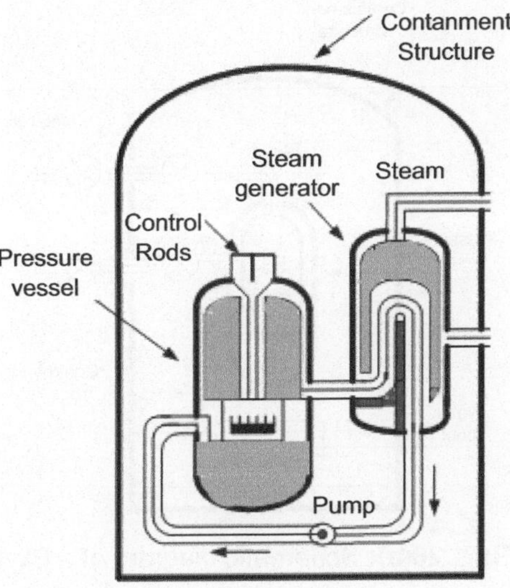

Fig.1.27 (a): Schematic diagram of PWR

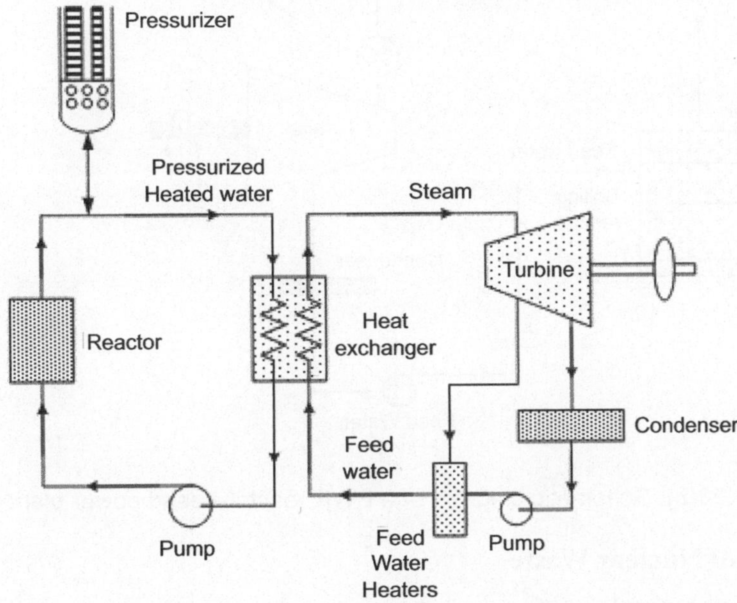

Fig.1.27 (b): schematic diagram of a PWR power plant

1.6.7 Disposal, Shielding, and Safe Practices of Nuclear Power Plant

The nuclear power plant needs special attention to nuclear disposal because of the danger of nuclear radiation. The emission intensity of radioactive waste is quite high. This waste emits gamma rays which are harmful to live animals and organisms. Solid waste materials are stored in shielded storage. This type of storage has borosilicate glasses and the glasses are stored in leak-proof tight capsules. The capsules are stored in deep salt mines. Sometimes large containers are placed at the bottom of the ocean.

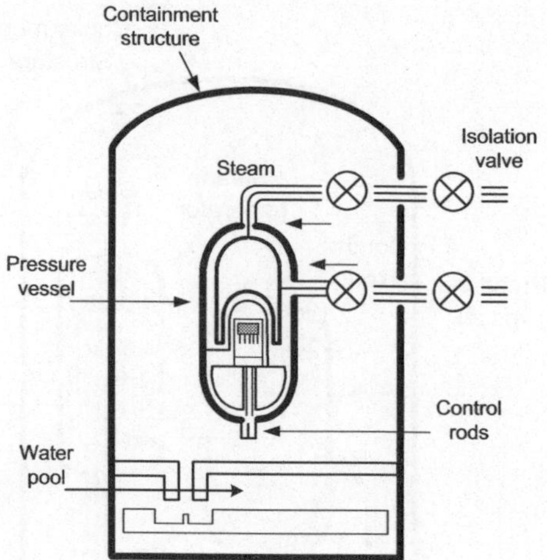

Fig.1.28(a): Schematic diagram of a BWR

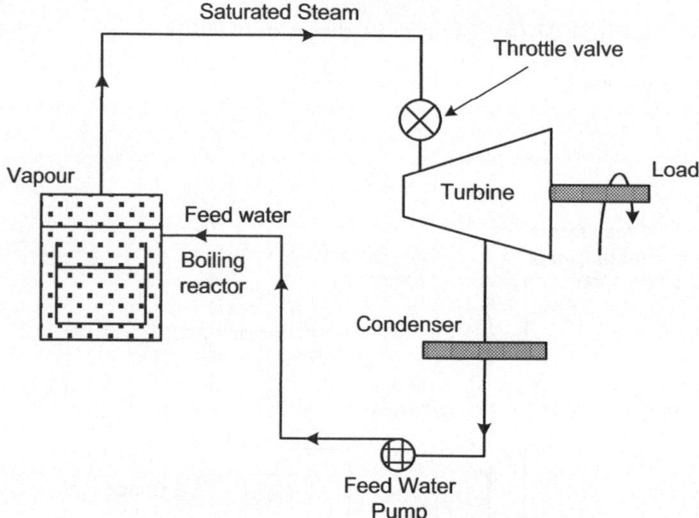

Fig.1.28(b): Schematic diagram of a BWR reactor-based power plant

1.6.7.1 Disposal of Nuclear Waste

Solid, liquid, and gaseous byproducts of nuclear plants create dangerous health hazards. These products are radioactive.

The gaseous products need to be filtered before exhausting into the atmosphere. There is less chance of fire in the fuel channel of the reactor. If somehow fire takes place, there is the possibility of release of a large volume of gaseous fission product. Hence, there must be a clean-up plant through which these gaseous products pass and remove the radioactive material. There may be a possibility of reduction of carbon dioxide near the reactor. It is extremely necessary to measure the carbon dioxide in the atmosphere near the reactor. Precautions must be taken against these toxic and radiological hazards.

There may be radioactive waste in the liquid effluents. The radioactivity must be removed from the liquid effluents. Proper records must be maintained so that the effluents do not create health hazards. Special precautions must be taken against the leakage of liquid effluents.

There are also some solid waste materials such as rejected control rods, small pieces of fuel material, etc. These must be stored in shielded concrete strong rooms. The waste materials are stored underwater for about 100 days so that radioactivity decays to a low level. They can also be stored in an air-cooled shielded area. The storage chamber should be cool and shield the waste material for a few years after which they are disposed of underground places.

1.6.7.2 Shielding

Shielding is provided in the nuclear plant to protect personnel, instruments, etc. from radioactivity. There are a few shielding materials such as lead, steel, cadmium, and concrete. Effective shielding depends on the density of the material. However, none of the above is effective against all types of radiation.

The density of lead, cadmium, concrete, and steel are 11.3g/m^2, 8.65g/m^2, 2.4g/m^2, and 7.8g/m^2 respectively. Lead is a more common material and cheap. Cadmium can absorb slow neutrons. Concrete is less efficient than lead. Steel has good structural properties but is not a good shielding material.

A nuclear reactor must have a shield. The shield comprises several centimeters of thick steel surrounded by a few meters (about 3m) of concrete.

1.6.7.3 Safe Practices of Nuclear Power Plant

The followings are the safe practices of nuclear power plants.

1. **Nuclear hazards:** Solid, liquid, and gaseous byproducts create dangerous health hazards. A necessary arrangement for the disposal of this material must be there in the plant. Suitable shielding must be provided to safeguard the instruments and personnel.
2. **Heat:** The exhaust pipelines carrying steam should be insulated to maintain safe working conditions.
3. **Noise:** Noise generated by the machinery and auxiliaries must be at a safe level.
4. **Vibration:** It is generated by tools and machinery and should be at a safe level.
5. **Electrical hazards:** Care must be taken for electrical hazards like an electrical shock, or burns from energized equipment.
6. **Fire and exposure:** Necessary firefighting measures must be provided.
7. **Other chemical hazards:** Necessary precautions must be provided in the plant for chemical hazards generated in the plant.

1.7 THERMAL POWER PLANTS IN MAHARASHTRA, INDIA

The state of Maharashtra is one of the largest producers of thermal power in India. The state share 13% of India's thermal power generation. There are a large number of coal mines in Maharashtra. This has aided the development of Coal - based thermal power facilities throughout the state. It has 75 numbers thermal power plants. As of Feb 28th, 2022 the installed capacity of the thermal plant in the state is 28766.91MW (excluding nuclear power generation). Table.1 shows the installed capacity of various power plants in Maharashtra.

Table 1.1: Installed capacity of various power plants in Maharashtra.

Ownership /Sector	Mode wise breakup									Grand Total
	Thermal (MW)					Nuclear (MW)	Renewable (MW)			
	Coal	Lignite	Gas	Diesel	Total		Hydro	RES* (MORE)	Total	
State	9540.00	0.00	672.00	0.00	10212.00	0.00	2850.84	388.13	3238.97	13450.97
Private	10856.00	0.00	568.00	0.00	11424.00	0.00	481.00	10121.56	10602.56	22026.56
Central	4858.18	0.00	2272.73	0.00	7130.91	690.00	0.00	123.00	123.00	7943.91
Sub-total	**25254.18**	**0.00**	**3512.73**	**0.00**	**28766.91**	**690.00**	**3331.84**	**10632.69**	**13964.53**	**43421.44**

The power plants are maintained by the state as well as other agencies. Chandrapur is the largest thermal plant under the Maharashtra state power generation company. The capacity of this station is 2920 MW. It has seven units, out of which two are 210MW each and five are 500MW each. The world's oldest thermal plant "Paras Thermal Power Plant" is found in Maharashtra.

UNIT SUMMARY

The coal based thermal plants are found extensively all over the globe. Maharashtra shares 13% of India's thermal power generation.

Steam turbines are used as the prime mover in coal-based and nuclear power plants. The prime mover for diesel-based and gas-based thermal plants are the diesel engine and gas turbine respectively. The alternator is common in all plants. The boiler is used in coal-fired plants for steam generation. There are two types of boilers namely fire tubes and water tubes. The heat generated is generated in nuclear fission in the nuclear reactor of the nuclear power plant. The generated heat is utilized to produce steam in the heat exchanger of a nuclear plant. Steam turbines are classified as impulse and reaction turbines. The condenser creates low pressure at the outlet of the steam of the turbines used in coal-fired and nuclear-based plants.

Diesel-based thermal plants have high operating costs and low efficiency at light load. Nowadays, diesel-based plants and gas-based thermal plants are also used for base load supply. A nuclear power plant is suitable for a base load plant.

Disposal of nuclear waste material and adequate shielding to guard personnel and other instruments is very important in a nuclear plant.

EXERCISES

Example 1.1

The overall efficiency of a coal-based thermal plant is 24%. In the plant, 800g of coal is required to generate 1 kWh of energy. Find the calorific value.

Solution:

The heat produced by burning 800g (= 0.80 kg) of coal

$$= \frac{\text{Output in heat units}}{\text{Overall efficiency}} = \frac{1 \times 860}{0.24} = 3583.33\text{kcal}$$

As, 1 kWh = 860kcal, hence

$$\text{The calorific value of coal} = \frac{3583.33}{0.80} = 4479.17 \text{ kcal} \quad \text{Ans.}$$

Example 1.2

The peak demand in a coal-based plant is 30,000MW. The load factor of the plant is 45%. The boiler and turbine efficiencies are 83% and 92% respectively. An amount of 800g of coal is burnt to generate 1 kWh of energy. The plant spends Rs.300 for 1000kg coal. Determine (a) thermal efficiency and (b) coal bills per annum

Solution:

(a) Thermal or mechanical efficiency = 0.83 0.92

= 0.763 or 76.3 % Ans.

(b) Unit generation/year = Peak load × load factor × Hours in one year

$= 30000 \times 0.45 \times 8760$

$= 118{,}26 \times 10^4$ kWh

Annual coal bill = Rs. 250 × 94608

= Rs. 23,652,000 Ans.

Example 1.3

The expenditure for coal in one year of a coal-based thermal plant is rupees 40 lakhs. The cost of coal per ton is rupees 400. The calorific value of coal is 6000 kcal/kg. The thermal and electrical efficiencies of the plant are 34 % and 85 % respectively. What is the average load on the plant?

Solution:

$$\text{Overall efficiency, } ç_O = 0.34 \times 0.85 = 0.289$$

$$\text{Coal used/year} = 40 \times 10^5 / 400 = 10^4 \text{tons} = 10^7 \text{kg}$$

$$\text{The heat of combustion} = \text{coal used/year} \times \text{calorific value}$$

$$= 10^7 \times 6000$$

$$= 6 \text{ x } 10^{10} \text{ kcal}$$

$$\text{Heat output from the plant} = \eta_O \text{ x Heat of combustion}$$

$$= (0.289) \times (6 \times 10^{10})$$

$$= 1734 \times 10^7 \, kcal$$

$$\text{Unit generation/year} = 1734 \times 10^7 / 860 \text{ kWh}$$

$$\therefore \text{Average load on station} = \frac{\text{Unit generated /year}}{\text{Hour in a year}} = \frac{1734 \times 10^7}{860 \times 8760} = 2301.68 \text{ kW } \textbf{Ans.}$$

Example 1.4

The fuel consumption of a diesel power plant is 0.26 kg to generate 1 kWh of energy. The alternator efficiency is 92%. The calorific value of fuel is 10000 kcal/kg. Calculate (i) the overall efficiency, and (ii) the engine efficiency.

Solution:

Heat produced by 0.26 kg oil $=10,000\times 0.26 = 2600$kcal

We know that the heat equivalent of 1kWh = 860kcal

$$\text{Overall efficiency}, \eta_o = \frac{\text{Electrical output (heat equivalent)}}{\text{Engine input (heat equivalent)}}$$

$$= \frac{860}{2600} = 0.3307 \times 100 = 33.07\% \quad \text{(Ans (i))}$$

$$\text{Engine efficiency}, \mu_{engine} = \frac{\text{Overall efficiency}}{\text{Electrical efficency or alternator efficiency}}$$

$$= \frac{33.07}{92} \text{x}100\% = 35.95\% \quad \text{(Ans. (ii))}$$

Example 1.5

The diesel consumption per day of a diesel power plant is 750kg. The unit generated per day is 3000kWh. The calorific value of the diesel oil is 12000 kcal. The alternator and engine efficiencies are 94% and 92% respectively.

Find (a) specific fuel consumption,

(b) Overall efficiency of the plant, and

(c) thermal efficiency of the engine

Solution:

(a) Specific fuel consumption = 750/3000 = 0.25 kg/kWh **Ans.**

(b) Per day heat produced by fuel = coal consumption/day×calorific values

$$= 750\times 12000 = 9\times 10^6 \text{kcal}$$

Electrical output in heat units/day = 3000 × 860

$$= 258\times 10^4 \text{kcal}$$

$$\text{Overall efficiency} = \frac{258\times 10^4}{9\times 10^6}\times 100 = 28.66\% \textbf{ Ans.}$$

(c) $\text{Engine efficiency} = \frac{\text{Overall efficiency}}{\text{Alternator efficency}} = \frac{28.66}{94}\times 100 = 30.49\%$

$$\text{Thermal efficiency} = \frac{\text{Engine efficiency}}{\text{Engine mech. efficiency}} = \frac{30.49}{92} \text{x}100\% = 33.14\% \ \textbf{(Ans.)}$$

Example.1.6

In a nuclear plant, the reactors delivered 400 MW of power. Find the mass of uranium fission per hour. It is given that the energy released due to nuclear fission is of each ${}_{92}U^{235}$ atom is 300 MeV.

Solution:

Energy received from the reactor = 400 MeV

$$= 4\times10^{8}\text{W (joule/s)}$$

$$\text{Energy received/ hour} = (4\times10^{8}) \times 3600$$

$$= 144\times 10^{10}\text{joule}$$

$$\text{Energy received per fission} = 300 \text{ MeV}$$

$$= 300 \times 10^{6}\times 1.6 \times 10^{-19}\text{joule}$$

$$= 4.8\times10^{-11}\text{joule}$$

$$\text{Number of atom fission /hour} = \frac{144 \times 10^{10}}{4.8 \times10^{-11}}$$

$$=3\times10^{22}$$

$$\text{Mass of } {}_{92}U^{235} = \frac{235}{6.023 \times 10^{23}} \times 3 \times 10^{22}$$

$$= 11.70 \text{ g}$$

Multiple Choice Questions

1. Coal in the steam thermal plant is shifted from storage with the help
   (a) Hoisting mechanism, (b) Conveyors belt
   (c) Hydraulic crane (d) Trolley car
2. A coal-fired plant generates 1000MW. Burning of coal releases 900x107 kilojoule/hour. The rate of heat rejection is
   (a) 600MW, (b) 900MW,
   (c) 1500MW, (d) 2200MW
3. In the vapor cycle in coal-fired thermal plant, regeneration yield efficiency is high since
   (a) increase in pressure inside the boiler,
   (b) addition of heat to the steam at the entry to the LP turbine,
   (c) the average temperature of heat addition increases in the boiler,
   (d) increase in total work by the turbine
4. Steam is called superheated, when
   (a) Actual volume is greater than saturated steam volume

(b) Actual volume is less than saturated steam volume
(c) Actual volume is equal to the saturated steam volume
(d) None of the above

5. In a steam turbine, the diaphragm refers to
   (a) Separating walls between rotors
   (b) Ring of guide blades
   (c) Partition between low- and high-pressure side
   (d) Flange connecting turbine outlet (steam) and condenser.
6. Cooling tower is for
   (a) Condensing steam
   (b) Reducing temperature of exhaust steam
   (c) Cooling exhaust gas
   (d) Reducing the temperature of water used for condenser
7. The amount of excess air for combustion of coal is between
   (a) 100% and 200%, (b) 30% and 70%.
   (c) 15% and 40%, (d) 3% and 10%
8. The type of induced draft fan in cooling towers are
   (a) Axial flow, (b) radial flow,
   (c) centrifugal, (d) propeller
9. The combustion system requires maximum excess air to is
   (a) Coal combustion (b) oil burner
   (c) Bas burner (d) chain grate stoker
10. In general, the induced draft fan is located at the
    (a) Outlet of the steam generator before dust collector
    (b) Outlet of the steam generator after the dust collector
    (c) Inlet of the steam generator before air preheater
    (d) Inlet of the steam generator after air preheater
11. Condenser condenses the steam exhausted from
    (a) Turbine (b) boiler
    (c) economizer (c) superheater
12. In a gas turbine plant, heat exchangers and reheating improves
    (a) Thermal efficiency
    (b) Specific power output
    (c) Both thermal and specific power output
    (d) Neither thermal efficiency nor specific power output
13. Gas turbine works on
    (a) Brayton cycle (b) Rankine cycle
    (c) striling cycle (d) otto cycle
14. Gas turbine cycle with regeneration
    (a) Increases pressure ratio (b) Decreases pressure ratio
    (c) Decreases work output (d) Increases heat input

15. Regeneration in gas turbine plant
(a) Increases efficiency but there is no effect on output
(b) Increases output but there is no effect on efficiency
(c) Both efficiency and output increases
(d) Efficiency increases but output decreases

16. Uranium -238 is represented by $_{92}U^{238}$ What does it represent?
(a) 92 neutrons and 238 protons
(b) 92 protons and 238 neutrons
(c) 92 neutrons and 146 protons
(d) 92 protons and 146 neutrons

17. The heavy water in the reactor of a nuclear plant is used as
(a) A coolant
(b) A moderator
(c) A coolant as well as a moderator
(d) A neutron absorber

18. The name of a commonly used moderator in a nuclear reactor is
(a) Heavy water
(b) Concrete
(c) Steel
(d) graphite

19. Nuclear shielding for protection against
(a) Excess electron
(b) X-rays
(c) α and β rays
(d) neutron and gamma rays

20. Moderator in nuclear plant
(a) Slows down the neutrons generated in fission
(b) Reduce nuclear pollution
(c) Control temperature
(d) Moderates the steam

21. India's first nuclear power plant is in
(a) Kota
(b) Tarapur
(c) Kalpakkam
(d) Narora

22. Feed water in the regenerative cycle is heated by
(a) Heater
(b) Drained steam
(c) Exhaust gases
(d) All the above

23. Efficiency of a thermal power plant is approximately
(a) 30 to 40%
(b) 45 to 50%
(c) 20 to 25%
(d) 60 to 70%

24. The pressure in the working fluid cycle of the thermal plant is developed by
(a) Condenser
(b) Superheater
(c) Feed water pump
(d) turbine

25. Water coming to the economizer is heated by
(a) HP steam
(b) LP steam
(c) Furnace
(d) flue gases

26. Select the correct sequence in which flow gas pas through after being exhausted from the boiler
(1) ID Fan
(2) Air preheater
(3) Economizer
(4) Electronic precipitator

(a) 4,3,2,1 (b) 3,2,4,1
(c) 2,1,4,3 (d) 1,4,3,2

27. The function of the Economizer is to
    (a) Heat the incoming water with steam
    (b) Heat the pulverized coal with exhaust gases.
    (c) Heat the incoming air with exhaust gases.
    (d) Heat the incoming water with exhaust gas

28. Air preheater of coal-fired power plant
    (a) Recovers heat from flue gases leaving the economizer
    (b) Improves combustion rate
    (c) Raises temperature of furnace gases
    (d) All the above

29. In the reactor of nuclear power plant thermal energy is obtained from
    (a) Fission of nuclear fuel (b) Fusion of nuclear fuel
    (c) Burning of the fuel rod in oxygen (d) All the above

30. In an ideal diesel cycle, the working substance is
    (a) Air (b) Diesel
    (c) Mixture of air and diesel (d) Any combustion gases

31. The range of thermal efficiency of the diesel engine is
    (a) 10-20% (b) 20-30%
    (c) 30-40% (d) 40-50%

32. Air filter is used in
    (a) Steam power plant (b) Nuclear power plant
    (c) Hydroelectric power plant (d) Diesel engine power plant

33. Gas turbine power plant not widely used
    (a) As peal load plant, (b) as standby plants,
    (c) base load plant, (d) in combination with a steam power plant

34. When we compare coal-fired and gas-based plants, gas-based plants have
    (a) Low initial cost but higher operating costs
    (b) High initial cost but lower operating costs
    (c) Initial and operating costs high
    (d) Initial and operating costs low

35. Gas turbine plant is used
    (a) Coal and peat (b) Kerosine oil, diesel oil, residual oil
    (c) Gas oil (d) Natural and liquid petroleum fuels

36. The work ratio of a closed cycle gas turbine plant depends on
    (a) On pressure ratio alone
    (b) Temperature ratio of the cycle and specific heat ratio
    (c) Pressure ratio, temperature ratio, and specific heat ratio
    (d) Pressure and specific heat ratio

ANSWERS															
1.	(b)	2.	(c)	3.	(c)	4.	(a)	5.	(a)	6.	(d)	7.	(d)	8.	(d)
9.	(d)	10.	(b)	11.	(a)	12.	(a)	13.	(a)	14.	(b)	15.	(a)	16.	(d)
17.	(c)	18.	(a)	19.	(d)	20.	(a)	21.	(b)	22.	(c)	23.	(a)	24.	(c)
25.	(d)	26.	(b)	27.	(d)	28.	(d)	29.	(a)	30.	(a)	31.	(c)	32.	(d)
33.	(c)	34.	(a)	35.	(d)	36.	(c)								

Short and Long Answer Type Questions

1. What are the factors that need to be considered for the selection of the site for a coal-based thermal power plant?
2. Draw the schematic diagram of a coal-based thermal plant and explain the function of each piece of equipment and the auxiliaries.
3. Briefly describe each part of the cola-based thermal plant and the working of the plant.
4. Write short notes on
   (a) Advantages of coal-based thermal plant (b) Economizer, (c) Superheater, (d) Air preheater,
   (e) types of turbines, (f) Safe working of thermal plants, (g) types of boilers
5. Discuss the advantages and disadvantages of diesel power plants.
6. Draw the schematic diagram of a diesel power plant and explain the function of each part.
7. Describe briefly the main components of the diesel power plant.
8. Discuss the applications of diesel power plants and gas turbine plants.
9. What are the advantages of a gas turbine plant?
10. List components of gas turbine plant.
11. Describe briefly the working of a Gas turbine plant.
12. Write short notes on (1) Open and closed cycle gas turbine plants, (2) methods of improving gas turbine efficiency
13. Describe nuclear fission. What are particles emitted during nuclear fission?
14. Define mass defect and binding energy.
15. Explain the nuclear chain reaction.
16. Name the main parts of the nuclear power plant.
17. Name some types of nuclear reactors.
18. Explain the working of a nuclear plant.
19. Draw a diagram to show the open cycle turbine plant with regeneration, intercooler, and reheating.
20. Write notes on (1) gas turbine fuels and (b) combined gas and steam cycle.

Numerical problems

1. A coal-based thermal power plant has an overall efficiency of 17% and 0.7 kg of coal is burnt per kWh of generated energy. Calculate the calorific value of coal.
2. A coal-based plant spends Rs25 lakhs in one year for coal combustion. The calorific value of coal is 5000kcal/kg. The cost of coal/ton is Rs. 500. The thermal and electrical efficiencies of the plant are 35% and 90% respectively. Calculate the average load.

3. A coal-based thermal plant of 500MW output. The calorific value of coal used is 6400kcal/kg. The thermal efficiency is 30% and the electrical efficiency is 92%. Determine the coal used per hour when the plant is working at full load.
4. The fuel consumption of a diesel-based power station is 0.28kg/kWh. The calorific value of diesel is 10000 kcal/kg. The alternator efficiency is 95%. Find (a) Overall efficiency, and (b) engine efficiency.
5. The fuel consumption in one day of a diesel power plant is 1000kg. The unit generated per day is 4000kWh. The calorific value of the diesel oil is 10000 kcal. The efficiencies of the alternator and engine are 96% and 95% respectively. Find (a) specific fuel consumption, (b) Overall efficiency of the plant, and (c) thermal efficiency of the engine.
6. There are three generating units in a diesel power plant. The capacity of one unit is 700KW, and the capacity of the other two units is 500KW each. The diesel consumption per kWh is 0.28. The calorific value of the fuel is 10200kcal/kg. The plant capacity factor is 40%. Find (a) fuel required for a month of 30 days, and (b) The overall efficiency of the plant.

   [Hints: Maximum energy in a month = plant capacity × hours in a month

   $$\text{Plant capacity} = \frac{\text{Actual energy produced}}{\text{Maximum energy that could have been produced}}$$]
7. An atomic reactor delivered 300 MW of power. It releases 200 MeV of energy by fission of each ${}_{92}U^{235}$ atom. Determine the mass of uranium fission per hour.
8. The half-life of an isotope is 41 days. Determine (1) decay constant, and (b) average life.

PRACTICAL

Experiment No.1

Title: Identify the routine maintenance parts of the coal-fired thermal power plant after watching a video program.

Apparatus used: Watch the video at,

1. https://www.youtube.com/watch?v=cTyL3yDfcJg
2. https://www.youtube.com/watch?v=wM81bIFkCLY
3. https://www.youtube.com/watch?v=eqn0VBVWS50

Objective: To identify the routine maintenance parts of the coal-fired thermal power plant.

Theory: In a coal-fired thermal plant, the following are the main parts.

(a) Coal storage
(b) Ash storage
(c) Boiler
(d) Superheater
(e) Economizer
(f) Turbine
(g) Alternator
(h) Condenser

(i) Cooling tower
(j) Chimney
(k) Electro static precipitator

The schematic diagram of the plant is shown in Fig. 1.1. The brief description of all the parts is given in section 1.3.3 and students are advised to describe briefly each part. The routine maintenance of each part of the plant is given below.

1. Coal storage: The coal is stored in a bunker. The bunker should be cleaned when it is empty. The bunker should be painted with varnish to increase its life at a regular interval of time.
2. Ash storage: The conveyer belt used for ash handling should be cleaned regularly so that it is always in working condition. The ash storage should also be cleaned at regular intervals so that space for new ash is created.
3. Boiler: The boiler should be cleaned regularly. The water tubes should also be checked and cleaned on regular basis. The insulation for the steam pipes must also check for the safety of the personnel.
4. Superheater: The superheater superheats the saturated steam. The proper functioning of this device is important. It should keep the temperature constant. It is necessary to check its function regularly and necessary measures must be taken if it not working properly.
5. Economizer: The economizer or the heat exchangers must be inspected regularly once in six months and repaired if necessary. It should be cleaned during the checkup so that the life of the device increase.
6. Turbine: To increase the life of the turbine it should be ensured that proper quality of steam enters the turbine. Proper expansion of steam in the turbine must be maintained and it should be checked. The insulation provided on the steam pipe should also be proper.
7. Alternator: The shaft of the alternator should be cleaned and greasing of the bearing must be done in a month. The wiring of the alternator should be inspected on regular basis.
8. Condenser: The condenser should maintain a low pressure at the exhaust of the turbine for proper expansion of the steam in the turbine. Each part of the condenser must be checked regularly so that it maintains constant low pressure at the exhaust of the turbine.
9. Cooling tower: The deposited scale from the cooling tower must be removed. It should be ensured proper airflow. The tubes must be cleaned. The water pump must be inspected. All the above activities must be done regularly.
10. Chimney: Smokestack must be done on the chimney. It facilitates the easy release of smoke and gases.
11. Electrostatic precipitator: The components of the precipitator must be checked regularly. The insulation of the transformer winding must be checked at regular intervals.

Conclusion: The parts of the coal-fired thermal power plant are identified for routine maintenance.

Experiment No.2

Title: Identify the routine maintenance parts of the gas-fired thermal power plant after watching a video program.

Apparatus Used: Watch the video at,

1. https://www.youtube.com/watch?v=wn4O7WlMf-M

2. https://www.youtube.com/watch?v=odZnOtJMleU
3. https://www.youtube.com/watch?v=usnnKAOvNnM

Theory: The main and auxiliary parts of gas turbine plants are as follows.

1. Gas turbine
2. The compressor
3. Combustion chamber
4. Alternator
5. Starting motor
6. Fuel system
7. Fuel pump
8. Lubricating pump

The schematic diagram of the plant is shown in Fig. 1.18, Fig. 1.19, and Fig. 1.20. A brief description of all the parts is given in section 1.5.4 and students are advised to write a brief theory of all the above parts from this section.

The routine maintenance of the parts is given below.

1. Gas turbine: Proper expansion of gas in the turbine must be maintained and it should be checked and recorded. The insulation provided on the gas pipes should also be checked.
2. The compressor: The air pipes must be checked regularly. It should be painted regularly to avoid corrosion. Reading of all the valves and their inlet and outlet pressures are to be recorded.
3. Combustion chamber: In the combustion chamber the combustion of fuel takes place. Hot gases are produced inside the chamber. It should be inspected at regular intervals.
4. Alternator: The shaft of the alternator should be cleaned and greased of the bearing as per the specification and as per the routine maintenance checklist. The wiring of the alternator should be inspected on regular basis including the cable trays.
5. Starting motor: The mechanical coupling with the alternator and connection terminals and control terminals from the turbine must be checked regularly. Greasing must be done as per the routine maintenance checklist.
6. Fuel system and fuel pump: It must be ensured that proper and clean fuel is entered into the fuel storage. There should not be any leakage of fuel to avoid chemical hazards. The pump should be checked regularly for any mechanical defect.
7. Lubricating pump: The lubricating pump must be checked for proper functioning.

Conclusion: The parts of the gas turbine plant are identified for routine maintenance.

Experiment No.3

Title: Assemble and dismantle a small diesel generator power plant

Apparatus Used: Watch the video at,

1. https://www.youtube.com/watch?v=6gvMn3eu8Jw

Theory: The parts and their working of the diesel generator power plant are explained in section 1.4.6. The students are asked to write the theory of this experiment in brief from this section.

Procedure for Dismantling

1. Disconnect the electrical power supply connections. Draw the connections of each on a paper and mark each.
2. Disconnect the battery charging lines and mark them on paper.
3. Remove the battery. Mark the cable terminals on paper.
4. Unscrew the bolts on each side of the same cover and keep them nearer to the site on a paper or plate.
5. Remove the control screen, all the wires, and support together.
6. Remove the diesel engine and ac generator together.
7. Diesel engine and the generator can be hoisted independently. In this case, the bolts that hold the set must be removed.

The assembly of the diesel generator set is just reversing the steps followed for dismantling. In this case, the following procedures were followed.

1. Assemble the diesel engine and the generator. Tighten the bolts on the frame.
2. Connect all wires of the control screen.
3. Screw the bolts on each side of the same cover.
4. Connect the battery.
5. Connect the battery charging lines.
6. Connect all the connections of the power supply.

Conclusion: Following the above procedure, it is learned how to assemble and dismantle a small diesel engine set.

Experiment No.4

Title: Identify the routine maintenance parts of the nuclear-fired thermal power plant after watching a video program.

Apparatus Used: Watch the video at,

1. https://www.youtube.com/watch?v=ElppoCeMSXM
2. https://www.youtube.com/watch?v=1U6Nzcv9Vws
3. https://www.youtube.com/hashtag/moderator
4. https://www.youtube.com/watch?v=Aia5zbMjf9o
5. https://www.youtube.com/hashtag/nuclear_power

Theory: Nuclear power plants use the process of nuclear fission to generate electricity. They do this by using nuclear reactors in combination with the Rankine cycle, where the heat generated by the reactor converts water into steam, which drives a turbine. The turbine is mechanically coupled with a generator. The followings are the main equipment of the nuclear power plant.

1. Nuclear reactor.
2. Heat exchanger.
3. Steam turbine.

4. Alternator.
5. Condenser.
6. Cooling tower.

The schematic diagram of the plant is shown in Fig.1.24. The parts of the plant are explained in section 1.6.6. Students are asked to read this section and write the theory in brief for all the above. The routine maintenance of the parts is given below.

(a) **Nuclear reactor:** The nuclear fission of the nuclear fuel takes place inside the reactor. Care must be taken for proper shielding as these materials are radioactive. Sensors for radioactive material are fitted on the reactor site and that need to be observed.

(b) **Heat exchanger:** The water circulating pump must be inspected for any defect and leakage.

(c) **Steam turbine:** To increase the life of the turbine it should ensure that proper quality of steam enters the turbine. Proper expansion of steam in the turbine must be maintained and it should be checked. All the valves and pressure measuring devices are to be checked regularly. The insulation provided on the steam pipe should also be proper and checked.

(d) **Alternator:** The shaft of the alternator should be cleaned and greased of the bearing as per the specification and as per the routine maintenance checklist. The wiring of the alternator should be inspected on regular basis including the cable trays.

(e) **Condenser:** The condenser should maintain a low pressure at the exhaust of the turbine for proper expansion of the steam in the turbine. Each part of the condenser must be checked regularly so that it maintains constant low pressure at the exhaust of the turbine and all the pressure valves and its reading are noted and recorded.

(f) **Cooling tower:** The deposited scale from the cooling tower must be removed. It should be ensured proper airflow. The tubes must be cleaned. The water pump must be inspected. All the above activities must be done regularly as per the checklist.

Conclusion: Following the above procedure, the student can identify the routine maintenance parts of the nuclear power plant.

KNOW MORE

1. Electrical power system is classified into three sections namely generation, transmission, and distribution. Electrical power is generated in the generation system, the transmission system transmits power to the load centre and the distribution system distributes the power to the customers.
2. The first power system was built by Thomas Edition in New York City. This system began operation in 1982 and supplies power to 59 customers in an area of a 1.5km radius at 110V DC. It consists of a steam engine-driven DC generator, cable fuses, etc. The load consists of incandescent lamps. In 1886, the transformer is tested commercially, and in 1888 polyphase ac transmission system was developed. By 1888 Tesla held several patents on ac motors, generators, and ac transmission.
3. Steam engine was the first practical device that convert thermal energy into mechanical energy. The first commercially successful steam engine is developed by Thomas Newcomen in 1712. The modern steam turbine was invented by Charles Parsons in 1984. The gas turbine was built in 1903.

4. Alternator is a doubly fed electrical machine that generates A.C from mechanical energy. It has two windings. They are armature winding and field winding. The field winding is supplied with DC and generated A.C is obtained from the armature winding. Alternators works on Faraday's law of electromagnetic induction.
5. Coal-fired thermal plant operates on the Rankine cycle. There are four processes of the vapor power cycle. They are (1) a constant pressure heating process to convert water into steam in the boiler, (2) a reversible adiabatic expansion of steam in the boiler, (3) a reversible constant pressure heat rejection in the condenser, and (4) a reversible adiabatic compression of liquid ending at initial pressure for the pump. When all these processes are ideal, the cycle is ideal and is called the Rankine cycle.
6. The demand for electrical energy is increasing day by day. The government of India has a fixed target of producing 63GW nuclear power by 2032.
7. Looking at the availability of gaseous fuel, it is necessary to pay attention to installing more gas turbine plants for supplying peak load.

REFERENCES AND SUGGESTED READINGS

1. National institute of occupational health, "Environment, Health and Safety Issues in Coal Fired Thermal ...http://www.nioh.org › publications › pdf
2. https://electricalshouters.com/thermal-power-plant
3. https://cea.nic.in/wp-content/uploads/pdm/2021/06/list_power_stations_2021.pdf
4. https://cea.nic.in/wp-content/uploads/installed/2022/02/installed_capacity.pdf
5. https://en.wikipedia.org/wiki/Steam_engine
6. Nag. P. K.Power Plant Engineering, McGraw Hill, New Delhi, ISBN: 978-9339204044 2. Tanmoy Deb, Electrical Power Generation, Khanna Publishing House, Delhi (Ed. 2018);
7. Gupta, B.R., Generation of Electrical Energy, S. Chand& Co. New Delhi.
8. Soni, Gupta, Bhatnagar, A Course in Electrical Power. - Dhanpatrai and Sons 11. The system, S.Chand & Co. New Delhi, 2005, ISBN: 9788121924962
9. Gupta, J.B. A Course in Electrical Power- S. K Kataria and Sons, New Delhi. 2014

□□

2 Large and Micro-Hydropower Plants

UNIT SPECIFICS

Through this unit we have discussed the following aspects:

- Introduction to hydropower plants;
- Factor for selection of a site for a hydropower plant;
- Energy conversion process of hydropower plant;
- Major Components of Hydro Plants and their functions;
- Classification of hydropower plants and turbines;
- Safe Practices for hydropower plants;
- Micro hydropower plants and their working;
- Hydrology;
- Large and Small hydropower plants in Maharashtra;
- Some experiments on hydropower plants.

The concept of hydropower generation and the process of energy conversion in large and micro hydropower plants are discussed. A brief description of various components of hydropower plants is presented. The classification and working of hydropower plants and hydro turbines for large and micro hydropower plants in detail are presented in this Unit. Further curiosity and creativity as well as improving the problem-solving capacity of the students are dealt with some numerical examples.

Besides giving a large number of multiple-choice questions as well as questions of short and long answer types marked in two categories following lower and higher order of Bloom's taxonomy, assignments through several numerical problems, a list of references, and suggested readings are given in this unit so that one can go through them for practice.

Some practical experiments related to the courses covered in Unit-2 are also appended at the end of this unit to make the students aware of the hands-on on these topics. In some of the experiments, some specific videos are provided.

After the related practical on the topic, based on the content, there is a "Know More" section appended. This section has been designed to supplement additional information and higher learning skills on the topic.

RATIONALE

This unit on large micro hydropower plants will help the students to get a fundamental idea behind the conversion of hydro energy into electrical energy. Different types of large and micro hydropower plants, the classification of hydro turbines, and their working are discussed. The factors that need to be considered while selecting a site for the hydropower plant are also presented. The hydrology for the hydropower plants is also presented. Furthermore, safe practice and use of hydropower plants in the modern day and its pros and cons also give up-to-date knowledge on the topic.

Some related problems are pointed out with their solutions which can help further for getting a clear idea of the concern topics on hydropower generation.

PRE-REQUISITES

Fundamentals of Electrical & Electronics Engineering (ES104)

UNIT OUTCOMES

After completion of Unit-2 students will be able to:

U2-O1: Describe the working of hydropower plants and their components

U2-O2: Classify large and micro hydropower plants, turbines for large and micro hydropower plants

U2-O3: Explain the working principle of working with various types of turbines

U2-O4: Realize the importance of safe practices in power generation in hydropower plants

U2-O5: Identify the routine maintenance parts of various hydropower plants.

Unit-2 Outcome	EXPECTED MAPPING WITH COURSE OUTCOMES (1 - Weak Correlation; 2 - Medium Correlation; 3 - Strong Correlation)				
	CO-1	CO-2	CO-3	CO-4	CO-5
U2-O1	3	3	3	2	2
U2-O2	3	-	3	2	-
U2-O3	3	-	1	-	2
U2-O4	3	1	-	-	-
U2-O5	3	2	3	-	-

2.1 INTRODUCTION

Hydropower relies on the *Water Cycle*. Hydropower is dependent on an understanding of the water cycle as portrayed in Fig.2.1. The water cycle consists of *three* stages:

1. Solar radiation heats the surface water of rivers, lakes, and oceans, causing it to evaporate.
2. Water vapor condenses to form clouds, which then fall as precipitation (rain and snow).
3. Precipitation accumulates in streams and rivers, which drain into seas and lakes, where this evaporates and the cycle begins again.

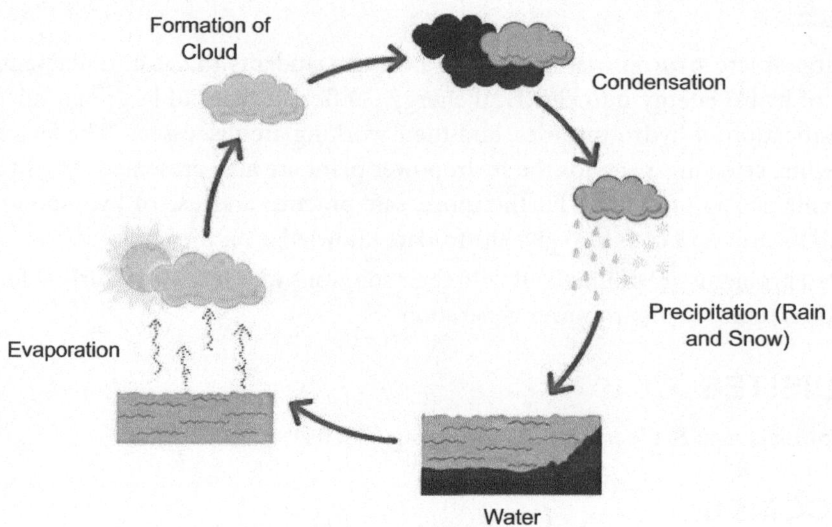

Fig. 2.1: Water Cycle

The level of precipitation that falls on rivers and streams in a given geographic area impacts the quantity of water for hydropower generation. The ability to produce hydropower can be significantly impacted by short-term variations in precipitation as well as long-term variations in precipitation trends, such as droughts.

2.1.1 Potential & Requirements for Hydropower Plant

A power plant that uses the potential energy of water for the generation of electrical energy is called a hydroelectric power plant or hydroelectric power station.

Hydroelectric power plants convert the *hydraulic energy* of a river, whether it is naturally occurring or artificially created, into clean, *renewable* electricity. The process consists of a series of stages and begins with the conversion of *potential energy* in masses of water that are positioned at higher altitudes than where the plant's turbines are located.

In general, this technique involves a barrier that blocks the water flow, such as a dam or crossbeam, and produces a body of water that can serve as a reservoir or a hydropower basin. The water is transported into charge basins and then diverted through tunnels and adduction channels to hydroelectric turbines via penstocks. Depending on the amount of energy needed, both flow-regulating devices (distributors) and injection valves are utilized here. The water flows over the turbines, which causes them to generate mechanical energy. The water then flows into a spillway, which directs it back into the waterway. The turbine is immediately connected to a revolving electric generator (alternator), which converts the mechanical energy of the turbines into electrical energy. To transmit this power over long distances, a transformation is required. The electrical energy must pass through a transformer before it can be sent over transmission lines; this lowers the current while increasing its voltage. Once the energy reaches its destination, it travels through a transformer once more, which rises the value of the current and lowers the voltage, making it ideal for industrial, commercial, and residential usage.

2.1.2 Different Types of Hydropower Plants

Hydropower plants are classified into three types based on the system used: *run-of-river* power stations, *conventional* hydropower stations, and *pumped storage* power stations.

In *run-of-river* power plants, the natural flow of a river between two distinct levels is used to make electricity. Without using penstocks, the water is transported by a diversion channel to the turbines. The power of the plant is mostly influenced by the river's flow and by how quickly water moves through the so-called jump, which connects two levels.

A *conventional hydropower* plant uses an upstream basin, the surge chamber, which can be natural- such as a lake, or built with a dam. Water from the dam flows through penstocks to hydraulic turbines, which turn and create mechanical energy. Then, the alternator converts this mechanical energy into electricity. There is a pool downstream where the turbulent water from the turbines is soothed before being restored to the river's normal flow. Unlike run-of-river systems, an upstream reservoir enables the control of water flows and, consequently, of the associated renewable power output.

Pumped storage power plants have two reservoirs at different heights i.e., upstream and downstream, the second one serves as an energy reserve. During times when there is less demand for energy, a pumping station pushes water from the downstream basin to the upstream basin. This lets the system handle times when there is more demand for energy safely. Some plants can use the fact that Francis turbines can be turned around to turn them into pumps and send the water back to the basin upstream.

2.2 FACTORS FOR SELECTION OF SITE FOR A HYDROELECTRIC POWER PLANT

The following points are considered for the selection of a site for a hydroelectric power plant.

(a) **Availabilityilty of water:** To estimate the power potential at a particular location, the river run-off data of many years must be available. The data includes maximum and minimum flows, and average flows at a particular period.

(b) **Storage of water:** A sufficient facility for creating storage of water must be available. Water is stored during high flow periods. Storage is important for almost all hydro plants to supply water during lean flow periods.

(c) **Head of water:** When the head increases, less amount of water is required to be stored in the reserver, and less amount of water to be handled by the penstock, screens, and turbine. This reduces the capital cost of the plant.

(d) **Types and cost of land:** There are many heavy machines required to be installed. The bearing capacity of the land should be sufficient for such machines.

(e) **Distance from load centers:** If the site is nearer to the load center, the cost of transportation is less. Hence, it reduces the overall per unit cost.

(f) **Transportation facility:** The site should have sufficient transportation facilities to carry heavy machines.

2.3 ENERGY CONVERSION PROCESS OF HYDROPOWER PLANT

The water in the reservoir has potential energy, which is turned into kinetic energy of water when it flows out of the reservoir. The motion of water flowing through the turbine causes it to rotate, which in turn causes the generator to produce power. Thus, the kinetic energy of water is turned into mechanical energy. The mechanical energy is then converted into electrical energy using an alternator or generator.

Because hydropower uses water to make electricity, plants are usually built on or near a water source. The available energy from moving water relies upon both the volume of water flow and the change in elevation, also known as the head, i.e., from one point to another. The amount of power that can be produced increases with the flow and head. At the plant level, water travels via a *pipe*, also known as a *penstock*, and spins the blades of a *turbine*, which ultimately turns a generator that generates electricity as per the layout of the traditional hydroelectric power plant shown in Fig.2.2. Most traditional hydroelectric facilities, including run-of-the-river and pumped storage systems, function in this manner. The schematic diagram of a hydroelectric power plant is also given in Fig. 2.3

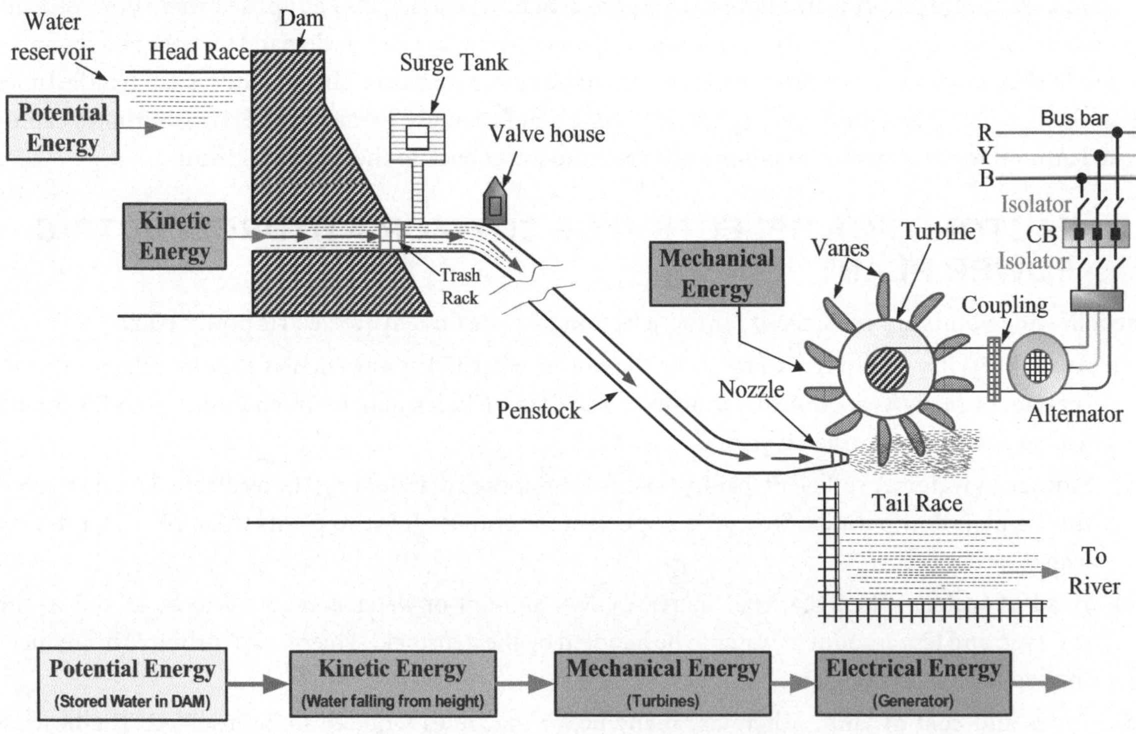

Fig.2.2: Layout of Hydropower Plant

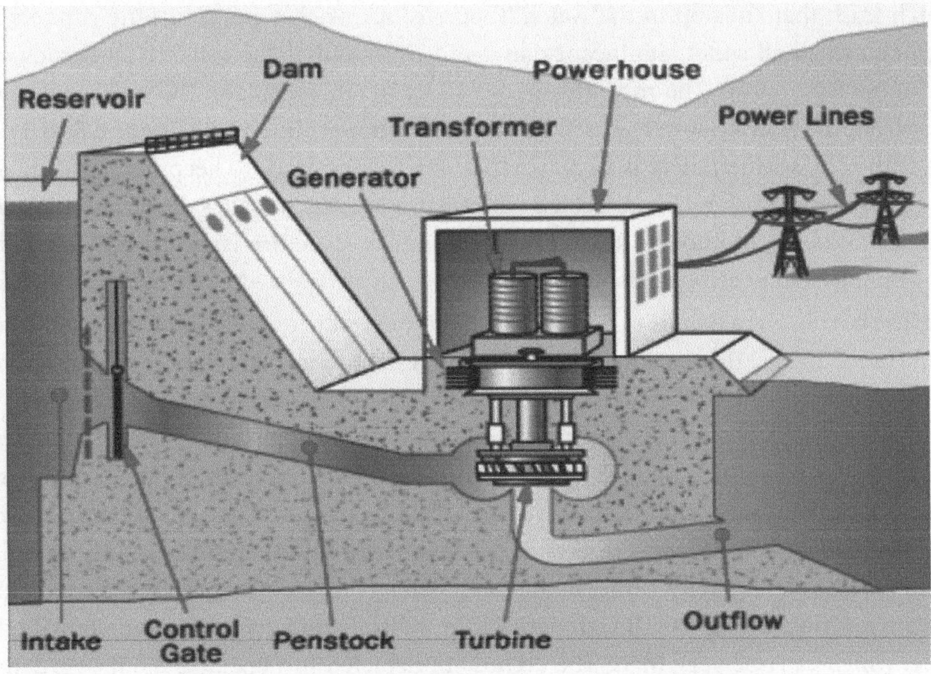

Fig. 2.3: Schematic diagram of Hydroelectric Plant

2.3.1 Major Components of Hydroelectric Plants and Their Functions

The majority of conventional hydropower plants have the following main components.

(a) Forebay
(b) Catchment Area
(c) Intake structure
(d) Dam
(e) Penstock
(f) Surge Chamber
(g) Hydraulic Turbines
(h) Power House
(i) Draft tubes
(j) Tail race

(a) Forebay: A hydroelectric plant would typically have a basin area known as a forebay, which is used to temporarily hold water before it is pumped into the intake chamber. The amount of water that must be supplied to a certain region influences how much water can be stored in the forebay. This is also employed when the intake load requirement is lower. We are aware that reservoirs are constructed across rivers to hold water, and that the penstocks are used to transport the stored water to the power plant from the dam's upstream side. The reservoir serves as the forebay in this instance.

(b) Catchment Area: Whenever a dam is constructed over a river or stream, the entire land behind the dam becomes part of the catchment area for the hydro plant.

(c) Intake structure: A structure known as an intake structure is responsible for directing water from the forebay into the penstocks. There are different kinds of intake structures, and the choice of which one to use depends on the conditions in the area. The trash racks are one of the most important parts of the intake structure. At the entrance to the penstock, there are trash racks to catch trash that ends up in the water. The penstock, wicket gates, turbine runners, and other components will all suffer significant damage if trash and water enter it. Steel rods are used to make these trash racks. The rods are spaced 10 to 30 cm apart, and the racks will segregate the debris from the flowing water, which has a maximum permitted velocity of 0.6 to 1.6 m/sec. In areas with cold weather, there is a chance that water will freeze. To keep the ice from getting into the penstocks, the trash racks are heated with electricity, which makes the ice melt when it reaches the trash racks. In addition to trash racks, the intake structure is equipped with rakes, trolley arrangements, and penstock closing gates, all of which are utilized to clean the trash racks.

(d) Dam: The purpose of a dam is to offer pondage, storage, or the ability to divert water into conduits in addition to raising the stream's water surface to establish an artificial head. The most costly and significant component of a hydro project is a dam. Dams are constructed using earthen or rock fill, concrete, or stone masonry. The geography of the site determines the type and arrangement. In a small canyon, a masonry dam might be constructed. A large valley might be the greatest place for an earth dam. The foundation characteristics, local transit options, the likelihood of earthquakes, and other dangers all influence the choice of the dam. There are three main classifications of masonry dams: solid gravity, buttress, and arch dams. The concrete gravity dam seen in Fig.2.4 is adequate for most locations. The strength of the subsoil strata will determine how high the dam can be, which can't be very high. The arch dam, depicted in Fig.2.5, is a curving dam that uses arch action to send a large percentage of its water pressure horizontally to the abutments. When a restricted canyon width is available, an arch dam is preferred. This dam is inherently stable and resists slippage. A large downward force produced by the water pressure on the buttress or deck dam's slanted upstream face prevents overturning or sliding. Such a dam as shown in Fig.2.6 is better suited to locations with shaky foundations and high earthquake risk. An earth dam has a much larger base than it does height. Due to the large base that creates a long seepage route, these dams are ideal for pervious foundations.

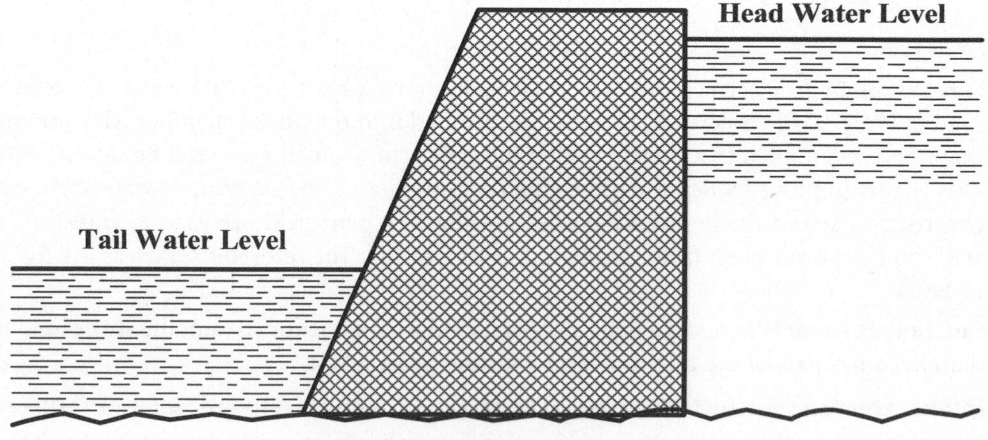

Fig. 2.4: Solid Gravity Dam

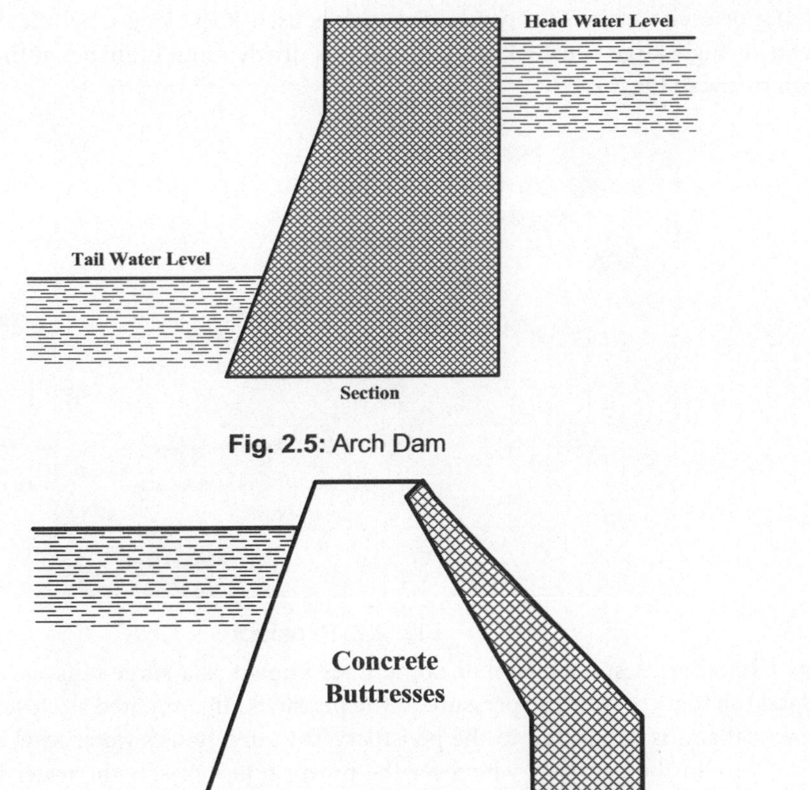

Fig. 2.5: Arch Dam

Fig. 2.6: Buttresses Dam

The following benefits are associated with earth dams:

(i) They cost less than dams made of stone.

(ii) They are most at home in natural settings.

(iii) If it is shielded from erosion, this kind of dam offers the most long-lasting style of construction.

But, earth dams also have the following limitations:

(i) Water seeps out of earth dams more than it does from masonry dams.

(ii) They are susceptible to water erosion.

(iii) They are not ideal for a spillway, hence an additional spillway with sufficient capacity is needed.

(e) Penstock: Penstocks act as large, sloping pipes that transport water from reservoirs or intake structures to the turbines. They operate under a certain amount of pressure, therefore abrupt closure or opening of penstock gates may result in water hammer on the penstocks. So, aside from the fact that the penstock is like a regular pipe, these are made to withstand the water hammer impact. To relieve this pressure, surge tanks are available for long penstocks and strong walls are available for short penstocks. Penstocks are produced using Steel or Reinforced Concrete Cement

(RCC). For each turbine, a separate penstock is used if the length is little. Similarly, if the length is great, a single large penstock is used, and it is divided into branches at the end. The penstock is shown below in Fig.2.7.

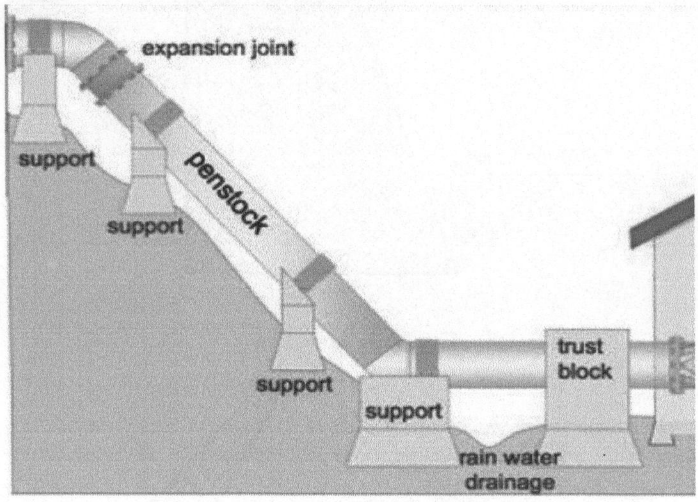

Fig. 2.7: Penstock

(f) **Surge Chamber:** A surge chamber, sometimes known as a surge tank, is a cylindrical tank with an open top that controls the pressure in the penstock. It is situated as close to the power house as is practical and is connected to the penstock. The surge tank's water level increases and controls the pressure in the penstock whenever the power house rejects the water load coming from the penstock. In the same way, when there is a big demand in the power house, the surge tank speeds up the flow of water into the power house, and then the water level goes down. The surge tank's water level stabilizes when the power house's discharge is consistent. Surge tanks come in a variety of varieties, and they are chosen depending on the needs of the plant, the length of the penstock, etc.

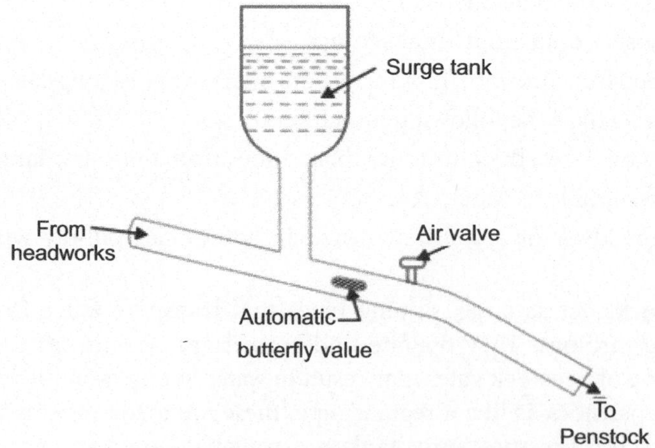

Fig. 2.8: Surge Chamber or Surge Tank

(g) **Hydraulic Turbines:** A hydraulic turbine is an apparatus that transforms hydraulic energy into mechanical energy, which is then transformed into electrical energy by connecting the turbine's shaft to the generator. The principle in this instance is that the generator generates electricity whenever the water from the penstock comes into contact with the revolving blades or runner under high pressure. In general, there are two types of hydraulic turbines: (a) Impulse turbine and (b) Reaction turbine. The velocity turbine is another name for an impulse turbine. An example of an impulse turbine is the Pelton wheel turbine. A pressure turbine is another name for a reaction turbine. The Francis turbine and the Kaplan turbine fall within this group.

(h) **Power House:** A facility known as a "power house" is set up to safeguard electrical and hydraulic machinery. In most cases, the substructure or foundation built for the power house supports the entire piece of equipment. In the case of reaction turbines, some machinery such as draft tubes, scroll casing, and so on are fixed within the foundation as it is being laid. Consequently, a large-scale foundation is laid. When it comes to the superstructure, generators are installed on the ground floor, beneath which are installed vertical turbines. Additionally, horizontal turbines are offered. On the first floor, a control room is available.

(i) **Draft tubes:** Draft tubes are required in the case of reaction turbines to link the turbine discharge to the tailrace. The diameter of the draft tube gradually increases to ensure that the water enters the tailrace at a safe rate of speed. Outlet gates are supplied at the draft tube's end and can be closed while repairs are being made.

(j) **Tailrace:** Water flowing from turbines to streams is known as a tailrace. It is preferable if the power plant is situated close to the stream. However, if it is positioned far from the stream, a channel must be built to transport water into a stream. Otherwise, the water flow could harm the plant in several ways, including cavitation, damaging the turbine blades, and diminishing turbine performance. This is due to silting or scouring produced by excessive water flow from the powerhouse. Therefore, correct tailrace design should be given greater priority.

2.3.2 How Much Power Does A Hydropower Plant Have The Potential to Generate?

Two factors determine how much electricity a hydroelectric plant generates:

(a) **The height of the waterfall:** The greater the height of the waterfall, the more force it possesses. The height of the waterfall is often proportional to the height of the dam from which it initiates. Hence, dam height determines how far water flows and how much power it generates. According to scientists, the force of falling water is "directly proportional" to the distance it falls. As a result, water that falls twice as far has twice as much energy.

(b) **Quantity of Water Falling:** The turbine will make more power if more water falls through it. The quantity of available water is dependent on the quantity of water flowing down the river. Larger rivers carry a greater volume of water and are therefore capable of generating a greater amount of power. Power is "directly proportional" to the flow of the river. A river that has twice as much water flowing through it as another river can make twice as much energy.

2.4 CLASSIFICATION OF HYDROPOWER PLANTS

The hydropower plants are broadly classified as follows.

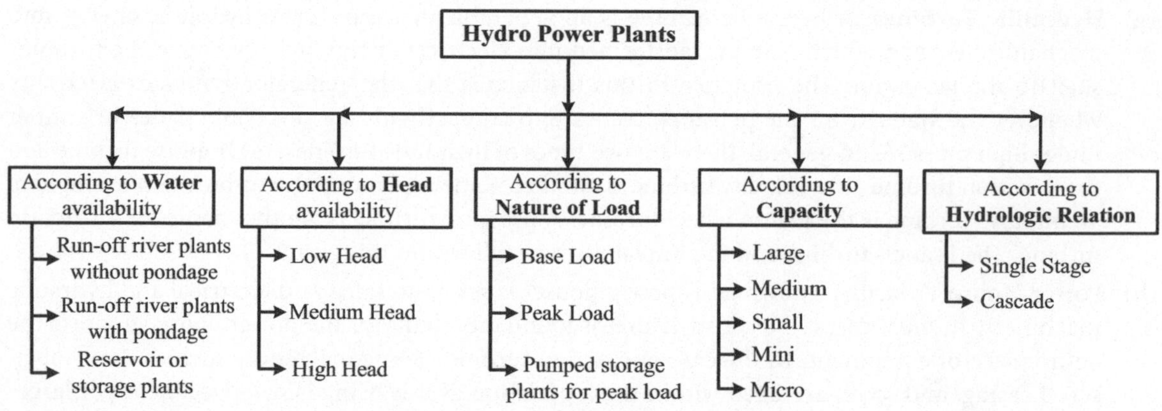

2.4.1 Classification of Hydro Plants According to Water Availability

There are three types of hydroelectric plants under this category

(a) **Run-off river plants without pondage:** Some hydropower plants are right next to rivers, so they can't store or collect water. These facilities are known as run-off river power plants without ponds. These plants can only use water when it is available. They can't be used whenever they want or fit any part of the load curve. In such plants, there is no water flow regulation. During periods of high flow and low load, water is wasted, while during periods of low flow, plant capacity is extremely low. As a result, the firm capacity of these plants is quite low. In these kinds of locations, the water is utilized most frequently for agricultural purposes or navigation, and the generation of electricity is a secondary concern at best. These plants can be built for a very low price, but the amount of power they make and the amount of water they can use are typically very low. During flooding, the tail water level may rise to an extreme level, rendering the plant dysfunctional. The primary objective of such plants is to generate energy from any available flow, hence reducing the amount of coal required by steam units. During times of high flow, these types of plants can deliver a substantial amount of the base load when they are put to use. The run-off-river plants without pondage are illustrated in Fig.2.9.

The run-off-river plants without pondage are illustrated in Fig.2.10. Pondage makes runoff river power plants even more useful. The term "pondage" refers to the storage that is available at the plant. This storage makes it possible for the plant to manage the hour-to-hour swings in the load that occur over a week or a lonperiodtime period amount of the pondage. If there is enough water in the pond, the power plant can make more electricity. This sort of power plant is more helpful than a plant that does not include pondage since it can be employed on segments of the load curve as needed, subject to certain limits. These power plants are more reliable and their ability to make electricity depends less on how fast the water flows. Depending on the flow of the stream, these power plants can be used as either base load or peak load power plants. During times of high flow, these plants may be used to support the base load, while during times of low flow, they might be used just to meet peak demand. When providing pondage, the tailrace condition must be such that floods do not elevate the tailrace water level, hence lowering the head on the plant and reducing its efficacy. When these plants are used with steam power plants, they save the most coal possible.

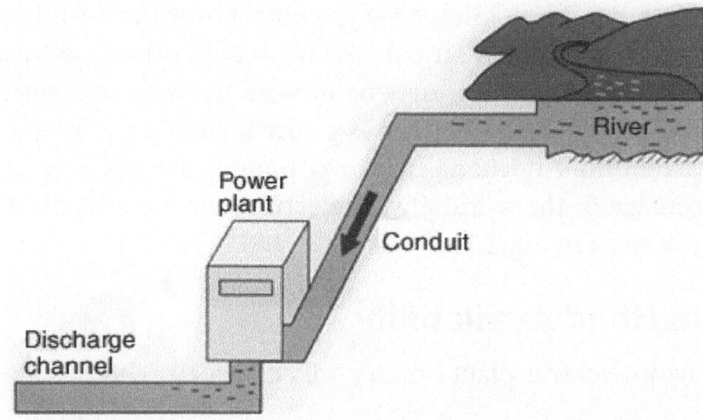

Fig. 2.9: Run-off-river plant without pondage

(b) Run-off river plants with pondage:

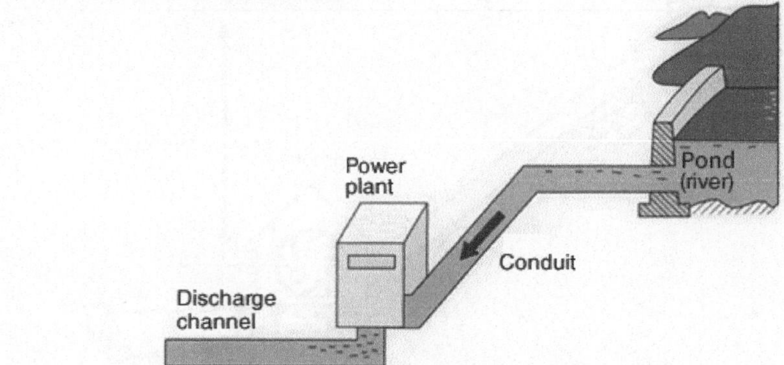

Fig. 2.10: Run-off-river plant with pondage

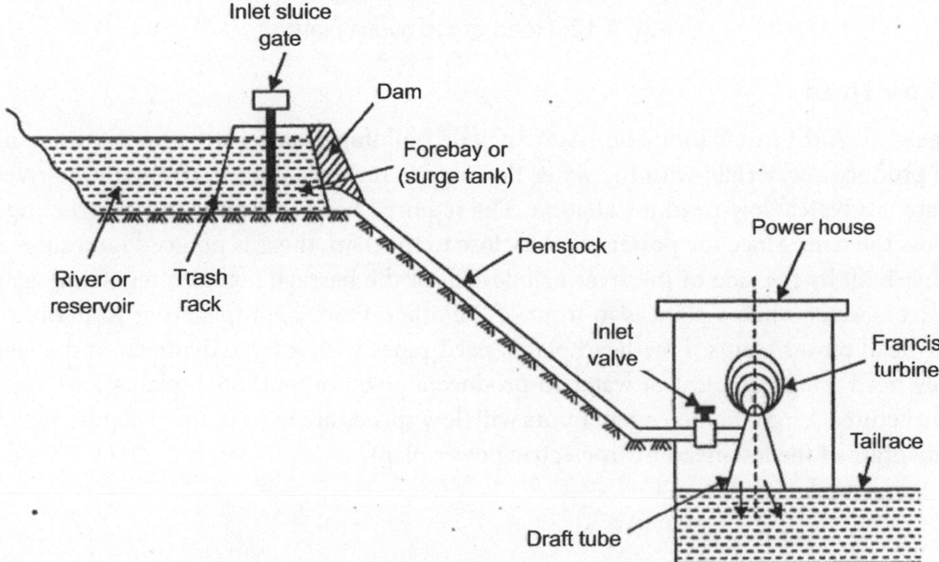

Fig. 2.11: Reservoir or Storage Plants

(c) **Reservoir or storage plants:** It is possible to keep control over the flow of water and make the most efficient use of it when it is kept in a large reservoir that is protected by a dam. The storage area adds to the plant's firm capacity, and it may be utilized to its full potential throughout the entire year. This type of plant can be utilized either as a base load or a peak load plant depending on the requirements of the situation. Additionally, it can be applied to any area of the load curve in a grid system. A large percentage of the world's hydroelectric power plants of this type. The reservoir or storage plants are illustrated in Fig.2.11.

2.4.2 According to Head Availability

There are three types of hydroelectric plants under this category. The head of the plant is shown in Fig. 2.12.

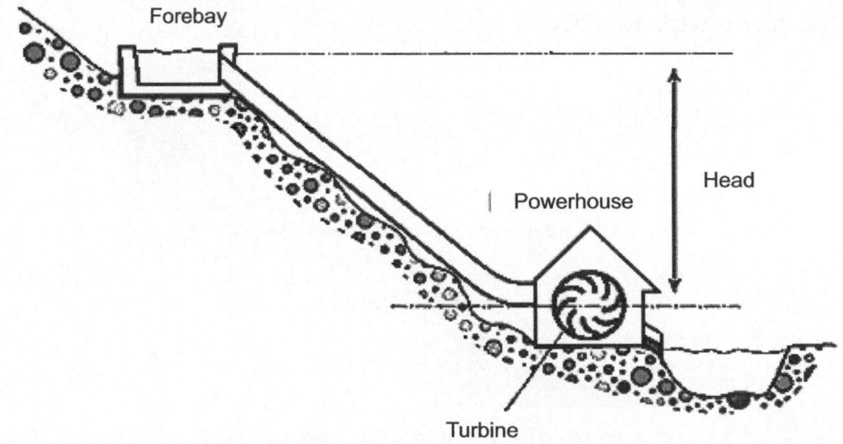

Fig. 2.12: Head of the hydro plant

2.4.2.1 Low Head

Most low-head (< 30m) installations on rivers include building a dam throughout the stream to hold it back and produce a waterfall, with the water flowing via turbines and returning to the river beneath the dam. here is a typical low-head installation. The required head is created by constructing a dam or barrage across the river. Since the power plant is close to the dam, there is no need for a surge tank. The plant is either built by the side of the river or one-half of the barrage includes regulating gates for the release of excess water while a plant is in front of the other. Francis, propeller, or **Kaplan** turbines are used in low-head power plants. Low-head plants need pipes with a large diameter and a short length because they need a high amount of water to produce a given output. Such plants have complex and expensive structures. Large-diameter generators with low speeds are used in these plants. Fig.2.13 shows the layout diagram of the low-head hydroelectric power plant.

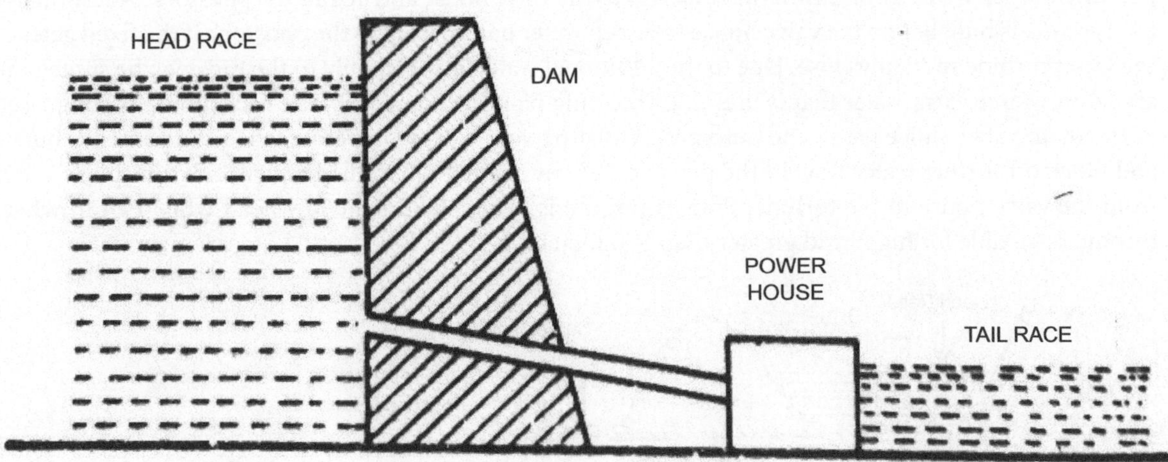

Fig. 2.13: Low-head hydropower plant

2.4.2.2 Medium Head

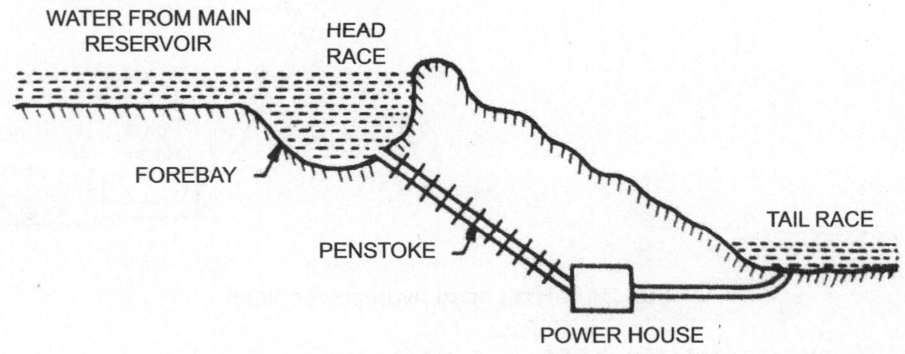

Fig. 2.14: Medium head hydropower plant

In these kinds of power plants, the stream water is typically diverted to a forebay that is located on one bank of the river, just like in the situation of a low-head plant. Penstocks are used to transport water from the forebay to the turbines. Such power plants use the forebay that is supplied at the start of the penstock as a water reservoir. In these types of plants, the process of transporting water from the main reservoir to the forebay and finally to the turbines via the penstock often takes place in an open channel. In this instance, the forebay itself acts as a surge tank. Francis, propeller, or Kaplan horizontal shaft turbines are employed in these facilities. In Fig.2.14, the configuration of a medium head plant (30m to 100m) is displayed.

2.4.2.3 High Head

Fig.2.15 shows the layout diagram of the high head hydropower plant (100m to 2000m). This power plant's head is generally higher than 300 meters. A dam is built at a level that creates the highest possible reserve water level. The valve house is connected to a pressure tunnel that is being built. Through this pressure tunnel, water travels from the reservoir to the valve house and begins the penstock. Additionally, a surge tank is built before the valve house to lessen water hammering to the penstock if the fixed gates of the water turbine suddenly close. Due to the additional water, it will supply to the turbine, the surge tank also stores some extra water that is useful for meeting pick-load demand. The valve house is comprised of the main valve, sluice gates, and automatic isolating valves, which operate when the penstock bursts and block off further water flow to the penstock. A connecting pipe called a penstock transports water from the valve house to the turbine. Francis turbine is beneficial for the low head while **Pelton wheel** turbine is suitable for high head greater than 500 meters.

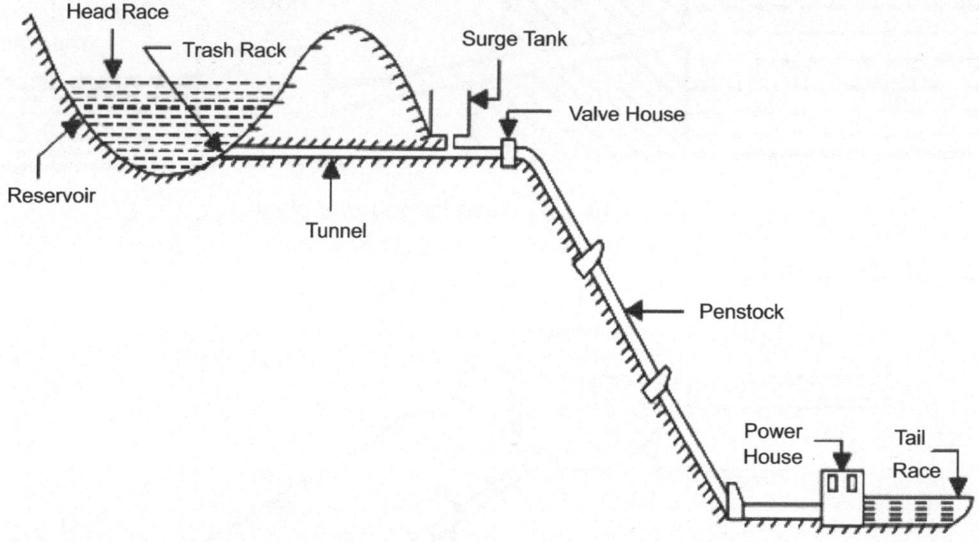

Fig. 2.15: High head hydropower plant

2.4.3 According to Nature of Load

There are three types of hydroelectric plants under this category such as base load, peak load, and pumped storage plants for peak load.

2.4.3.1 Base Load Plant

The power plants that can supply base load are referred to as base load power plants. These plants often have huge capacities. The load factor of such plants is high since they are maintained running essentially on block load (i.e., the load that is essentially constant). Base load plants consist of reservoir and run-off river plants without ponds. Plants with significant storage capacity are best employed as base load plants, especially during rainy seasons when rain water raises the reservoir's water level. The cost per unit of energy that is generated by a plant needs to be relatively low for the plant to be considered for usage as a base load plant.

2.4.3.2 Peak Load Plant

Peak load plants are those utilized to supply the system's peak load, which corresponds to the load at the peak of the load curve. Peak load plants can be made using runoff river plants with pondage. If the pondage is sufficient, a substantial percentage of the load can be provided by such a plant when necessary. Naturally, reservoir plants can also be employed as peak load plants. Large seasonal storage is available at peak load facilities. They conserve water during periods of low demand and operate during periods of high demand. Such plants have a low load factor.

2.4.3.3 Pumped Storage Plants for Peak Load

This peak load plant has a distinctive design. Here, there are two different kinds of water ponds: the upper head water pond and the tail water pond. By a penstock, two ponds of water are joined to one another. The lower end is the main generating pumping plant. During the off-load period, the plant's extra energy is used to pump water from the lower head pond to the upper head pond. It is utilized to generate electricity at peak times when water is abundant. This setup allows for repeated usage of the same water. The only additional water needed is to deal with seepage and evaporation. The Pumped storage plants for peak load are illustrated in Fig.2.16.

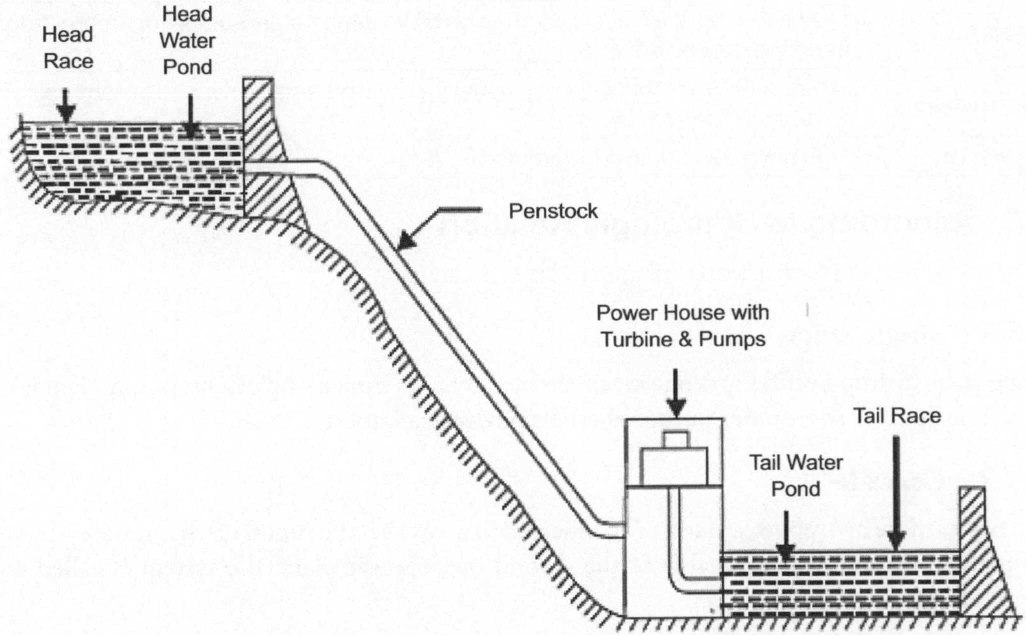

Fig. 2.16: Pumped storage plants for peak load

2.4.4 According to Capacity

In addition to the classifications presented above, hydroelectric power plants can also be classified based on their capacities. They are as follows.

(a) Large hydropower plant.

(b) Medium hydropower plant

(c) Small hydropower plant

(d) Mini hydropower plant

(e) Micro hydropower plant.

(f) Pico hydropower plant

The terms "mini," "micro," and "pico" hydro plants are typically grouped as "small hydro plants." In addition to the aforementioned categorization, a new class of very large hydropower plants with capacities ranging from more than 5,000 MW to 10,000 MW are also emerging as a result of significant investment and improved technology. However, when it comes to small hydro, each country has a different upper and lower limit for defining the term. Small hydropower is commonly defined by its output in kilowatts around the world. Different countries have different rules, but the upper limit is always between 5 and 50 MW. The classification is shown in Table. 2.1.

Table 2.1: Classification of hydroelectric power plants based on capacity

Large Hydro	More than 100 MW, and typically connected to a large power grid
Medium Hydro	15 to100 MW, usually connect to a grid.
Small-Hydro	1to15 MW, usually connect to a grid.
Mini-Hydro	Above 100 kW, but less than 1 MW; either stand-alone or, more frequently, connecting to the grid.
Micro-Hydro	From 5kW to 100kW, they usually powered small towns or rural businesses in an area far from the grid.
Pico-Hydro	From a few hundred Watts to 5kW.

2.4.5 According to Hydrologic Relation

There are two types of hydroelectric plants under this category.

2.4.5.1 Single Stage

A single-stage hydropower setup is one in which the discharge from a single hydropower plant is returned to a river or used for some other purpose besides power generation.

2.4.5.2 Cascade

When two or more hydropower plants are connected in a way that the runoff discharge of one hydropower plant is used as the intake discharge of the second hydropower plant, the system is called a cascade hydropower plant.

2.5 CLASSIFICATION OF TURBINES FOR HYDROPOWER PLANTS

Electricity is generated by a variety of turbines that convert hydraulic energy into mechanical energy. There are numerous ways to describe the different types of turbines. The classification methods include the manner of momentum exchange between the fluid and the turbine, the fluid flow path thru the turbine, the hydraulic activity range of the turbine, and the turbine's specific speed. Various other types of turbines may also exist. The turbines are classified in various aspects as shown below.

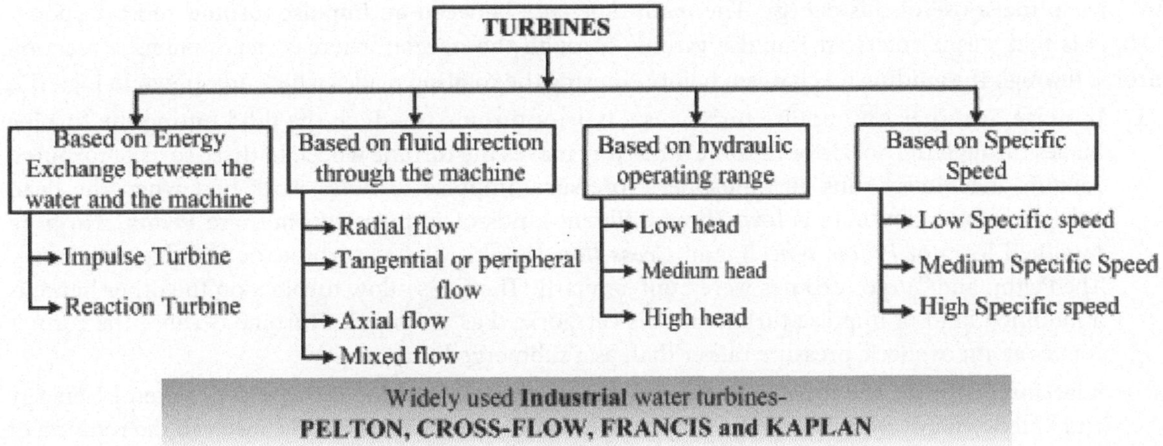

2.5.1 Based on Energy Exchange Between Water and Machine

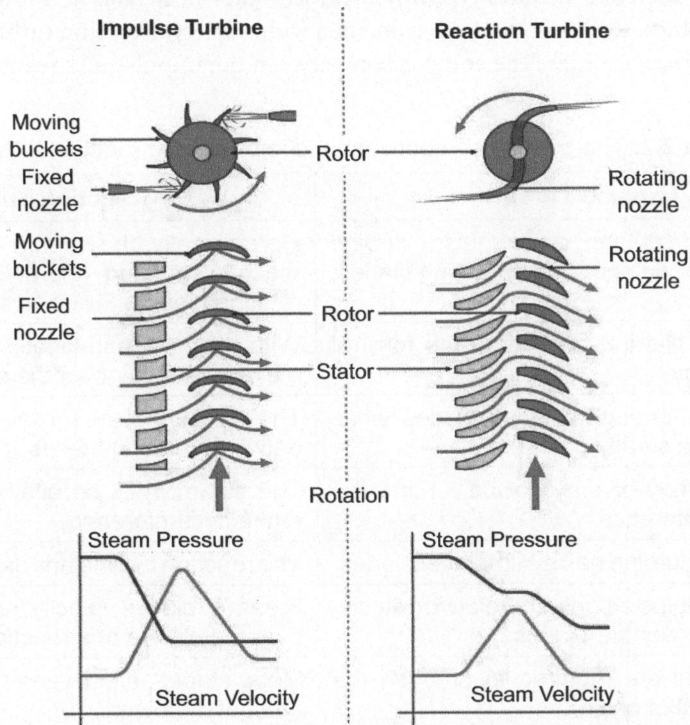

Fig. 2.17: Difference between Impulse and Reaction turbine

Hydro turbines can be divided into two groups based on how the fluid flow affects the turbine blades: **Impulse** and **Reaction.** The main difference between an impulse turbine and a reaction turbine is how the potential energy is changed into kinetic energy to turn the turbine wheel. The pressure head of a working fluid stores potential energy, while the velocity head stores kinetic energy. The fluid can be compressible or incompressible. Different physical concepts are employed by impulse and reaction turbines to make use of this energy. The *main difference* between an impulse turbine and a response turbine is that steam enters an impulse turbine through the nozzle, whereas steam enters a reaction turbine through the guiding mechanism before entering the rotating blades which are shown in Fig.2.17.

(a) **Impulse Turbine:** An impulse turbine is a type of turbine in which the fluid hitting the turbine blades through the nozzle or in some other way moves the turbine wheel. In these sorts of turbines, rotating machinery runs at atmospheric pressure. Impulse turbines work best when the head is high and the flow rate is low. Three different kinds of impulse turbines are ***Pelton***, ***Turgo*** (a modified form of *Pelton Wheel*), and ***Cross-flow*** (Banki-Michell turbine, or Ossberger turbine). The Pelton and Turgo turbines were built similarly. The Cross-flow turbine, on the other hand, is a modified kind of impulse turbine that is categorized as an impulse turbine because the runner rotates at atmospheric pressure rather than as a submerged turbine.

(b) **Reaction Turbine:** The turbine is referred to as a reaction turbine if the water's potential energy and kinetic energy, which are caused by pressure and velocity respectively, result in the rotation of the turbine blades. In these kinds of turbines, power exchange occurs as a result of changes in water pressure and the kinetic energy of the water. The turbine as a whole is submerged in the water. Applications for reaction turbines typically include higher flow rates and lower heads than those for impulse turbines. Reaction turbines come in a wide variety. Reaction turbines include ***Francis***, ***Kaplan***, and ***Deriaz*** turbines. The comparison between the impulse and reaction turbine is shown in Table 2.2.

Table 2.2: The comparison between the impulse and reaction turbine

S. No	Impulse Turbine	Reaction Turbine
1.	The stream enters an impulse turbine through a nozzle and strikes rotating blades.	Here, initially, the stream flows via the guide mechanism and then flows through the rotating blades.
2.	The stream hits the buckets in the form of kinetic energy.	With pressure and kinetic energy, the steam moves smoothly over the spinning blades.
3.	Steam flows through rotating blades while maintaining a steady pressure.	The pressure of steam decreases as it passes between rotating blades.
4.	The steam may or may not be let into the entire circumference.	The steam must be allowed to circulate the entire circumference.
5.	The impulse turbine has symmetrical blades.	The reaction turbine has asymmetrical blades.
6.	Steam maintains a constant relative velocity as it passes over the blades.	Steam's relative velocity increases as it glides over the blades of a reaction turbine.
7.	Fewer stages are required to produce the same amount of power.	More stages are needed to get the same amount of power.
8.	The direction of steam flow in a turbine wheel is radial to the wheel's rotation.	Steam flows axially and radially toward the turbine wheel.
9.	Less maintenance is necessary.	It necessitates greater maintenance.
10.	It is conducive to low discharge.	It is ideal for both medium and high discharges.
11.	Newton's second law applies to the impulse turbine.	Newton's third law applies to the reaction turbine.

12.	Impulse turbine rotor construction is disc or wheel type.	Reaction turbine rotor construction is drum type.
13.	The degree of reaction is zero.	The degree of reaction is greater than zero (between 0 and 1)
14.	An example of an impulse turbine is the Pelton Wheel.	Francis and Kaplan turbines are examples of reaction turbines.

A more detailed analysis of both turbines is found in the given following video link https://www.youtube.com/watch?v=3AD_Hiy2QjM.

2.5.2 Based on Fluid Direction Through Machine

The movement of water through the turbine classifies these turbines into four types. They are

(a) Radial flow

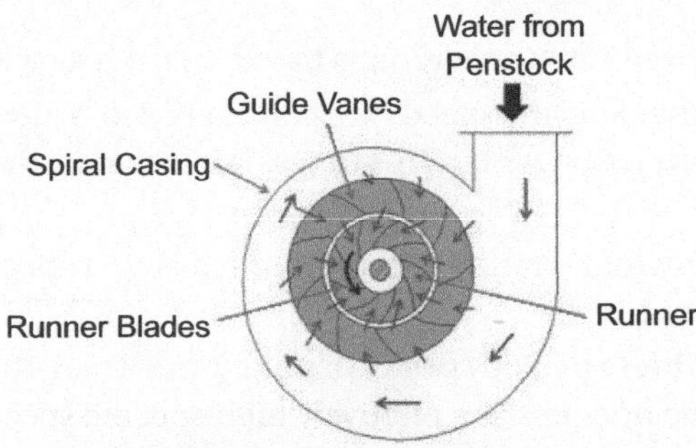

Fig. 2.18: Radial flow

A radial flow turbine is one in which the flow in the runner flows in a radial direction. These turbines can be classified as either inward radial flow or outward radial flow turbines, depending on the direction of the radial flow. Francis turbines are radial flow turbines. The radial flow can be illustrated as shown in Fig. 2.18. Inward radial flow turbines are those in which water flows from the outward to the inward of the runner. Outward radial flow turbines have a runner that allows water to flow from the inward to the outward.

(b) Tangential flow: Water flows tangentially to the runner in these turbines. **Pelton** turbines belong to this class of turbines.

(c) Axial flow: The fluid in this kind of turbine moves parallel to the turbine shaft (turbine axis). These turbines include Kaplan.

(d) Mixed Flow: A mixed flow turbine, such as a modern Francis turbine, is a type of turbine in which the flow enters the turbine in a radial direction and exits the turbine in an axial direction.

2.5.3 Based on Hydraulic Operating Range

Consequently, three types of water turbines exist. They are low head turbines, medium head turbines, and high head turbines.

(a) Low Head turbines: Low-head hydraulic turbines are those that have a head range of less than 30 meters. These turbines include the **Kaplan** turbine. An ultra-low head is one with a head height of under 3 meters.

(b) **Medium Head turbines:** Medium heads have an effective range between 30 and 300 meters. In such cases, Francis turbines are commonly used.

(c) **High Head turbines:** Turbines with heads more than 300 meters, like the Pelton Turbine, are called "high-head turbines."

2.5.4 Based on Specific Speed

The specific speed of a turbine (N_s) is the speed at which a turbine with geometric similarity can produce one unit of power under one head unit. The specific speed of a turbine (N_s) is given by (2.1).

$$N_S = \frac{N\sqrt{P}}{H^{5/4}} \tag{2.1}$$

Where, N = normal working speed in r.p.m., P = power output of the turbine, and H = effective head (m)

Water turbines are categorized into three groups based on this criterion.

(a) **Low specific speed turbine:** Specific speeds are considered to be low when the value is between 1 and 10. Impulse turbines function within this range. For instance, the **Pelton** turbine typically runs at a speed of around 4.

(b) **Medium specific speed turbine:** Francis turbines, which have a specific speed between 10 and 100, have a medium specific speed.

(c) **High specific speed turbine:** Specific speeds that are more than 100 are regarded as having high values. The Kaplan turbine operates at a relatively high specific speed.

2.6 MOST WIDELY USED INDUSTRIAL WATER TURBINES

There are three types of water turbines widely used in electricity generation. They are the **Pelton wheel** or **Pelton Turbine, Francis** Turbine, and **Kaplan** Turbine.

2.6.1 Pelton Turbine

The **Pelton turbine**, also known as the **Pelton Wheel**, was initially developed by an American carpenter and inventor named *Lester Allan Pelton* in 1879. A Pelton turbine is a type of *impulse* turbine used for *high head* and low flow rate, in which the flow strikes the wheel *tangentially*. The flow of potential energy and high pressure travels through the Penstock and up to the nozzle while the complete set is at atmospheric pressure. This nozzle bottleneck moves the water flow while increasing the water's velocity, as Nozzles transform high-pressure flow into a very fast flow. The water jet from the nozzle strikes the spoon-shaped blades (buckets) of the impeller, which turns the turbine. A Pelton turbine converts the kinetic energy of an incoming water jet to rotational energy. To achieve higher velocities, Pelton turbines are used for height differences of 300 to 2000 m and water capacity of less than 50 m^3/s. They are defined as *low specific-speed* turbines. They come in a variety of sizes, and some have been used to power up to 200 MW. The Pelton turbine is shown in Fig.2.19 and Fig.2.20 for clear understanding. Some of the components of the Pelton wheel turbine are portrayed in Fig.2.21, such as (a) Casing, (b) Spear, (c) Buckets or vanes, (d) Break nozzle, (e) Runner, and (f) Governing Mechanism, etc.

(a) **Casing:** The Pelton wheel casing keeps water from splashing, and it allows water to flow from the nozzle to the tailrace. When compared to a reaction turbine, the casing of the wheel does not have any hydraulic function to carry out.

(b) **Spear:** There will be very little energy loss since the Needle Spear controls the water flow, travels inside the nozzle, and offers smooth flow. When the nozzle is entirely closed by sliding the spear forward, the amount of water impacting the runner is decreased to zero, yet the runner continues to rotate for an extended period owing to inertia.

(c) **Bucket or vanes:** The bucket is the most important part of the Pelton wheel. To prevent fatigue failure, buckets are cast as a single solid piece. It is evident that the force pushing on the turbine bucket changes with time. If you track a specific bucket, it will experience significant force for a brief period (during the impingement of the jet), followed by a longer period of inactivity during which no jet interaction occurs. As a result, the force pushing on the bucket is likewise variable. Although it changes over time, it is cyclical. Such cyclic fore will readily result in premature fatigue failure if the bucket were constructed out of sections joined together by welding. A splitter is used to divide a water jet into two equal parts. The jet turns almost 180 degrees due to the unique design of the bucket. As a result, the bucket experiences an impulsive force. Newton's second law of motion can be used to calculate the force in this situation. Typically, a blade outlet angle of around 180 degrees is employed to increase impulsive force. The bottom part of each bucket has a cut. This ensures that incoming buckets will not interfere with the water jet.

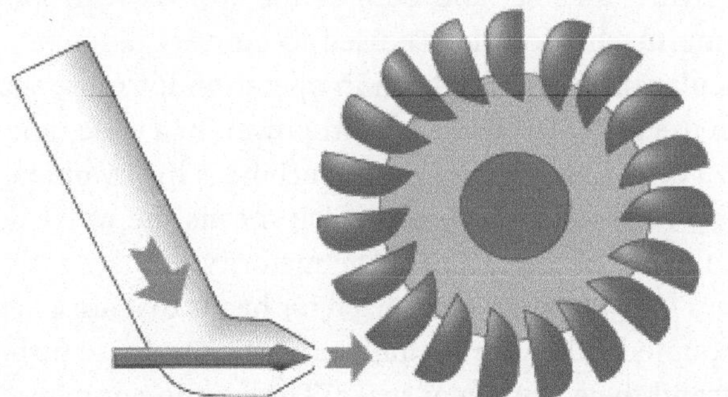

Fig. 2.19: Water flow toward buckets of Pelton turbine

Fig. 2.20: Pelton turbine

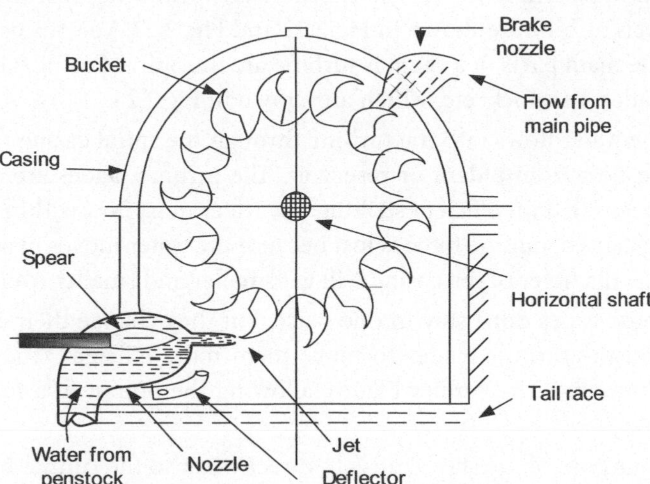

Fig. 2.21: Layout of Pelton turbine

(d) **Break Nozzle**: A breaking jet is provided, which directs the flow of water onto the bucket so that the runner can be stopped and allowed to rest in a relatively short amount of time.

(e) **Runner**: A Pelton wheel possesses a runner that rotates and contains kinetic energy, and around the periphery of the runner are equally spaced buckets that are either hemispherical or double ellipsoidal. Before hitting the rotor blades, all of the potential energy is transformed into kinetic energy.

(f) **Governing Mechanism**: The Pelton turbine is controlled by an oil pressure governor, which is made up of the following components: The oil sink, the spear's needle or rod, pipes connecting the control valve with the servomotor and the oil sump, the centrifugal governor, often known as a pendulum, which is powered by a turbine shaft-driven belt or gear, the control or distribution valve, or the relay valve, and the relay cylinder is another name for the servomotor, etc. When the generator's load falls, the generator's speed increases. This causes the turbine's speed to exceed its typical value.

2.6.2 Francis Turbine

Francis turbines are the most common type of hydro turbine, and 60% of the world's hydropower capacity is made up of them. This is a big rotating mechanical device used to convert potential and kinetic energies into hydroelectricity. These particular turbines have been in operation for more than a century to provide industrial power and are still in use today to produce hydropower. In a wide range of operating conditions, these turbines perform well. The definition of a Francis turbine is the combination of an *impulse* turbine and a *reaction* turbine. It is a mixed-flow turbine, which means the water flows radially toward the blades of the impeller and axially out of the turbine. The majority of these turbines are utilized in medium to large hydropower plants. These turbines are utilized for heads that are a height of 2m low and 300m high. Because they can be mounted either horizontally or vertically, these turbines offer a significant advantage in terms of efficiency and the economy of space. The reaction and impulse water forces that are applied throughout the turbine's blades cause each blade to rotate. As a result, the turbine's efficiency improves, and more energy is generated within the hydroelectric plant. The layout and picture of the Francis turbine are shown in Fig.2.22 and Fig. 2.23. Various parts can be used to build a Francis turbine. So the main parts of a Francis turbine are the Spiral Casing, Guide Vanes, Stay Vanes, Draft Tube, Runner Blades, Penstock, etc. which are shown in Fig.2.24.

(a) **Spiral casing:** The water flows into the turbine through the spiral casing. This pipe permits high-pressure water to flow from a dam or reservoir. The turbine blades are constructed in a round pattern, which means that for efficient striking, the water must flow within the circular axis. This is why spiral casing is used, but the force is lost because the water moves in a circle. So that the force stays the same, the diameter of the casing will get smaller and smaller over time.

(b) **Guide Vanes**: These vanes don't stay in one place, but they change their angle based on how the water needs to hit the turbine blades to make them more efficient. They also regulate the rate at which water flows into the runner blades, allowing the output of a turbine to be adjusted in response to the load.

(c) **Stay Vanes:** The purpose of the stay vane is to direct water to the runner blades. Because of radial flow, these vanes remain stationary and reduce water swirling. When it reaches the runner blades, the turbine becomes extremely efficient.

(d) **Draft tube:** In most turbines, the force exerted at the exit of the runner is negligible in comparison to the force exerted by the surrounding atmosphere. The water that comes out of the outlet cannot be sent straight to the tailrace. So, water goes from the turbine's outlet to the tailrace through a pipe or tube. This tube is called a "Draft Tube," and one end is directly connected to the runner's exit while the other end is submerged in water in the tail race.

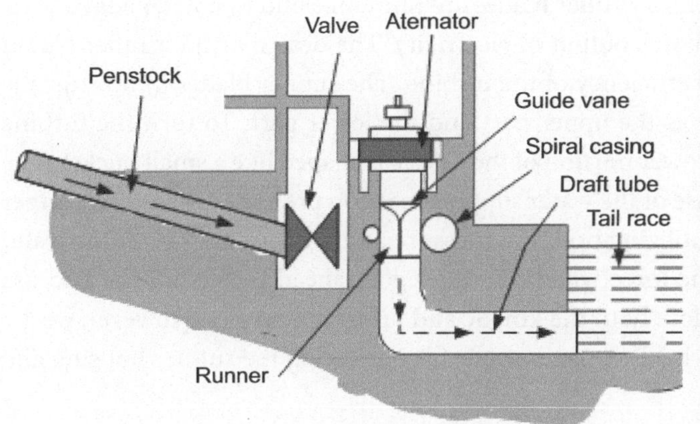

Fig. 2.22: Layout diagram of Francis turbine

Fig. 2.23: Francis turbine

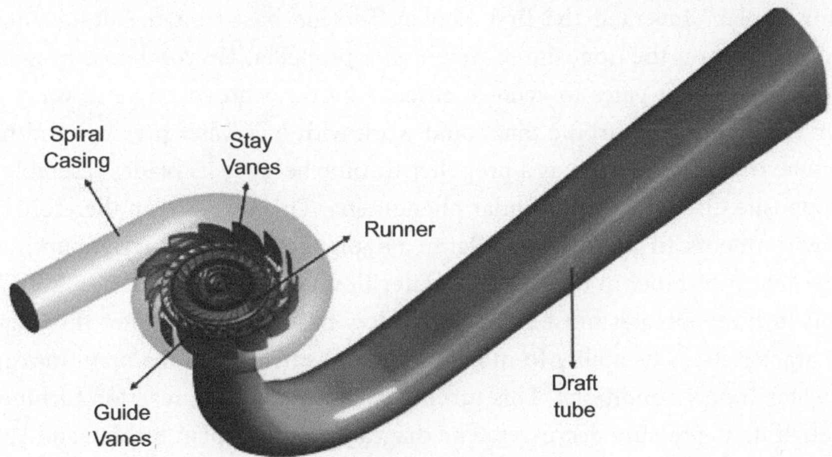

Fig. 2.24: Francis turbine

(e) **Runner Blades:** The runner blades are an important part of this turbine. These are set up in the middle of the turbine, where the water hits. The tangential force of the water's impact turns the shaft, which makes torque. These blades are mostly made up of two parts. The lower half is shaped like a small bucket and turns the turbine with the help of the water supply's impulse action. The reaction power of the water that is provided through the turbine is utilized by the upper part of the turbine blades. Therefore, the runner turns due to these two forces.

(f) **Penstock:** The water flows from the dam to the Francis turbine through the penstock, which is made of cement or cast steel.

The water from the penstock flows into the turbine's spiral casing. It then flows through the guide vanes and stay vanes. To maintain water pressure, the diameter of the turbine's spiral casing is gradually decreased. The stay vanes are stationary in their position and work to reduce the spins in the water supply that the spiral casing creates and to make the water flow more linear so that it can be diverted using movable guide vanes. The water supply will be struck at the runner blades at an angle determined by the angle of the guiding vanes. Because the turbine's runner blades are immobile and unable to adjust their position, the guiding vanes regulate the turbine's output of electricity. The design of the runner blades has a major impact on the performance and efficiency of the turbine. The runner blades in this turbine are primarily divided into two halves, such as the upper part and the lower part. To turn the turbine using the water supply's impulse action, the lower portion of the device is shaped like a small bucket. The top or higher portion of the turbine makes use of the water supply's reaction pressure. Therefore, runner blades turn the runner most effectively by utilizing both the pressure and kinetic energies of the water supply. We use the draft tube to increase the force when the water goes ahead to the tailrace because once the water exits the runner blade it will lose both the kinetic and pressure energies. However, we are still unable to increase the force to a point where we can stop air from entering the runner housing and leading to cavitation.

2.6.3 Kaplan Turbine

In 1913, "Viktor Kaplan" invented the first Kaplan Turbine based on the design of the turboprop engine. Thus, it operates on the opposite principle as a propeller. He combined propeller blades with automatically-adjusted wicket gates to achieve efficiency over a broad range of water flow and level. This was the first hydroelectric turbine that could work with low water pressure and high water flow. The Kaplan turbine is also referred to as a propeller turbine because its blades resemble propellers and operate in the opposite direction using similar phenomena. This turbine can therefore be used in river and low head environments. In hydroelectric plants, a Kaplan turbine is a reaction turbine or a particular kind of propeller hydro turbine. In this turbine, water flows in an axial direction both into and out of the turbine. This turbine operates most effectively at low head and high water flow rates. The Kaplan turbine's key characteristic is its ability to move its blades as needed to maintain maximum efficiency under various water supply conditions. This turbine is considered as a reaction turbine because when water runs through it, its pressure decreases. The diagram of the Kaplan turbine and layout diagram is shown in Fig.2.25 and Fig.2.26.

The operating principle of a Kaplan Turbine is primarily based on the axial flow reaction principle, because in axial flow turbines, water is supplied throughout the runner in a direction parallel to the runner's rotating axis. The water entering the turbine has the pressure and kinetic energy needed for the blades to rotate efficiently inside a hydroelectric plant.

Kaplan turbines can be designed to allow massive amounts of water to pass through them without breaking. These turbines are made slightly differently from other types of turbines. These turbines include many rotor blades that are directly attached to the turbine's core shaft. The connection between these rotor blades and the variable joints allows for positional modification. Because the external half of the rotor blade rotates much faster than the internal part, it is crucial to observe that the rotor blades in this turbine are not horizontal but rather slightly twisted. The major parts of a Kaplan turbine are its runner or impeller, hub, draft tube, runner blades, shaft, and guide blades as shown in Fig.2.27. A brief description of each part is given below.

(a) **Runner blades**: The runner blades are crucial parts of this turbine, which resembles a propeller. These turbines don't have plane blades like other axial flow turbines do; instead, they have twisted blades that allow water to flow from the input to the exit. Once the water contacts these blades, they begin to rotate, which causes the shaft to revolve even more.

(b) **Hub**: This turbine has a vertical shaft, and the larger part at the bottom is called a hub. The turbine's blades are situated on the turbine's hub to manage the rotational speed of the blades.

(c) **Shaft**: One end of the shaft in the turbine is simply attached to the runner, while the other end is connected to the generator coil. When the runner rotates due to the blades' rotation, the shaft also rotates, and this rotation can be conveyed to the generator coil. Electricity is produced when the generator coil spins. Because the turbine shaft rotates at a high speed between 1800 and 3600 rpm, it should have heat-resistant features. The shaft of the turbine is made out of structural steel.

(d) **Guide Vane**: The guide vane is a regulating part of the turbine that turns ON and OFF depending on how much power is needed. Guide vanes rotate at a precise angle to regulate water flow. When there is a greater need for power, it opens wider, allowing more water to hit the rotor blades. It opens less as a result of a reduction in power needs, which means that less water strikes the blades. Through guide vanes, the turbine's efficiency can be increased. Without guide vanes, the turbine would not work well.

(e) **Runner:** In a turbine, the role of the runner or impeller is crucial. It is a revolving part that aids in the production of energy. The rotation of the shaft can be caused by the impeller turning due to the axial flow of water across the blades of the turbine.

Fig. 2.25: Kaplan turbine

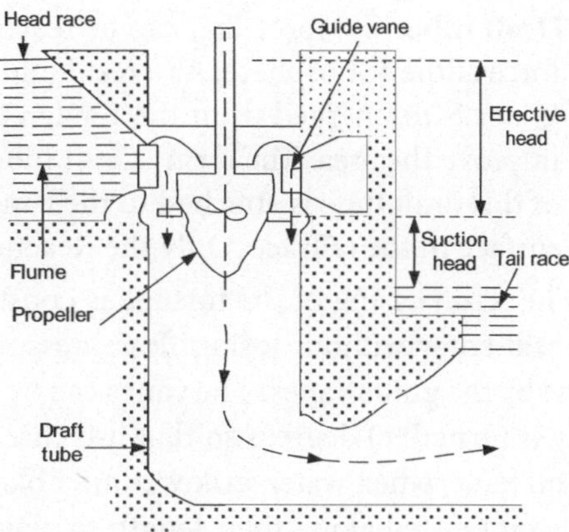

Fig. 2.26: Layout of Kaplan turbine

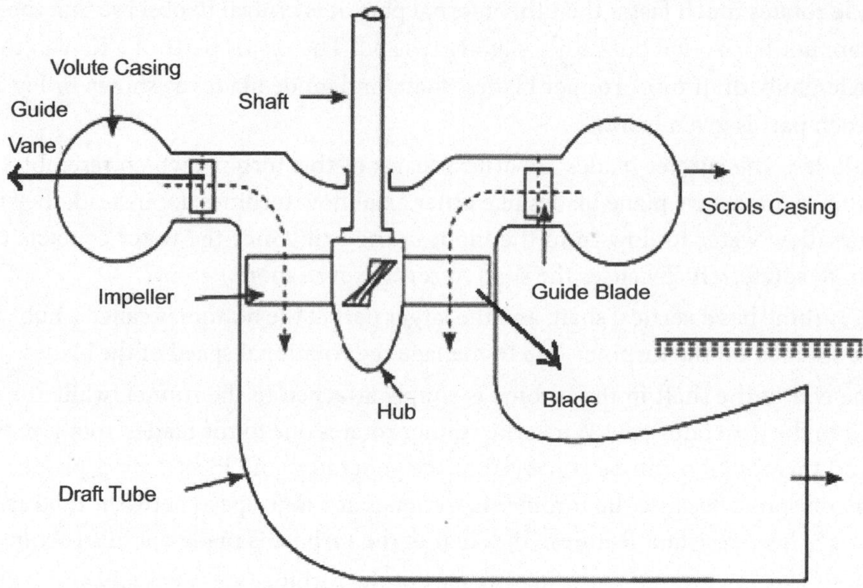

Fig. 2.27: Constructional layout of Kaplan turbine

(f) **Mechanism of blade control:** At the point where the blade is attached to the turbine, there is a moveable axis. The movable blade connection, which causes the attack angle, is controlled by the blade control mechanism. It contains crucial parts of the Kaplan turbine.

(g) **Scroll casing or volute casing:** The entire turbine can be encased in a scroll casing to reduce its cross-sectional area. The water initially flows from the penstock to the volute casing before entering the guide vane area. The water is axially pumped via the impeller after turning up to a 90-degree angle from the blade of the guide. Here, the turbine's casing protects the vital parts from damage caused by an external load, including the impeller blades, guiding vanes, and a runner.

(h) **Draft tube:** The force that can be reached at the end of the turbine's runner is usually less than the force of the atmosphere. As a result, the exit water cannot be dumped into the tailrace immediately. Water is discharged from the Kaplan turbine to the tailrace through a tube, which can gradually improve the area. The term "Draft tube" thus refers to the tube's expanding surface area. One end of this draft tube is attached to the runner's exit, and the other end is submerged under the water's surface in the tailrace. Only the Reaction turbine uses the Draft tube.

The scroll casing of the turbine is constructed in such a way that the water coming from the penstock will enter without losing flow pressure. The water will be forced into the runner blades of the turbine by the guide vanes. The vanes can be adjusted to meet the needs of the water flow rate. The water supply is turned 90 degrees so that it is directed axially at the runner blades. Due to the water supply's reaction force, when water strikes runner blades, they begin to rotate. To increase efficiency, these blades have been twisted along their length to always incorporate the best angle of attack for all blade cross-sections. Wherever the kinetic and force energy of the water is lowered, the water enters the draft tube from the runner blades.

Water pressure can be raised when kinetic energy is converted into pressure energy. The generator's shaft can be turned by the turbine spinning to produce power.

2.7 SAFE PRACTICES FOR HYDROPOWER PLANTS

Although hydropower plants might present serious safety concerns to the people who work there, there is never a good reason for an accident or fatality to occur at work. Hydropower plant developers, owners, and operators all need to demonstrate a strong commitment to workplace health and safety. There are several risks. In most cases, access to hydropower installations is restricted, and there is no natural lighting. Many lower floors are underground and frequently below the surface of the water.

(a) **Designing safety in hydropower plants:** When developing and implementing a new hydropower scheme or updating an old station, we must carefully evaluate the needed standard of worker health and safety, as well as the scope of work required to reach that standard. This includes a thorough awareness of the applicable laws, construction codes, and insurance needs. The division of duties between the various parties — the designer, developer, owner, contractors, etc. — must also be made clear. While standards, rules, and guidelines are fine places to start, the ultimate solution must be adapted to the specific conditions and amount of risk at the station in the issue.

(b) **Planning ahead to control risks:** A basic strategy for reducing workplace risks entails planning ahead of time to reduce workplace accidents, injuries, and illnesses. To do this, we make sure that work systems are secure and the equipment is well-maintained. Information on health and safety must be provided to workers, together with training and proper supervision.

(c) **Safety enhancements for aging hydropower plants:** New hydropower plants are often well-designed and in compliance with relevant safety requirements and regional construction rules. Larger hydropower plants may feature safety measures that are as complex and comprehensive as those seen in modern multi-story office buildings. Older plants, however, were frequently not designed with safety in mind and now require urgent modification to meet current occupational health and safety regulations. While safety features are easily implemented into new hydropower projects, adapting them to existing stations may be more challenging. The scope of work must account for the interfaces with existing infrastructure and the modification necessary for the particular site and location.

(d) **Station evacuation:** People must be able to exit a hydroelectric facility safely, regardless of the severity of the situation. There should be at least two separate exits for each station. There should always be a backup emergency escape route available in case the primary route is blocked. Lighting must be sufficient for emergency exits. There is more to safety at hydroelectric plants than just having the right hardware or equipment on hand. The provision of safety facilities to safely evacuate employees from a hydroelectric plant before the conditions inside become hazardous should be the top priority. The provision of facilities to securely remove people from unsafe situations should be the second factor to be taken into account. Then, we consider the safety features that will protect the plant from damage.

(e) **Flood Protection:** Hydroelectric dams can and do overflow. The failure of the drainage pumps can result in a gradual rise in the water level, which could eventually cause the station to be flooded. Alternately, a plant malfunction and leak that drainage pumps are unable to control can quickly flood the station. Alarms for flood, water level, and evacuation are therefore an absolute requirement. To try and drain the headworks and penstocks of water to control flooding, flood protection schemes can be put in place. These schemes can also automatically stop the hydro plant before the water levels become dangerous.

(f) **Fire and smoke control:** We must detect flames as early as feasible, prevent their spread, notify all staff, and offer safe, well-lit evacuation routes as quickly as possible. Smoke control and airflow are also very important. A fire will quickly fill a hydro station with thick, black, and pungent smoke. This smoke is often a bigger danger to the people working there than the fire itself because it makes it hard to see (preventing occupants from finding safe escape routes, as well as hindering search and rescue operations). People can be killed or poisoned by smoke or asphyxiation long before they are hurt by the heat of the fire. A comprehensive fire protection system must take into account all passive measures (such as using fire-rated building materials and construction techniques), active measures (such as using sprinklers, vents, and firefighting equipment), and operational measures (e.g. plans, systems, and training for fire prevention and response).

(g) **Emergency and Crisis management:** To ensure worker safety in hydroelectric power plants, it is not enough to have the right tools and hardware on hand. It entails a continual dedication on the part of the owner, management, operator, and staff to establish and uphold a safe and healthy working environment. This pledge ought to be made in writing and included in a workplace health and safety policy that is backed by safe work practices and documentation. A written risk control program, fire protection program, hazard register, site induction protocols, attendance boards, permit to work systems, neighborhood safety teams, and a comprehensive crisis and emergency plan should all be included.

2.8 MICRO HYDROPOWER PLANT

Micro hydro is a type of hydroelectric power that typically produces from 5 kW to 100 kW of electricity using the natural flow of water. These installations can provide power to an isolated home or small community, or are sometimes connected to electric power networks, particularly where net metering is offered. There are many of these installations around the world, particularly in developing nations as they can provide an economical source of energy without the purchase of fuel. A schematic diagram of micro hydropower plant is shown in Fig.2.28. The following are the main components of the Micro hydropower plant.

1. Intake and waterway
2. Sedimentation basin
3. Headrace
4. Head tank (Forebay)
5. Penstock
6. Turbine
7. Generator
8. Load stabilizer
9. Transformer

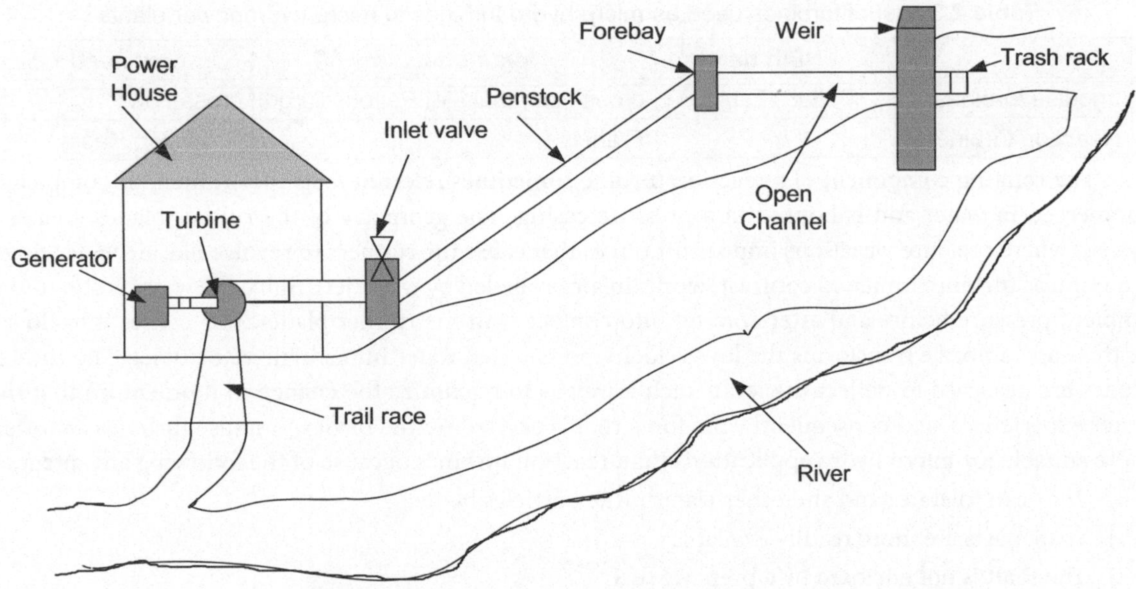

Fig. 2.28: Schematic of a micro hydropower plant

2.8.1 Classification of Micro Hydro Turbines for Different Heads

The kind of turbine that can be utilized in a micro hydro installation relies on several variables, including head of water, flow rate, and the accessibility of local maintenance and equipment delivery. A turbine converts energy from falling water into mechanical energy. The choice of a hydro turbine is determined by

(a) Site parameters.
(b) Available head
(c) Water flow
(d) Speed of the generator or other components.

Every turbine has a power-speed characteristic that tends to operate most effectively at a specific combination of speed, head, and flow. The operating head of a turbine has a significant impact on its design speed.

We know that there are two types of turbines. They are impulse turbines and reaction turbines. With an impulse turbine, the water jets that interact with the runner blades turn the turbine runner while it is operating in the air.

The turbine runner of a reaction turbine is completely submerged in water and covered in a pressure casing. Its blades are positioned in such a way that pressure differences between them produce lift forces similar to those on an airplane wing, which drive the runner to rotate. Table 2.3 shows a list of turbines used as micro hydro turbines in micro hydropower plants.

Table 2.3: List of turbines used as micro hydro turbines in micro hydropower plants

	High head	Medium head	Low head
Impulse turbines	Pelton, Turgo	cross-flow, multi-jet Pelton, Turgo	cross-flow
Reaction turbines		Francis	Propeller, Kaplan

The rotating component of a reaction turbine sometimes referred to as the "runner," is completely submerged in water and is housed in a pressure casing. The geometry of the runner blades creates a system where pressure variations impose lift forces that cause the runners to revolve like airplane wings. An impulse turbine runner, in contrast, works in air propelled by water jets. Since the water is still under ambient pressure before and after coming into contact with the runner blades, this causes it to do so. In this case, a nozzle transforms the low-velocity pressurized water into a high-velocity jet. The runner blades are designed to deflect the jet in such a way as to maximize the change in momentum that the water experiences, and consequently, the force that is exerted on the blades. Impulse turbines are often more suitable for micro hydro applications than reaction turbines because of the following advantages:

(a) They can tolerate sand and other waterborne particles better.
(b) Spare parts are more readily available.
(c) The shaft is not enclosed by a pressure seal.
(d) They are simpler to manufacture and maintain.
(e) They are more efficient in terms of part flow.

Despite these benefits, the main drawback of impulse turbines is that they are typically not suited for low-head sites due to their low specific speeds. This is because a significant increase in transmission speed is needed to permit coupling to a normal alternator. At medium heads, the crossflow, Turgo, and multi-jet Pelton are appropriate.

2.8.1.1 Pelton Turbine

It comprises of a group of buckets with unique shapes mounted around the edge of a disc. The buckets are spun by water jets from one or more nozzles that strike them. The buckets are divided into two halves to prevent the centre portion from acting as a dead spot ineffective for deflecting water away from the oncoming jet. The lower lip cutaway allows for a smoother entry of the bucket into the jet as well as allowing the next bucket to advance further before cutting off the jet that is propelling the bucket in front of it. The Pelton bucket is designed to deflect the jet via a maximum angle of 165 degrees (not 180 degrees), which is the maximum angle feasible without interfering with the following bucket for the oncoming jet.

Pelton turbines are typically considered for large-scale hydro installations with heads above 150 m, however, for micro-hydro applications, they can be used effectively with heads as low as 20 m. At lower heads, Pelton turbines are not employed because their rotational speeds become very sluggish and the runner required is quite huge and bulky. A Pelton turbine can be utilized effectively with relatively low heads if the installation's runner size and low speed are not an issue.

2.8.1.2 Turgo Turbine

This is an impulse machine that operates in a manner analogous to that of a Pelton turbine, although it was developed to achieve a higher specific speed. In this instance, the jets were pointed at the runner's plane from one side and the exits from the other. As a result, the ejected fluid's ability to interfere with the entering jet does not limit the flow rate (as is the case with Pelton turbines). As a result, a Turgo turbine can use a runner with a smaller diameter with an equivalent power than a Pelton turbine. It is more likely possible to link Turgo turbines directly to the generator rather than needing to go via an expensive speed-increasing transmission with smaller, faster-rotating runners. The Turgo, like the Pelton, is effective over a broad speed range and has the main traits of impulse turbines outlined for the Pelton, including the ability to be installed either horizontally or vertically. Turgo runners are more challenging to construct than Pelton runners, and their vanes are more delicate than Pelton buckets.

2.8.1.3 Cross-Flow Turbine

A crossflow turbine, also known as a Michell-Banki turbine, features a drum-shaped runner made up of two parallel discs joined near their rims by a sequence of curving blades. A crossflow turbine's runner shaft is always horizontal (unlike Pelton and Turgo turbines which can have either horizontal or vertical shaft orientation). A rectangular nozzle operates to steer the jet along the whole length of the runner. The majority of the water's kinetic energy is transferred when it hits the blades. The energy is subsequently reduced as it exits the turbine after passing through the runner and striking the blades once more. Even though it is technically an impulse turbine, there are also hydrodynamic pressure forces at play, so a more accurate term would be "mixed flow."

2.9 ADVANTAGES & DISADVANTAGES OF HYDROELECTRIC POWER PLANT

The advantages of hydroelectric power plants are:

(a) Hydropower has a significant impact on lowering Greenhouse Gas emissions (GHG).
(b) There is very little pollution because fuel is not burned.
(c) The power plant relies on water that is provided for free by nature.
(d) It is renewable since rainfall refills the reservoir's water, therefore the fuel is generally always available.
(e) It is possible to save the water and then use it when there is a higher demand.
(f) The dams have a longer lifespan (50 years approximately), which makes it possible to produce electricity more cheaply.
(g) Lowest operating and maintenance expenses.
(h) Hydroelectric Power Plant may be immediately put into operation.
(i) This power plant can reliably deliver energy to variable demand.
(j) The lowest possible cost per kWh of generation can be achieved.
(k) The location of the plant is generally in a remotareasea, hence the cost of the land is low.
(l) Overall efficiency is higher.
(m) The disadvantages of hydroelectric power plants are:
(n) Since dams are constructed on a large scale and must be well-guarded, their construction is quite costly. Any small damage will result in enormous destruction both inside the dam and nearby.
(o) The dam investments have a considerable payoff period before they start to pay off. As a result, the dam must be active for many years to be profitable.

(p) During the construction of hydroelectric power dams, local residents and business owners are relocated. This causes an unpleasant scenario.

(q) There will be geological damage from the construction of these dams. For example, during the building of the Hoover Dam in the United States, there were numerous earthquakes and depressions on the earth's surface.

(r) Dams cause some sort of disruption to adjacent nations or states that connect the rivers. Since the dams are formed by obstructing the river, the water supply is irregular.

(s) Erection of the Dam is difficult.

2.10 HYDROLOGY

2.10.1 Precipitation

This comprises all of the water that falls to the earth's surface from the atmosphere. It primarily comes in two variants, such as (i) Liquid precipitation (Rainfall) and (ii) Solid precipitation (Snow, Hail).

2.10.2 Run-off

It is the part of rain or snow that ends up in rivers, lakes, or the ocean. Runoff can only happen when the rate of rain falls faster than the rate at which water soaks into the ground, and when small and large depressions on the surface of the ground fill up with water. Evaporation losses must also be taken into account. Typically, the run-off is determined using (2.2), where R = Run-off, P = Precipitation, E = Evaporation

$$\mathrm{R = P - E} \tag{2.2}$$

2.10.3 Evaporation

It is the process of water changing from its liquid form to its gaseous state.

2.10.4 Hydrograph

It is a graph that shows the relationship between discharge and time. For a hydrograph, the ordinates can be measured in terms of the gauge height, the number of cubic meters per second per square kilometer, the power in kilowatts that can be generated theoretically per meter of fall, or the energy in kilowatt-hours recorded at the switchboard, while the abscissae can be measured in hours, days, or weeks. In a few words, a hydrograph shows how the flow changes over time. Additionally, it shows the amount of energy that can be drawn from the stream at various periods of the day or year. It resembles the load curve that is employed in the investigation of electrical power.

2.10.5 Unit Hydrograph

It is a hydrograph with a volume of 1 meter or (cm of runoff) from a rainstorm of a certain duration and a real pattern. A unit hydrograph can be made from a hydrograph of the actual runoff when there is uniform rainfall intensity and real uniform distribution. The total runoff volume (area under the hydrograph curve) is first determined before creating a unit hydrograph. By dividing the ordinates of real run-off by the entire volume of run-off (in metres or centimeters) over the drainage area, the ordinates of the unit hydrograph are then calculated. There are several restrictions on the application of unit hydrographs. Theoretically, an infinite number of unit hydrographs exist for a given basin. In practice, only a few unit hydrographs are utilized for a given basin.

2.10.6 Flow Duration Curve

This is a plot illustrating the flow available during a given period against the percentage of time. Flow or discharge can be measured in cubic meters per second, per week, or another time unit. If the available flow head is known, the discharge in cubic meters per second or per week, or the discharge for the time, can be converted to power in kilowatts. As a result, the flow duration curve is transformed into the load duration curve for the hydroelectric plant. With the aid of a flow duration curve, it is possible to determine the site's total available power. The minimum and maximum flow conditions can be found using a flow duration curve. A plant's maximum capacity can be determined based on minimum flow circumstances, but a flow duration curve can be enhanced by storing water on the upstream side to be used during off-peak hours.

2.10.7 Mass Curve

A mass curve is a graph that shows how much water can be stored from a stream's flow over a certain amount of time (in days, weeks, or months). The cubic meter or the day-second meter are the units used to indicate storage. A day-second-metre is the flow rate of 1 m³/sec for one day, equal to $60 \times 60 \times 24 = 86{,}400$ m³. By using storage, the water flow can be adjusted to meet the needs of the plant, increasing the plant's generating capacity for the same mass flow. Pondage* is the water in the plant behind the dam. Storage is the water kept in reservoirs upstream. A reservoir's main function is to store water that can be used when there is a shortage. A mass curve is used to analyze a reservoir's ability to provide the appropriate amount of water flow.

2.10.8 Hydro Electric Potential

Storage improves the form of the flow duration curve, increasing the hydroelectric station's primary power capacity. A power duration curve with various scales can be created from the flow duration curve. The power (P) is calculated using Bernoulli's equation given by (2.3).

$$P = \frac{0.736}{75} Qwh \ kW \tag{2.3}$$

(Recall that 75 kg-mt/sec = 1 metric HP = 0.736 kW)

$$P = 9.81 \times 10^{-3} \ Qwh \ \text{kW} \tag{2.4}$$

Where, Q = discharge in m³/sec; w = density of water = 1000 kg/m³; h = head in meters.

However, because every energy exchange is inevitably accompanied by losses, not all of the gross power determined by the aforementioned equation is converted into electrical power. The term η can be used to account for the losses (overall efficiency of the plant). Thus

$$P = 9.81 \ Qh\eta \ \text{kW} \tag{2.5}$$

[⊠ = 10^3 kg/mt³, hence it is canceled with 10^{-3} terms present in the expression of P], and the total energy in kWh produced over a time interval of T hours is given by (2.6).

$$\text{Energy} = 9.81\ Qh\eta \times T\ \text{kWh} \tag{2.6}$$

For instance, a river with a head of 20 mt and a discharge of 6000 m³/sec. With an overall efficiency of 70%, the generated power is

$$P = 9.81 \times 6000 \times 20 \times 0.7\ \text{kW} = 824040\ \text{kW} = 824.04\ \mu\text{W}$$

2.11 LARGE AND SMALL HYDROPOWER PLANTS IN MAHARASHTRA

The Maharashtra Government's Water Resource Department (WRD) was responsible for the design, construction, and commissioning of the hydroelectric projects in the state. Following the completion of the commissioning process, the hydro projects were leased out to Mahagenco for an extended period so that they could be operated and maintained. There are currently 25 hydro projects with a combined capacity of 2580 MW.

The first hydroelectric power-producing station in India was built by Tata Power in 1915 and was commissioned at Khopoli with a capacity of 40 MW before being increased to 72 MW. The Company has a hydro capacity of 693 MW installed, with 65% of that capacity being generated for the domestic market. The hydro stations were the first to use cheap, clean, and pollution-free energy. They are mainly used to power the industrial areas around them, including Bhira.

The Koyna Hydroelectric Project is India's second-biggest hydroelectric power plant, after the Tehri Dam Project. It is a complicated project consisting of four dams, the largest of which is located on the Koyna River in Maharashtra and is thus referred to as the Koyna Hydroelectric Project. The project site is in the district of Satara. The Koyana Dam is located near Koyananagar village. Koyana River. The project has a total capacity of 1,960 MW. The project includes four phases of energy generating. All of the generators are in underground powerhouses that have been dug deep into the Western Ghats mountains. The electricity is also generated by a dam foot powerhouse. The Koyna River is regarded as Maharashtra's lifeline due to the project's capacity for producing electricity. The project makes use of the Western Ghats' height. As a result, a very large hydraulic head can be achieved over a relatively small distance.

In the more remote parts of our country, a river or stream that flows seasonally or perennially (i.e. all through the year) can be a good source of energy. People in the area are now able to properly operate and maintain the technologies used in small hydropower projects. The total amount of electricity that could be made in our country through small hydropower projects has been estimated to be 15,000 MW. This potential is 732.63 MW in Maharashtra alone, and projects with a potential of 292.525 MW have been already installed by the Water Resources Department. The Maharashtra Energy Development Agency (MEDA) has taken the initiative to establish such small hydropower projects in the remote tribal territory of Asli in the Nandubar district. The agency has found 60 possible locations. MEDA has submitted thorough project papers for the construction of two minor hydropower projects on the Warana River, each with a capacity of 300 KW, at the Mauje Mangale-Saavarde and Chincholi dams. MEDA has been tasked with the responsibility of developing small hydropower (SHP) power projects of up to 5 MW on the Run of the River, Waterfalls, and K.T. Weirs.

UNIT SUMMARY

It is possible to create electricity from the kinetic energy of falling water. Electricity generated by hydroelectric plants is completely fuel-free. Furthermore, water inflows throughout each monsoon indicate that it is a renewable source of energy. They have low operational costs overall. Hydroelectric plants have numerous advantages. The other side is that there are drawbacks to them as well. A hydrograph displays the change in stream flow over time in m3/sec. Similar to a load duration curve is a flow duration curve. A mass curve shows the total runoff volume in m3 up to a specific period. The hydrograph can be used to calculate storage requirements. An essential and crucial part of any hydro project is figuring out how much space you'll need for storage. Hydro project site selection should take into account water supply, storage demand, head of water, geological characteristics, sedimentation, site access, and environmental impacts. Hydro plants can be divided into three categories: low head, medium head, and high head. The civil engineering work includes the reservoir, dam, forebay, intake structures, surge tank, penstock, spillway, etc. There are three types of hydro turbines: Pelton, Francis, and Kaplan. Hydro turbines are equipped with a governor and speed regulation to maintain a consistent speed regardless of load changes. Some hydropower plants are underground. Small hydro plants have numerous benefits, including rapid construction, modest civil engineering tasks, small financial requirements, etc. Peak load supply is a perfect use for a pumped storage facility. The water is recycled repeatedly. During the off-season, water is pumped back from the tail race to the head water pond. India's total hydro potential is projected to be 84044 MW. So far, only about 29,000 MW has been built.

EXERCISES

Example 2.1

A hydroelectric power plant operator with a 50 m effective head. Consider a discharge of 400 m³/sec. Determine the amount of power produced by an electric turbine if the efficiency of its alternator set is 0.9.

Solution:

The power generated is given as,

$$P = \left(\frac{735.5}{75}\right) Q \cdot h \cdot \eta = \frac{735.5}{75}(200) \cdot (50) \cdot (0.9) = 176.52 \times 10^6 W = 176.52 MW$$

Example 2.2

The average flow rate for the last 12 months is indicated below

1000 m³/sec in Jan. 500 m³/sec in apr. 2500 m³/sec in Jul. 500 m³/sec in oct. 900 m³/sec in Feb. 300 m³/sec in May. 2200 m³/sec in Aug. 300 m³/sec in Nov. 500 m³/sec in Mar. 1100 m³/sec in Jun. 1200 m³/sec in sept. 1000 m³/sec in Dec. If the operating effective head is 150 m and the turbine-alternator set efficiency is 0.85, calculate the average river input and the power generated.

Solution:

The average flow of the river is given by,

$$Q = \frac{1}{12}[1000 + 900 + 500 + 500 + 300 + 1100 + 2500 + 2200 + 1200 + 500 + 300 + 1000]$$

$$= 1000 \ \text{m}^3/\text{sec}$$

The power developed is given by

$$P=\left(\frac{735.5}{75}\right)Q\cdot h\cdot\eta=\frac{735.5}{75}(1000)\cdot(150)\cdot(0.85)=1250.35\times10^{6}W=1250.35MW$$

Example 2.3

It has been determined that a minimum run-off of 95 m^3/sec. will be available in a hydroelectric plant with a head of 40 m. Determine the firm's capacity and annual gross output.

Solution:

The minimum run-off available (Q) = 95 m^3/sec

But the weight of 1 m^3 of water = 1000 kg

So the weight of 95 m^3 of water = 95,000 kg

Head of water = 40 m

Work done in one second = Weight of water/sec × Head of water = 95000 × 40 kgm

1 metric HP = 75 kg m/sec. so, 0.746 kW=75 kg. m/sec. then,

$$1\,kW = \frac{75}{0.746} = 100.54\ kg.\ m\ /\ sec.$$

$$\text{Hence, power (kW)} = \frac{95000\times40}{100.54} = 37796\ kW$$

i.e., the firm capacity is 37796 kW for the power plant. Yearly gross output can be calculated as follows:

$37796 \times 8760 = 331\times10^{6}$ kWh.

Example 2.4

Show that the average power in a hydropower plant is given as P = 3.14·η·K·A·F·H × 10-4 kW when A is the catchment area in sq. km., F is the Annual rainfall in mm., H is the effective head in m, η = Plant efficiency and K = Yield factor.

Solution:

Catchment area = A × $(10^3)^2$ × $(100)^2$ sq. cm., Annual rainfall = F × 10^{-1} cm.

The volume of water annually available is calculated as

$$v=\left(A\times\frac{F}{10}\times10^{10}\times K\right)c.c.=\left(A\times F\times K\times10^{3}\right)m^{3}$$

As 1 m^3 of water weighs 1000 kg, Hence v m^3 of water weighs

$$\left(A\times F\times K\times10^{3}\right)\times10^{3}\,kg=A\cdot K\cdot F\times10^{6}\,kg$$

The weight of water available per second is given as

$$\frac{AKF\times10^{6}}{365\times24\times60\times60}kg=\frac{AKF}{31.5}kg.$$

It is given that the effective head of water is H m.

$$Workdone/\sec = (wt.\ \text{of}\ water/\sec) \times H = \frac{AKFH}{31.5} kgm$$

$$Power = \frac{AKFH}{31.5} kgm,$$

but 1 metric $HP = 75$ kgm,

$$\text{Hence, total HP developed} = (Power / 75) \times \eta = \frac{AKFH}{31.5} kgm \times (1/75) \times \eta$$

$$\text{Hence power in kW} = \frac{AKFH\eta}{31.5 \times 75} \times 0.746 \ [\because 1HP = 746W]$$

So it is proved that the average power in the hydro plant is given as

$$P = 3.14 \cdot \eta \cdot K \cdot A \cdot F \cdot H \times 10^{-4} \text{ kW.}$$

Example 2.5

Determine the hydroelectric station's continuous power availability, from the given data, where the Catchment area is 200 sq. km., Annual rainfall is 1000 m., the effective head is 200 m., yield factor to allow runoff and loss by evaporation is 50%, and plant efficiency is 80%.

Solution:

As found above the power in kW is given as $3.14 \cdot \eta \cdot K \cdot A \cdot F \cdot H \times 10^{-4}$ kW, by substituting the given data, $P = 3.14 \times 0.8 \times 0.5 \times 200 \times 1000 \times 200 \times 10^{-4} = 5024$ kW

Multiple Choice Questions

1. Hydroelectric power plant site selection does not involve which of the following?
   (a) Large Catchment area (b) Rocky land
   (c) Sedimentation (d) Availability of water
2. The factors that determine how much electrical energy a hydroelectric power plant can produce include __________
   (a) Efficiency of Alternator (b) Quantity of water
   (c) Head of water (d) Specific weight of water
3. The majority of hydroelectric power plants are in __________
   (a) Hilly areas (b) Deserts
   (c) Plain areas (d) Deltas
4. In a hydroelectric plant, spillways are employed for ________
   (a) To discharge all surplus water
   (b) To discharge surplus water on the downstream side of the dam
   (c) Water is not available in sufficient quantity
   (d) None of the above
5. A dam with a wide base in comparison to its height is referred as
   (a) Arch Dam (b) Earth Dam
   (c) Buttress Dam (d) Solid Gravity Dam

6. A hydroelectric station's surge tank is situated close to the ________
   (a) Reservoir (b) Turbine
   (c) Tailrace (d) None of the above
7. The function of a surge tank is
   (a) To produce surges in the pipeline
   (b) To supply water at constant pressure
   (c) To supply water at different pressure
   (d) To relieve water hammer pressures in the penstock pipe
8. Penstock in a hydroelectric power plant is ___________
   (a) The nozzle that releases high-pressure water on turbine blades
   (b) a conduit connecting forebay to scroll case of turbine
   (c) a pipe connected to runner outlet
   (d) a pipe connecting surge tank to dam
9. Kaplan turbine is _____________
   (a) Axial flow turbine (b) Mixed flow turbine
   (c) Tangential flow turbine (d) None of the above
10. Which turbine converts water pressure energy into kinetic energy first using a nozzle placed close to the runner?
    (a) Reaction Turbine (b) Impulse Turbine
    (c) Both a and b (d) None of the above
11. Gross head is the difference between __________
    (a) head race and friction losses (b) net head and friction losses
    (c) head race and tail race (d) head race and net head
12. Pelton turbines are mostly ________
    (a) Inclined (b) Vertical
    (c) Horizontal (d) None of the above
13. The speed at which an imaginary turbine, similar to the one in use, would turn to produce one unit of power at one unit of the head is referred to as?
    (a) specific velocity (b) specific speed
    (c) unit speed (d) none of the above
14. In a Francis turbine runner, the number of blades is generally between __________
    (a) 16 to 24 (b) 8 to 16
    (c) 4 to 8 (d) 2 to 4
15. Which of the following claims regarding hydroelectric plants is false?
    (a) Its capital cost is very high
    (b) A long duration of time is needed for building a hydroelectric power plant
    (c) Per unit cost of the hydropower plant is higher than diesel plant
    (d) A hydroelectric power plant can supply power to fluctuating loads

16. Which power plant has instant starting
    (a) Hydropower plant (b) Diesel power plant
    (c) Both b and c (d) None of the above
17. Hydroelectricity accounts for ______ of the world's total energy consumption.
    (a) 35% (b) 17%
    (c) 7% (d) 3%
18. Which is the biggest hydroelectric power plant in the world?
    (a) Vajont Dam (b) Sand Dam
    (c) The Three Gorges Dam (d) Banasura Sagar Dam

ANSWERS															
1.	(c)	2.	(b)	3.	(a)	4.	(b)	5.	(b)	6.	(a)	7.	(d)	8.	(b)
9.	(a)	10.	(b)	11.	(c)	12.	(c)	13.	(b)	14.	(a)	15.	(c)	16.	(c)
17.	(b)	18.	(c)												

State whether the following are True (T) or False (F)

1. A hydroelectric plant's output is inversely proportional to the sum of its discharge and head.
2. Hydropower plant operating expenses are substantial.
3. A hydrograph is a graph that plots runoff in m^3/s versus calendar months.
4. A flow duration curve plots each point's percentage of time where the flow was either equal to or greater than the specified flow.
5. A mass curve shows the runoff in m^3/s during several months.
6. The mass curve cannot be used to estimate storage needs.
7. A high head plant has a 50 m or greater head of water.
8. The base of an earth dam is narrow.
9. Surge tanks are designed to handle abrupt variations in water usage.
10. Power output of a hydraulic turbine is directly inversely related to its specific speed.
11. A Pelton turbine is appropriate for systems with high head and low water flow.
12. Reaction turbines include Francis turbines.
13. The nozzles of a reaction turbine are numerous.
14. For modest hydroelectric projects, bulb turbines are appropriate.
15. A base load plant uses pumped storage.
16. For pumped storage systems, reversible turbines and pumps are ideal.
17. A pumped storage plant has a very quick start-up period.
18. India's total hydro potential is projected to be 84000 MW.

ANSWERS															
1.	T	2.	F	3.	T	4.	T	5.	F	6.	F	7.	F	8.	F
9.	T	10.	F	11.	T	12.	T	13.	F	14.	T	15.	F	16.	T
17.	T	18.	T												

QUESTIONS AND PROBLEMS

Short and Long Answer Type Questions

1. What variables affect a hydroelectric plant's electricity output?
2. Why are hydroelectric plants more dependable?
3. Describe the hydrograph.
4. What steps go into creating a flow duration?
5. Describe the mass curve.
6. How can the amount of storage needed for a potential hydroelectric project be calculated?
7. Describe pondage.
8. What variables affect the location of hydroelectric plants?
9. What types of hydro plants are there?
10. List the many kinds of dams.
11. What does the surge tank do?
12. What does specific speed mean?
13. How are hydroelectric generators categorized?
14. List a few hydro plants' auxiliary equipments.
15. Describe a small hydroelectric facility. What benefits does it offer?
16. What exactly is a pumped storage facility? What use does it serve?
17. Why are some hydroelectric facilities buried?
18. List a few Indian river basins.
19. What is India's estimated overall hydro potential?
20. What does a system's risk cost?
21. Describe a hydrograph. What details does it offer?
22. How can a hydrograph be used to create a flow duration curve?
23. Describe a mass curve. What details does it offer? What does it serve?
24. How can the amount of storage needed for a hydro project be calculated?
25. How may hydro plants be categorized in terms of (a) regulating water flow, (b) head, and (c) load?
26. Discuss whether a pumped storage plan is economically feasible.
27. Write a brief essay on India's pumped storage facility development.
28. What civil engineering tasks are required for a project involving hydroelectricity? What are they used for?
29. What varieties of hydro turbines are there? What uses do they have? Describe the key elements of their construction.
30. Explain how a Pelton turbine and a Francis turbine operate differently.
31. What does a turbine's "specific speed" mean? How may turbines be categorized based on a particular speed?
32. What features set a Francis turbine's speed control mechanism apart from a Pelton turbine? Create diagrams to support your responses.

33. What criteria are used to choose a location for hydroelectric stations?
34. "Run-off" – what is that? Describe the "hydrograph" in detail.
35. Calculate the hydroelectric potential using the water outflow and water head.
36. How are hydel plants categorized? Talk about it briefly.
37. Describe the fundamental structure and workings of a hydroelectric plant.
38. Give a basic classification and description of water turbines.
39. What features distinguish a water turbine?
40. Give a brief explanation of how a water turbine is run.
41. Describe briefly: a) Penstock; b) Water hammer and surge tank; c) the hydroelectric generator; d) cavitation, and e) the structure of a hydroelectric power plant.

Numerical problems

1. A turbine in a hydroelectric facility produces 2400 horsepower with a 400-foot head. If the turbine needs to run at 500 rmp, figure out what that speed is specifically.
2. The available head of a river is 100 mt, and its discharge is 500 lit/sec. Will using a Pelton wheel spinning at 500 rpm be wise? Assume a 90% machine efficiency.

PRACTICALS

Experiment No.1

Title: Identify the Routine Maintenance Parts of the Large Hydropower Plant after Watching a Video Programme.

Aim: To identify the parts of a Large hydropower plant

Apparatus/ software required: Watch the video at,

(a) https://www.youtube.com/watch?v=3ixtdPORwsw
(b) https://www.youtube.com/watch?v=MSR7Acw_Q6U

Theory: A hydropower plant captures the potential energy of water and generates electrical energy. A hydro turbine is used as a prime mover. The hydro turbine converts the potential energy into mechanical energy. The turbine shaft is mechanically coupled to the alternator. The alternator converts the mechanical output of the hydro turbine into electrical energy. The hydro plant works on the principle that the potential energy of stored water at a suitable height is converted to kinetic energy. In this process, the falling water attains a very high speed and the high-speed water runs the turbine. The followings are the parts of the plants.

(a) Dam/Barrage: The Dam provides storage of water from which the potential energy of water is obtained and the kinetic energy of falling water from the storage is utilized to run the hydro turbine.

(b) Head Race Tunnel: The headrace conduit, conveys the water from the reservoir to the turbine. The conduit can be a channel, flume, penstock, tunnel, or combination of these.

(c) Surge Tank: Surge tanks are constructed for intermittent water reservoirs near to turbine. It reduces the length of the water column. This provides a high-pressure force to the water column.

(d) Penstock: These are pipes or long channels. The penstock carries water from the reservoir to the turbines.

(e) **Sluice Valve:** This controls the amount of water allowed to flow through the penstock. This is simply a gate. It can be raised or lowered the water entering the turbine and thus control the power output of the turbine.

(f) **Power House:** It is a building that housed hydraulic and electrical equipment. The turbine, alternator, step-up transformer, and control panels are included in the powerhouse.

(g) **Turbine:** Turbines convert the energy of falling water into mechanical energy to drive an alternator.

(h) **Alternator:** It converts mechanical energy into electrical energy. It is mechanically coupled with the turbine.

(i) **Tailrace channel or tailrace tunnel:** This channel carries water from hydro plants.

The schematic diagram of the plant is shown in Fig.2.2. The details of all the components are already explained in the section 2.3

The parts of the plants which need to undergo routine maintenance are as follows.

(a) Turbine functional checks and inspection.
(b) Turbine bearing lubrication and inspection.
(c) Gearbox inspection.
(d) Gearbox oil condition analysis and oil changes.
(e) Gearbox bearing inspection and lubrication.
(f) Drive belt inspection and replacement.
(g) Drive coupling inspection.
(h) Generator inspection
(i) Generator bearing inspection and lubrication.
(j) Hydraulic system inspection.
(k) Hydraulic system oil condition analysis and oil changes.
(l) Check all sensors operate correctly.
(m) Check controller functions correctly.
(n) Inspection of intake area, impounding structures, pipeline, sluice(s)

Procedure for routine maintenance:

The above-listed routine maintenance must be done periodically. The numbers of visit depend on the capacity of the plant. For a small capacity numbervisitsisit is less but for a large capacity p, lant it is more. The maintenance of the equipment of the plant is done periodically, say daily, monthly, weekly, yearly, and five yearly basis as per the manufacturer's instruction.

The followings are the routine maintenance works to be carried out during each shift

(a) Cleaning of all panels, instruments, and equipment installed in the power station.
(b) Oiling and greasing of all equipment as per the manufacturer's instructions.
(c) Topping up of oil in bearing, oil pressure unit pump.
(d) Replacement of lamps, fuses, etc.
(e) Cleaning of trash racks.

(f) Inspection of forebay, bye-pass gates, and intake gates.
(g) Draft tube gates and appurtenant works, and
(h) Any other works as assigned.

The inspection and observation carried out during each shift shall be logged daily in the control room log book.

Discussion: After completion of this experiment, the students can identify the parts of the large hydropower plant and also be able to know the routine maintenance of the parts.

Experiment No.2

Title: Identify the routine maintenance parts of the micro hydropower plant after watching a video program.

Aim: To identify the parts of the micro hydropower plant

Apparatus/ software required: Watch the video at,

(a) https://www.youtube.com/watch?v=Rc23N6wDeNY
(b) https://www.youtube.com/watch?v=_uNoditN-yI

Theory:

Micro hydro is a type of hydroelectric power that typically produces from 5 kW to 100 kW of electricity using the natural flow of water. These installations can provide power to an isolated home or small community, or are sometimes connected to electric power networks, particularly where net metering is offered. There are many of these installations around the world, particularly in developing nations as they can provide an economical source of energy without the purchase of fuel. Following are the main components of the Micro hydropower plant which need to go through maintenance

1. Intake and waterway
2. Sedimentation basin
3. Headrace
4. Head tank (Forebay)
5. Penstock
6. Turbine
7. Generator
8. Load stabilizer
9. Transformer

The schematic diagram of a micro hydropower plant is shown in Fig.2.28

The daily maintenance of the parts is as follows.

1. Intake and waterway: The suspended trash at the screen must be removed at any time. The water leakage from the weir and gate must be recorded and if required repairing needs to be done. Flush the sand sedimentation out if necessary. The deformation cracks the in structure mustcheckedheck recorded or if required need to go for repair.
2. Sedimentation basin: If there is sand sedimentation, it is required to flush the same.
3. Headrace: Suspended materials along the canal need to be flushed out at any time. The leakage, deformation, and crack in the structure must be recorded and repaired if necessary. A landslide along the headrace must be removed.

4. Head tank (Forebay): The suspended trash at the screen must be removed at any time. Flush the sand sedimentation out if necessary. Water leakage must be recorded and if necessary, repairing must be done.
5. Penstock: Leakage and deformation must be recorded.
6. Turbine: Abnormal sound and vibration must be checked and recorded and need to find the cause of the same. Leakage from housing must be checked and recorded repaired pair if necessary
7. Generator: Abnormal sound and vibration must be checked and recorded and need to find the cause of the same. The temperature must be recorded. The damaged belt must be replaced if necessary.
8. Load stabilizer: The performance must be checked. The damaged heater must be replaced.
9. Transformer: Leakage of oil must be checked and if required replaced the oil.

Discussion: After seeing the videos student to identify the main parts which need routine maintenance of a Micro hydropower plant.

Experiment No.3

Title: Assemble a micro hydropower plant and then dismantle it.

Aim: To assemble and dismantle the component the of micro hydropower plant

Apparatus/ software required: Watch the video at

https://www.youtube.com/watch?v=pZ4z4qmYur8

Theory:

Micro hydro is a type of hydroelectric power that typically produces from 5 kW to 100 kW of electricity using the natural flow of water. These installations can provide power to an isolated home or small community, or are sometimes connected to electric power networks, particularly where net metering is offered. There are many of these installations around the world, particularly in developing nations as they can provide an economical source of energy without the purchase of fuel. Following are the main components of the Micro hydropower plant.

1. Intake and waterway
2. Sedimentation basin
3. Headrace
4. Head tank (Forebay)
5. Penstock
6. Turbine
7. Generator
8. Load stabilizer
9. Transformer

The schematic diagram of a micro hydropower plant is shown in Fig.2.28

The procedure for assembling a micro hydropower plant

1. Install the turbine and the generator set.
2. Closed the inlet valve.
3. Connect the pipes and tighten the

4. Adjust the pressure by adjusting the water inlet valve.
5. Connect the generator terminals
6. Switch on the supply to load.

The dismantling procedure is as follows.

1. Switch off the supply to load.
2. Disconnect the generator terminals.
3. Close the water inlet valve.
4. Loosen the pipe connector.
5. Unscrew the Foundation bolt.
6. Remove the turbine and generator set.

Conclusion: Using the above procedure a micro hydropower plant can be assembled and dismantled.

KNOW MORE

1. Hydropower plants supply one-sixth of the world's total electricity.
2. In the year 1770, Bernard Forest de Belidor, a French engineer published the architecture of hydraulics in which vertical and horizontal machines were described. The water wheel was used for industrial power for more than a century and nowadays it is not used because of size limitations. The term "Turbine" was developed in the 19th century. At the beginning of 20th century, many small hydroelectric power plants were constructed in France. Later on in the same century large hydropower plants were constructed in US.
3. The hydropower plants are suitable for both base and peak load.
4. No country is endowed with ample water resources or abundant coal reserves. This requirement can be made by the combined operation of thermal and hydropower plants. This is called hydro thermal co-ordination. The hydro-thermal co-ordinations yields many advantages such as flexibility in operation, econmic power genearation, secured supply, etc.
5. Surge tank is an open tank used with pressure conduit of considerable length. The function of surge tank is to reduce the water hammer. There are various types of surge tank such as simple type, Inclined type, expansion chamber and gallery type, retricted orifice or throttle type, and differential type of surge tanks.
6. Hydraulic turbine are directly connected to the electric generator or alternator. The generators are always runs at constant speed irrespective of the variations in load. This constant speed is called synchronous speed. It is given by $N_S = \dfrac{120f}{P}$, where frequency in Hz or cycle/second, P is the number of poles of the generator. The speed of the generator can be maintained constant only when the speed of the turbine runner is maintained constant. If the load on the generator varies and the input to the turbine is constant, the speed of the turbine tends to increase if the load goes down or it tends to decrease if the load goes up. Hence, the speed of the generator or the frequency varies accordingly, which is not desired. Thus, the speed of the runner must be maintained constant at all loads. This is done by a governor who regulates the quantity of water. This is a separate study on a power system called automatic generation control or load frequency control.

7. Like frequency, the voltage at the terminal must be maintained constant. It is done by the automatic voltage regulator. The automatic voltage regulator received a signal corresponding to the output voltage and it is compared with that of the signal corresponding to the desired voltage level. If there is errors in this comparison, the automatic voltage regulator sends a signal to the excitation system of the generator, and accordingly, the required DC voltage is applied to the field winding of the generator to maintain the terminal voltage constant.

REFERENCES AND SUGGESTED READINGS

1. Soni, Gupta, Bhatnagar, A Course in Electrical Power. - Dhanpatrai and Sons 11. The system, S.Chand & Co. New Delhi, 2005, ISBN: 9788121924962.
2. Gupta, B.R., Generation of Electrical Energy, S. Chand& Co. New Delhi.
3. Gupta, J.B. A Course in Electrical Power- S. K Kataria and Sons, New Delhi. 2014.
4. Nag. P. K.Power Plant Engineering, McGraw Hill, New Delhi, ISBN: 978-9339204044 2. Tanmoy Deb, Electrical Power Generation, Khanna Publishing House, Delhi (Ed. 2018);
5. https://www.mahaurja.com/meda/en/grid_connected_power/small_hydro
6. https://www.tatapower.com/businesses/hydro.aspx
7. https://en.wikipedia.org/wiki/Koyna_Hydroelectric_Project.
8. http://www.doed.gov.np/storage/listies/December2019/guidelines-for-operation-and-maintenance-of-hydropower-plants.pdf
9. https://cea.nic.in/wp-content/uploads/2020/04/chapter-6.pdf
10. https://www.publications.usace.army.mil/Portals/76/Users/182/86/2486/EC%201130-2-216.pdf?ver=2019-05-30-143437-757
11. https://policy.asiapacificenergy.org/sites/default/files/GUIDELINE%20FOR%20THE%20T%26C%20OF%20SMALL%20HYDRO_2015.pdf
12. https://policy.asiapacificenergy.org/node/3334
13. https://openjicareport.jica.go.jp/pdf/11737046_17.pdf
14. ttps://www.ppa.org.fj/wp-content/uploads/2020/10/Micro-Hydropwer-System-Install-Guideline-V1.pdf

❑❑

3 Solar and Biomass-based Power Plants

UNIT SPECIFICS

Through this Unit, we have discussed the following aspects:

- Global solar power radiation;
- Solar map- solar map of India;
- Solar power technology;
- Basics behind the solar cell;
- Solar thermal power plants;
- Flat plate collectors;
- Concentrated solar power plants;
- Construction and working of the power tower, parabolic trough, parabolic dish, and fresnel reflectors;
- Construction and working of solar photovoltaic (PV) power plant;
- Biomass-based power plants;
- Layout of a bio-chemical based (e.g., biogas) power plant;
- Layout of a thermo-chemical- based (e.g., Municipal waste) power plant;
- Layout of an agro-chemical based (e.g., bio-diesel) power plant;
- Features of the solid, liquid, and gas biomasses as fuel for biomass power plants;
- Some experiments on solar thermal power plants and biogas plants.

The concept of renewable power generation using solar energy in terms of thermal and photovoltaic is discussed. Clean, green, and sustainable power generation using biomass, biowaste, and other bio-product is discussed in detail. Further curiosity and creativity, as well as improving the students' problem-solving capacity, are dealt with through numerical examples.

Besides giving a large number of multiple-choice questions as well as questions of short and long answer types marked in two categories following the lower and higher order of Bloom's taxonomy, assignments through several numerical problems, a list of references, and suggested readings are given in this unit so that one can go through them for practice.

Some practical experiments related to the courses covered in this unit are also appended at the end of this unit to make the students aware of the hands-on on these topics. In some of the experiments, some specific videos are provided.

After the related practical on the topic, based on the content, there is a "Know More" section appended. This section has been designed to supplement additional information and higher learning skills on the topic.

RATIONALE

This unit on solar and biomass-based power plants will help the students to get a fundamental idea behind the conversion of solar energy into electrical energy directly and indirectly by heat energy. Different types of solar thermal power technologies and direct solar energy using solar photovoltaics are discussed in the chapter. Various issues related to solar energy, including its radiation, are also discussed.

The use of biomass for the production of electrical energy is discussed in this unit. Different types of biomass are used for different processes of producing useful energy, like biogas and biodiesel. Bio-chemical and bio-thermal process, including fermentation and digestion, is also illustrated.

Some relevant numerical problems with solutions and suggested questions will be helpful for students in preparing course work and competitive examinations.

The set of practical/ experiments is designed to help students understand the topic deeply.

PRE-REQUISITES

Fundamentals of Electrical & Electronics Engineering (ES104)

UNIT OUTCOMES

After completion of Unit-3, students will be able to:

U3-O1: Describe solar radiation and its usefulness

U3-O2: Explain solar energy and its harvesting using different types of solar thermal plants

U3-O3: Explain the working principle of solar PV and the working of SPV power plant

U3-O4: Realize the importance of biomass energy for a clean, green, and sustainable environment

U3-O5: demonstrate the use of solid, liquid, and gaseous biomass in different types of power plants

Unit-3 Outcome	EXPECTED MAPPING WITH COURSE OUTCOMES (1 - Weak Correlation; 2 - Medium Correlation; 3 - Strong Correlation)				
	CO-3	CO-2	CO-3	CO-4	CO-5
U3-O1	1	1	1	-	-
U3-O2	3	3	3	-	-
U3-O3	3	3	2	-	-
U3-O4	2	2	2	-	1
U3-O5	3	2	2	-	-

3.1 INTRODUCTION

Power generation for this modern world has become a challenging issue in the last few decades because of increased demand and deployment of natural resources by other energy sources. In the past century, electrical power generation mainly depended on fossil fuels like coal, oil, and gas. Coal-fired thermal power station shares the maximum generation of the globe, and of late and for the last few decades, thermal stations using nuclear fuel have taken the front seat of electrical power generation. These sources of electrical power generation are non-renewable, and these resources take millions of years to create by the natural process itself. For sustainable growth and a better future, renewable sources are the only alternative for electrical power in addition to thermal and hydropower. Solar energy and Biomass fuels play a significant role in generating commercial electricity by about 4% of total electricity generation today and increasing their participation every year globally. The most commonly known fact about solar energy is that it represents a clean and green source of energy. Most thermal power generation releases harmful greenhouse gases, which are very harmful to our environment. Solar power is a great way to reduce the carbon footprint. Solar power is safe, renewable, free, cost-effective, and abundantly available. The only technical challenge is harvesting the same as required for useful work. Solar power can be made available at remote corners to crowded areas in the range of watts to gigawatts, depending on size, requirement, and capacity. The commercial and economic viability of solar power plants is already proven. Capital investment and location may be an issue but running, and maintenance cost is minimum. Biomass fuels are renewable as they can be replaced quickly without permanently depleting natural resources. Biomass fuels consist of trees, plants, crops, grass, some type of algae, and municipal waste. These sources can be managed sustainably and economically. Biomass helps the climate by reducing greenhouse gases as the emission level is far smaller than fossil fuels. Municipal wastes and garbage pollute the ecosystem with a negative impact on human health, and this waste can easily be converted to electricity, bio-fertilizers, and other valuable products. Biomass fuel is widely available, and combining economic and environmental factors with energy sources; is at the top of the list. This unit deals with various energy sources using solar and biomass in detail.

3.2 SOLAR ENERGY

Solar energy is the most important source of energy available to the Earth. This energy is the primary source of life on Earth and drives photosynthesis. The energy from the sun in the form of radiation is solar energy. Solar energy can be used in many ways to convert to electricity, directly and indirectly. This energy received from the sun can be utilized in three ways. They are

(a) Converting solar energy into thermal energy.

(b) Converting solar energy into electricity.

(c) Photosynthesis.

Various types of solar collectors are used to convert solar energy to thermal energy. Different types of solar collectors are discussed in detail in section 3.5. These solar collectors collect solar energy in terms of heat, and heat is used to heat fluids (like water, other suitable liquids, gas, air, etc.), and this fluid is used to run the turbine to generate electricity. Other commercial use of solar thermal energy includes solar cooker, solar water heating system, solar air heating system, crop drying, refrigeration, water pumping, timber seasoning, water desalination, etc. Solar photovoltaic is the direct conversion of solar energy to electricity. Across the globe and in India, the generation of electricity using photovoltaics is increasing day by day in a very rapid way. Harvesting solar energy as a sustainable alternative to fossil fuel is taken up globally in most countries. Especially in India, many schemes are taken by the central and respective state governments to develop an alternative and sustainable energy source through various ministries and nodal agencies. Photosynthesis is plants' chemical conversion of carbon dioxide and water into carbohydrates in the presence of sunlight and chlorophyll. The detailed process of photosynthesis is not part of this section.

3.2.1 Solar Map of India

A solar map, in general, is a map of a city, state, country, or any piece of land that illustrates information about how much a certain piece of land, building, or home experiences a certain amount of sunlight. Though solar maps are illustrated in many forms, a solar map essentially records where and to what extent a certain location experiences a certain amount of sunlight or radiation. It normally combines topographic, meteorological, and sometimes financial data to help scholars or consumers, and investors in promoting awareness of the potential of solar power. The solar map of India is shown in Fig.3.1. This map shows the daily total and yearly total of solar radiation in kWh/kWp. Values such as kilowatt-hour tell about how much equivalent electricity the radiation can generate, and the kilowatt-peak provides information about how high its output is and how much maximum output in kilowatts a solar panel can produce. Fig.3.2 shows the global horizontal radiation in KW/m^2. Making a solar map is a complicated process. It requires sophisticated instruments to measure certain environmental conditions, including solar radiation. Meteorological and topographical data are used for the solar map. Meteorological data includes measurement of the position of the sun, atmospheric conditions, latitude, and shading. Topographical data includes the measurement of the area exposed to the sun with a degree of radiation and how much area is directly receiving radiation from the sun.

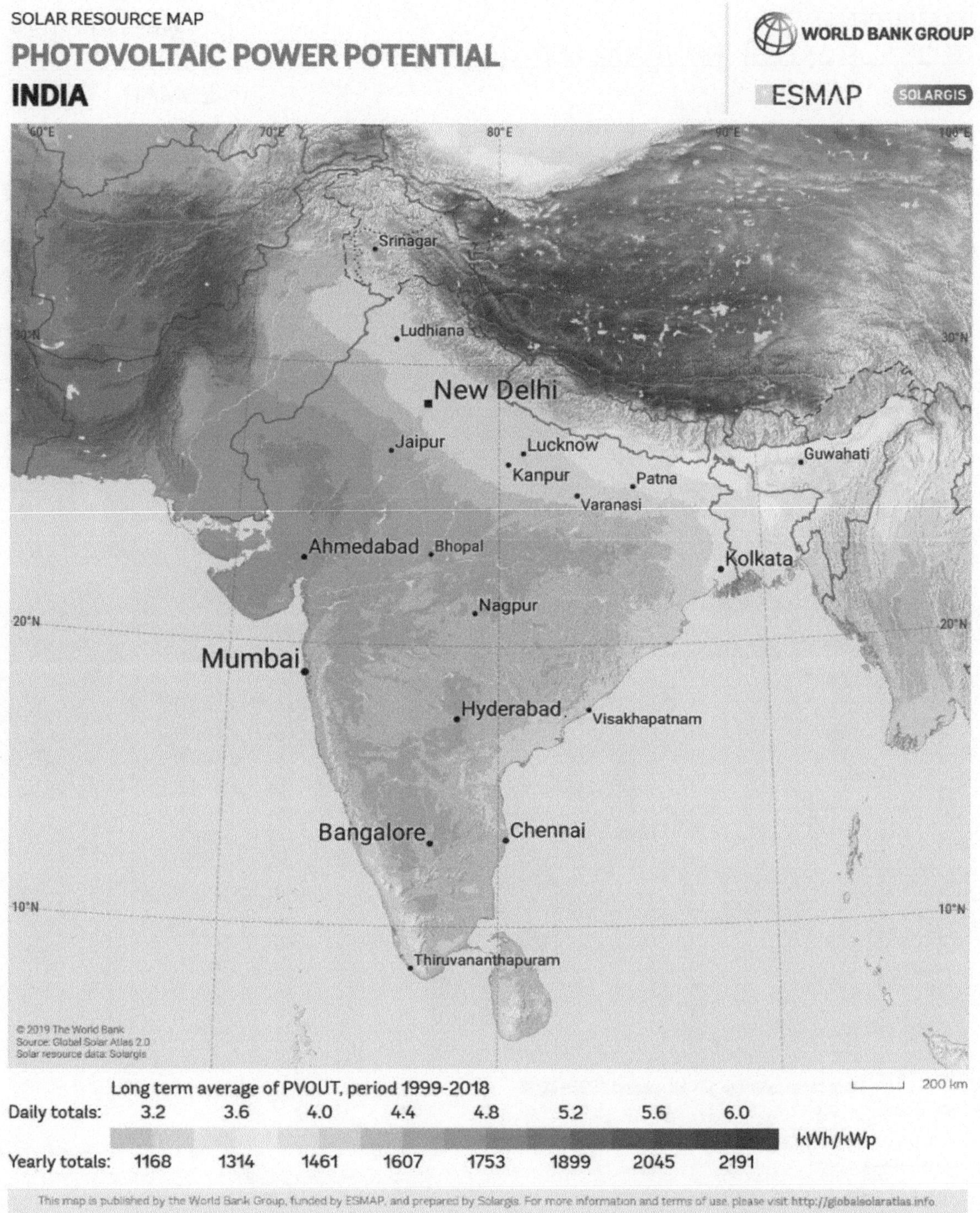

Fig. 3.1: Solar Map of India with photovoltaic power potential (Courtesy: https://solargis.com/)

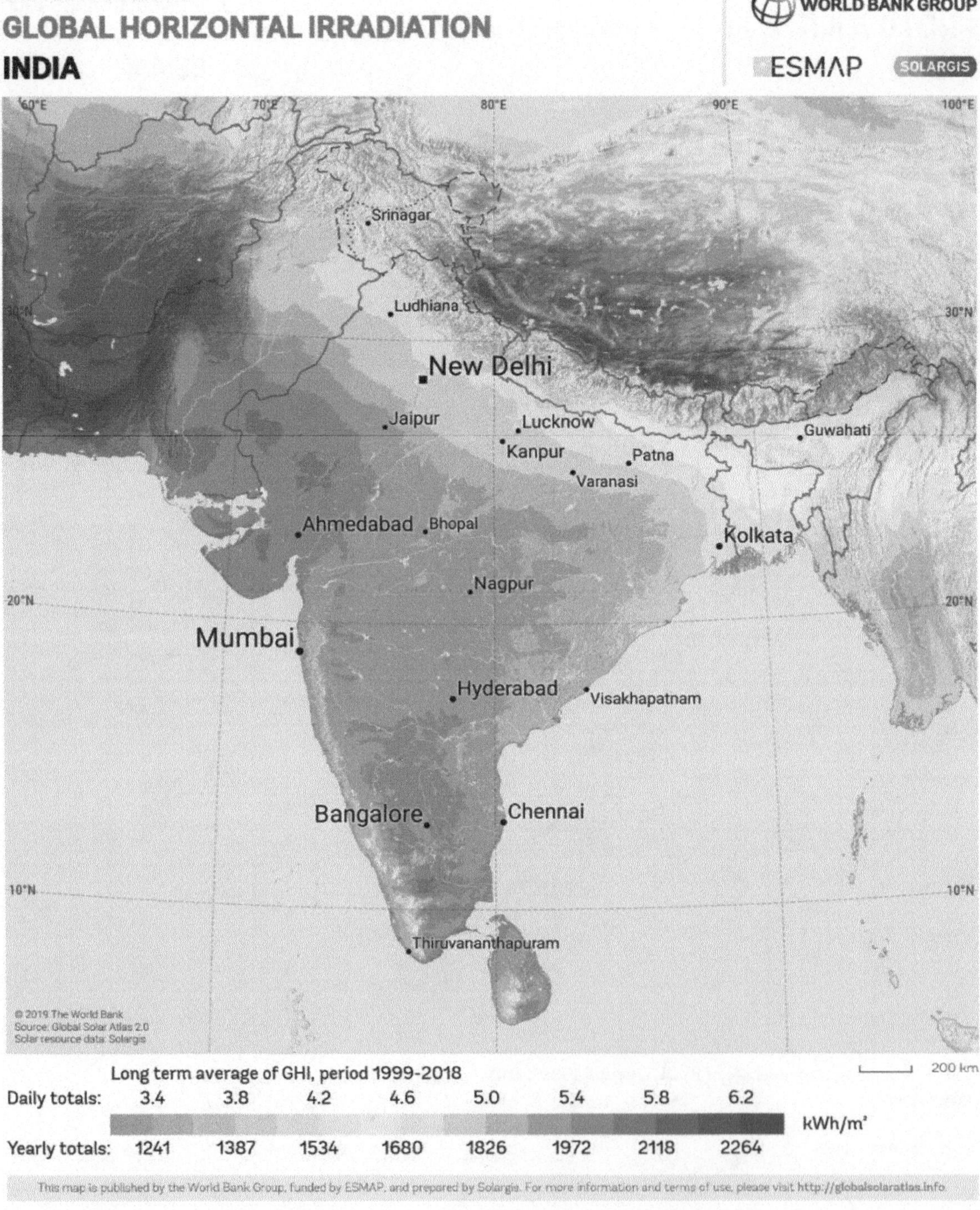

Fig. 3.2: Solar Map of India with global horizontal radiation (Courtesy: https://solargis.com/)

Some complex tools or instruments used in developing Solar Maps include LiDAR Technologies, the ESRI ArcGIS server, Solar Automated Feature Extraction (SAFE) technologies, and several other instruments. All these technologies are used in collecting, processing, and developing the solar map itself. According to policymakers, a solar map serves multiple roles. According to government officials, solar maps help keep track of progress on sustainability goals for the city or area in which they live. If they prefer to establish a more eco-friendly environment, a solar map, in their minds, would be the right tool to use in measuring this goal. Another idea why a local government may want to provide a solar map online is to promote self-awareness of citizens' electrical consumption and educate citizens about the possible rewards of using solar power instead of other conventional sources of power.

3.2.2 Global Solar Power Radiation

The amount of solar energy available on the Earth's surface is considerably smaller than that of arriving at the top of the atmosphere. The amount that reaches the Earth's surface is dependent on atmospheric conditions and the composition of atmospheric constituents and including absorption and scattering.

Solar radiation is the electromagnetic radiation emitted by the sun. This radiation can be converted into useful forms, such as heat and electricity, using different types of technologies. The electromagnetic radiation emitted by the sun shows a wide range of wavelengths. It can be divided into major regions - ionizing radiation, like X-rays and gamma rays, and non-ionizing radiation, including ultraviolet, visible, and infrared. Solar radiation has a spectral, or wavelength, distribution from short wavelength radiation too long wavelength radiation. Short-wavelength radiation has a higher energy level than long-wavelength.

As sunlight passes through the atmosphere, some part of it is absorbed, scattered, and reflected by air molecules, water vapors, clouds, dust, and pollutants. This is called diffuse solar radiation. The diffused solar radiation does not have a unique path. The solar radiation that reaches the surface of the Earth without being diffused is called direct beam solar radiation. The sum of the diffused and direct solar radiation is called total radiation or global solar radiation.

For any area on Earth's surface, the amount of energy it receives will vary hourly, daily and seasonal. The angle of the sun's position in the sky relative to a point on the Earth's surface determines the intensity of sunlight reaching that area.

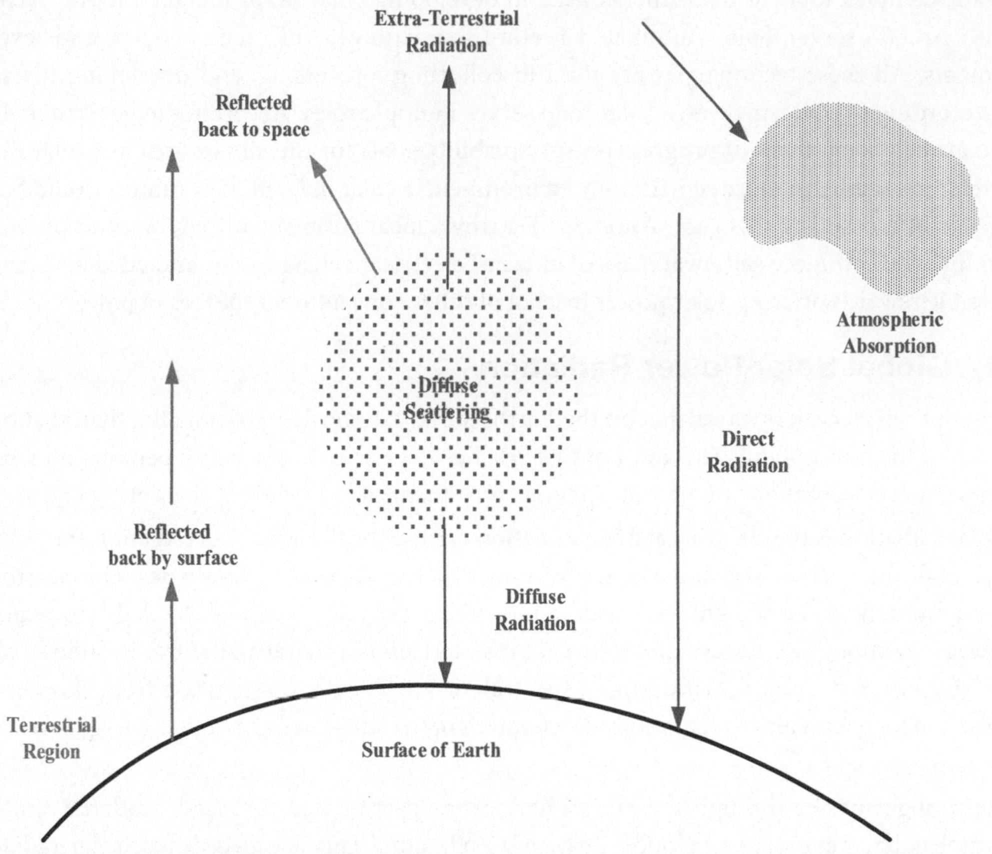

Fig.3.3: Direct, diffuse, and total solar radiation

Direct solar radiation is generally most intense at any one spot on the surface of the Earth at solar noon since it is most perpendicular in the sky and has the least amount of the atmosphere to travel through. Fig.3.3 shows the direct, diffuse, and total solar radiation. For locations at and north of 23.5° north latitude, it is most intense at solar noon on June 21 (the summer solstice). At that point, the sun is at the highest point in the sky that it will reach during the year, and it is at this point, sunlight passes through the least amount of the Earth's atmosphere. The summer solstice is the longest day of the year. The shortest day of the year is December 21, and the sunlight is the least intense during the winter solstice. For points on the equator, the sun will be most intense around March 20 and September 21, as these are the days when the sun is directly overhead are shown in Fig.3.4.

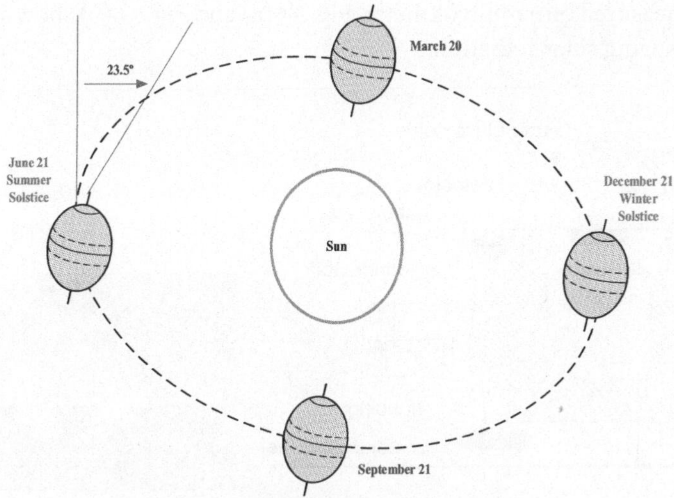

Fig. 3.4: Earth's orbit around the sun

The total solar radiation incident on a surface has three components. They are

(a) Beam radiation (R_b).

(b) Diffuse radiation (R_d).

(c) Reflected radiation from ground and surroundings (R_r).

Fig.3.5 shows the three components of solar radiation on a tilted surface.

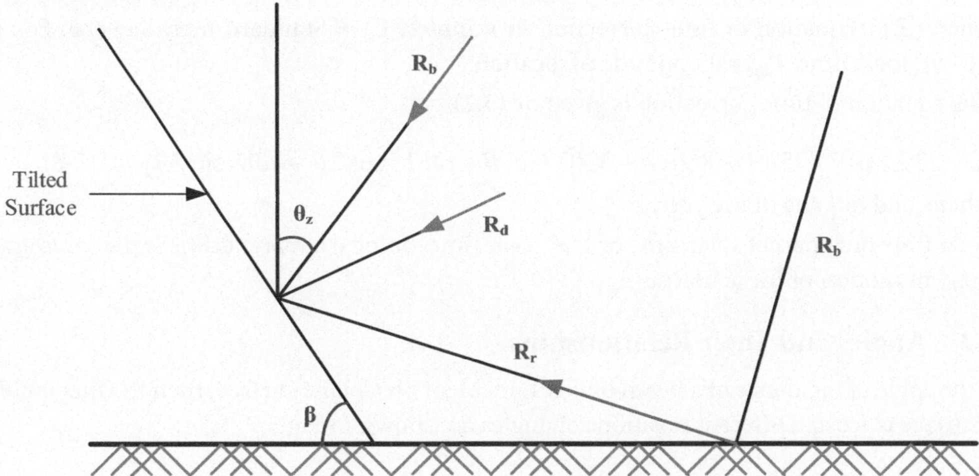

Fig. 3.5: Solar radiation on a tilted surface

3.2.2.1 Pyranometer

The pyranometer is used to measure global solar radiation from the Sun and sky on a horizontal surface, consisting of a thin blackened surface supported inside a relatively massive, well-polished case. When exposed to solar radiation, the blackened surface rises in temperature until its heat loss rate by all causes is equal to the rate of gain of heat by radiation. The rise in temperature sets up a thermal electromotive force (emf) which is measured on a millivoltmeter. Fig. 3.6(a) and Fig.3.6(b) show a typical thermoelectric pyranometer for measuring solar radiation.

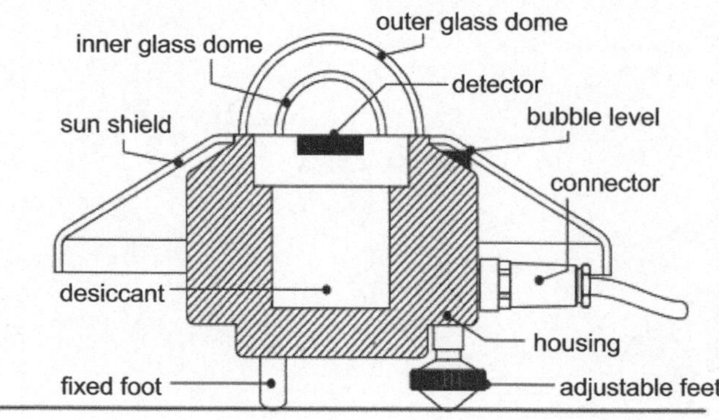

Fig. 3.6 (a): Thermoelectric Pyranometer

Fig. 3.6 (b): Thermoelectric Pyranometer

3.2.2.2 Solar Time

This is the time based on the apparent angular motion of the sun across the sky. Solar noon is the time the sun crosses the meridian of the observer. Solar time and standard time are not the same, and the relationship is given by (3.1),

$$\text{Solar time} = \text{Standard time} + 4\left(L_{st} - L_{loc}\right) + E \tag{3.1}$$

where E = Equation of time correction in minutes, L_{st} = Standard meridian (eg. For India, it is 82.50°E) for local time, L_{loc} = Longitude of location.

The equation of time correction is given by (3.2),

$$E = 229.2x10^{-6}(75 + 1868\cos B - 32077\sin B - 14615\cos 2B - 4089\sin 2B) \tag{3.2}$$

where and n = day of the year,

Solar time or apparent solar time or true solar time, or local apparent time is the same and based on the apparent motion of the actual sun.

3.2.2.3 Angles and Their Relationships

If q is the angle of incidence of a beam of flux I, incident on a plane surface, then the flux incident on the plane surface is *Icosq*. Different positions of angles are shown in Fig.3.7

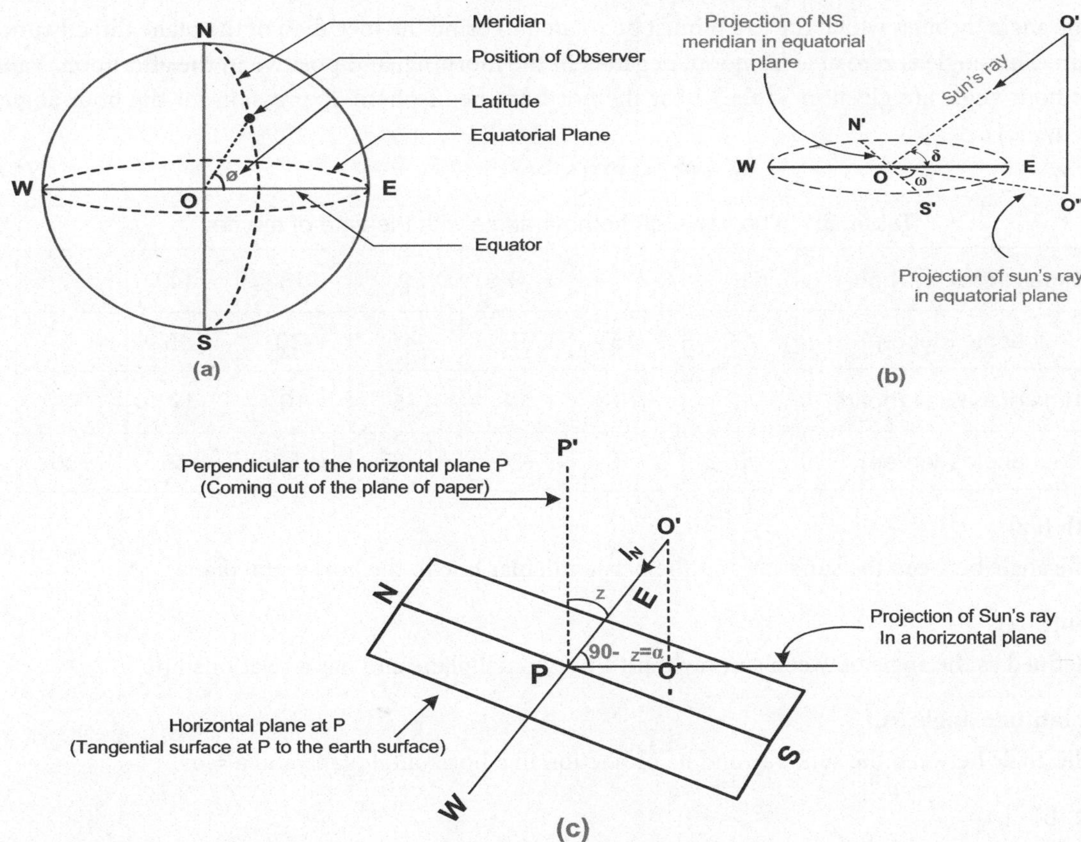

Fig. 3.7: View of different angles (a) Latitude (f), (b) Declination (d) and hour angle (w), (c) Zenith (θ_z) and altitude (a)

Latitude (ϕ)

The latitude of a location is the angle made by the radial line, joining the given location to the centre of the earth. The latitude is positive in the northern hemisphere and negative in the southern hemisphere.

Declination (δ)

Declination may be defined as the angle between the line joining the centres of the sun and the earth and its projection on the equatorial plane. Declination is due to the rotation of the earth about its axis, which makes an angle of 66.5°. The declination varies from a maximum value of 23.45° on 21 June to a minimum value of –23.45° on 21 December. The following equation can calculate this

$$A = \pi r^2$$

$$= 23.45 \sin\left[\frac{360}{365}(284+n)\right] \quad (3.3)$$

Where n is the nth day of the year

Hour angle (ω)

It is the angle through which the earth must be rotated to bring the meridian of the plane directly under the sun. This angle is zero at solar noon, negative in the morning, and positive in the afternoon. Values of the hour angle are given in Table.3.1 for the northern hemisphere. Expression for the hour angle is given by (3.4).

$$\omega = (ST - 12)15^\circ \tag{3.4}$$

Table. 3.1: The value of the hour angle with the time of the day

Time of the day (hour)	6	7	8	9	10	11	12
Hour angle (degree)	-90	-75	-60	-45	-30	-15	0
Time of the day (hours)	12	13	14	15	16	17	18
Hour angle (degree)	0	+15	+30	+45	+60	+75	+90

Zenith (θz)

It is the angle between the sun's ray and the perpendicular line to the horizontal plane.

Altitude (α)

It is defined as the angle between sun rays and a horizontal plane and has a relationship .

Solar latitude angle (α_s)

It is the angle between the sun's ray and its projection in a horizontal plane and a = αs.

Slope (β)

It is the angle between the plane surface, under consideration, and the horizontal. It is taken as positive for the surface sloping towards the south and negative for the surface sloping towards the north.

Surface azimuth angle (γ)

It is the angle in the horizontal plane between the line due south and the projection of the normal to the surface on the horizontal plane. By convention, the angle will be taken negative if the projection is east of south and positive if west of south for the northern hemisphere and vice versa for the southern hemisphere. The variation of g for some orientations is given in Table. 3.2.

Table. 3.2: Surface azimuth angle (g) for various orientations in the northern hemisphere.

Surface orientation	g
Sloped towards South	0°
Sloped towards North	–180°
Sloped towards East	–90°
Sloped towards West	+90°
Sloped towards south-East	–45°
Sloped towards South-West	+45°

Solar azimuth angle (γs)

It is the angle in a horizontal plane between the line due south and the projection of beam radiation on the horizontal plane.

Angle of incidence (θi)

It is the angle between beam radiation on a surface and the normal to that surface. The angle of incidence can be expressed as (3.5).

$$\cos\theta i = (\cos\phi\cos\beta + \sin\phi\,\sin\beta\,\cos\gamma)\,\cos\delta\,\cos\omega + \cos\delta\,\sin\omega\,\sin\beta\,\sin\gamma + \sin\delta(\sin\phi\,\cos\beta - \cos\phi\,\sin\beta\,\cos\gamma) \quad (3.5)$$

(a) For a surface facing due south, $\gamma = 0$

$$\cos\theta i = \cos(\phi - \beta)\ \cos\delta\,\cos\omega + \sin\delta\,\sin(\phi - \beta) \quad (3.6)$$

(b) For a horizontal plane facing due south, $\gamma = 0, \beta = 0, \theta i = \theta z$ (zenith angle)

$$\cos\theta z = \cos\phi\ \cos\delta\,\cos\omega + \sin\delta\,\sin\phi \quad (3.7)$$

(c) For a vertical surface facing due south, $\gamma = 0, \beta = 90°$

$$\cos\theta z = \cos\phi\ \cos\delta\,\cos\omega + \sin\delta\,\sin\phi \quad (3.8)$$

Equation (3.6) can be solved for the sunset hour angle $\omega = \omega s$ for $\theta s = 90°$

$$0 = \cos\phi\ \cos\delta\,\cos\omega_s + \sin\phi\ \sin\delta$$

$$\omega_s = \cos^{-1}(-\tan\phi\,\tan\delta)$$

The total angle between sunrise and sunset is given by (3.9).

$$2\omega_s = 2\cos^{-1}(-\tan\phi\,\tan\delta) \quad (3.9)$$

Since 15° change is equal to 1 hour, the number of daylight (sunshine) hours (*N*) is given by (3.10).

$$N = \frac{2}{15}\cos^{-1}(-\tan\phi\tan\delta) \quad (3.10)$$

Latitude, longitude, and elevation for different places in India are shown in Table.3.3. The equation of time correction (E) for different months is shown in Table. 3.4.

Table. 3.3: Latitude, longitude, and elevation of different places in India (Courtesy: Tiwari, G. N., "Solar Energy")

Place	Latitude (ϕ)	Longitude (L_{loc})	Elevation (E_0) above mean sea level
Bangalore	12°58′ N	77°35′ E	921 m
Chennai	13°00′ N	80°11′ E	16 m
Jodhpur	26°18′ N	73°01′ E	224 m
Kolkata	22°32′ N	88°20′ E	6 m
Mt. Abu	24°36′ N	72°43′ E	1195 m
Mumbai	18°54′ N	72°49′ E	11 m
New Delhi	28°35′ N	77°12′ E	216 m
Simla	31°06′ N	77°10′ E	2202 m
Srinagar	34°05′ N	74°50′ E	1586 m

Table. 3.4: Time correction (E) in (minutes: second)
(Courtesy: Tiwari, G. N., "Solar Energy")

Month	1	8	15	22
January	-(3:16)	-(6:26)	-(9:12)	-(11:27)
February	-(13:34)	-(14:14)	-(14:15)	-(13:41)
March	-(12:36)	-(11:04)	-(9:14)	-(7:12)
April	-(4:11)	-(2:07)	-(0:15)	1:19
May	2:50	3:31	3:44	3:30
June	2:35	1:15	-(0:09)	-(1:40)
July	-(3:33)	-(4:48)	-(5:45)	-(6:19)
August	-(6:17)	-(5:40)	-(4:35)	-(3:03)
September	-(0:15)	2:03	4:29	6:58
October	10:02	12:11	13:59	15:20
November	16:20	16:16	15:29	14:02
December	11:14	8:26	5:13	1:47

3.3 PHYSICS BEHIND SOLAR CELLS

Solar cells are the basic component of a solar photovoltaic system. Solar cells are made of semiconductor materials and are photosensitive. Silicon is primarily used as a semiconductor. When the photon incident the surface of the solar cells, the electron-hole pairs are ionized, and due to this, the flow of electricity is observed. This is the basic principle of solar cells.

Intrinsic semiconductors are usually not used for solar cells. A p-n junction diode is formed on the base of p-type material, and a thin film of n-type material is diffused on it. A basic model of solar cells is shown in Fig.3.8.

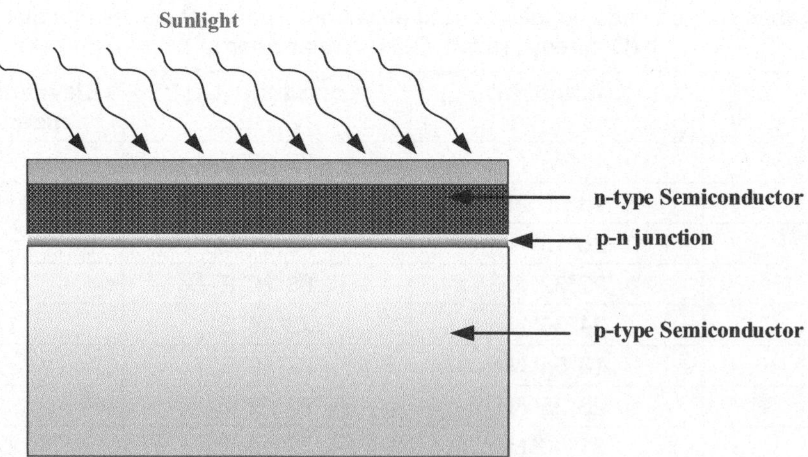

Fig.3.8: Basic solar cell

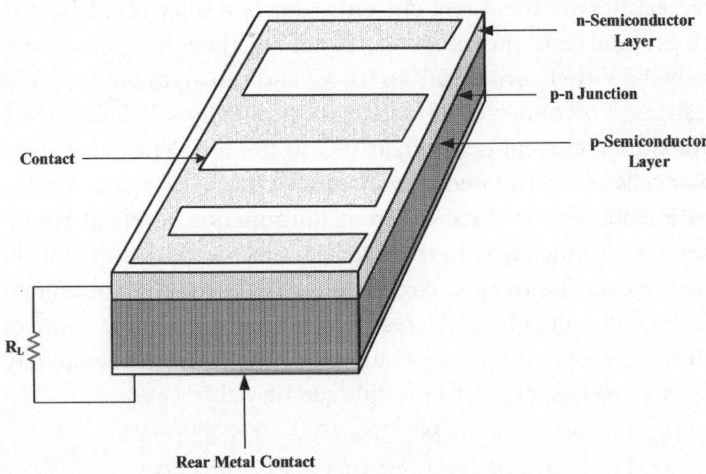

Fig. 3.9: Model of a crystalline solar cell

These solar cells work on the principle of the photovoltaic effect, which is a process of generating an emf utilizing the incident sun rays on these cells. In a p-n junction, photons are absorbed, and the free electrons of n-type material will tend to flow through the junction to p-type material, and the holes from p-type material will tend to flow through the junction to n-type material. This diffusion of charged particles through the junction creates an electric field E_f from the n-type region to the p-type region. A model of a crystalline solar cell is shown in Fig.3.9, where external electrical connections are made through load resistance. Both the terminals of semiconductors are connected externally, and electrons will flow from the n-type material through the resistance to the p-type material. Due to this flow of electrons, electron-hole pairs will be formed and neutralized. This process of forming free electrons and holes continues till solar radiation is present in the cells. This flow of electrons constitutes an electric current through the external circuit, and this current depends upon the intensity of solar radiation as well as the surface area of the cells receiving the radiation. A typical I-V characteristic of a solar cell is shown in Fig.3.10.

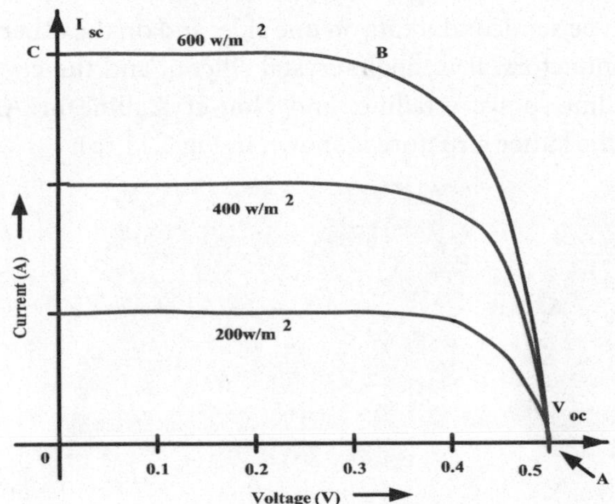

Fig. 3.10: Typical I-V characteristics of a solar cell

Voltage (V) characteristics are the direct currents (dc) in a solar cell. When the terminal is open-circuited, or a very high external resistance is connected as load, then the open circuit voltage (V_{OC}) across the cells is approximately 0.5 V (between 0.55 V to 0.6 V) and shown as point A. When the terminals are shorted, or very low resistance is connected as load, then these cells will deliver the maximum current at zero voltage, and the maximum current is shown as ISC as point C. The curves between points B and C are almost flat, and solar cells are considered to work best in that region as a constant dc current source. Three different curves are shown for three different illumination levels at room temperature. Open circuit voltage increases logarithmically with the intensity of solar radiation, but short circuit current is a linear function. There is a decrease in open circuit voltage (V_{OC}) with increasing module temperature. For each solar cell, the open circuit voltage decreases by 2.3mV per degree approximately. If ΔT equals the difference between the cell operating temperature and the reference temperature, the open circuit voltage and optimum power voltage (V_m) of a module can be written as

$$V_{OC}\,(T)(mV) = V_{OC}\,(28°\text{ C})(mV) - \Delta\text{T} \times 82\ (mV)$$

$$V_m\,(T)(mV) = V_m\,(28°\text{ C})(mV) - \Delta\text{T} \times 82\ (mV)$$

The cell temperature to be determined experimentally depends on the solar insolation (the flux of solar radiation per unit of horizontal area for a given locality), the ambient temperature, the wind speed, and the encapsulation type. The following approximation holds good for the same as

$$T_{cell} = T_{ambient} + kP_{in}\ (wm^{-2})$$

where $k = 0.02$ to 0.03 (deg.m^2w^{-1}), P_{in} is the incident solar radiation.

3.4 TYPES OF SOLAR CELLS

The most common type of solar cells is silicon solar cells. Silicon solar cells are classified into three categories according to their crystalline structure. The categories are given below.

(a) Monocrystalline structure silicon cell.

(b) Polycrystalline structure silicon cell.

(c) Non-crystalline or Amorphous silicon cell.

A Monocrystalline silicon cell is a single structure, as suggested by their names, and boron is doped with silicon to produce p-type semiconductors on one side, and on the other side, phosphorous is doped to produce n-type semiconductors. It is single-crystal silicon, and the crystal lattice is continuous. A schematic of monocrystalline, polycrystalline, and Non-crystalline or Amorphous silicon cells are shown in Fig.3.11(a), and the lattice structure is shown in Fig.3.11 (b).

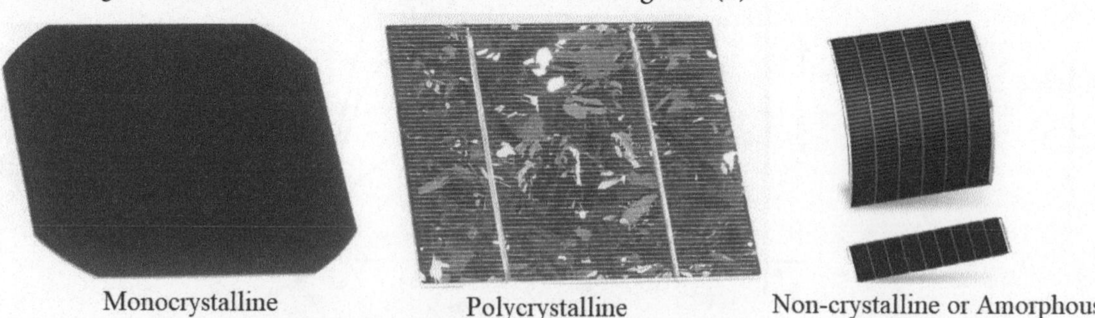

Fig. 3.11 (a): Different silicon cells as per the crystalline structure

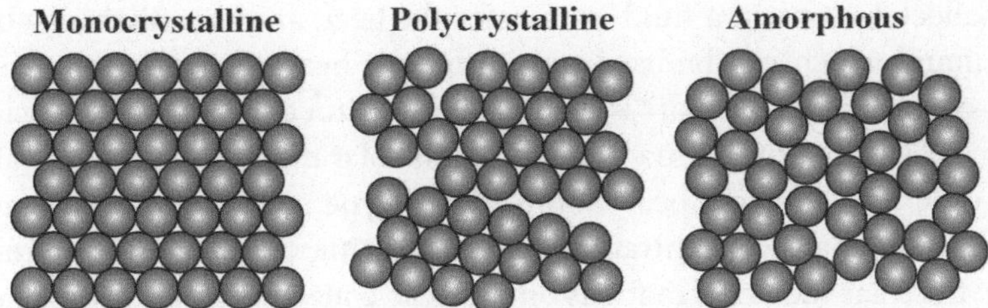

Fig. 3.11 (b): Typical lattice structure of different silicon cells

Polycrystalline or multi-crystalline silicon cells used in solar panels consist of several crystals of silicon in a single photovoltaic cell. During the solidification of the material, various sizes of crystals are formed. Several portions of silicon are melted and form the wafer after colling, and the crystalline structure depends upon the cooling condition. Monocrystalline cells are more efficient as they are from the same source, and polycrystalline structures are sourced from multiple silicon. The formation of the junction is the same as the monocrystalline structure. Amorphous or non-crystalline silicon solar cells are thin-film solar cells. Silicon film is deposited on glass or other material and forms a very thin layer. The efficiency of amorphous solar cells is higher than that of the two. Various technology has been adopted to increase the efficiency, including an amorphous silicon carbide layer which increases the gap between conduction and valence band and thereby increases efficiency. The second type of solar cells is thin-film solar cells and which are made from very thin layers of semiconductors. Materials used for thin-film solar cells are cadmium telluride or copper indium gallium diselenide. These cells are flexible and lightweight. The third type of solar cell is termed as III-V Solar cell. They are mainly constructed from the elements in group III (gallium and indium) and group V (arsenic and antimony) of the periodic table. These solar cells are expensive but more efficient than silicon and thin-film solar cells. Various research is underway for developing the next generation solar cells with higher efficiency, compactness, and flexibility. The new generation of solar cells made from organic materials, quantum dots, and hybrid organic and inorganic materials are cost-effective, easy to manufacture, and more reliable. Further research in the field of developing different solar cells must fulfill the requirement of humanity.

3.5 SOLAR POWER TECHNOLOGY

Solar power is useful broadly in two categories- Solar photovoltaic (PV) and Solar thermal. Both solar PV and solar thermal power are used to produce clean and green electricity. For solar PV, silicon is used extensively. Silicon is the most commonly available element on Earth and makes up 27% of the Earth's crust by mass, and is the second most abundant element after oxygen. Approximately 90% of solar cells are produced from silicon. Electronic-grade silicon is used mostly for semiconductors, and all other types of silicon are used for solar cells. Production of solar PV modules has increased more than 1000 times in the last four decades. In the last ten years, the growth of solar PV has been about 30%, and a huge quantity of silicon is required for producing solar cells. Silicon is mostly available in the form of oxide and is commonly available as quartz, sand, and silicates. The naturally available silicon contains impurities, and various steps are taken to purify the silicon wafers. For semiconductor electronic use purest form of silicon is required at the level of parts per billion, but for solar applications, the impurity level in silicon is compromised to parts per million. Details of solar PV and its technology and use will be discussed in further sections. A solar collector absorbs solar radiation and converts it to useful heat energy. The solar collectors contain a fluid to transfer the heat, and this fluid may be water, oil, air, or any other suitable liquid which can be used to transfer the heat efficiently for a useful purpose. The basic characteristic of solar heat collectors is the high absorption and low heat emission. This process of collecting heat from solar radiation is broadly classified as solar thermal. There are various types of solar thermal collectors used for collecting heat. Some are flat-type collectors where a maximum of 100°C may be obtained, and some are concentrating collectors using optical lenses or reflectors, which are used to concentrate the solar radiation to focus on the heat-collecting fluids. These heated/ superheated fluids are used for useful purposes. Each of the different types of solar thermal collectors and their use is discussed in the following sections.

3.5.1 Flat Plate Collectors

A solar flat plate collector consists of a transparent sheet cover, and under that, there are a series of copper or aluminum tubes that carry a liquid to transfer heat, and these are based on a large heat-absorbing plate. The tubes containing fluids are made of good conductors and are painted with black or dark colors or chemically etched black to absorb maximum solar radiation. A flat solar plate collector is shown in Fig. 3.12

On the thick absorber plate, a series of parallel tubes are soldered, and all the pipes are connected in series or parallel in such a manner that the fluid inside the tubes gets heated and naturally flows from the inlet to the outlet. The plate and the tubes are painted black to absorb the maximum amount of sunlight. Also, one or more glass or plastic sheets are placed on top of the black sheet to avoid heat loss by radiation. This whole structure is now placed under the sun to absorb solar radiation at a proper inclination so that the sun's rays are incident for the whole day. The heat absorbed by radiation is taken away by circulating fluid through the pipes and tubes. The temperature achieved by a flat plate collector may be within the range of 40 to 70°C depending on the season, time, and inclination, and efficiency may be within 30 – 50%. The efficiency of the flat plate collector may be significantly increased by selecting the proper coating of the collector surface. Instead of simple black paint, an anti-reflecting coating will improve the efficiency of the collectors. The flat plate collectors absorb both the direct and diffused radiations. Using a solar tracker and with automatic movement of the flat collector, efficiency also may be improved.

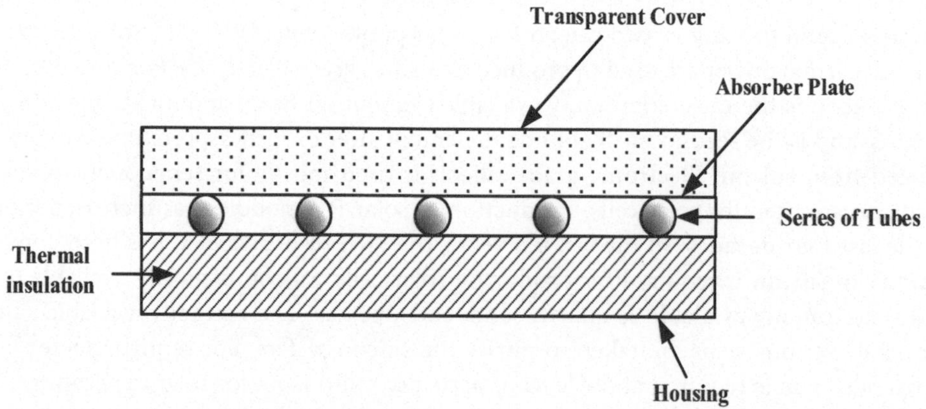

Fig. 3.12: Solar flat plate collector

A flat plate collector is mainly used for water heating, room heating, or reducing room temperature keeping the collectors at the top of the room. Alternatively, using a low boiling point fluid, a turbine can also be used for electric power generation with these vapors. Different types of flat plate collectors are shown in Fig.3.13. Different types of materials are used for solar plates and tubes. These may be classified as follows:

(a) **Thermophysical properties**: Thermal conductivity, heat capacity, radiation coefficient, thermal conductivity, etc.

(b) **Physical properties**: Density, tensile strength, melting point, ductility, etc.

(c) **Environmental properties**: Corrosion resistance, moisture absorption, degradation due to pollution, amination, etc.

A solar plate collector and the absorber plate should have higher thermal conductivity, high heat capacity, adequate tensile strength, and corrosion resistance. As explained above, fluid tubes are made of copper, and absorber materials are iron, brass, zinc, aluminum, or other metals, which have better thermal conductivity and all other properties, as explained above. The selection of insulation materials is critical for flat plate collectors as these materials should have low thermal conductivity and be chemically stable under varied environmental conditions. Most of the common insulation materials commonly used are glass, glass wool, mica or calcium silicate for moderate and high temperatures, polyurethane foam, and thermocouple (polystyrene) for low-temperature use. Forced flow of air, fluid, or liquid is also used with or without fins to achieve higher efficiency for various domestic and industrial applications.

The advantages and disadvantages of flat plate collectors are listed below.

Advantages of flat plate collectors

(a) It absorbs both direct and diffused radiations.

(b) It does not need to be oriented toward the sun.

(c) It requires less maintenance.

(d) Its mechanical design and arrangement are simple.

(e) It is comparatively less expensive.

Disadvantages of flat plate collectors

(a) It requires anti-freeze protection for reflectors.

(b) More and wide materials are necessary for reflecting surface.

(c) The greater area of the absorber surface limits the insolation intensity.

(d) As the area of the absorber is more, the heat loss in the surroundings is also more.

(e) The temperature attained by the working fluid is comparatively low.

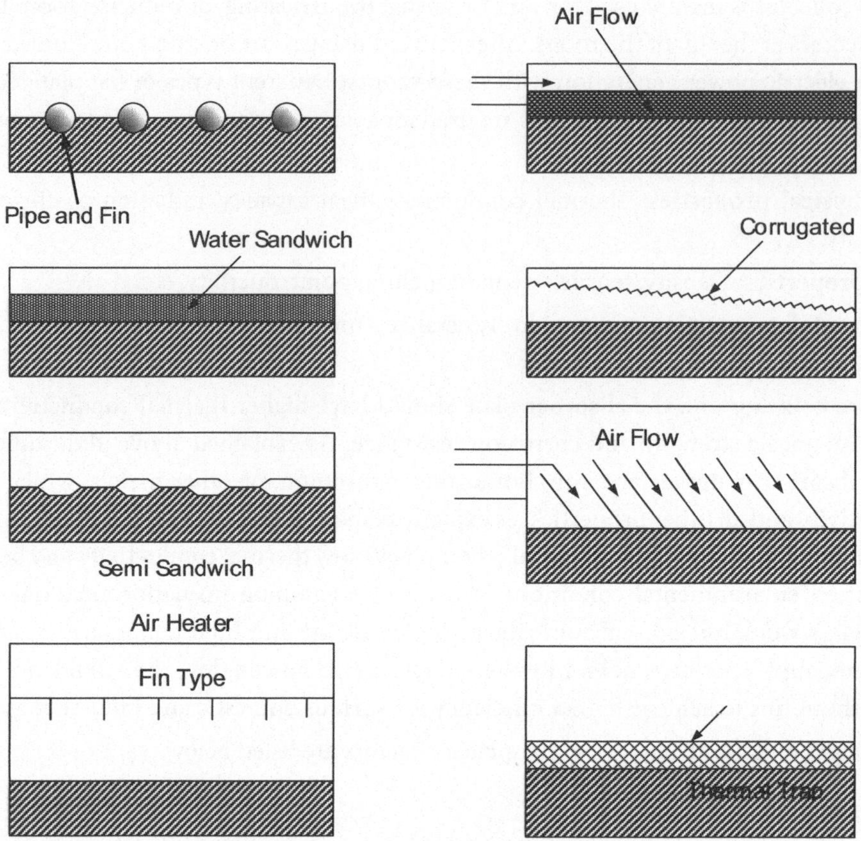

Fig. 3.13: Different types of flat plate collectors

3.5.2 Concentrated Solar Power Plant

To generate high-temperature solar energy applications such as solar thermal power generation, solar energy is to be concentrated optically or using mirrors before being transferred into heat. Concentrating collectors are also known as focusing collectors. The concentrating or focussing collectors are classified as (i) Line focusing type collectors and (ii) Point focussing type collectors. The line focusing collectors include a line of collector pine. The main line focussing collectors are parabolic trough reflectors, mirror strip collectors, and Fresnel lens collectors. The point focussing collectors include a point which is a small volume through which heat transport fluid flow. The main type of point, focusing solar collector, is a parabolic dish or heliostat field.

The reflected or refracted light is concentrated in a focal point, thus increasing the energy flux in the receiving target. With these concentrating collectors, a temperature of 200 - 300°C or above may be obtained. However, some mechanism of tracking the sun or a sun tracker should be provided to track the sun seasonally. Cylindrical parabolic concentrating mirrors are medium-range temperature concentrators within the range of 100 to 250°C, and the paraboloid type concentrating mirrors are for high temperatures and generally above 200°C. The concentrator increases the solar radiation by a concentration ratio of C, which is defined as the ratio of aperture area A_a of the concentrator to receiver area A_r.

$$C = \frac{A_a}{A_r}$$

This value of C varies from 20 to 100 for line-focusing type collectors, and a high value of C, like more than 100 to 3000 or sometimes up to 4000, can be achieved from a point focussing type solar collectors. For point focussing type collectors, the area of the absorber is very small, and by making a small absorber surface, C values can be increased.

For parabolic reflectors, the focal axis is aligned in an East-West (E-W) direction so that the collectors are efficient throughout the whole day. On the other hand, Parabolic trough mirrors receive the energy at a focal point, and the concentration ratio is very high to give rise to a very high temperature. Fresnel lens concentrators are made of glass or transparent plastic material, and it contains linear grooves on one surface so that after the refraction of the rays, they are concentrated. These lenses also can be used for medium temperature rise, and grooves are either facing the sun or facing downward. Various types of solar concentrator collectors are shown in Fig.3.14.

A heliostat is a device that continually tilts a mirror or multiple mirror facets to track the sun's movement to reflect sunlight toward a predetermined target—such as a receiver sitting on top of a solar tower. Heliostats are a critical component of CSP and concentrating solar-thermal power tower technologies. A central stationary receiver receives solar radiation from a heliostat. Heliostats are placed in open space, and the concentration ratio is very high, about 3000. In some applications, heliostats and parabolic reflectors and their combinations are used for better efficiency. Heliostat-based collectors are more suitable for solar thermal power plants as the temperature and pressure are adequate for driving a turbine for power generation.

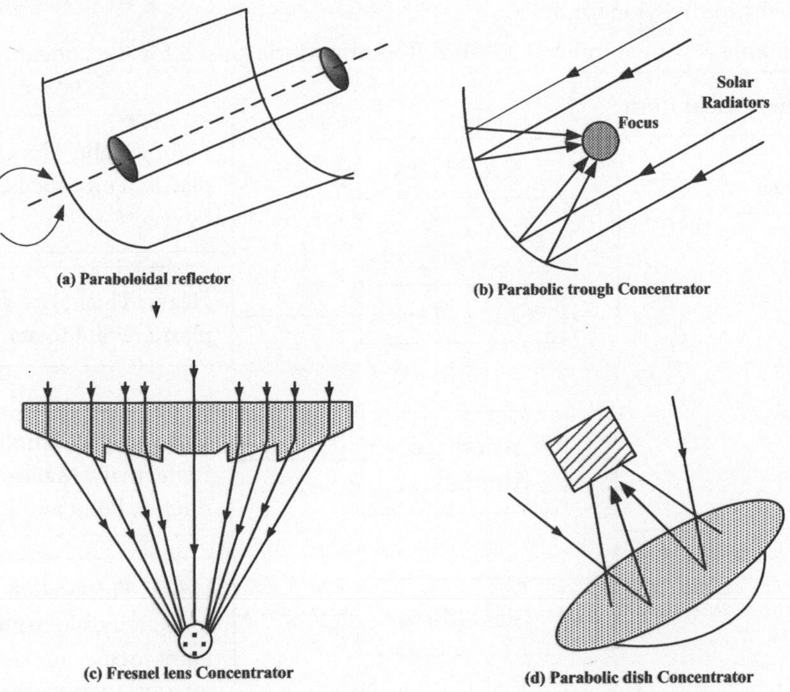

(a) Paraboloidal reflector

(b) Parabolic trough Concentrator

(c) Fresnel lens Concentrator

(d) Parabolic dish Concentrator

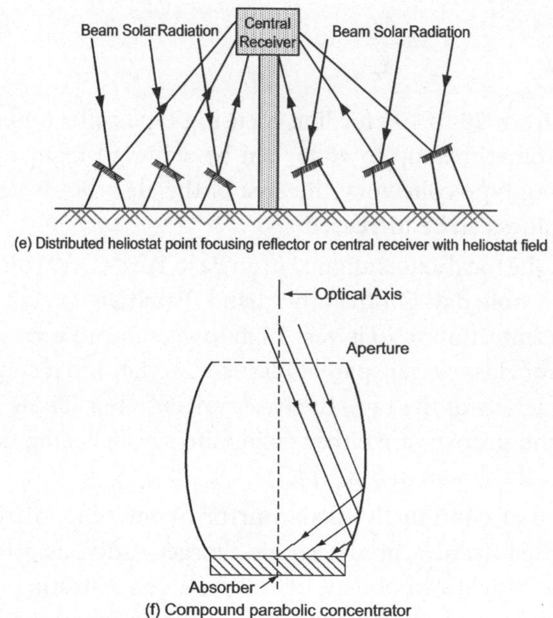

Fig. 3.14: Various types of concentrated solar power reflectors

A compound parabolic concentrator consists of two parabolic segments and is arranged in such a way that the focus of one is located and the bottom end of the other vice versa. The receiver is a flat surface. It is a non-imaging concentrator, and they have the capability of reflecting the absorber of all the incident radiation within the wide limit.

A comparison table is shown in Fig.3.15 for different materials used for the concentrator.

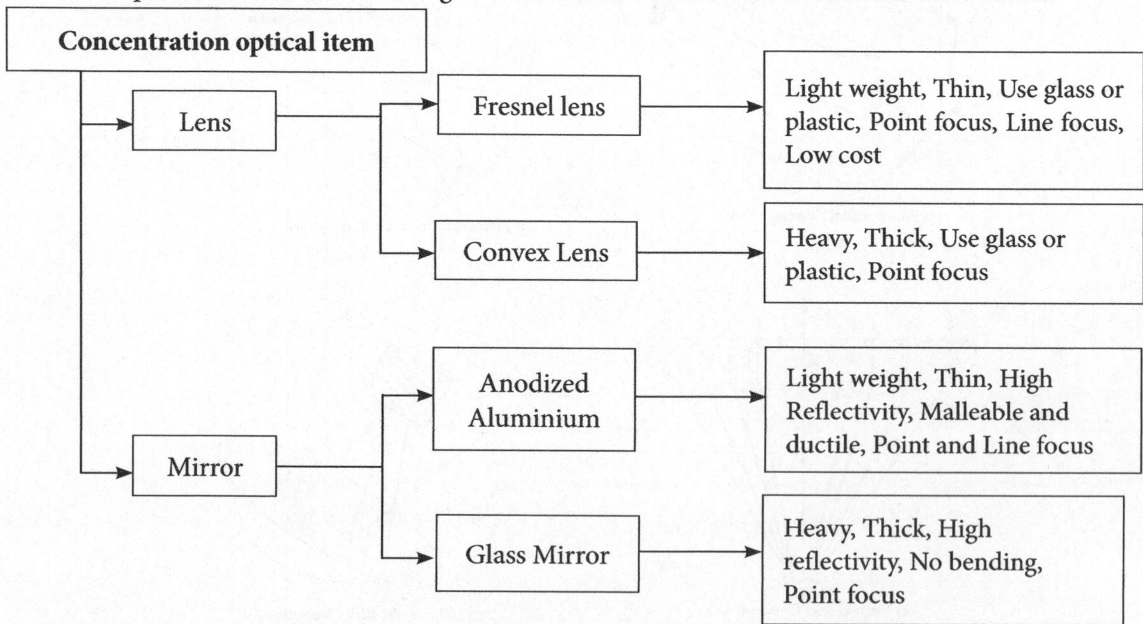

Fig. 3.15: Comparison of different materials used for concentrator

3.5.2.1 Parabolic Trough

A parabolic trough reflector is used to concentrate sunlight on solar cells or at a focal point. The solar cell collects the sun's energy and converts it to electrical energy. This is the most mature and commercialized concentrated solar power technology. This system uses a linear parabolic reflector to focus the sunlight, and a pipe or tube with fluids runs on this focal line, and the steam generated by this process can be used to run a turbine. Parabolic trough collectors can also be used for low solar radiation. The sun tracking system of the parabolic trough collector is driven in a single-axis mode. A schematic is shown in Fig.3.14 (b). This is one of the important types of solar collectors and is most widely used in solar plants. An absorber is a collector pipe with a coating of selected absorbing material. The dimension of a trough is roughly 3 to 6 meters in length and 1.5 to 2.5 meters in width. The advantages and disadvantages of parabolic trough collectors are listed below.

Advantages of parabolic trough collector

(a) The material required for the reflecting surface is less.
(b) The absorber area is smaller; hence insolation intensity is higher.
(c) The working fluid can attain a comparatively higher temperature as the insolation on the absorber is more concentrated, and heat losses are less.
(d) The collector efficiency is comparatively higher.
(e) The amount of heat stored per unit volume is immense; thus, heat storage costs are less.
(f) Anti-freeze protection for the absorber is not required.

Disadvantages of parabolic trough collector

(a) It collects only the beam component of solar radiation.
(b) It needs a tracking system to track the sun to collect more radiation; thus, the system becomes expensive.
(c) Regular maintenance of the reflecting surface is necessary.
(d) The flux on the absorber is non-uniform.
(e) The capital investment is high.
(f) It has an additional loss like reflectance loss, intercept loss, etc.

3.5.2.2 Parabolic Dish

A parabolic reflector could be used to concentrate sunlight on the solar cells. A parabolic dish mainly consists of a receiver, a parabolic reflector- parabolic-shaped concave mirrors, a solar tracker, the mounting structure, and a tube to carry the heated fluid. This parabolic dish is mounted on the dual-axis solar tracker that keeps it always oriented towards the sun. The reflector is made of glass or an anodized aluminum plate. A parabolic dish is a point-focus system with paraboloid geometry by the revolution of one-half of a parabola around its normal. The receiver is placed at the focal point of the dish. Fig.3.14(d) shows a schematic of a parabolic dish. As the collected and focused thermal energy from the sun falls on the receiver, it gets heated to a very high temperature reaching approximately 700 - 1200°C. This hot fluid inside the tube is directly used to run the turbine, and the crankshaft drives the electric generator producing electricity. Due to this high temperature and high concentration ratio, this is one of the appropriate systems for photovoltaic application. However, this system is very bulky and cost-intensive. On average, optical efficiency lies between 0.90 to 0.93, and the concentration ratio is typically maintained between 2000-5000 with a lifetime of 30 years.

3.5.2.3 Fresnel Reflector

Fresnel reflectors are similar to parabolic troughs in that solar radiation heats a receiver pipe, which contains the heat transfer fluid. This reflector system simplifies the parabolic trough design. Instead of using a single parabolic reflector, it mimics the parabolic shape with a set of flat mirrors mounted at ground levels. A schematic of this type of plant is shown in Fig.3.16.

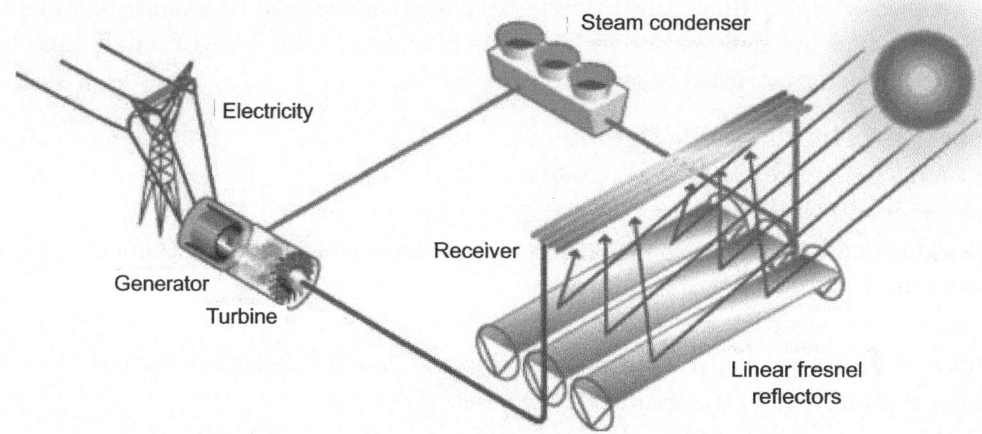

Fig. 3.16: A schematic of the Fresnel reflector power plant (Source: US Department of Energy)

Light concentration is used using lenses. Fresnel's lenses are used for concentrating the rays. Fresnel lenses are made of several prisms in a linear formation or a concentric circle formation. A typical Fresnel lenses use 10 – 20 individual, long reflecting segments instead of a single reflector. This system is made of rotating about its long axis and oriented north-south so that they can track the movement of the sun from east to west. As compared to parabolic trough, Fresnel lenses are light in weight as they are made of polymer materials, thin, flat mirrors, and are easy to handle and which reduces the cost because of its ground-level mounting; the system reduces the wind resistance. Another advantage of Fresnel's lenses is that they have a large aperture area and short focal length, which makes these lenses suitable for high-concentration applications. Both lenses and mirrors are used for concentrator photovoltaics. These lenses are suitable for smaller concentrator assemblies, whereas the mirrors are suited for line assemblies.

3.5.3 Power Tower

The power tower system is comparatively a newer technology compared to other solar energy collection methods and is most suitable for large-scale power plants. The power tower system employs large flat mirrors, called heliostats, which track the sun throughout the day and focus its concentrated rays onto a receiver located at the top of a centrally located and elevated tower or sometimes termed a central receiving system. Within the receiver, the concentrated solar rays heat the fluid, and that flows to the thermal storage tank, where it is stored and maintained at 98% of thermal efficiency. This fluid is used to rotate the turbine shaft and the steam generator for electricity. A typical power tower is shown in Fig.3.17.

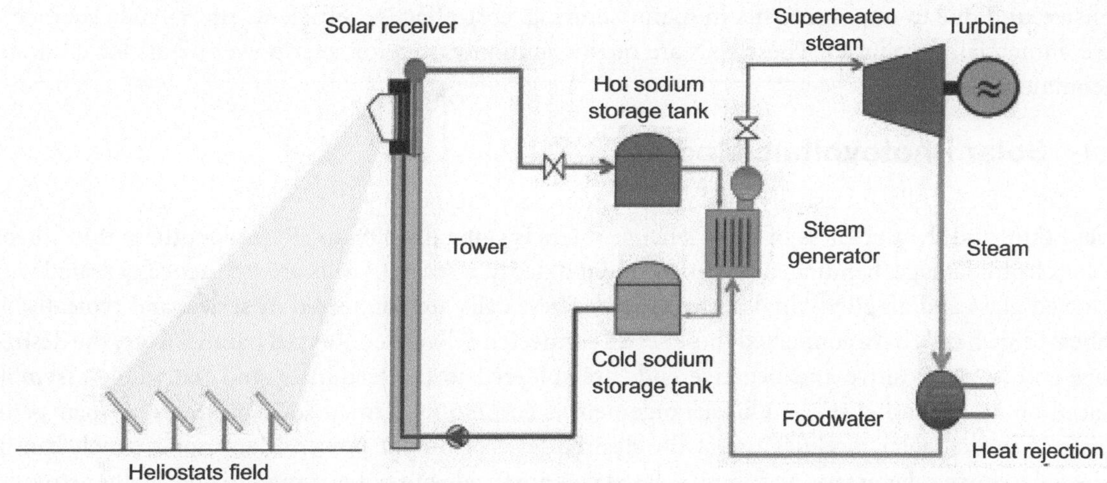

Fig. 3.17: A schematic of the power tower (Courtesy: US Department of Energy)

The main advantage of this type of power plant is that a very high temperature can be achieved as thousands of mirrors onto a receiver. Thermal energy at higher temperatures can easily be converted to electricity. The power tower is unique among solar technologies because it can store energy efficiently and cost-effectively. They can operate whenever the consumer needs power, even when the sun is not present at night time and during cloudy weather. The working principle of the solar tower is similar to the design of a steam power plant, and the only difference is that the steam is replaced by molten salt. The process is as follows: sunrays heat the salt in the receiver, the molten salt is stored in the hot storage, the hot salt is pumped through the steam generator, and the steam drives the turbine, and this turbine produces electricity using the generator. After this process, the salt is pumped to cold storage, and the system is in a closed loop. This process of producing green electricity is commercially available in the USA with a capacity of up to 900 MW (multiple series of plants) in Southern California and many more in Spain, Israel, South Africa, and Morocco.

3.6 SOLAR PHOTOVOLTAIC POWER PLANT

The concept of solar cells and their electricity generation technology are briefly discussed in previous sections. Solar cells are made of semiconductor devices like silicon or other semiconductor materials. Different types of solar cells are also discussed in section 3.4. When the solar rays fall on the surface of the semiconductor, electricity is produced, and this generated electricity depends on the intensity of solar radiation, incident angle, size and type of solar cells, and ambient temperature. A small solar cell can produce only a small fraction of electricity, and a combination of series and parallel connections of similar solar cells can generate a considerable amount of electricity at desired voltage with the required power output. This system of having a combination of many solar cells for producing electricity is broadly termed solar photovoltaic (SPV) or photovoltaic (PV) modules. These SPV are capable of producing a considerable amount of electricity for domestic, commercial, and industrial use. The first commercial photovoltaic cells were manufactured in the late 1950s, and after that, till the 1970s, there was primarily used as a power source for satellites, and after 1980, these cells were extensively used for consumer electronic products as the primary power source. During its initial days, solar cells were very expensive, and due to improvements in manufacturing, cost-effective, efficient, and reliable solar cells were commercially produced. These cells are most commonly used for solar power plants for domestic and commercial use.

3.6.1 Solar Photovoltaic Module

Solar photovoltaic cells are usually made out of monocrystalline or polycrystalline silicon. These cells are very thin, and the thickness of these silicon wafers is generally 300μm. To protect these thin silicon film cells from damage, bending, and environmental decay, a series of cells are hermetically sealed with toughened glass and an ethyl-vinyl acetate sheet. These cells are connected in series, and typically, 36 numbers of such cells have connected these series connected cells are connected parallel to get the desired voltage and levels. Positive and negative ends are soldered to the terminals, and the whole assembly is placed on an insulating sheet. This arrangement is commonly termed solar modules. A solar panel consists of several solar modules to get the desired level of output power. Many solar panels can be connected to form solar arrays, and these solar arrays are fixed with outer frames to give further strength and enable easy mounting on structures. A schematic diagram of solar cells, solar modules, solar panels, and solar arrays is shown in Fig. 3.18.

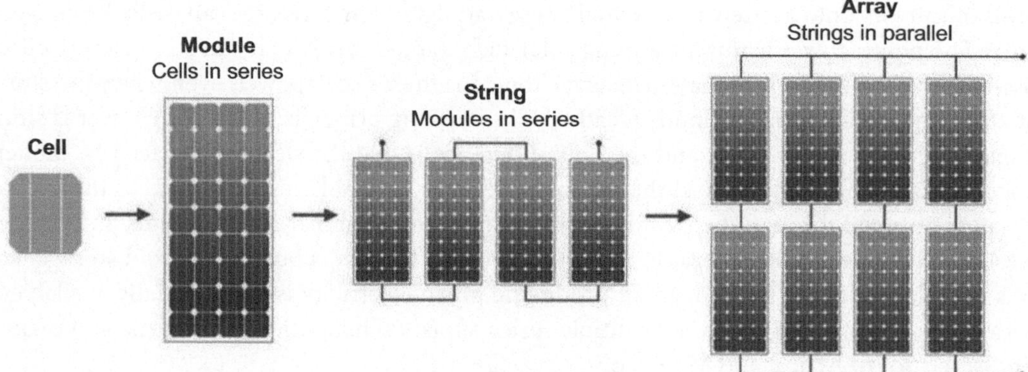

Fig. 3.18: Basic building blocks for PV systems include cells, modules, panels, and arrays.

3.6.2 Solar PV Generation

The generation of electricity using a solar PV system is not the same as conventional electromagnetic generators. In fact, solar PV power generation system is much simpler than conventional generators. The solar panels or solar arrays are placed to face the sun's rays, and the solar cells produce electricity. The phenomenon of producing electricity is already discussed earlier.

Solar panels are mounted in either fixed, freestanding positions or with directional movements for tracking. When these solar panels are mounted to generate electricity, they must be mounted at the best angle to receive the maximum sun rays. A directional solar tracking system is attached to achieve the maximum output to these plates. There are two types of tracking systems. One is preset with time, height, and angle, and the other one is automatic as per the position of the sun from east to west with automatic sensor-based control gears. The daily energy output of solar panels can be increased from 25% to 40% using solar tracking. However, directional tracking arrays are not suitable due to excessively high cost and complex mounting systems.

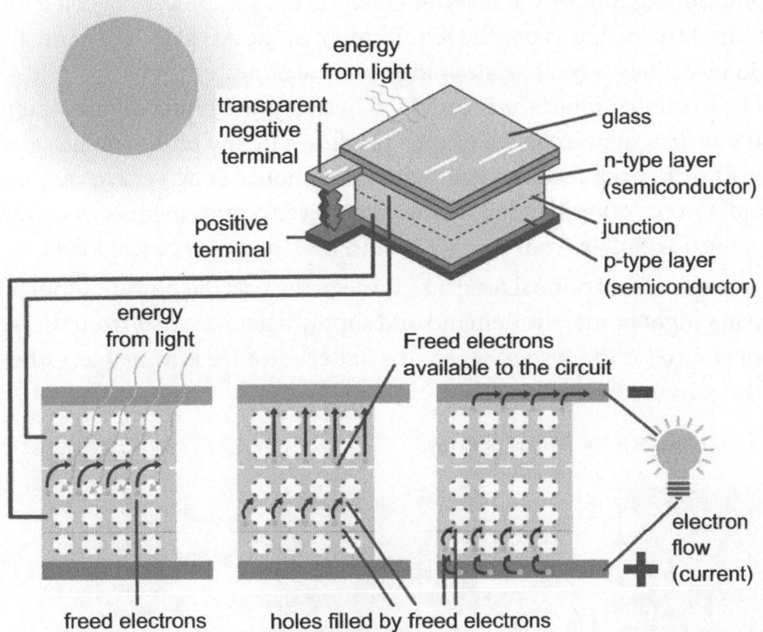

Fig. 3.19: Inside a Solar PV (SPV) cell (Courtesy: U.S Energy information administration)

Several different components are required for an SPV system. These basic components are the configuration of the solar PV system, including solar panels, DC to AC inverter, optimizer, battery bank, battery controller, and sometimes auxiliary energy sources and electrical loads. In addition to these, an arrangement for different connectors, wires, surge protection devices, equipment for measuring power, disconnect devices, and power processing circuits are also part of solar power generation. The inner view of solar PV can be seen as shown in Fig.3.19.

3.6.3 Types of Solar PV Systems

Photovoltaic systems are classified according to their functional and operational requirements and configurations. Based on the above, there are mainly two types of solar PV systems - grid-connected solar PV systems and stand-alone solar PV systems. Photovoltaic systems are also classified by how the equipment is connected to other power systems and electrical loads. Photovoltaic systems can be designed to feed DC loads to electrical utility or AC loads using DC – AC inverter and can also be operated with or independent utility grid or connected with other energy sources with energy storage devices like batteries.

3.6.3.1 Grid-Connected Photovoltaic System

Grid-connected photovoltaic systems are increasingly attracting the attention of the industry and power-generating companies as they can directly be connected to the electric utility grid. This is the common alternative to fossil-fuel power generation and is extensively used. The primary component of a grid-connected photovoltaic system is the solar panels, connectors, inverter, power conditioning unit, charge controller, measuring instruments like meters, AC grid or bus, and battery storage (optional for some systems). A typical grid-connected photovoltaic system is shown in Fig.3.20.

The power conditioning unit or the inverter converts the DC power collected by the solar panels to AC power at the desired frequency as per the requirement of the AC grid. This unit also controls the flow of power to the grid in various ways, like stopping the flow of power to the AC grid when the AC grid is not energized. A bi-directional interface is provided between the photovoltaic system and the AC grid. This bi-directional interface allows the AC power produced by the photovoltaic system to either supply on-site electrical load or to back feed the grid when the photovoltaic system output is greater than the on-site load demand. On the other hand, if the on-site power requirement is more than the photovoltaic power output, the power will flow from the AC grid to the on-site electrical loads.

A battery storage system is optional for grid-connected PV as the power output is directly connected to the AC grid. During night hours, the demand and supply balance is met from the storage system as the photovoltaic output is zero for the system where the battery storage is available. Otherwise, the balanced demand will be met from the AC grid.

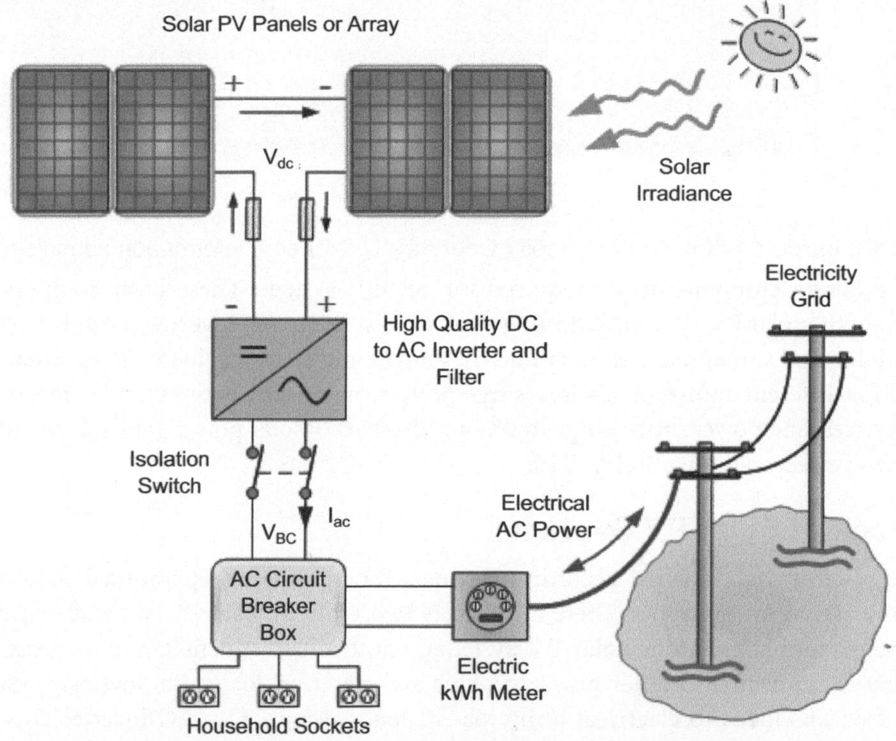

Fig. 3.20: Diagram of a grid-connected photovoltaic system

3.6.3.2 Stand-Alone Photovoltaic System

A stand-alone solar photovoltaic system is designed to operate independently without a grid connection. These are mostly used in rural electrification at isolated places or at remote locations where the common grid is not reachable or available. This type of system consists of all the components needed for the grid-connected system except the bi-directional controller and the utility AC grid. If the electrical loads are AC in nature, then an inverter is required to invert the DC power collected by the solar panels to the desired frequency. The simplest form of a stand-alone photovoltaic system is the direct coupled system, where the DC output of the PV module is directly connected to the DC load. A direct coupled system (See Fig.3.21) does not have battery storage, and the load can only be operated during day time. A sun-tracking system may be employed with this system to obtain maximum power from the PV panels. In many domestic, agricultural, and industrial utilities, this direct-coupled system is used where their loads are operated during sunlight hours.

In many stand-alone PV systems, batteries are used for energy storage. Fig.3.22 shows a diagram of a typical stand-alone photovoltaic system powering DC and AC loads.

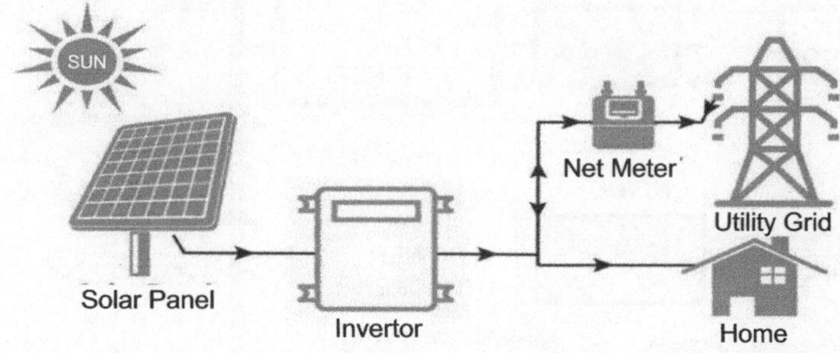

Fig. 3.21: Direct-coupled photovoltaic system

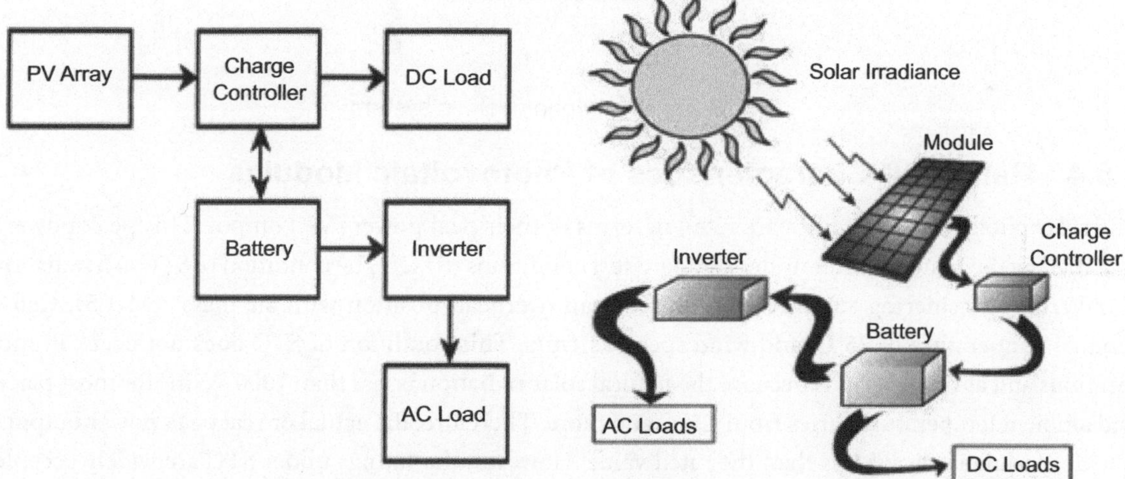

Fig. 3.22: Stand-alone photovoltaic system with battery storage

3.6.3.3 Hybrid Photovoltaic System

The hybrid photovoltaic system most commonly uses the power source from photovoltaic systems combined with wind and another source of energy. A hybrid photovoltaic system is either grid-connected or stand-alone and with battery storage or without battery storage. The pros and cons of having a storage battery are already summarised earlier. The basic advantage of a hybrid PV system is that the generated electricity is not solely dependent on solar power, and during the winter season or rainy days, the required demand may be met from other sources and may be from the utility grid. A typical schematic of a hybrid photovoltaic system is shown in Fig.3.23. A hybrid PV system can cater to both types of DC and AC loads provided the system contains an inverter and other power conditioning components. The reliability of the system can be increased by incorporating weather-independent sources like diesel generators or fuel cells.

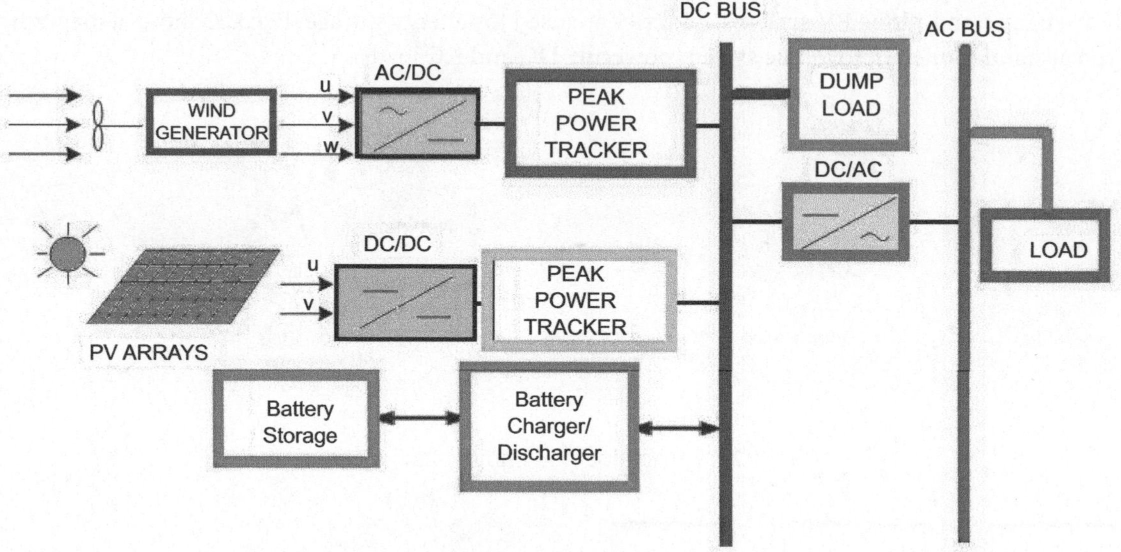

Fig. 3.23: Hybrid photovoltaic system

3.6.4 Ratings & Characteristics of Photovoltaic Modules

The solar photovoltaic modules are rated in terms of their peal power (W_p) output. This peak power is specified by the manufacturer under standard test conditions (STC). The condition of STC is Irradiation-1000W/m^2 (considering sun at about 48° from an overhead position with air mass AM 1.5), Cell or module temperature of 25°C, and wind speed as 1m/s. This condition of STC does not occur in most locations and at times. This is because the natural solar radiation is less than 1000 W/m^2 for most places, and ambient temperature varies from 25°C and more. Therefore, the actual or real peak power output of a solar module is always less than the rated value. However, the ratings under STC are widely accepted by the manufacturer and by the user.

3.6.4.1 I-V characteristic of PV Module

The I-V characteristic of a photovoltaic module is shown in Fig.3.24. For different irradiation levels, different graphs are plotted for a 75 Wp module at different loads. The maximum power point is shown as dots. The power output of solar PV modules strongly depends on solar irradiation. The power of a module decreases almost linearly with the decrease in the intensity of solar radiation. Again solar irradiation is not constant over the day, and the power output varies at different times of the day.

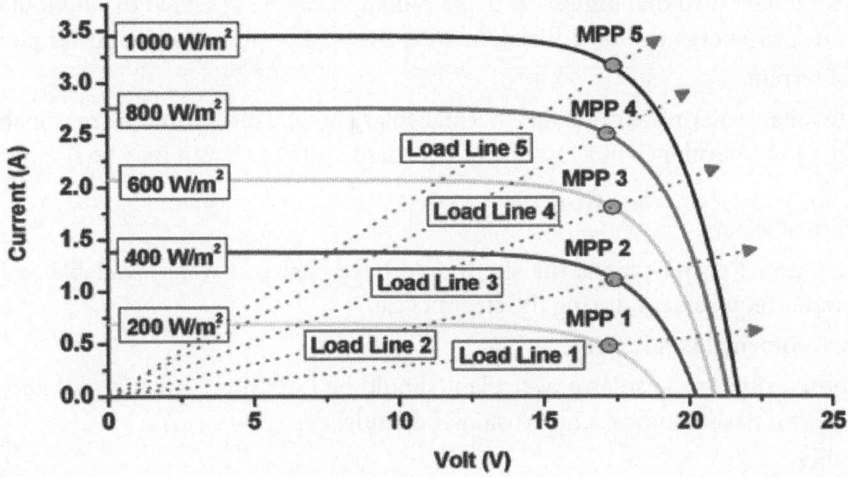

Fig. 3.24: I-V characteristic of a 75 W_p PV module (Maximum Power Point (MPP))

3.6.4.2 P-V Characteristic of PV Module

The P-V characteristic of a photovoltaic module is a nonlinear curve (logarithmic) curve plotted between the power output of a PV module with the voltage in Fig.3.25. The maximum power point is shown in each curve shows the maximum power points. However, drop-in module voltage is not significant for a large change in radiation intensity as the voltage is a logarithmic function of the radiation intensity.

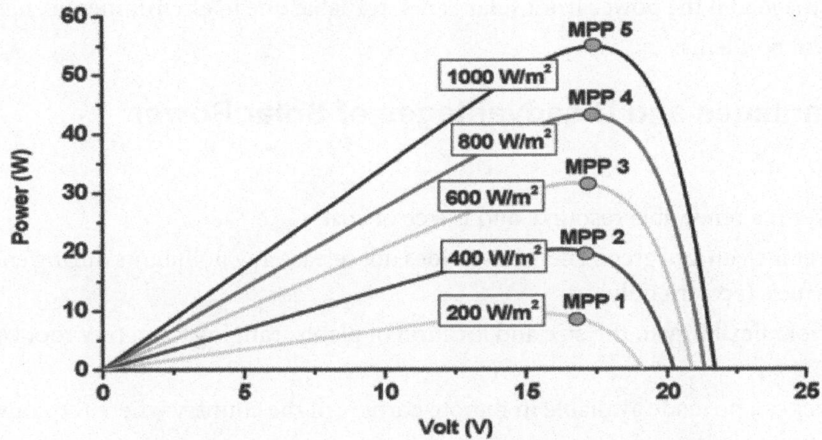

Fig. 3.25: P-V characteristic of a photovoltaic module

3.6.5 Selection of Site for Solar Power Plant

There are various factors affecting the site selection of a solar power plant. The major concern is the solar irradiation in that area, and all other elements are similar to conventional power plants. Solar energy is also not location specific, as the sun is available in almost all places on Earth. The factors are listed below:

(a) Availability of solar radiation

(b) The site should be such that high solar beam radiation can be obtained throughout the year so that maximum solar energy can be utilized for solar thermal or photovoltaic power plants.
(c) Nature of terrain
(d) For photovoltaic solar plants or solar thermal solar plants, land should be reasonably flat so that a large area can be developed at a lesser cost. The nature of the terrain may be sloppy and even rocky or sandy.
(e) Availability of water
(f) For solar thermal power plants, the site should have plenty of water available easily to fulfill the cooling water requirement during the steam cycle.
(g) Local environmental condition
(h) The proposed site for the solar power plant should be free from excessive fall and dust, from the flood zone and flash flooding, and erosion and landslide.
(i) Accessibility
(j) The site should be accessible by rail and road for transporting heavy machinery and equipment for power plants.
(k) Near to load center
(l) The site should be located as close as possible to the load so that the power generated by these plants can be delivered to load centres avoiding the cost of transmission and transmission loss.
(m) Availability of backup power
(n) The site should be located such that a backup power source is readily available, which assures power to the load if the power from solar is not available due to environmental, natural calamities, or technical problems.

3.6.6 Advantages and Disadvantages of Solar Power

Advantages

(a) Solar power is a renewable resource and is free of cost.
(b) Solar power is clean and green energy as it does not release any pollutants during energy generation like fossil fuels (eco-friendly).
(c) There is more flexibility in the size and location of plants, ranging from tiny rooftop plants to large power plants.
(d) Solar power can be made available in remote corners of the country where the conventional power grid is not accessible.
(e) Machinery and equipment used for solar power result in low maintenance and repair (easy fabrication). Only supporting items like inverters and batteries need more maintenance.
(f) Solar power can be used very efficiently for heating and thermal operations.
(g) Solar photovoltaic modules are durable in nature and have been designed for more than 20 years (longer operating life).
(h) Suitable for mobile loads such as cars, buses, and satellites.
(i) Modularity in operation.

Disadvantages

(a) Solar radiation is not always completely predictable because of changes in weather and other climatic conditions; hence reliability is relatively low.

(b) During the night-time, solar radiation is not available, and hence power availability during that time needs proper planning or storage.

(c) Solar power plants are expensive, and capital investment is very high compared to conventional power plants for similar output. Solar power plants are not currently cost-competitive.

(d) The efficiency of the solar power plant is low and around 10%, and energy payback time are considerable compared to other conventional power plants.

(e) Solar power plants require large areas, and the especially large and medium solar photovoltaic system requires more area.

3.7 BIOMASS-BASED POWER PLANTS

Biomass is organic matter obtained from plants (terrestrial and aquatic), animals, and microorganisms grown on land and water and their derivatives. Biomass accounts for 15% of world energy use. In most developing and underdeveloped countries, biomass is used as the primary source of energy for cooking and heating. The form of energy obtained from biomass is terms as biomass energy. Biomass is renewable in nature because organic materials are generated regularly and are a constant process of nature. It is also noted here that coal, oil, and natural gas are not considered biomass because nature takes more than several million years to reproduce it again at a certain temperature and pressure, and these items are termed as non-renewable.

Biomass is considered to be greenhouse gas neutral. This is because while the combustion of biomass will generate carbon dioxide just as would the combustion of fossil fuel when that biomass is regrown, it will reabsorb the same amount of carbon dioxide as it released during combustion. Thus, the growing, burning, and re-growing of biomass simply cycle carbon dioxide between the atmosphere and biosphere.

Biomass is mainly produced from solar energy as it is used to grow green plants by photosynthesis. Solar energy is, in turn, stored in the form of chemical energy. Biomass energy is primarily classified into three groups, (i) Biomass from forests, cultivated crops, etc., (ii) Biomass from waste like municipal waste, kitchen waste, animal dung, etc., and (iii) Biomass converted into liquid fuels.

The biomass conversion to energy varies from one type of biomass to other. Primarily direct combustion and gasification have been used for the first group of biomass to convert to energy. However, pyrolysis is also developed for energy purposes. For the rest of the groups, different processes are involved in converting them to useful energy. Biomass can be converted into biogas or biofuel using two basic processes (i) Anaerobic digestion and (ii) Fermentation.

Energy from biomass is green energy, and conversion of biomass to electricity is the best option for the environment and ecology. Most countries of the world are investing and announcing lucrative schemes and various incentives to producers for the production of electricity from biomass and waste. Challenges of converting biomass to electricity are met with new technological developments and new initiatives. This form of energy is of low running cost and has no adverse environmental impact and is hence promoted globally.

Wood, straw, and other forest products are under dry biomass. Fast-growing trees and waste for agricultural products like straws of all types of grains, sugarcane, and similar products are cultivated.

Similarly, starch and oil reach plants, cereals, herbaceous crops, and aquatic crops grown in freshwater or seawater are also cultivated. Algae is also cultivated for extracting energy at a large scale and can be converted to methane. The process of extracting energy for different cultivated crops is different.

Organic wastes can be converted to energy. The waste can be classified as municipal or urban waste, household waste, industrial waste, forest waste, fishery and poultry waste, animal waste, and animal and human excreta. These wastes may be converted into heat, biogas, and biochemical by various processes. These processes will be discussed in later sections briefly.

3.7.1 Site Selection for Biomass Power Plant

While selecting a site for a biomass power plant, the following must be considered.

(a) **Location**: The site of the biomass plant should be located far away from the residential areas. Bad smells and noise are unavoidable for a biomass plant. The plant should not be situated near a freshwater well, as the fermented slurry may pollute the water on the other well.

(b) **Open and sunny space:** The gas generating station should be located in an open and sunny space where direct sunlight will fall on the plant at a temperature between 15°C to 30°C, the rate of generation of gas is, and the plant will be more efficient.

(c) **Size of plant**: Generally, 10 to 20 m^2 area is required per m^3 of gas according to the standard guidelines. The site should be such that sufficient space is kept for fermenter, gas storage, and collection of digestate.

(d) **Distance from the consumer**: To achieve maximum efficiency in gas pumping and minimize gas leakage, the distance between the biogas plant and biogas consumption centers should be minimum. As per guidelines, for a plant of $2m^3$ plant, the distance should not be greater than 10 meters.

(e) **Minimum gradient**: For the pipeline, a minimum gradient of 1% must be available for conveying gas.

(f) **Availability of water**: Plenty of water should be available as the biomass plant uses lots of water to make a slurry for digestion.

(g) **Availability of input material**: The material used in the biomass power plant should be readily available near the site so that the transportation cost may be reduced.

(h) **Accessibility**: The plant should be accessible by rail or road for the transportation of machinery and raw material for input.

3.7.2 Bio-Chemical-Based Power Plants

Biomass biochemical conversion technologies refer to the conversion of a certain type of biomass into biofuels or other useful products through a controlled environment and chemical, physical and biological treatments. This conversion of biomass to corresponding products using micro-organisms. There are broadly three types of biochemical processes. They are

(a) Fermentation.

(b) Anaerobic digestion.

(c) Composting.

These processes occur at lower temperatures and lower reaction rates compared to thermochemical processes.

(a) **Fermentation:** Fermentation is a process of decomposition of organic matter by micro-organisms. For example, the decomposition of sugar to form ethanol and carbon dioxide by yeast and ethanol forming acetic acid in making vinegar. Biogas and ethanol are commonly used for domestic and industrial use as well as fuel for vehicles and as an energy source for generating electricity. Biogas and ethanol production is achieved using microbial destruction and reconstruction (also termed fermentation) of the hydrocarbons containing biomass in the absence of air. This process of an absence of air is termed the anaerobic condition. For mesophile bacteria, the duration for fermentation is 20 to 30 days at a temperature range of 30°C to 40°C, and for thermophile bacteria, it is 3 to 6 days at 40°C to 60°C in the presence of CO_2 as a source of carbon with other material. Biogas can be produced by fermenting organic materials in the absence of air using mesophilic or thermophilic bacteria to break them down into alcohols or fatty acids and then into methane.

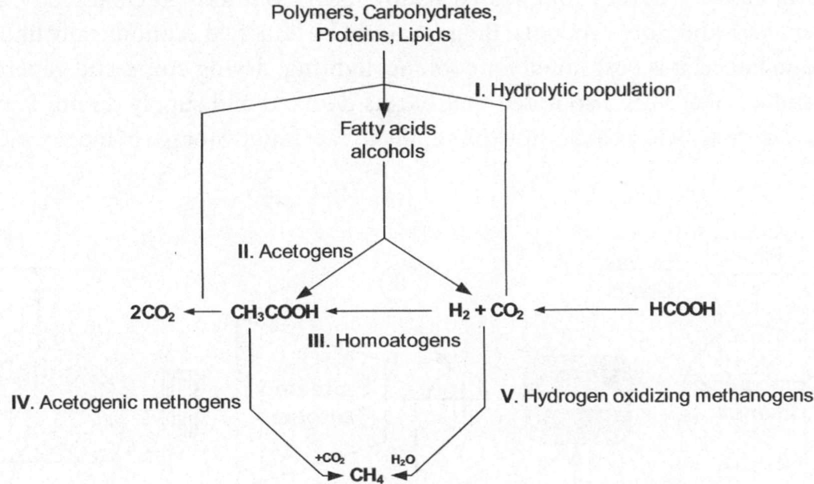

Fig. 3.26: Schematic of forming useful biogas from biomass

(b) **Anaerobic digestion:** Anaerobic digestion is a sequence of processes through which bacteria break down organic matter in the absence of air, like animal manure, wastewater biosolids, food wastes, and other biodegradable wastes. The anaerobic digestion process is used to treat biodegradable wastes (such as organic polymers like carbohydrates) broken into fatty acids, amino acids, methane, and carbon dioxide. This process is divided into two phases – acidogenic and methanogens. Acidogenic (acid-forming) bacteria convert sugars and amino acids into carbon dioxide, ammonia, and organic acids, and this is termed as acetogenesis process. Finally, methanogens (bacteria producing methane as a metabolic byproduct) convert these products to methane and carbon dioxide. A schematic of producing methane from biomass is depicted in Fig.3.26. Biogas mainly consists of 50% - 70% methane and 35% - 40% carbon dioxide with some impurities like ammonia, hydrogen sulfide, and water vapor. Anaerobic digestion is widely used as a source of renewable energy.

(c) **Composting:** Compost is an aerobic (with air- or oxygen) method of decomposing organic material or organic solid waste into useful matters like manures. This composting process is mainly used to recycle biodegradable products and also produce a new resource for energy fuel. However, this process is not widely used for renewable energy sources.

3.7.2.1 Components of Bio-chemical-Based Power Plant

A schematic of a bio-chemical-based (biogas) based power plant is shown in Fig.3.27. The organic input may be one or more and their combinations from animal waste, cow dung, food waste, and other organic waste and which are fed to the mixing chamber. From this mixing chamber, it goes to the pressurization unit and then to the fermenter unit. In the fermenter, digestion is done using micro-organisms as discussed earlier, at a controlled pressure and set temperature as per the micro-organism used. After certain time biogas is generated, this gas is fed to the boiler, and the boiler is attached to the prime mover- turbine. The turbine drives the generator to produce electric energy output. If required, some gas may be taken out from the fermenter, or heat may be taken from the boiler for other drying and boiling processes. This plant can also be used as a multi-purpose plant to produce heat from biomass electricity from the generator, natural/ CNG (Compressed natural gas) from fermenters directly, and byproducts as high-quality fertilizer and fiber products. Biogas cannot be liquefied economically like LPG (liquefied petroleum gas), and hence, it is best suited for cooking, lighting, drying crops, and generating electricity using a turbine and a boiler. It is also noted that biogas demand and supply do not always match as it depends on many external factors, including the supply of raw input. Storage of biogas within a gasholder is required.

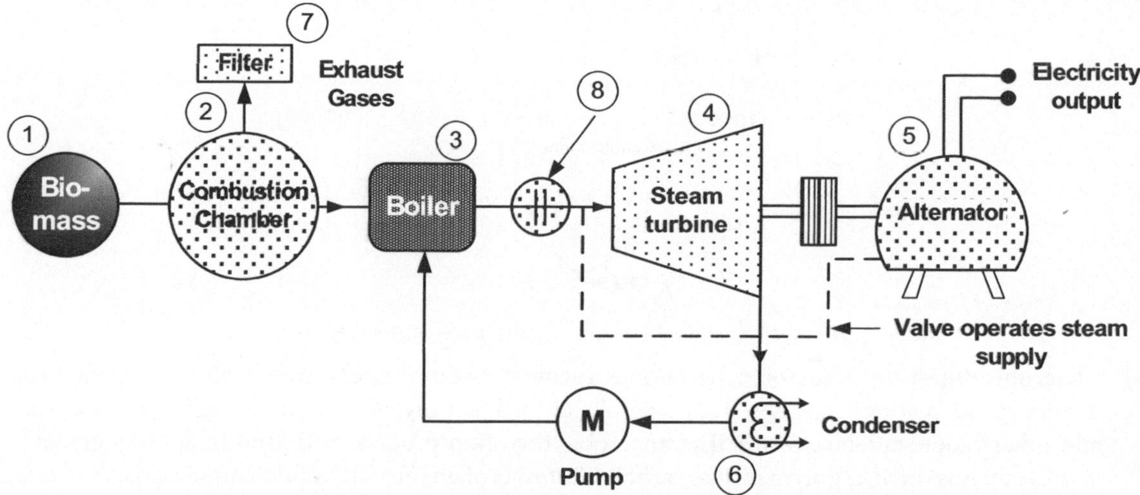

Fig. 3.27: Block diagram of bio-chemical-based (biogas) power plant

3.7.2.2 Advantages and Disadvantages of Bio-Chemical-Based Power Plant

Advantages

(a) Employment creation in villages/small towns and rural areas

(b) Byproducts are useful and can be used as multi-purpose plants.

(c) Low cost- capital cost moderate, cost of micro-organism is minimum and can be reused, and cost of collection of waste is sustainable.

(d) Organic residues, waste material, cow dung, and other bio-degradable can be used, which is available in many areas at no cost or less cost.

(e) It comes from renewable energy sources.

(f) It supplies electric power, heat, and gas, which are the needs of modern society.
(g) Biogas manure is good fertilizer.
(h) Land requirement is minimum.

Disadvantages

(a) The major disadvantages of biochemical-based power plants are
(b) It is expensive.
(c) It requires a lot of space.
(d) It still releases greenhouse gases.
(e) It can have a negative impact on the surrounding environment, and
(f) It is inefficient in terms of how much energy it takes to create electricity.
(g) In addition to these, large-scale biochemical-based power plants may adversely affect the life cycle system, but adequate study is required to overcome and address these issues.

3.7.3 Thermo-Chemical-Based Power Plants

Bio-degradable biomass can be converted to useful energy products by two processes: using micro-organisms and thermo-chemical conversion. The process of anaerobic digestion using micro-organisms is already discussed in the previous section. Thermal conversion is the use of heat, with or without the presence of oxygen or air, to convert biomass into other forms of energy and useful chemical products. In thermo - chemical process, the plant matter is heated but not burned; it breaks down into various gases, liquids, and solids. These products can further be processed to be refined into various useful fuels and other products, including methane and alcohol. Biomass gasifiers capture methane released from the process and can be used for gas turbines to produce electricity. It is also mentioned here that the energy efficiency of biomass plants may be anywhere between 7 and 27%. However, if biomass is mixed with any fossil fuel, especially coal, efficiency goes up to 30-40%. Burning biomass along with conventional fossil fuel, especially coal, is called Co-firing. These thermo-chemical processes include direct combustion, pyrolysis, and torrefaction, and the plant is shown in Fig.3.28.

Combustion

Combustion is the burning of biomass in the presence of oxygen. This involves high-temperature exothermic oxidation and produces hot flue gas. The first stage of combustion is drying to remove the moisture content, then it is heated to break the chemical bonding within the biomass, and after that, combustion takes place. The waste heat is used for hot water, heat, or with a waste heat boiler to operate a steam turbine to produce electricity. Biomass also can be co-fired with existing fossil fuel power stations.

Pyrolysis

Pyrolysis converts biomass feedstocks under controlled temperatures and absent oxygen into gas, oil, and biochar (used as a valuable soil conditioner or manure and also to make graphene). The gases and oil can be used to power a generator, and some technologies can also make diesel and chemicals from the gases. Generally, there are three types of pyrolysis - slow pyrolysis (350-800°C, slow process-hours to days), fast pyrolysis (400-600°C, very fast at vacuum or atmospheric pressure), and flash pyrolysis (300-800°C, fast at moderate pressure).

Torrefaction

Torrefaction is similar to pyrolysis but in a lower operating temperature range (200-300°C) and slow process. In the first stage, torrefaction removes the moisture content and some other volatile from the biomass and makes the biomass easier to grind, transport, and store. This helps to transform biomass into a more easily manageable feedstock that is available around the year as fuel to the power plant. The final product is an energy-dense solid fuel often referred to as "bio-coal." Thermochemical conversion is commonly referred to as gasification. This technology uses high temperatures in controlled partial combustion to form a producer gas and charcoal followed by chemical reduction. A major use for biomass is for agriculture residues with gas turbines. Advanced uses include the production of diesel, jet fuel, and useful chemicals.

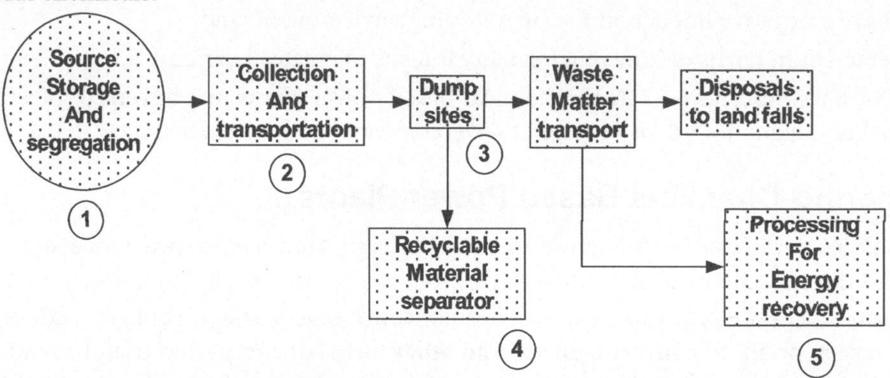

Fig. 3.28: A schematic diagram of a thermo-chemical-based power plant

3.7.3.1 Components of Thermo-Chemical-based Power Plant

A schematic diagram of a thermo-chemical-based power plant is shown in Fig.3.29. As discussed above, a thermo-chemical reaction converts organic biomass into useful byproducts. These byproducts are gaseous or liquid fuels or residue as solid. These products are collected at different temperatures and pressures from the gasifiers. Gasses mostly contain carbon monoxide, methane, nitrogen, hydrogen, and carbon dioxide; liquids so produced are oil, acetic acid, methanol, and tar; the solid is charcoal. The biomass and waste products are collected from the plant and stored at a designated place. Hazardous and recyclable materials are separated. The materials are ready for combustion and gasification for energy conversion. In some cases, municipal wastes are directly fed to the unit, and the combustion process starts. The next steps are common like other electricity generation processes – steam turbine to generate electrical energy. The heat generated can be used for other purposes.

The direct firing (combustion) of biomass involves the burning of fuel with excess in the air (or oxygen) inside a furnace and which delivers heat directly. A schematic of a direct combustion power plant is shown in Fig.3.27. The heat is absorbed by the boiler, and the boiler produces the steam to run the turbine. The turbine shaft is connected to the generator to produce electricity. The components like the turbine, generator, condenser, and cooling towers are already discussed in the previous chapter.

Gasifier:

There are two types of gasifiers- a fixed bed and a fluidized bed gasifier. A fixed bed-type gasifier is the simplest one with a cylindrical vessel with a gate at the bottom. Biomass is introduced at the top and air from the bottom, and the heat in the form of flue gas is collected from the side. Ash is removed from the bottom. A schematic of the fixed bed gasifier is shown in Fig.3.30.

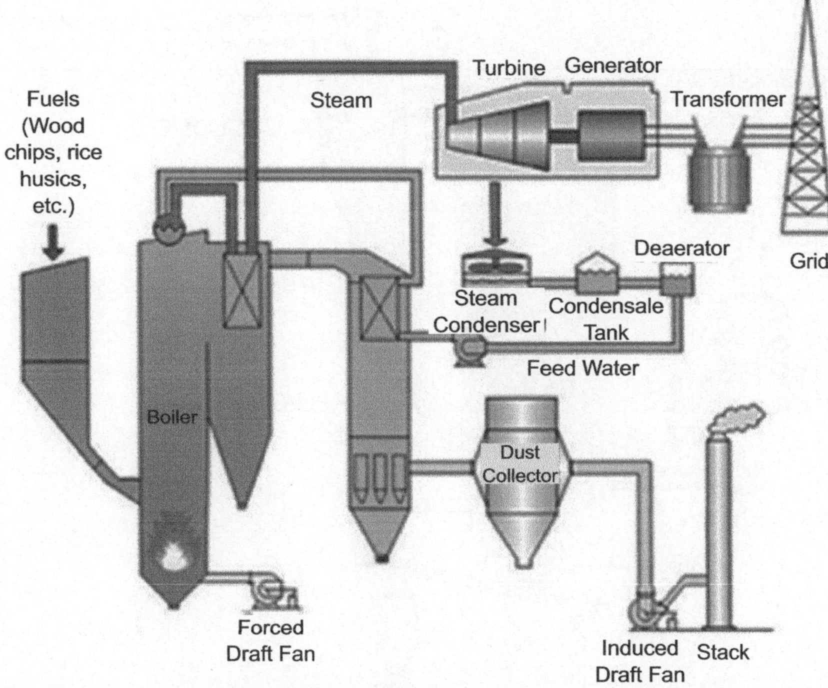

Fig. 3.29: Schematic of a direct-fired power plant

(Courtesy: Power generation technologies, Paul Breeze, Newnes, 2014)

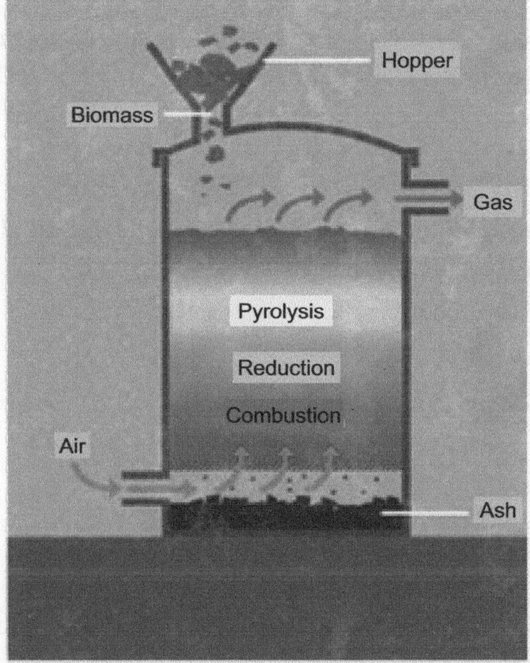

Fig. 3.30: Cross section of a fixed bed gasifier

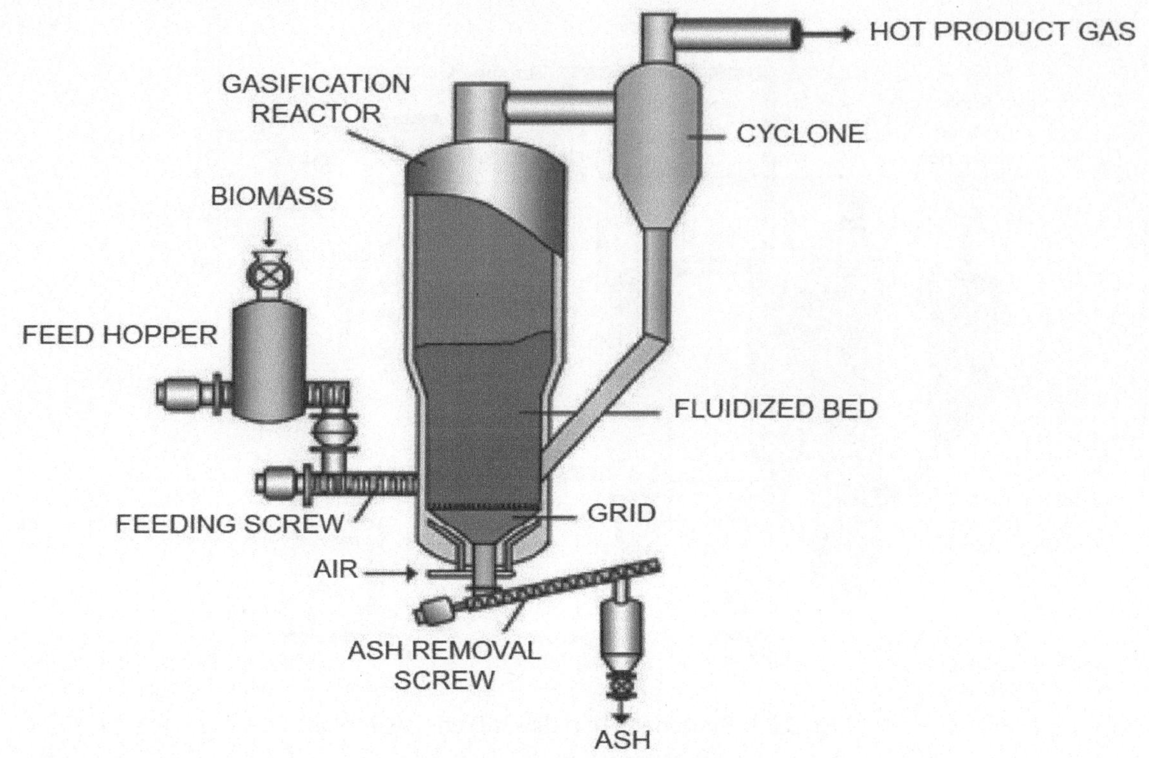

Fig. 3.31: A schematic of a fluidized-bed biomass gasifier

Alternatively, a fluidized bed gasifier is operated with a reduced air supply so that the combustion does not complete. The gas from the fluidized bed gasifier can be used directly in a gas turbine or a reciprocating engine. A schematic is shown in Fig.3.31.

3.7.3.2 Advantages and Disadvantages of Thermo-Chemical-Based Power Plant

Various advantages which are common for biofuel and biogas plants are already discussed. In addition to those, the following are the specific advantages:

(a) Residue can be used in landfill.

(b) Reduces waste volume by 90%.

(c) The heat produced can be used for various purposes.

(d) Stand-alone electricity generation.

(e) Community service for sustainable development.

(f) Eco-friendly co-generation of electricity.

(g) Employment creation in the area.

In a thermo-chemical plant, all the processes are used, including combustion, gasification, pyrolysis, and torrefaction, and these processes have their individual disadvantages.

For the process of combustion, the main disadvantages are

(a) Air pollution and greenhouse gas emissions.

(b) Low energy efficiency.

(c) Flue gas cleaning.

For the gasification process, the major drawbacks are

(a) complex technology,

(b) high investment and operating costs and

(c) extensive gas cleaning of the syngas.

Similarly, for pyrolysis and torrefaction processes, the major disadvantages are

(a) High investment cost.

(b) Extensive gas cleaning of the syngas.

(c) Feedstock sensitivity.

3.7.4 Bio diesel

In general, agrochemical commonly includes chemical products comprised of all types of fertilizers, pesticides - all kinds of plant protection chemicals, plant-growth hormones, and soil conditioners. In the context of agrochemical power plants, biofuel or biodiesel are focal to be discussed in this section.

Biofuel

Biofuel is an alternative to fossil fuel that can be produced over a short period compared to the formation of fossil fuels. Biofuel can be produced from plants or agriculture, domestic or industrial waste. The two common types of biofuel are bioethanol and biodiesel. The process of producing bioethanol is briefly discussed in the previous section. Bioethanol is an alcohol made by fermentation, mostly from carbohydrates produced in sugar.

Biodiesel

Biodiesel is produced from plant fats or oils and animal fats using transesterification and esterification. Transesterification is a process of exchanging the organic material of the ester group with alcohol in the presence of an acid or base catalyst. This chemical reaction can also be achieved with the help of enzymes like lipases. A block diagram for producing biodiesel is shown in Fig.3.32. Common input for biodiesel is vegetable oil without any impurities, including dirt and water. After cleaning vegetable oils, transesterification is done to react with fatty acid and alcohol to produce biodiesel. The separation of glycerol and biodiesel is very important to form a stable emulsion. This is done by gravitational settling, decantation, filtration, or purification using water or acid, or ether. Fig.3.33 shows a schematic of an agrochemical-based power plant. The only difference with the other type of biomass-based power plant is that the fuel used here is biodiesel. Biodiesel as a fuel alone can be used in a biodiesel power plant, or biodiesel can be blended with other petroleum oils in proper proportion.

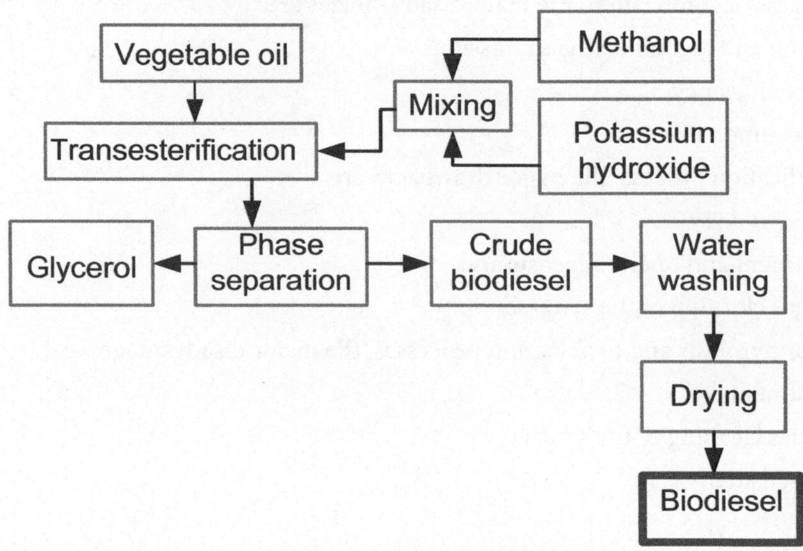

Fig. 3.32: Schematic process flow of biodiesel production.

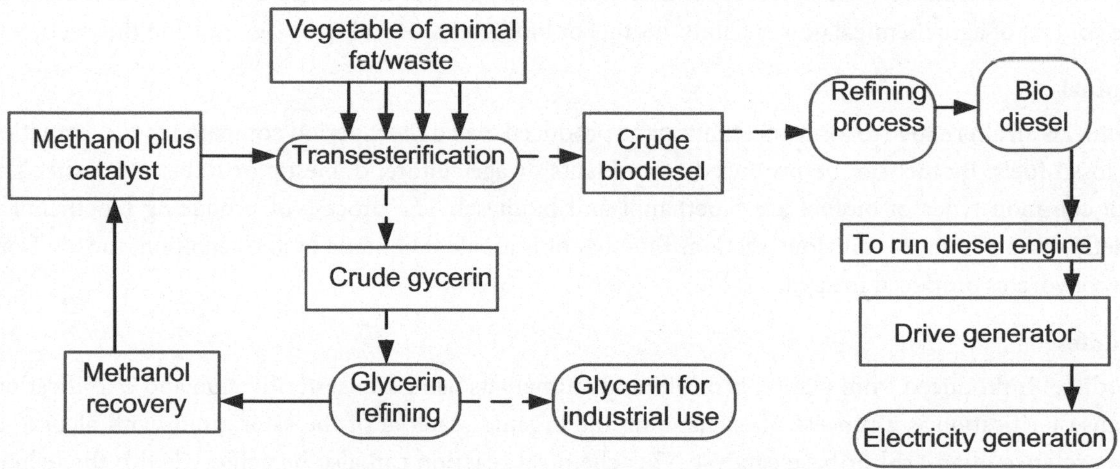

Fig. 3.33: A schematic of an agrochemical-based plant

3.7.4.1 Advantages of Biodiesel

In addition to the advantages of biomass power plants, as mentioned above, the followings are the specific Advantages of Bio-Diesel Plants.

(a) Pollution reduction- reduces greenhouse gases.

(b) Clean, renewable substitute to petroleum diesel.

(c) Sustainable environment.

3.8 FEATURES OF SOLID, LIQUID, AND GAS BIOMASS

The most important property of biomass with regard to combustion and for all other thermo-chemical processes is its moisture content. This moisture content directly influences the energy content of the fuel. Moisture content is the property for mostly solid fuels. Other important characteristics like heat value, moisture level, chemical composition, size, and density of the fuel affect biomass fuel performance. Biomass is an organic material that comes from plants or animals. For solid biomass, the major components are cellulose, hemicellulose, and lignin. The four major types of biomass are Wood and agricultural products, Solid wastes, Landfill gas and biogas, and alcohol fuels. Chemically biofuel consists mainly of fatty acid methyl (or ethyl) esters (FAMEs). Feedstocks for biodiesel include animal fats, vegetable oils, soy, rapeseed, jatropha, mahua, mustard, flax, all types of oil seeds, and algae. The three significant compositional properties are (i) ash content, (ii) susceptibility to slagging and fouling, and (iii) percent volatiles. Ash content is an important parameter for biomass, as low ash content is better. Slagging and fouling are problems that occur when the ash begins to melt inside the combustor and form deposits on the surface of the combustor. The "percent volatiles" in fuel is a less commonly known property that refers to the fraction of the fuel that will readily volatilize (turn to gas) when heated to a high temperature. Fuels with "high volatiles" will tend to vaporize before combusting ("flaming combustion"), whereas fuels with low volatiles will burn primarily as glowing "char." This property affects the performance of the combustion chamber and should be taken into account when designing a combustor. The size and density of the biomass fuel particles are also important. They affect the burning characteristics of the fuel by affecting the rate of heating and drying during the combustion process. Fuel size also dictates the type of handling equipment that is used. The wrong size of fuel will have an impact on the efficiency of the combustion process and may cause jamming or damage to the handling equipment. Smaller-sized fuel is more common for commercial-scale systems because smaller fuel is easier to use in automatic feed systems and also allows for finer control of the burn rate by controlling the rate at which fuel is added to the combustion chamber. Fuel size and density are probably the most overlooked factors affecting fuel performance and should be given careful consideration when selecting a fuel type. The general features of solid, liquid, and gas biomass as fuel are

(a) Fuels for biomass power plants should have a high calorific value.
(b) It should have low moisture content.
(c) Biomass should have a moderate ignition temperature.
(d) Products obtained after the complete combustion of fuel should not be harmful or hazardous to the environment.
(e) It should be easy to transport and low cost.
(f) It should produce a large amount of heat/ energy after conversion.
(g) For liquid fuel, viscosity and temperature dependence are to be taken care of.
(h) Ash composition of the fuels after combustion or other process and its further use and analysis.
(i) The proper size and density of biomass.
(j) Handling and storage capacity of all types of fuels.

Wood and forest residue, residue from agriculture, food crops, municipal waste, plant oils or animal fats, grass used in biomass power plants, and biomass fuels are renewable sources of fuel. It is a carbon-neutral, sustainable energy source that can be used to create electricity or renewable fuel, or other forms of energy. Solid biomass fuels can be used at the nearest possible stations so that the transportation cost and handling costs may be minimized. Storing solid biomass is also important. For liquid and gaseous biomass, transportation, handling, and storage is cost-intensive and need to be economical in all respect.

UNIT SUMMARY

Solar radiation is electromagnetic radiation emitted by the sun, which is not equal in all parts of the globe and depends on the latitude and longitude of the places and seasons. Solar cells are semiconductor devices that directly convert solar radiation to electricity. Actual power delivered from the solar cells depends on the intensity of sunlight and local climatic conditions, and the size of the cells. Solar collectors absorb solar radiation and convert it to useful heat, which is used for heating a fluid. Flat plat collectors consist of transparent covers, absorber plates, tubes containing fluid, and fitted with insulating materials. Concentrated collectors mainly consist of reflectors or mirrors which collect solar radiation at a concentrated focal point to heat the fluid for a useful purpose. Solar thermal power plants are of two types: solar distributed collector power plants and solar central receiver power plants. Crystalline solar cells have more efficiency than thin-film solar cells. Photovoltaic power systems are generally classified according to their functional and operational requirements and component configuration. Grid-connected and stand-alone solar PV systems can be developed as per the requirement. Organic matter derived from the biological organism is called biomass, and the energy derived from biomass is termed biomass energy. Biomass resources may be cultivated or maybe from various wastes. Waste biomass resources are classified as municipal waste, industrial organic waste, rural animal waste, forest waste, agricultural waste, household waste, and human and animal excreta. Cultivated biomass resources are various plants used as wood, sugar cane crops, non-woody plants, algae, and see weeds. The biomass conversion process depends on the temperature, pressure, micro-organism, and culture condition. The biomass conversion processes are direct combustion, thermochemical, and biochemical. In direct combustion, biomass is burnt in the presence of air/ oxygen. In thermochemical conversion, the organic matter is converted into gaseous or liquid fuels under various conditions. Biochemical conversion includes anaerobic digestion and fermentation. In anaerobic digestion using micro-organisms and without external oxygen, biomass is digested into other useful byproducts. In fermentation, the decomposition of biomass is done using bacteria. Biogas can be produced by fermenting organic materials in the absence of air with the help of bacteria to break down biomass into alcohol and fatty acids and, finally, methane, carbon dioxide, and water. Biogas is also known as swap gas, fuel gas, marsh gas, and gobar gas. The primary component of biogas is methane, and methane cannot be liquefied at ambient temperature. Biogas can be stored in a tank for use in a gaseous state. There are different designs of biogas plants depending on the input material and type. Biofuel and biodiesel are sustainable green alternatives for petroleum fuel. Biochemical and thermochemical power plants are alternatives to conventional power plants. Characteristics of biomass as fuel are heat value, moisture content, chemical composition, size, and density.

EXERCISES

Example 3.1

Calculate the angle of incidence of beam radiation on a surface located at New Delhi at 1:30 (solar time) on February 16, 1995, if the surface is tilted 45° from the horizontal and pointed 30° west of south (1°=60′).

Solution:

In the given problem, the value of n is 47.

$\delta = -13.0°$ (from eq. (3.3)); $\omega = +22.5°$ (from Table 3.1)

$\gamma = 30°$; $\beta = 45°$; $\phi = +28°35'$ (from Table 3.3)

The angle of incidence can be calculated by using eq. (3.5)

$$\cos\theta_i = \cos(28°35')\cos 45° + \sin(28°35')\sin 45°\cos 30°)\cos(-13.0°)\cos(22.5°) + \cos(-13.0°)\sin(22.5°)\sin 45°\sin 30° + \sin(-13.0°)(\sin(28°35')\cos 45° - \cos(28°35')\sin 45°\cos 30°) = 0.999$$

$$\theta_i = \cos^{-1}(0.999) = 2.56°$$

Example 3.2

Calculate the number of daylight hours in Delhi on December 22 and June 22, 2015.

Solution:

From Table 3.3, $\phi = 28°35'$N. For December 22, 2015, $n = 356$ and $\delta = -23.44°$ (Using Eq. (3.3))

From Eq. (3.10), we have,

$$N = \frac{2}{15}\cos^{-1}(-\tan(2835)\tan\delta(-23.44))$$

$$= \frac{2}{15}\cos^{-1}(-(-0.434)(0.545)(28°35')$$

$$= \frac{2}{15}\cos^{-1}(0.237)$$

$$= 10.18 \text{ hours}$$

Similarly, for June 22, 2015, $n = 173$; $\delta = 23.44°$

From Eq. (3.10), we have N = 13.82 hours

Example 3.3

Calculate the zenith angle of the sun in New Delhi at 2.30 PM on February 20, 2019.

Solution:

We have, $n = 51$; From Table 3.3, $\phi = 28°35'$N and $\omega = 37.5°$ (from Eq. (3.4))

Using Eq. (3.3), we have
$$\delta = 23.45\sin\left[\frac{360}{365}(284+n)\right]$$

$$= 23.45\sin\left[\frac{360}{365}(284+51)\right] = 11.58$$

From Eq. (3.7), we have, $\cos\theta_z = \cos\phi\ \cos\delta\cos\omega + \sin\delta\sin\phi$

$$\cos\theta_z = \cos 28°\ 35'\ \cos(-11.58°)\cos\omega + \sin(-11.58°)\ \sin 28°35' = 0.587$$

$$\theta_z = \cos^{-1} 0.587 = 54.03°$$

Example 3.4

Determine the local apparent time corresponding to 1430 hours on July 1, at Mumbai (latitude 18°54′ N, longitude 72°49′ E). Equation for time = –4′.

Solution:

Using Eq. (3.1), we have, Solar time = standard time + 4 ($L_{st} - L_{loc}$) + E

Here standard time = 1430 hours, standard time longitude = 82.50°E and the longitude of location are 72°49′E.

Local apparent time = 1430 – 4′–4(82.5 – 72.85) minutes = 13 hour 47 minutes 24 seconds

Note: in local time calculation, hours, minutes, and seconds are to be converted to the decimal system.

Example 3.5

Calculate the number of daylight hours (sunshine hours) in Delhi on December 22 and June 22, 1995.

Solution:

Here the latitude of new delhi (ϕ) = 28°35', for December 22, 1995, n = 356 and δ = -23.44°,

As we know

$$N = \frac{2}{15}\cos^{-1}\left[-\tan\left(-23.44°\right)\tan\left(28°35'\right)\right]$$

$$N = \frac{2}{15}\cos^{-1}\left[-(-0.434)(0.545)\right]$$

$$= (2/15)\cos^{-1}\left[0.237\right] = 10.18 \text{ hours}$$

Similarly, for June 22, 1995, n = 173; δ = 23.45°

Therefore

$$N = \frac{2}{15}\cos^{-1}\left(-\tan 23.45° \cdot \tan 28°35'\right) = 13.82 \text{ hours}$$

Multiple Choice Questions

1. Which of the following energy has the greatest potential among all the sources of renewable energy?
   (a) Solar energy
   (b) Wind Energy
   (c) Thermal energy
   (d) Hydro-electrical energy
2. What is the rate of solar energy reaching the earth's surface?
   (a) 1016W
   (b) 865W
   (c) 2854W
   (d) 1912W

3. Which is the most common source of energy from which electricity is produced?
   (a) Hydroelectricity (b) Wind energy
   (c) Coal (d) Solar energy
4. Complete the reaction: $H_2O + CO_2 \rightarrow$ _______
   (a) $CH_2O + O_2$ (b) $CO_2 + O2$
   (c) $H + CO_2 + O_2$ (d) $CH_2O + H_2O + O_2$
5. In what form is solar energy radiated from the sun?
   (a) Ultraviolet Radiation (b) Infrared radiation
   (c) Electromagnetic waves (d) Transverse waves
6. Solar radiation which reaches the surface without scattering or absorbed is called ____________
   (a) Beam Radiation (b) Infrared radiation
   (c) Ultraviolet radiation (d) Diffuse radiation
7. The scattered solar radiation is called ___________
   (a) Direct Radiation (b) Beam Radiation
   (c) Diffuse radiation (d) Infrared Radiation
8. Solar radiation received at any point of the earth is called ____________
   (a) Insolation (b) Beam Radiation
   (c) Diffuse Radiation (d) Infrared rays
9. Insolation is less ___________
   (a) when the sun is low (b) when the sun is right above the head
   (c) at night (d) at sunrise
10. What is solar radiation?
    (a) Energy radiated from the sun in all directions
    (b) Energy radiated from the earth in all directions
    (c) Radiation traveling in space
    (d) Energy radiated from the sun travels in ether
11. What are three relevant bands of solar radiation?
    (a) UV, infrared, and far infrared (b) UV, visible and infrared
    (c) Ultrasonic, infrared, and visible (d) UV, ultrasonic and near-infrared
12. Which two bands of solar radiation are the majority in the total solar radiation reaching earth?
    (a) UV and visible (b) Visible and ultrasonic
    (c) Visible and infrared (d) Infrared and UV
13. Which of the following affects the amount of solar radiation received by a location or water body?
    (a) The shape of the water body (b) Time at night
    (c) The rotational speed of the earth (d) Altitude and latitude
14. What is direct solar radiation?
    (a) Solar radiation directly received by the earth's surface from the sun
    (b) Cosmic radiation directly received by the earth's surface
    (c) Solar radiation received by the earth's surface after reflection
    (d) Cosmic radiation received by the earth's surface after reflection

15. What is indirect solar radiation?
    (a) Solar radiation directly received by the earth's surface from the sun
    (b) Solar radiation received by the earth's surface after scattering
    (c) Cosmic radiation directly received by the earth's surface
    (d) Cosmic radiation received by the earth's surface after reflection
16. What type of radiation does earth emit?
    (a) UV (b) Visible
    (c) Infrared (d) Longitudinal
17. What is the electromagnetic spectrum?
    (a) The radiation spectrum consists only of UV and visible rays
    (b) All rays falling in the category of infrared and UV rays
    (c) All rays falling in the category of gamma and x-rays
    (d) Radiation spectrum encompassing all types of radiation
18. Which of the following is responsible for thermal energy?
    (a) UV (b) Infrared
    (c) Gamma (d) UV-A
19. How does infrared radiation cause heat?
    (a) By exciting neutrons of the substance that absorbs them
    (b) By de-exciting electrons of the substance that absorbs them
    (c) By exciting electrons of thc substance that absorbs them
    (d) By exciting protons of the substance that absorbs them
20. Which of the following is used to measure the flux of outgoing long-wave radiation?
    (a) Watt/square meter (b) Watt
    (c) Joules (d) Watt/cubic meter
21. Which of the following process is involved in long-wave radiation?
    (a) Adsorption (b) Scattering
    (c) Evaporation (d) Condensation
22. What is solar irradiance?
    (a) Solar radiation received by the earth
    (b) Solar radiation is directly received by the earth's surface
    (c) Solar radiation received by the earth's surface after scattering
    (d) The intensity with which solar radiation enters the earth's atmosphere
23. Solar irradiance is measured in ______
    (a) watts (b) meters/sec
    (c) newtons (d) watts/square meter

.24. Beam radiations are measured with the help of
    (a) Anemometer (b) Sunshine recorder
    (c) Pyrheliometer (d) None of the above
25. Solar radiation flux is usually measured with the help of a
    (a) Pyranometer (b) Anemometer
    (c) Sunshine recorder (d) None of the abov

26. Reflecting mirrors used for exploiting solar energy are known as

(a) Mantle (b) Ponds
(c) Diffusers (d) Heliostats

27. A pyranometer is used for the measurement of

(a) Direct as well as diffuse radiation (b) Direct radiation only
(c) Diffuse radiation only (d) None of the above

28. The most widely used solar material is

(a) Arsenic (b) Silicon
(c) Cadmium (d) Steel

29. Diffused radiation has

(a) no unique direction
(b) unique direction
(c) short wavelength as compared to beam radiation
(d) large magnitude as compared to beam radiation

30. Solar energy can be directly converted into electrical energy by

(a) photoelectric cell (b) dry cell
(c) rechargeable cell (d) battery

31. Solar energy can be used to cook food in

(a) solar cooker (b) woodstove
(c) gas oven (d) traditional oven

32. Solar energy can be converted into

(a) thermal energy only
(b) electrical energy only
(c) both thermal energy and Electrical energy
(d) none of the above

33. Global radiation is given by

(a) Direct radiation/ Diffuse Radiation (b) Direct radiation - Diffuse Radiation
(c) Diffuse Radiation /Direct radiation (d) Direct radiation + Diffuse Radiation

34. The complement of the zenith angle is

(a) Solar altitude angle (b) Surface azimuth angle
(c) Solar azimuth angle (d) Slope

35. Angle made by a plane surface with horizontal is called ________.

(a) Altitude angle (b) Zenith angle
(c) Slope (d) Hour Angle

36. The angle is measured from a plane and which is equal to the angle between the beam of rays and normal to the plane is called __________

(a) Declination (b) Azimuth angle
(c) Hour angle (d) Incident angle

37. High-temperature collectors use ___ for fulfilling heat requirements.

(a) un-glazed collectors (b) flat plate collectors
(c) mirrors or lenses (d) any of the above

38. Glazed solar collectors are designed primarily for
(a) space heating (b) crop drying
(c) pre-heat makeup ventilation air (d) all of the above

39. Unglazed solar collectors are designed primarily for
(a) space heating (b) crop drying
(c) pre-heat make-up ventilation air (d) all of the above

40. Which of the following also serves as the exterior wall surface of the building?
(a) Glazed solar collector (b) Un-glazed solar collector
(c) both (A) and (B) (d) none of the above

41. The following fluid is used in a parabolic trough power plant.
(a) molten salt (b) synthetic oil
(c) pressurized steam (d) all of the above

42. The ___ focus concentrated sunlight on a receiver that sits on top of the tower.
(a) heliostats (b) heliocentric
(c) heliosphere (d) none of the above

43. The function of a solar collector is to convert.......
(a) Solar Energy into Electricity (b) Solar Energy Radiation
(c) Solar Energy, thermal energy (d) Solar Energy, mechanical energy

44. Flat plate collector absorbs.......
(a) Direct radiation only (b) Diffuse radiation only
(c) Direct and diffuse both (d) All of the above

45. Solar cells, for power generation, entail the following significant disadvantages........
(a) Variable power (b) High cost
(c) Lack of availability (d) Large area requirement

46. By which of the following arrangements the maximum temperature can be achieved
(a) Photovoltaic (b) Flat solar collector
(c) Solar tower (d) Paraboloidal reflector

47. Production of bioethanol is through fermentation of ________ and starch components
(a) Alcohol (b) Sugar
(c) Milk (d) Acid

48. Bio-chemical process for producing biogas mainly consists of these two processes.
(a) Composting and feeding (b) Acidogenesis and methanogens
(c) Pyrolysis and combustion (d) Combustion and torrefaction

49. This is also called a biogas
(a) Biobutanol (b) Biodiesel
(c) Bioethanol (d) Biomethane

50. The aerobic digestion of sewage is utilized in the production of
(a) Metal articles (b) Biofuels
(c) Biomass (d) Synthetic fuels

51. The term biomass most commonly refers to
(a) Inorganic matter (b) Chemicals
(c) Ammonium compounds (d) Organic matter

52. The process of usage of organic material to generate energy is known as
(a) Biomass energy (b) Hydrothermal energy
(c) Geothermal energy (d) Nuclear energy

53. The process of usage of organic material to generate energy is known as
(a) Biomass energy (b) Hydrothermal energy
(c) Geothermal energy (d) Nuclear energy

54. Which of the following are commonly used in the fermentation process?
(a) Yeast (b) Bacteria
(c) Mushrooms (d) Virus

55. Which of the following is an example of a thermo-chemical conversion technique to convert biomass into usable forms of energy?
(a) Composting (b) Gasification
(c) Anaerobic digestion (d) Extraction with esterification

ANSWERS

1.	(a)	2.	(a)	3.	(c)	4.	(a)	5.	(c)	6.	(a)	7.	(c)	8.	(a)
9.	(a)	10.	(a)	11.	(b)	12.	(c)	13.	(d)	14.	(a)	15.	(b)	16.	(c)
17.	(a)	18.	(a)	19.	(c)	20.	(a)	21.	(b)	22.	(d)	23.	(d)	24.	(c)
25.	(a)	26.	(d)	27.	(a)	28.	(b)	29.	(a)	30.	(a)	31.	(a)	32.	(c)
33.	(d)	34.	(a)	35.	(c)	36.	(d)	37.	(c)	38.	(a)	39.	(c)	40.	(b)
41.	(d)	42.	(a)	43.	(c)	44.	(c)	45.	(b)	46.	(c)	47.	(b)	48.	(b)
49.	(d)	50.	(b)	51.	(a)	52.	(a)	53.	(a)	54.	(a)	55.	(b)		

Short and Long Answer Type Questions

1. Distinguish between global radiation and diffuse radiation.
2. Explain the importance of solar energy.
3. Explain the photovoltaic effect briefly. Explain the principle of operation of the photovoltaic cell.
4. Explain with the help of neat diagram construction of the solar cell.
5. List the materials used to form solar cells.
6. Describe the operation of a solar cell.
7. What are the different types of solar cells?
8. Write short notes on a solar power plant.
9. List the factors to be considered while selecting a site for a solar power plant.
10. Describe the principle of solar photovoltaic energy conversion.
11. What is the advantage and disadvantage of photovoltaic solar energy conversion?
12. What materials are used for solar concentrators?

13. Draw a schematic of a solar thermal power plant and briefly explain its working.
14. What is the major component of a solar PF system?
15. Explain different types of solar PV systems.
16. State various routes of biomass energy conversion to other forms of energy.
17. What is biomass? How is it useful?
18. Discuss the availability of biomass.
19. Explain the process of production of biomass.
20. What are the factors which affect the generation of biogas?
21. Draw and explain the use of a gasifier.
22. Explain the different characteristics of biomass as fuel.

Numerical Problems

1. Calculate the hour angle (ω) at 2.30 PM.
2. Calculate the number of daylight hours in Delhi on December 18 and June 18 in a leap year.
3. Determine local apparent time and declination at Kolkata corresponding to 1240 hours IST on September 12. Given E = 5′13″)
4. Calculate the sunset hour angle and day length at a location of latitude 35°N, on March 13, 2020.
5. Calculate the sun's altitude and azimuth angles at 10 am solar time on September 12 at a latitude of 27°N.
6. Determine the sunset hour angle and day length for a location with latitude 24°25′N and longitude 81°58′E on February 1, 2020.
7. Calculate the angle made by beam radiation with the normal to a flat plate collector, pointing to the due south location of (28°38′N, 77°17′E) at 9.00-hour solar time on December 1. The collector is tilted at an angle of 36° with horizontal. Also, find out the day length on that day.
8. Calculate the zenith angle and solar azimuth angle for a place with a latitude of 53°12′N at 9.00 hour solar time on June 1, 2019.

PRACTICALS

Experiment No. 1

Title: Assemble and dismantle the parabolic trough Concentrated Solar Power (CSP) plant.

Aim: To assemble and dismantle the parabolic trough concentrator.

Apparatus/ Software required: A complete set of parabolic trough concentrator solar power plants is to be available for this experiment.

Alternatively, students may watch a video for the parabolic trough concentrator power plant.

Theory:

A parabolic trough concentrator uses the mirrored surface of a linear parabolic reflector to focus direct solar radiation onto an absorber pipe that runs along the focal line of the concentrator with a fluid that is heated to produce steam for a steam turbine. The key component of a parabolic trough concentrator consists of a collector, receiver, trough stand, and tracking system. Ancillary components include piping for the fluid, instrumentation and safety mechanism, and storage system (optional). In India, there are five different types of commercial parabolic troughs available

(a) Large Aperture Parabolic Trough SharperSun (29.22m^2) by Leveragenet
(b) Optitrough300 (28.75m^2) by Ultra Conserve
(c) SolPac P60 (6.41m^2) by Thermax
(d) SG1000 (2.06m^2) by GreenEra and
(e) PTC (1.7m^2) by Oorja Energy.

Different types of parabolic trough concentrators are shown below from Fig. 3.34 to 3.38.

Fig. 3.34: Large Aperture Parabolic Trough ShaperSun (29.22m^2) by Leveragenet

Fig. 3.35: Optithrough300 (28.75m^2) by ultra conserve

Fig. 3.36: SolPac P60 (6.41m^2) by Thermax

Fig. 3.37: SG1000 (2.06m^2) by Green Era

Fig. 3.38: PTC (1.7m^2) by Oorja Energy

A parabolic trough is used for low and medium heat applications up to a maximum temperature of 250°C. The configuration of an industrial process heat system depends mainly on the specific application. It may consist of one or more parabolic troughs in a system.

Collector: The collector of a parabolic trough is an assembly of curved shaped reflectors arranged on a structural steel framework. The reflectors are arranged so as to give a parabolic shape and reflect the incident solar radiation onto a tubular receiver. The sample structure of the collector is shown in Fig.3.39.

Fig.3.39: Sample picture of collectors

Receiver: The receiver of the parabolic trough is placed at the line focus of a trough so as to capture the solar radiation and transfer the same to the thermal medium used in the system. In India, the receiver being used is an evacuated/non-evacuated type comprising a linear absorber constructed of a metallic tube surrounded by a glass tube. The sample structure of the receiver is shown in Fig.3.40.

Fig.3.40: Sample Picture of receivers

Trough stand: The basic framework of a trough stand is a steel structure. The structure is designed so as to withstand wind speed in an operating condition as well as in a parked stage as per the existing structural design code. The overall system rests on a civil foundation made for the purpose. The sample structure of the Trough stand is shown in Fig. 3.41.

Fig. 3.41: Sample structure of the Trough stand

Tracking System: The tracking system enables the trough to remain focused on the sun so as to capture the maximum possible direct radiation during the day. The single-axis tracking system is provided with either north-to-south or east-to-west tracking. The tracking system may include the following few sets of equipment – An electrical motor, Gearbox, Gear & Pinion, Shaft, Solar radiation sensor, Wind sensor, and Timer. Balance of the plant includes a number of components such as heat transfer pipes & support structure, instrumentation & safety mechanism, and storage tank (optional) to control fluid flow and temperature. The heat transfer pipes carry fluid and thus transfer the heat received by it to an end-user application. Fluid circulates in the system at a certain desired rate. The sample structure of the Gear Box, shaft, and Gear & Pinion is shown in Fig. 3.42.

Fig.3.42: Sample structure of the Gear Box, shaft, and Gear & Pinion

Storage System: The thermal storage subsystem is a part of the circulation system. It extracts heat from the circulating fluid when the temperature becomes too high. When the temperature is too low, it supplies the stored heat to the fluid. Insulation should be provided both on the tank and supporting structure. This ancillary is optional. The sample structure of the Storage system is shown in Fig.3.43.

Fig. 3.43: Sample structure of the Storage system

Procedure for assembling:

The following steps are followed to assemble a parabolic trough concentrator.

1. Unpack the reflector.
2. Unpack the mounting structure.
3. For a fixed location, the base mounting structure is to be fixed with cement concrete. For mobile or temporary locations, the mounting structure should have bearings with wheel or flexible structure.
4. Once the mounting structure is erected, the reflectors are fitted with the mounting structure using nuts and bolts provided in the box.
5. The solar tracking gears are to be placed accordingly as per the instructions at the bottom of the mounting structure.
6. The solar tracking sensors are to be placed at the top four corners of the reflector.
7. The fluid tube is to be fitted longitudinally across the reflector.
8. If there are more numbers of reflectors, then the fluid tubes are to be connected hermetically.
9. The steam turbine is to be connected to the fluid tube. The working fluid is connected in a closed circuit with the input to the reflector absorber from the turbine.
10. The generator is coupled already with the turbine, and both are to be fitted using a spirit level so that the turbine shaft and the generator shaft are horizontal. This whole assembly is to be mounted on a rigid structure.
11. The connection from solar tracker sensors and the control panel is to be connected using flexible wires, and the wires are to be bound with the structure using a wire-binder stip.
12. The output terminal of the generator is to be connected to the load as per the requirement (either through a transformer or directly to the load).
13. An optional insulated storage tank is provided with some system for storing the hot working fluid. If this storage tank is available, then it should be connected to the fluid circuit.

Precautions and observations during assembling:

The following are to be taken care of during installation:

1. The concrete base is to be made as per the shape, size, and weight of the reflector to support for rigid structure as per the measurement. The base structure for the reflector and the base structure for the turbine and generator are to be different. Both structures are to be placed at a minimum possible distance.
2. The mounting structure should be rigid and horizontal and use a spirit level for the same.
3. Utmost care should be taken to protect the reflector surface from damage or deface.
4. The fluid pipes are to be sealed hermetically so that the fluid inside is insulated or protected from outside influences.
5. The solar tracker gears and the motor are to be connected as per the instructions manual provided with the assembly by the manufacturer.
6. The electrical wires connected with the control panel fitted under the reflector should be fixed with the structure with a strip and should not be kept loose.
7. The site should be protected from trespassers.
8. Generator terminals are to be protected.

Procedure for dismantling:

The following steps are followed in brief for dismantling a parabolic trough concentrated solar power plant. Most of the steps are in reverse of assembling, but few are different from assembling.

1. All the electrical connections from the generator and the other control circuit should be disconnected from the respective pins or bolts.
2. The turbine and generator assembly are to be disconnected from the steam pipe (or the fluid pipe).
3. The working fluid pipe is to be disconnected from the reflector assembly and kept aside. The fluid inside the tube is to be protected using the valve fitted on each joint.
4. The reflector dismounted from the structure and unbolted it. Care should be taken for any external damage or defacing.
5. The mounting structure is to be unbolted and kept separately so that the pairs of bolts and screws are the same.
6. The solar tracker gear assembly and the motor are to be unbolted from the mounting structure.
7. All the parts and their different accessories are to be packed separately and labeled so that these can be used at a later time without any mismatch.

Precautions and observations during dismantling:

The precautions are the same as the precautions of assembling. Care should be taken to protect the reflector and all the other accessories from damage during dismantling.

Observation:

Assembling: A log book are to be maintained to describe all the procedure of the installation with date and time with the signature of the working staff and station-in-charge.

Dismantle: A log book are to be maintained to describe all the procedure of dismantling, and all the parts and their accessories are to be labeled in a separate packing/ box. The content of the packet/ box is to be listed clearly. After completing the dismantling procedure, a signature may be obtained from the working staff and station-in-charge.

Discussion:

After completion of the installation and dismantling, the students are to write a note on the working principles of various parts of the assembly and its maintenance

Experiment No. 2

Title: Assemble and dismantle the parabolic dish Concentrated Solar Power (CSP) plant.

Aim: To assemble a parabolic trough or parabolic dish concentrator.

Apparatus/ Software required: A complete set of parabolic dish concentrator solar power plants are to be available for this experiment.

Alternatively, students may watch a video for the parabolic trough concentrator power plant.

Theory:

Parabolic dish solar concentrators are a dual/ two-axis tracking system that concentrates the solar radiation towards a thermal receiver located at the focal point, and heat is absorbed by a working fluid to run a sterling engine.

A paraboloid Dish consists of reflectors mounted on a truss structure such that the incident sunlight is reflected onto a cavity receiver in a similar way, reflecting a telescope that focuses starlight or a dish antenna that focuses radio waves. The receiver, which is insulated on the outside, is held in a fixed position in relation to the reflectors by means of a suitable structure. The heat of the sun collected at the receiver is transferred to the thermal fluid used in the system. Light from the sun arrives at the Earth's surface almost completely parallel. So the dish should be aligned with its axis pointing at the sun, allowing almost all incoming radiation to be reflected toward the focal point of the dish. This is achieved by moving the entire array of reflectors and receivers to track the sun at all times with the help of a dual-axis tracking system. The paraboloid dishes are shown in the below figures in Fig. 3.44 to 3.46.

Fig.3.44: Square Paraboloid dish (25 m^2 collector Area by ATE Enterprises) [Image Source: ATE Enterprises website]

Fig.3.45 Circular Paraboloid dish (90 m^2 & 55 m^2 collector Area by Megawatt Solution) [Image Source: Megawatt Solution]

Fig. 3.46: Square Paraboloid dish with Solar PV power generation (2 x 16 m^2 aperture Area) by Forbes Solar [Image Source: Forbes Solar Website]

Key components of a Paraboloid dish-based concentrated solar thermal (CST) system can be subdivided as parabolic dish collector, receiver, dish mounting system, solar tracking system, piping for the working fluid, instrumentation and control circuit, and storage system (optional). Different types of parabolic trough concentrators are shown in the attached Figure. A paraboloid dish is used for the low to medium process heat application. It can attain a maximum temperature of up to 350°C as per requirement in industries, commercial & residential complexes, religious places, etc. A typical parabolic dish of 90 m^2 reflective area has a thermal output capacity of 50 kW at 1000 W/m^2 solar insolation. (Courtesy: CSH India). The configuration of an industrial process heat solar system depends mainly on the specific application; it may consist of one or more Paraboloid dishes in a system. Paraboloid dishes have been installed in various thermal applications across industries, including food processing in food parks, thermic fluid heating in scientific laboratories, and ironing application, amongst others.

Collector: The collector of a paraboloid dish is an assembly of flat/curved reflectors of high reflectivity arranged on a structural steel framework. The reflectors are arranged in a parabolic shape to reflect the incident solar radiation to a common point, i.e., the receiver. An actual Figure of the collector is shown in the diagram. The supporting structure is also shown in Figure. The supporting structure is different for different types of solar receivers and depends on the size and shape of the collector. This supporting structure is also attached to the solar tracker gear and motor assembly.

Receiver: The receiver of the paraboloid dish is placed at the focus of the dish to capture the solar radiation and transfer the same to the thermal medium used in the system. This critical component is generally a cavity-type absorber as per the design codes used in the manufacture of similar thermal equipment using conventional heat sources. The receivers are supported on a steel structure. A diagram is shown in the attached Figure. The supporting structure for the receiver is also mounted on the receiver on the same structure. The sample receiver is shown in Fig.3.47 and Fig.3.48.

Fig. 3.47: Receiver support structure

Fig. 3.48: Cavity Receiver

Fig. 3.49: Support structure with stand

Dish Stand: The basic framework of the dish stand is a steel structure. The structure is designed to minimize wind speed in operating conditions as well as in parked stages as per the structural design code. The overall system rests on a foundation that provides elevated support. The foundation is of two types: (i) Civil foundation & (ii) structural foundation. The support structure is shown in Fig.3.49.

Tracking System: The paraboloid dish is provided with a two-axis tracking mechanism that enables it to be focused continuously toward the sun in order to capture the maximum possible direct radiation at any point in time and avoid cosine losses. The tracking system may consist of an electrical motor, gearboxes, sprockets and chains, shaft, solar radiation sensor, wind sensor, etc. A Figure is attached for clarity in Fig. 3.50. Tracking mechanism is a two-axis tracking. It is programmed and sensor-based. There are various safety features attached to the system, like alarm indicators and limits for angular movement. The heat transfer pipes carry fluid and transfer the heat received by it to an end-user application. Fluid circulates in the system at a certain desired rate to quickly and efficiently transfer the received heat from the solar field to end-use application. The thickness of the fluid pipe depends on the pressure and temperature of the application. Normally mineral wool and glass wool are used as insulating materials for the fluid pipe, and aluminum or galvanized steel sheets are used as cladding materials for thermal shielding.

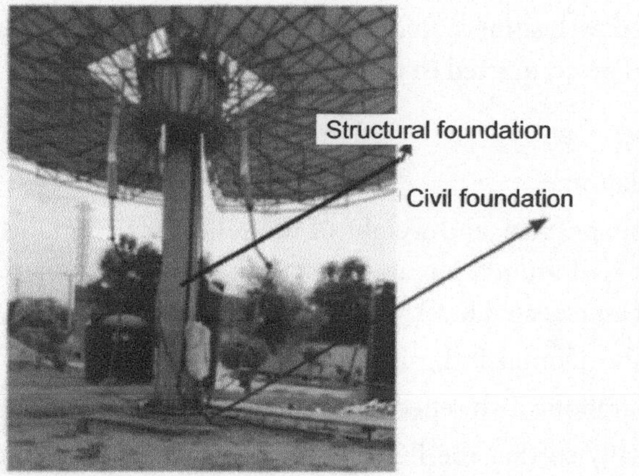

Fig. 3.50: Tracking system

Procedure for assembling:

The following steps are followed to assemble a parabolic dish concentrator.

1. Unpack the reflector from the box.
2. Unpack the mounting structure from the box.
3. For a fixed location, the base mounting structure is to be fixed with cement concrete. For mobile or temporary locations, the mounting structure should have bearings with a wheel or flexible structure for movement.
4. Once the mounting structure is erected, the parabolic dish reflectors are fitted with the mounting structure using nuts and bolts provided in the box. Need to follow the steps provided in the instruction manual from the manufacturer.
5. The solar tracking gears, electrical motor, gearboxes, sprockets and chains, and shaft are to be placed accordingly as per the instructions, with the rigid structure at the bottom of the mounting structure with mechanical and electrical systems.
6. Solar tracking sensors like solar radiation sensors and wind sensors are to be placed at the center area of the dish.
7. The cavity-type absorber with the thermal fluid is to be fitted at the focus of the dish. This is the most critical component of the system. The receivers are supported on a steel structure and are to be fitted with great care.
8. The turbine, which will be running using this thermal fluid, is at the focal point with the generator. The working fluid is connected in a closed circuit with the input to the cavity absorber from the turbine.
9. The generator is coupled already with the turbine (or heat engine). This whole assembly is to be mounted on a rigid structure.
10. The connection from solar tracker sensors and the control panel is to be connected using flexible wires, and the wires are to be bound with the structure using a wire-binder stip.
11. The output terminal of the generator is to be connected to the load as per the requirement (either through a transformer or directly to the load).
12. An optional insulated storage tank is provided with some system for storing the hot working fluid. If this storage tank is available, then it should be connected to the fluid circuit.

Precautions and observations during assembling:

The following are to be taken care of during installation:

1. The concrete base is to be made as per the shape, size, and weight of the reflector to support for rigid structure as per the measurement. The civil foundation and structural foundation are made with steel structure and are wind resistant at an elevated level.
2. The mounting structure should be rigid and horizontal and use a spirit level for the same.
3. Utmost care should be taken to protect the parabolic dish reflector surface from damage or deface.
4. The thermal fluid pipes are sealed hermetically so that the fluid inside is insulated or protected from outside influences.

5. The solar tracker gears and the motor are to be connected as per the instructions manual provided with the assembly by the manufacturer.
6. The electrical wires connected with the control panel fitted under the reflector should be fixed with the structure with a strip and should not be kept loose.
7. The site should be protected from trespassers.
8. Generator terminals are to be protected.

Procedure for dismantling:

The following steps are followed in brief for dismantling a parabolic dish concentrated solar power plant. Most of the steps are in reverse of assembling, but few are different from assembling.

1. All the electrical connections from the generator and the other control circuit should be disconnected from the respective pins or bolts.
2. The cavity absorber, turbine (or heat engine), and generator assembly are to be disconnected from the top elevated stand very carefully.
3. The mounting structure for the cavity absorber is dismantled from its base and to be removed without damaging the dish and its curvature.
4. The working fluid inside the tube is to be protected using the valve fitted on each joint, and before dismantling, the valves are to tightened.
5. The parabolic dish reflector dismounted from the structure and unbolted it. Care should be taken for any external damage or defacing.
6. The mounting structure is to be unbolted and kept separately so that the pairs of bolts and screws are the same.
7. The solar tracker gear assembly and the motor are to be unbolted from the mounting structure.
8. All the parts and their different accessories are to be packed separately and labeled so that these can be used at a later time without any mismatch.

Precautions and observations during dismantling:

The precautions are the same as the precautions of assembling. Care should be taken to protect the reflector and all the other accessories from damage during dismantling. For the dismantling process, if the parts are heavy, a crane may be used.

Observation:

Assembling: A log book are to be maintained to describe all the procedure of the installation with date and time with the signature of the working staff and station-in-charge.

Dismantle: A log book are to be maintained to describe all the procedure of dismantling, and all the parts and their accessories are to be labeled in a separate packing/ box. The content of the packet/ box is to be listed clearly. After completing the dismantling procedure, a signature may be obtained from the working staff and station-in-charge.

Discussion:

After completion of the installation and dismantling, the students are to write a note on the working principles of various parts of the assembly and precautions taken.

Experiment No. 3

Title: Assemble the solar PV plant to produce electric power and then dismantle it.

Aim: To assemble and dismantle a solar PV plant.

Apparatus/ Software required: A complete set of solar photovoltaic power plants with all their accessories are to be available for this experiment.

Alternatively, students may watch a video for the parabolic trough concentrator power plant.

Theory: The basic building block of a photovoltaic system is the Solar Cell, a semiconductor device having a simple p-n junction and which, when exposed to sunlight, produces DC electricity. The solar cell is made up of "Semi-Conductor" materials that are processed to make the device photovoltaic. The detailed theory portion is discussed in section 3.6. The operation of solar cells involves these major processes:

(a) Absorption of sunlight into semiconductor materials
(b) Generation of charge carriers.
(c) Separation of +ve & -ve charges to different regions of the cell to produce e.m.f.

The power generated by a single cell is small, and therefore, several cells are interconnected in series/ parallel combinations to get the required voltage and current. When a number of solar cells are connected in series to get a specific voltage, the unit so formed is called a Solar Module. Charging batteries is the primary use of the SPV module. Therefore normally, 36 cells are joined in series to form a standard module, which is capable of charging 12 volts battery. A terminal box is provided on the backside of the module for external connections. A Bypass diode is connected across +ve and –ve in the terminal box. The cathode of the diode will be at the +ve terminal, and Anode will be at the –ve terminal of the module. This diode protects the module cells from overheating due to the shadowing of the module or any cell breakage. Generally, the rating of the bypass diode is 1.52 times the maximum current of the module. The Repetitive Reverse Peak Voltage V_{rrm} of the diode should be double the string open voltage.

Description of Items in Solar PV power plant

Main Components of Solar Photo Voltaic System

The solar power system consists of the following components:

(a) Solar array.
(b) Battery Bank
(c) Solar Charge Controller
(d) Field Junction Box
(e) Solar Module Mounting Structure
(f) Earthing kit
(g) Cables.

(a) Solar Array: Solar array consists of a series/parallel combination of modules, which are mounted on the metallic structure in a sunny and shadow-free area at a fixed angle as recommended by the designer. All the modules will face the South in the Northern hemisphere. Cables from the array area will come to the control and battery room through junction boxes from panels of modules. The solar Array is shown in Fig. 3.51.

Fig.3.51: Solar Array

(b) Battery Bank: The Sun is not always available, and it is not regular. However, loads are to be fed at any time of the day. Therefore power should be stored in a battery bank. Low maintenance Lead acid battery or any other storage battery as per the specification is used. The capacity of this battery bank is given in Ampere - Hour (AH) and bus bar voltage. The bus-bar voltage is decided by the voltage requirement of the load. The solar Array is shown in Fig. 3.52.

Fig.3.52: Picture of a Battery Bank

(c) Solar Charge Controller: The charge controller is the interface between Array and the battery bank. It protects the battery from overcharging and moderate charging at the finishing end of the charge of the battery bank. Therefore it enhances the life of the battery bank. It also indicates the charging status of batteries like battery undercharged, overcharged, or deep discharged through LEDs indications. Some switches and MCBs are also provided for the manual or accidental cut-off of charging. In some charge controllers, load terminals are also provided through a low battery charge cut-off device so that it can protect the battery bank from deep discharge. Charge controllers are designed as per the specific requirement. The sample structure of the solar charge controller is shown in Fig. 3.53.

Fig. 3.53: Solar Charge Controller

(d) **Field Junction Box (FJB):** Field junction box is the interface between Solar panels and the Charge Controller. All the incoming/outgoing cables/wires from the Solar panel to Charge Controller are terminated at FJB. The field junction box of the solar PV system is shown in Fig. 3.54

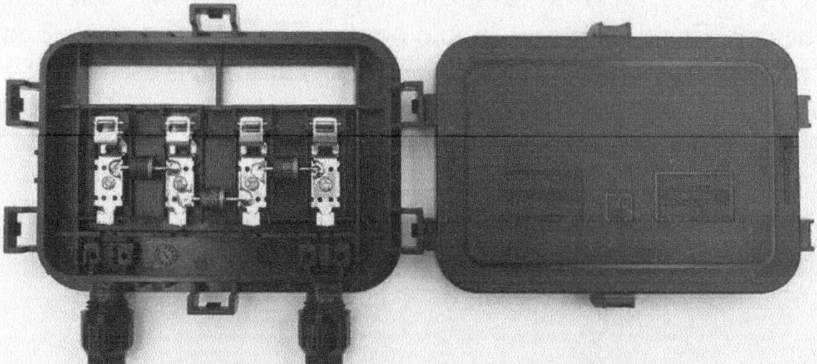

Fig. 3.54: Field junction box

(e) **Solar Module Mounting Structure:** This is made up of galvanized iron frames and angles. In this structure, flexibility is provided to change the module-mounting angle seasonally. This structure is grouted by small civil work, and modules are subsequently mounted. Also, this mounting structure should be earthed suitably at several places if the voltage of the array is more than 50 Volts. The solar module mounting structure is shown in Fig. 3.55.

(f) **Earthing kit:** Earthing kit is provided to earth the mounting structure. The provision of earthing shall be made as follows: The installation shall have proper earth terminals and shall be properly earthed. In general, the earth's resistance shall not be more than 2 ohms. Earth provided shall preferably be maintenance-free using earth resistance improvement material like charcoal and salt.

(g) **Cables:** Different types of cables are necessary to connect module to module, modules to charge controller, charge controller to the battery, or connect the battery to load as required. The cable size used for interconnection of the SPV module, Charge Controller, and battery shall be a minimum of 2 × 2.5 sq. mm Cu. Cable. As far as some hardware is concerned, the screws and bolts/nuts are of Chrome plated, stainless steel, and brass, so rusting should not take place.

Operation and Technical specification:

The following parameters shall be clearly specified by the manufacturer for a different types of Solar modules:

(a) Peak power output (Pm)
(b) Current at peak power output (I_m)
(c) The voltage at peak power output (V_m)
(d) Short circuit current (I_{sc})
(e) Open circuit voltage (V_{oc})
(f) The conversion efficiency of the module (n)

The values of parameters from (a) to (f) above shall be specified under standard test conditions of

(a) The cell junction temperature of 25 ± 2°C.
(b) The irradiance of 1000 Watt/M.Sq. as measured with a reference solar cell (duly certified by a recognized national/international test house/lab. Nominated for this purpose.
(c) Standard Solar spectral energy distribution.
(d) Air Mass of 1.5.

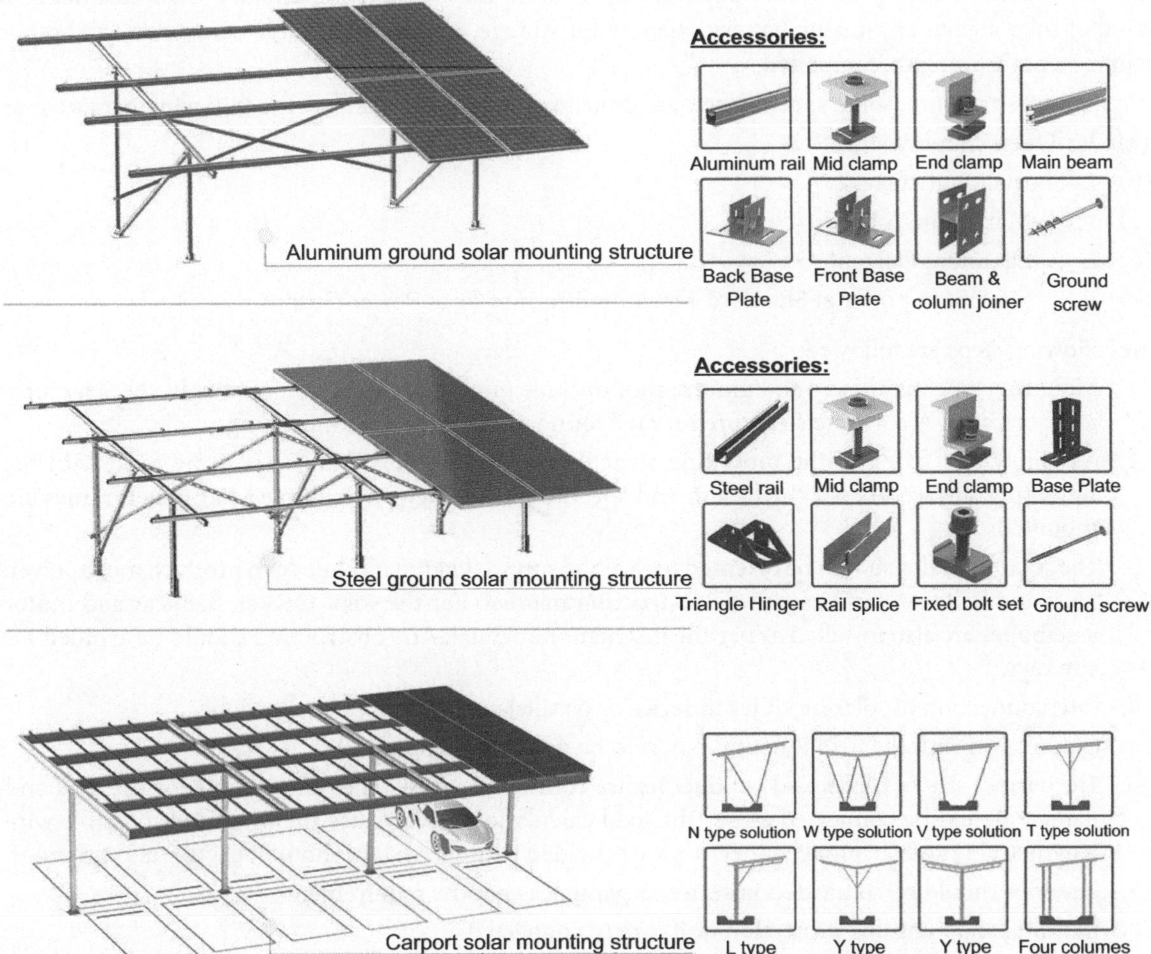

Fig. 3.55: Solar module mounting structure

The frame of the mounting fixture shall be made of anodized aluminum with a 20-micron anodization thickness. All other parts, such as fasteners, etc., shall be made of galvanized or stainless steel to make them weatherproof. In addition to holes provided for fixing onto the mounting structure, extra holes are to be provided suitably in the frame for cable routing.

The solar module shall be able to withstand a maximum mean hourly rainfall of 40 mm. The solar module shall be able to withstand a humidity level of up to 95%. The conversion efficiency of the modules up to 35W shall not be less than 8%, and for modules greater than 35W shall not be less than 12%.

The cell efficiency of the solar cells shall be greater than 12%. If required by the purchaser, the back plastic laminate shall be replaced by a toughened glass sheet to make the module suitable for use in coastal areas/industrially polluted areas/places where the plastic laminate is likely to get corroded.

Assemble steps of Solar PV power plant:

All the components and accessories are already available at the site. The planning for the solar PV plant, collection of information like load, application, climatic data, user compatibility, load calculations, sizing of solar arrays, optimizing battery capacity for storage, selection of charge controllers, and other requirements are already completed.

Before installation, some specific tests are done for solar panels to check the following parameters:

(a) V_{oc}-Open circuit voltage
(b) I_{sc}-Short circuit current
(c) V_{max}- Maximum Voltage
(d) I_{max}- Maximum Current
(e) P_{max}- Maximum power at Standard Test Conditions or Peak Power Output.

The following steps are followed:

1. Mounting type may be ground mount, rooftop, pole mount, or tracker. Accordingly, the structures are fabricated. A concrete structure for civil foundations is used for mounting.
2. Assembly and fixing of the mounting structure. The mounting frames are to be fixed with the mounting surface. As per the design and specifications, single or multiple solar panel frames are mounted.
3. The solar modules should be oriented to face the sun so that the modules can produce more power. Nuts and bolts are fixed as per the instruction manual. For the solar tracker, the gear and motor assemblies are also installed as per the instruction manual. Any obstruction should be avoided for sun rays.
4. Interconnection of solar modules in series or parallel configuration is to be done.
5. Connection with the field junction box is to be done for each module.
6. The correct size of cables and conductors are connected neatly. The output cable for the load and battery should be connected as per the load calculation. Always use the minimum possible wire length. Cable and terminal connectors are provided with the system should be water and fireproof.
7. Batteries should be connected in series or parallel as per the requirement
8. Earthing and lightning protection units are to connected.

Precautions for Solar PV power plants during installation:

The following issues related to solar PV systems are to observed.

1. Solar panels should be installed South facing in the Northern hemisphere and North facing in the Southern hemisphere. Since India is in the Northern hemisphere, Solar panels will always be installed- South facing in our country. The directions North-South may be found with the help of a Magnetic Compass.
2. The support for Solar panels needs to be robust and should not be accessible to the general public. It should be so installed that rainwater, bird dropping, leaves, etc., do not accumulate, and the top surface can be cleaned easily.
3. Distance between adjacent rows of structures has to be maintained so that the shadow can be avoided.
4. All exposed wiring must be in conduits/capping casing. Wiring through roofing must be waterproof. Where the wiring is through flammable materials like a thatched roof, they must be in a metal conduit.
5. Fencing may be provided for the protection of the site if mounted on the ground.

Steps for dismantling with precautions:

The steps for dismantling are much easier than its installation. The following steps are generally followed with the precautions for not damaging the items during uninstallation.

1. The battery voltage is to be checked before initiating the uninstallation, and it should be rated at the time of installation.
2. The charge controller is to be made OFF condition. No electrical loads are connected.
3. Batteries are disconnected, and terminals are sealed with grease.
4. The connecting cables and wires are disconnected, unbolting the lugs from the terminal and kept pair-wise.
5. The solar panels are unmounted from the mounting structure and kept aside with care.
6. Mounting structures are to be unbolted and kept separately. The nuts and bolt pairs are kept separately with proper labeling for future use.

Observation:

Assembling: A log book are to be maintained to describe all the procedure of the installation with date and time with the signature of the working staff and station-in-charge.

Dismantle: A log book are to be maintained to describe all the procedure of dismantling, and all the parts and their accessories are to be labeled in a separate packing/ box. The content of the packet/ box is to be listed clearly. After completing the dismantling procedure, a signature may be obtained from the working staff and station-in-charge.

Discussion:

After completion of the installation and dismantling, the students are to write a note on the working principles of various parts of the assembly and precautions taken.

Experiment No. 4

Title: Assemble a small biogas plant to generate electric power

Aim: To assemble a small biogas plant to generate electric power.

Apparatus/ Software required: A complete set of all accessories of a biogas power plant is available at the site for this experiment.

Alternatively, students may watch a video or construction of a medium-sized biogas plant and its various activities.

Suggested web pages: https://www.instructables.com/Constructing-a-Medium-Sized-Biogas-Plant-Using-Kit/ (some diagrams are also taken from this page for easy understanding)

Theory:

Biogas is a mixture of gases, primarily consisting of methane, carbon dioxide, and hydrogen sulfide, produced from raw materials such as agricultural waste, manure, municipal waste, plant material, sewage, green waste, and food waste. It is a renewable energy source. As discussed in section 3.9.2, biogas is produced by anaerobic digestion. Microorganisms, in the absence of air, digest the organic material and release a mixture of gases. The gases thus produced contain mostly methane along with other gases like Carbon dioxide, Nitrogen, and Hydrogen Sulphide in small quantities.

The major component of a biogas plant:

1. The Biogas plant consists of a digester tank, where the organic material is stored, and the microorganisms work on them and release gas.
2. The gas thus produced is collected in a tank known as a gas collector. In a floating-type model, this tank is floating in the slurry and moves up and down based on the amount of gas stored in it
3. A guide pipe helps the gas collector tank to move up and down inside the digester tank.
4. Waste is fed through a feed pipe inside the digester tank.
5. The fully digested slurry drains out through the outlet pipe. This can be collected, diluted, and used as fertilizer for plants.
6. A gas pipeline from the Gas collector tank helps in utilizing the gas for cooking and lighting

Steps to install a biogas plat:

1. **Site preparation**: The site should guarantee plant safety. A biogas plant should not be located further than 5 meters from the field. The digester chamber must be in an open area and should not be near any water source or natural water, as animal excrement may seep into underground water, as shown in Fig 3.56.

Fig. 3.56: Site of biogas plant

2. **Size of the biogas plant**: The biogas plant size is dependent on the average daily feedstock and expected hydraulic retention time of the material in the biogas system. The capacity of the plant should be designed based on the availability of raw materials. The capacity of the plant indicates the quantity of gas produced in a day. Based on the study, 1 kg of cow dung, along with an equal quantity of water (1:1) under anaerobic conditions in a day, produces 0.04 m3 or 40 litres of biogas.
3. **Selection of tanks**: Size is already calculated, and as per the size, the tank should be selected. As a thumb rule, for 4 kg of daily bio waste, the size of the tank may be 750 litre. Similarly, for 5 kg waste, the size of the tank may be 1000 litre. This tank is made of PVC and rubber with no leakage. For the bigger size of plants, the tank may be made of leak-proof concrete.
4. **Materials required for connection**: PVC elbow of different diameters, PVC pipe of different diameters, the threaded coupler of different diameters. Bigger size pipes are needed for the feeding waste and digester slurry waste outlet, and smaller size pipes and connecting accessories are needed for the digester guide system, gas tank connection, and digester guide system. Adhesives are required for pipe joints and connections for leak-proof. Generally, commercial adhesives like Araldite epoxy adhesive, M-seal, and PVC solvents are used as Fig. 3.57 and 3.58.

Fig. 3.57: PVC Elbow

Fig. 3.58: PVC pipes

5. **Tools required**: General tools like a Hackshaw for cutting the pipes at the required size, a sharp knife for fixing and fitting, a medium-sized hammer, and a set of spanners to tighten the gas pipe connector.
6. **Preparing the gas tank**: The top portion of the tank needs to be cut and removed. The width of the cutting should be just enough for the free movement of the gas tank. No need to place the removed top portion of the gas holder on top of the digester tank.
7. **Fixing the feed pipe to the digester**: The bigger PVC pipe is to be fixed by cutting the portion of the tank using Hackshaw and fixing it with epoxy resin adhesive. Similarly, the slurry outlet pipe should be fixed with the tank. Some guides are to be provided for easy up and down movement of the gas holder tank, and for this, a portion of PVC pipes are cut and fixed at the ridges of the tank, as shown in the diagram. These pipes are to be extended after placing the gas holder tank. Fig.3.59 shows such arrangement.

Fig.3.59: Fixing the feed pipe to the digester

8. **Preparation of gas pipes**: Gas pipes are used to transport gas from the tank to the power plant. These include a piece of gas pipes, ball valves, the required number of bends, gas nipples, gas adapters, and some more accessories like clamps and screws to hold the gas pipe on the wall. The length of the pipe is just sufficient from the gas tank to the gas turbine. The connection of the gas pipeline should be leak-proof. Adhesives are used in joints.
9. The gas holder tank should be placed over the digester tank so that the guide couplers fixed on the sides of the gas tank sits over the digester. Units should be placed.
10. Feed the biowaste to the digester. Initially, 80 kg of biowaste, like cow dung, is mixed with approximately 300 liters of water with 250g of jaggery. Jaggery helps to multiply the microorganism at a faster rate.
11. The gas formation will start after 2 to 3 days, and the gas holding tank will rise. Initial gas is to be released as it contains a mixture of air and other impurities. After releasing the first time, the gas produced can be used directly.
12. In order to burn the biogas in the Gas Engine, the gas pressure has to be increased with the aid of a gas compressor. The output of the gas compressor is regulated. In order to limit noise emissions, the Gas Engine is mounted in a noise-insulated cabin. The biogas is burnt in the gas engine, and the resulting energy is converted to electricity by the generator.
13. The combustion air is drawn in from the outside via the feed air fan. The inlet air generates an overpressure in the noise-insulated cabin of the Gas Engine. The exhaust air flows out via the silencer. In order to limit noise emissions, the Gas Engine is mounted in a noise-insulated cabin. The air inlet and outlet channels are equipped with sliding block absorbers for noise reduction. The inlet channel is additionally equipped with a dust filter.
14. Once the tank is full of the feed, the slurry will be oozed out from the slurry outlet pipe, and the slurry will be used as organic fertilizer.

Precautions to be taken during installation:

1. Water should be available near the site.
2. The digester tank should be placed in a more sunlight area.

3. Easier access for feeding waste.
4. Easy to remove the slurry and properly use it as fertilizer or for other use.
5. Minimum distance from the biogas plant to the power plant
6. Do not use chlorinated water for feed, as it kills the microorganism.
7. Avoid using biomaterials like dry skin of the onion, egg shells, coconut husk, boned, etc.
8. Protect all the gas pipes from leakage.
9. Do not use any kind of flame near the plant, and the plant should be provided with a fire extinguisher.
10. The plant site should be protected from trespassers.

Dismantle the biogas plant:

Most of the steps are in reverse of installation. However, during installation, in many pipe connections and gas pipe connections, epoxy adhesive is used. The joins where epoxy adhesives are used cannot be separated, and they will crack. Therefore, the pipe connections for dismantling a working plant may be damaged from future use.

The digester unit and the gas unit need to dismantle by separating both tanks.

The gas engines are too disconnected, including the gas compressor, and all the accessories, including nuts and bolts, are to be kept with the label for future use. The digester tanks are to be cleaned and kept safely without damage.

Observation:

Assembling: A log book are to be maintained to describe all the procedure of the installation with date and time with the signature of the working staff and station-in-charge.

Dismantle: A log book are to be maintained to describe all the procedure of dismantling, and all the parts and their accessories are to be labeled in a separate packing/ box. The content of the packet/ box is to be listed clearly. After completing the dismantling procedure, a signature may be obtained from the working staff and station-in-charge.

Discussion:

After completion of the installation and dismantling, the students are to write a note on the working principles of various parts of the assembly and precautions taken.

KNOW MORE

Solar energy is a very vast subject with its numerous applications and various technologies. The followings are the issues related to solar energy, which may be interesting for students to know more on the topic of solar energy.

- Details analysis of solar radiation.
- The concept of heat transfer in terms of solar energy as solar energy is commonly used as thermal energy in addition to the generation of electrical power.
- Different types of solar collectors and their advantages and disadvantages over each other.
- Solar energy is commonly used as water heating for industrial and domestic use. The technology related to the water heating system may be of interest.

- Solar cookers and solar crop drying is used extensively. The thermal modeling of such dryers and the use of solar cookers for community services are topics for discussion.
- The solar photovoltaic system is discussed briefly in this chapter. Different efficient solar photovoltaic materials have been developed very recently, and advanced researches are on developing materials, including the composition of modules.
- Financial analysis of different solar power plants attracts attention.

A list of some books is listed in the further reading section for the advanced topics.

Biomass energy has been attracting attention from researchers in the last few decades. It is renewable and green energy, which is biomass energy's most significant advantage. Renewable sources are used extensively, and as far as possible, this energy is used to replace fossil fuels. The following issues may be discussed to know more about the topic of biomass energy.

(a) Optimum use of biomass resources.
(b) Cultivation of biomass economically on land and aquatic culture.
(c) Analysis and use of biofuel for the transportation sector.
(d) Economic analysis and commercial use of bio-thermal power plant and bio-chemical power plant.
(e) Purification of biomethane/biogas.

REFERENCES AND SUGGESTED READINGS

1. https://en.wikipedia.org –internet source for various topics.
2. Nag. P. K., Power Plant Engineering, McGraw Hill, New Delhi
3. Tanmoy Deb, Electrical Power Generation, Khanna Publishing House, Delhi (Ed. 2018)
4. Gupta, B.R., Generation of Electrical Energy, S. Chand& Co. New Delhi,
5. Solanki, Chetan Singh, – Solar Photovoltaics: Fundamentals, Technologies, and Applications, PHI Learning, New Delhi, ISBN: 9788120351110
6. Gupta, J.B. A Course in Electrical Power– S. K Kataria and Sons, New Delhi. 2014,
7. Solar Electricity Handbook; Michael Boxwell; Greenstream publishing ltd, UK-2011
8. Solar Power Hand Book, Dr. H. Naganagouda (2014)
9. Fundamentals of Renewable Energy Systems Paperback – D.Mukherjee, New Age International Publisher; First edition (2011)
10. Renewable energy Technologies; A Practical Guide for Beginners, Chetan Singh Solanki, PHI School Books (2008)
11. K. Hasan Saeed & D. K. Sharma, Non-conventional Energy Sources, S.K. Kataria & Sons, New Delhi.
12. D. S. Chauhan, S. K. Srivastava, "Non-conventional Energy Sources", New Age International publishers, Third Ed, 2012
13. Non-conventional Sources of Energy, G.D Rai, Khanna Publishers, Delhi, 2012
14. Tiwari, G. N., "Solar Energy-Fundamentals, Design, Modelling and Applications" Narosa Publishing House, Fourth reprint 2019.
15. Renewable Energy Sources and Emerging Technologies, Kothari D.P. and Signal K.C –PHI; 2 Edition (2011)

16. The Climate Solution; Mridula Ramesh; neelkamal publication - 2009
17. " Green Power: Eco-Friendly Energy Engineering", Khartchenko . N.V, Tech Books, and New Delhi, 2008.
18. Handbook of energy and environment in India; Banerjee B. P. , Oxford University Press 2005 India
19. "Environmental Science", Cunningham .W.P,11th ed., McGraw-Hill, 2010.
20. Report on Material and component specification Dual axis tracked parabolic dish, and Single axis tracked parabolic trough, UNDP-GEF CSHP, Ministry of New and Renewable Energy, Government of India, December 2015.

Further Reading

For further reading, the following books are useful

1. Tanmoy Deb, Electrical Power Generation, Khanna Publishing House, Delhi (Ed.2018)
2. Renewable energy Technologies; A Practical Guide for Beginners, Chetan Singh Solanki, PHI School Books (2008)
3. K. Hasan Saeed & D. K. Sharma, Non-conventional Energy Sources, S.K. Kataria & Sons, New Delhi.
4. D. S. Chauhan, S. K. Srivastava, "Non-conventional Energy Sources", New Age International publishers, Third Ed, 2012
5. Tiwari, G. N., "Solar Energy-Fundamentals, Design, Modelling and Applications" Narosa Publishing House, Fourth reprint 2019.

❑❑

4 Wind Power Plants

UNIT SPECIFICS

Through this unit we have discussed the following aspects:

- Introduction to wind energy and related terms and its importance.
- Wind power density.
- Wind map of India.
- Operating characteristics of the wind turbine.
- Factors affecting the performance of wind turbine rotors.
- Main components of a wind.
- Classification of wind turbines and electric generators used in wind power plants.
- Layout of various wind power plants.
- Some experiments on hydropower plants.

The concept of wind power generation and the process of energy conversion in large and small wind power plants are discussed. A brief description of various components of wind power plants is presented. The classification of wind power plants and electric generators for wind power plants in detail are presented in this Unit. Further curiosity and creativity as well as improving the problem-solving capacity of the students are dealt with through numerical examples.

Besides giving numbers of multiple-choice questions as well as questions of short and long answer types marked in two categories following the lower and higher order of Bloom's taxonomy, assignments through several numerical problems, a list of references, and suggested readings are given in this unit so that one can go through them for practice.

Some practical experiments related to the courses covered in this Unit are also appended at the end to make the students aware of the hands-on on these topics. In some of the experiments, some specific videos are provided.

After the related practical on the topic, based on the content, there is a "Know More" section appended. This section has been designed to supplement additional information and higher learning skills on the topic.

RATIONALE

This unit on wind power plants will help the students to get a fundamental idea behind the conversion of wind energy into electrical energy. Different types of wind power plants, the classification of wind turbines, and their working are discussed. Various types of generators used in wind power plants are presented. Furthermore, wind power plants in the modern day and their pros and cons also give up-to-date knowledge on the topic. Some related problems are pointed out with their solutions which can help further for getting a clear idea of the concern topics on wind power generation.

PRE-REQUISITES

Fundamentals of Electrical & Electronics Engineering (ES104)

UNIT OUTCOMES

After completion of Unit-4 students will be able to:

U4-01: Explain the concept of conversion of wind energy to electrical energy.

U4-02: Describe the working of wind power plants and their components.

U4-03: Classify wind power plants, wind turbines, and electrical generators, towers for wind power plants.

U4-04: Explain the working principle of different generators used in wind power plants.

U4-05: Identify the routine maintenance parts of large and small wind power plants.

Unit-4 Outcome	EXPECTED MAPPING WITH COURSE OUTCOMES (1 - Weak Correlation; 2 - Medium Correlation; 3 - Strong Correlation)				
	CO-1	CO-2	CO-3	CO-4	CO-5
U4-O1	1	3	3	2	2
U4-O2	2	3	1	-	-
U4-O3	2	2	3	1	1
U4-O4	2	3	1	-	-
U4-O5	3	2	2	-	-

4.1 INTRODUCTION

The air has mass. The mass of air contains solid, liquid, and gas particles. Cold air contains more of these particles than hot air. Thus, cold air is heavier than hot air. The cold air creates higher atmospheric pressure than hot air. The reason for this difference is the solar radiation of the Sun. The high-pressure air moves towards the low-pressure area. The moving air is called wind. The wind is freely available in nature. The Sun heats the atmospheric air as well as the earth's surface. When the earth is heated, the air above it raises and a low-pressure zone is created. On the other hand, the air above the non-heated parts of the earth is cold and creates high pressure. Thus, the wind is developed. The heating of air and the earth's surface are uneven and hence the speed of the wind is variable. When air moves, it attains kinetic energy. This energy is utilized for the production of electrical energy. The plant in which this electrical energy is produced from wind energy is called a wind power plant.

4.1.1 Importance of Wind Energy

(a) It is a clean and freely available source of energy. The wind source is inexhaustible.
(b) The wind is the first natural source of energy used by mankind. It is non-conventional as well as renewable. Enormous energy is associated with wind.
(c) Wind power generation does not pollute air and water. It also does not emit carbon dioxide (CO_2).
(d) The harnessed mechanical energy from the wind source can be utilized for (a) mechanical devices say water pumps, and (b) electrical power generation.

4.1.2 Types of Wind

There are two sources of wind. They are (a) Local wind, and (b) Global wind.

Local wind:

This type of wind is produced due to uneven heating and cooling of land and water surfaces during the day and night. The land area of the earth comprises a plain surface, valleys between hills, hills of different heights, and buildings of unequal heights. Due to these reasons, the lands of a particular region are not equally heated by the sun's radiation. Also, the land and water bodies are not equally heated. During day hours the land is heated more quickly than the water bodies. Hence, winds blow from water to land. At night the land cools more quickly than water and hence, winds move from land to water. The winds generated in this way due to the above are called local winds.

Global winds:

The global wind is also called the planetary wind. These winds are produced due to the rotation of the earth and unequal temperature differences between polar and equatorial regions. We know that earth is divided into some circles called latitudes and longitudes. The latitudes are parallel to the equator and the longitudes are the circles that pass through the north and south poles. There are unequal temperatures in polar and equatorial regions. If we follow the longitudes, the solar radiation is perpendicular to the equator. If we move to the northern hemisphere, the solar radiation is inclined and the amount of radiation is spread over a large area hence heating is not the same as that of the equator. Similarly, in the case of the southern hemisphere. The earth rotates once a year around the sun. This creates a temperature difference in the eastern and western regions. The rotation of the earth about its axis also creates temperature differences. Thus, due to all the above reasons, the uneven temperature difference and hence pressure difference develop global winds.

4.1.3 Some Commonly Used Terms in Wind Technology

Following are some commonly used terms in wind technologies.

(a) **Weather:** Weather represents the instantaneous state of the atmosphere in a particular region of the earth. The state may be temperature, pressure, rain, clouds, wind speed, etc.
(b) **Wind climate:** It is the climate in a wide sense. It may be the sum of weather at a particular location over the year.
(c) **Laminar wind:** The wind that flows in parallel with the ground surface is called laminar wind flow. The laminar flow of wind is the best-suited flow for electrical power generation.
(d) **Turbulence:** When the laminar flow of air is disturbed, it is called turbulence. The turbulence occurs

due to many effects like obstacles, the roughness of the surface, thermal effect, hills, buildings, etc. Thus, the wind speeds disturb due to turbulence. The winds take a different direction from the prevailing direction. These winds are called turbulent. Due to turbulence, the output power may be disturbed and may cause damage to the wind power plants.

(e) **Turbulence index:** It is used to measure the turbulence of wind as compared to average wind speed. It is given by equation (4.1), where σ is the standard deviation of wind speed and $\bar{v}$ is the mean wind speed.

$$\text{Turbulence index, TI}=\frac{\sigma}{\bar{v}} \tag{4.1}$$

(f) **Wind shear:** It is the change in wind speed and wind direction with height and is defined as the change in horizontal wind speed with the change in height.

4.1.4 Wind Profiling

Wind speed is affected by heights. To extract power from wind, winds power plants are situated about 150m to 200m above the ground. Wind profile or wind gradient is the variations of wind speed with height. This profile also changes with changes in the region like high rises, countryside, plains, or sea area. The roughness of the earth's surface changes the wind speed. Thus, the wind has a changing profile. Fig.4.1 shows some of the wind profiles. A factor called wind shear exponent or power law index, denoted by α is determined for each site. The magnitude of α carries the site-specific information. The expression for α is given by equation (4.2).

$$\alpha = \frac{\log_{10}\left(\frac{v_2}{v_1}\right)}{\log_{10}\left(\frac{h_2}{h_1}\right)} \tag{4.2}$$

where, v_1 = wind speed at height h_1, v_1 = wind speed at height h_1

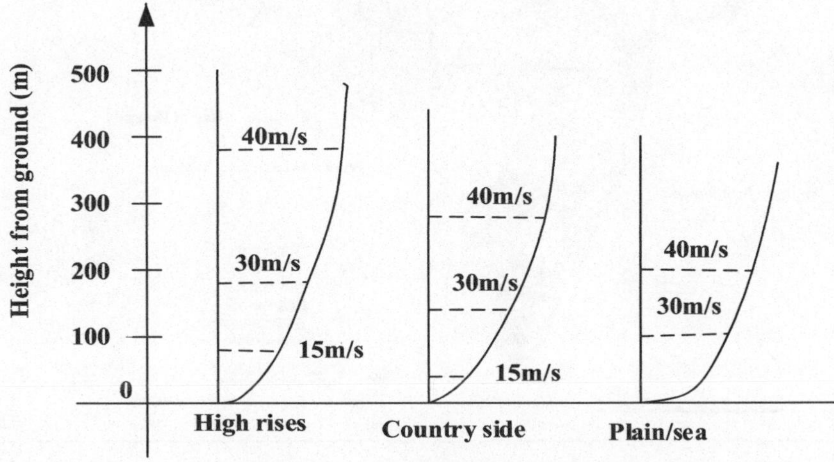

Fig.4.1: Wind gradient or profile

For long-term wind, a model called the power law model given by equation (4.3) is used.

$$\frac{v_2}{v_1} \left(\frac{h_2}{h_1}\right) \tag{4.3}$$

The value of α depends upon the roughness class. Its value is 0.1, 0.15, 0.2, and 0.3 for roughness class 0, 1, 2, and 3 respectively. The roughness is referred to the terrain and vegetation density of the land.

4.1.5 Wind Map of India

The national institute of wind energy (NIWE) in Chennai, India made regional surveys and wind resource maps at more than 97 sites that are suitable for wind power development at 30m and 50m heights. The map is shown in Fig.4.2. The NIWE is doing wind measurements at the greatest height at particular locations. The height is always specified on the wind map because the wind speed increases with height.

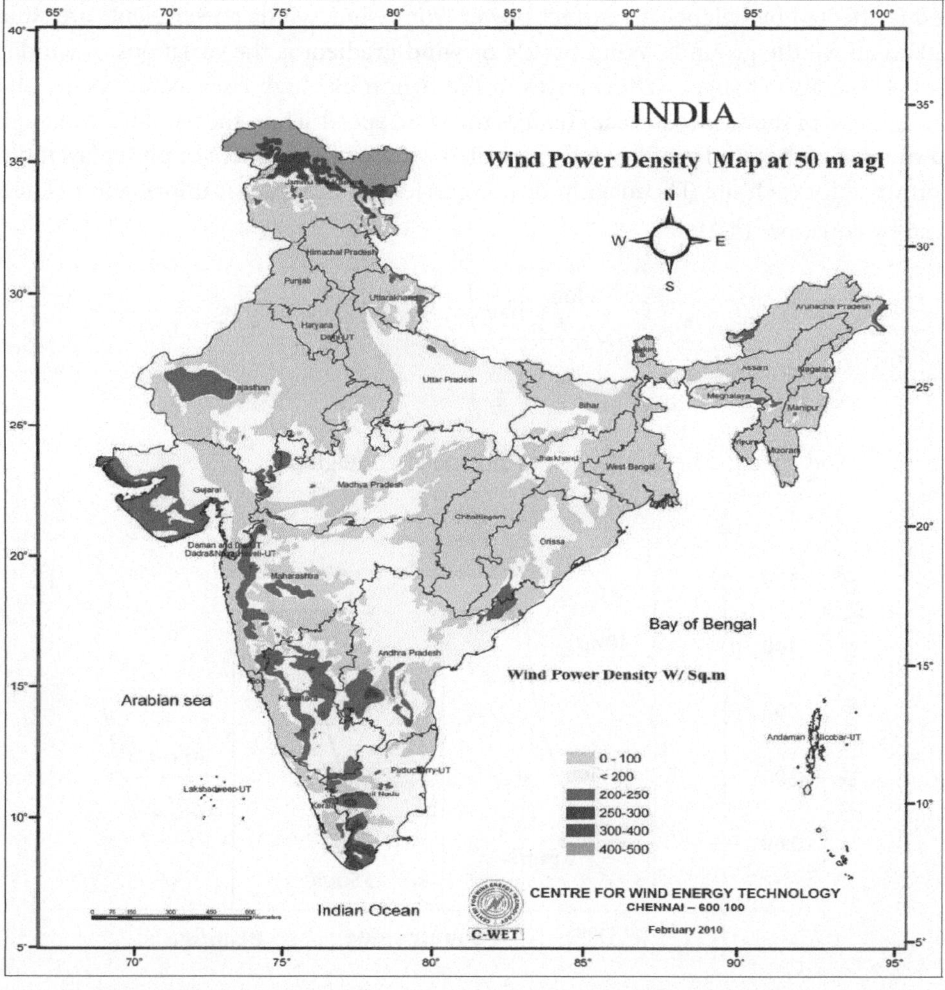

Fig. 4.2: Wind power generation in India (wind map) (Courtesy: www.niwe.nic.in)

4.2 ROTATION PRINCIPLE

There are two strategies for converting the kinetic energy of wind into mechanical energy. They are named as lift and drag principle. In both methods, the wind is slowed down to capture the kinetic energy. These principles will work only when there is a relative velocity between a moving fluid and an object. In the case of wind energy conversion, the wind is the moving fluid and the turbine blades are the objects. The drag is the force created by the drag principle and lift is the force created by the lift principle. The drag force is developed by creating turbulence in the flowing fluid (i.e wind). Drag force depends on exposing the wind to the flat or curved area on one side of the rotor and shielding the other side. The resulting differential drag force rotates the rotor. The drag force is a result of viscous frictional forces at the aerofoil surface and unequal pressure on the aerofoil surface facing towards and away from the oncoming flow. Modern large wind power plant works on the lift principle. The lift principle applies to streamlined objects such as fish, aircraft fuselage, and wing sections of aircraft, helicopters, etc. A wind turbine blade is also a streamlined object. When the air passed through the wind turbine blade, the air pressure on one side of the blade is reduced compared to another side. This causes the lift and drag force on the blade. The magnitude of both forces is different. The force of lift is stronger than the force of drag. Fig.4.3 depicts the lift and drag forces. The force parallel to the air steam is called the drag force. The force produced perpendicular to the air steam is called lift force.

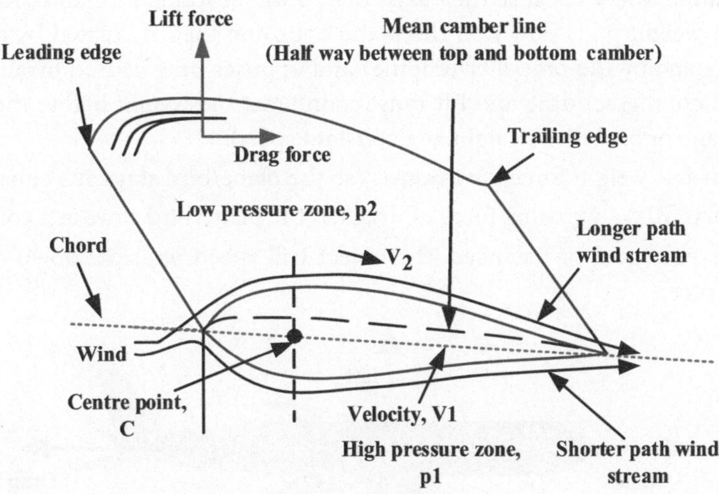

Fig. 4.3: (a) Aerofoil lift action

What is the relationship between lift and drag?

Drag is the price paid to obtain lift. The lift-to-drag ratio (L/D) is the amount of lift generated by a wing or airfoil compared to its drag. The L/D ratio is used to express the relation between lift and drag and is determined by dividing the lift coefficient (LC) by the drag coefficient(DC) (LC/DC).

How are lift and drag generated?

Fluid: Lift only generates when there is an interaction between a solid object and a fluid.

Motion: Lift only occurs when there is a difference in velocity between the solid object and fluid. This motion also introduces drag, which is called induced drag.

The science behind a flight or a bird

Four forces are acting on the Airplane. They are weight, lift, thrust and drag. It is known that gravity is a force that pulls everything toward the Earth's surface. This pull is called the weight force. Airplanes and birds have to be able to provide enough lift force to oppose the weight force. Lift is caused by the variation in air pressure when air flows under and over an airplane's wings. It acts upwards against weight and must be greater for the aircraft to fly. The power source of a bird or airplane provides the thrust. Thrust is the force that moves the object forward. Thrust is provided by

(a) Muscles – for birds and other flying animals
(b) Engines – for flying machines
(c) Gravity – for gliders that fly by always diving at a very shallow angle (birds do this too when they glide).

The force working against thrust is called drag. It is caused by air resistance and acts in the opposite direction to the motion. The amount of drag depends on the shape of the object, the density of the air, and the speed of the object. Thrust can overcome or counteract the force of drag. An object in flight is constantly engaging in a tug of war between the opposing forces of lift, weight (gravity), thrust, and drag. The flight depends on these forces – whether the lift force is greater than the weight force and whether the thrust is greater than the drag (friction) forces. The forces are shown in Fig.4.3 (b). Lift and drag are considered aerodynamic forces because they exist due to the movement of an object (such as a plane) through the air. The weight pulls down on the plane opposing the lift created by air flowing over the wing. Thrust is generated by the propeller (engine) and opposes drag caused by air resistance. During take-off, thrust must counteract drag and lift must counteract the weight before the plane can become airborne. If an airplane or bird flies straight at a constant speed:

(a) Lift force upwards = weight force downwards (so the plane/bird stays at a constant height)
(b) Thrust force forwards = opposing force of drag (so the plane/bird stays at a constant speed)

If the forces are not equal or balanced, the object will speed up, slow down or change direction toward the greatest force.

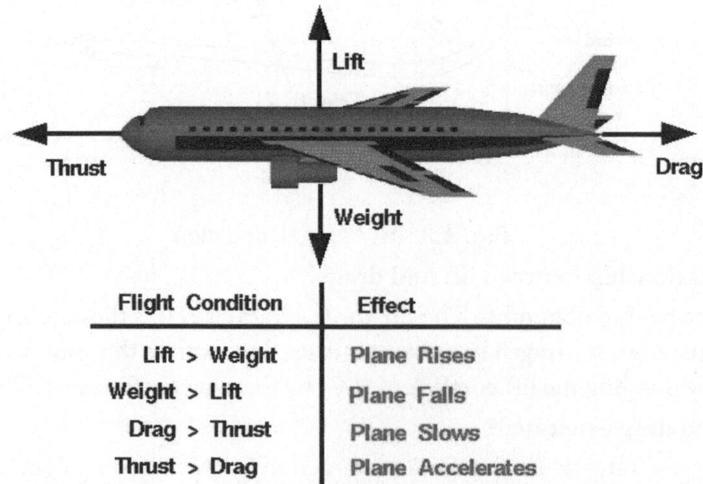

Flight Condition	Effect
Lift > Weight	Plane Rises
Weight > Lift	Plane Falls
Drag > Thrust	Plane Slows
Thrust > Drag	Plane Accelerates

Fig. 4.3: (b) Forces that govern the flight movement

(Courtesy: https:www.grc.nasa.gov/www/k-12/BGP/smotion.html)

4.3 WIND POWER AND ENERGY

4.3.1 Wind Power

According to the energy conversion theory, energy can neither be created nor destroyed but it can transform from one form to another. Wind energy is a special form of kinetic energy. The wind turbine rotor converts this kinetic energy into mechanical power. It is not possible to 100% kinetic energy of the wind into mechanical power. The speed of wind before it reaches the rotors is called upstream speed and the speed at which wind leaves the rotor is called downstream speed. The kinetic energy (E) of the wind depends on the moving air mass (m) and speed (v) and is calculated using (4.4).

$$E = \frac{1}{2} m v^2 \tag{4.4}$$

Wind power (P) is defined as the rate of change of wind energy (E) and is given in (4.5)

$$P_w = \frac{dE}{dt} = \frac{1}{2} \dot{m} v^2 \tag{4.5}$$

However, a small portion of wind power is converted into electrical power. When wind passes through the wind turbine and drives the blade to rotate, the corresponding mass flow rate ($\dot{m}$) is calculated using equation (4.6),

$$\dot{m} = \rho A v \tag{4.6}$$

where ρ is the air density factor (= 1.225 kg/m³), *A* is swept area (m²) of the blades as shown in Fig.4.4 (a) and *v* is the wind speed (m/s). Substituting (4.6) into (4.5), the available wind power (P_W) is obtained as (4.7).

$$P_w = \frac{1}{2} \rho A v_w^3 \tag{4.7}$$

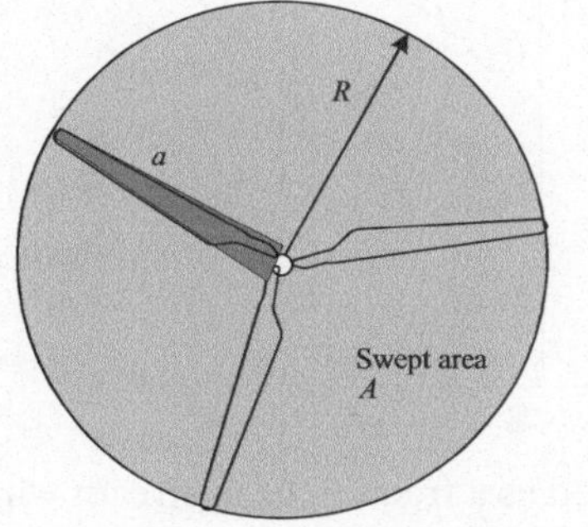

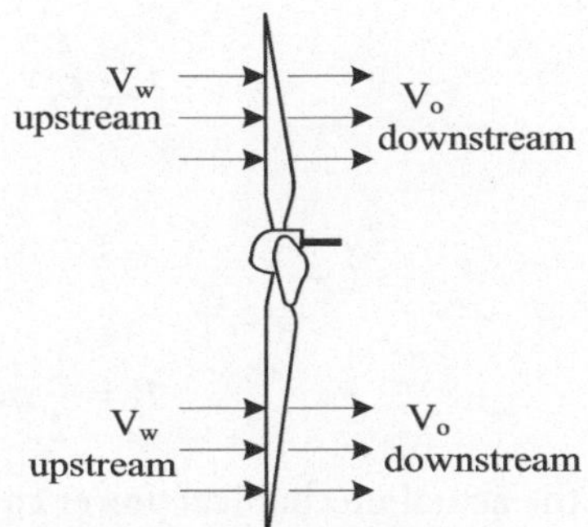

Fig. 4.4: (a) Swept area of wind turbine **Fig.4.4: (b)** Wind turbine with wind velocity

From equation (4.7), the wind power or undisturbed wind power depends on the swept area and the wind velocity of the location along with the air density. The upstream wind (i.e. wind just before reaching the wind turbine blade) or undisturbed wind power is directly proportional to the cubic power of the wind speed. Hence, the small variation in wind speed affects the huge change in wind power.

This power is called upstream wind power. The downstream wind means the wind which is after just leaving the wind turbine blade. It is not possible to extract all the upstream wind power from the wind turbine blades into downstream wind power because the downstream wind speed is less compared to the upstream wind speed.

4.3.2 Actual Wind Turbine Power

The upstream wind power is more than the downstream wind power. The difference between these two power is extracted by the wind rotor blades and is called actual mechanical power. This actual mechanical power is used for electric power generation via an induction generator. Fig.4.4(b) shows the upstream and downstream velocity of the moving air. The turbine output power (P_o) is given by (4.8), where v_w = upstream wind velocity, and v_o = downstream wind velocity.

$$P_o = \frac{1}{2} \times mass\ flow\ rate\ per\ second \times \left(v_w^2 - v_o^2\right) \tag{4.8}$$

The velocity of moving air is not continuous from the upstream wind velocity to the downstream wind velocity. The average velocity of the wind passing through the wind turbine rotor blades is calculated using equation (4.9).

$$v_{avg} = \frac{v_w + v_o}{2} \tag{4.9}$$

The mass flow rate of the moving air passing through the swept area (A) having an air density (ρ) is determined using (4.10).

$$\text{Mass flow rate second} = \rho A v_{avg} \tag{4.10}$$

Substituting (4.10) into (4.8), the actual mechanical power of the wind turbine rotor becomes as follows:

$$P_o = \frac{1}{2}\left[\rho A \frac{v_w + v_o}{2}\right] \times \left(v_w^2 - v_o^2\right) \tag{4.11}$$

Equation (4.11) can be rearranged as (4.12) and (4.13).

$$P_o = \frac{1}{2} v_w \left[\rho A \frac{1 + \left(\frac{v_o}{v_w}\right)}{2}\right] \times v_w^2 \left(1 - \frac{v_o^2}{v_w^2}\right) \tag{4.12}$$

$$P_o = \frac{1}{2} \rho A v_w^3 \times \frac{\left(1 + \frac{v_o}{v_w}\right)\left[1 - \left(\frac{v_o}{v_w}\right)^2\right]}{2} \tag{4.13}$$

Typically, the actual mechanical power can be expressed as a fraction of upstream wind power and is given by (4.14)

$$P_o = \frac{1}{2} \rho A v_w^3 C_p \tag{4.14}$$

where

$$C_p = \frac{\left(1 + \frac{v_o}{v_w}\right)\left[1 - \left(\frac{v_o}{v_w}\right)^2\right]}{2} \tag{4.15}$$

The factor C_p is called the power coefficient of the wind turbine rotor or the efficiency of the wind turbine rotor. This factor is the fraction of the upstream wind power, which is captured by rotor blades. It is also defined as the ratio (given by (4.16)) between the actual mechanical power outputs of the rotor blades to the upstream wind power.

$$C_p = \frac{P_o}{P_w} \tag{4.16}$$

There is an optimum downstream wind velocity, $v_{o,opt}$ that results in maximum output power, P_{max} which can be obtained as follows:

$$\frac{dP_o}{dv_o} = 0 \tag{4.17}$$

Where, $P_o = \frac{1}{4}\rho A(v_w + v_o)(v_w^2 - v_o^2)$, $\frac{dP_o}{dv_o} = \frac{1}{4}\rho A(-2v_w v_o + v_w^2 - 3v_o^2)$

After simplification, the expression for $v_{o,opt}$ is obtained as $v_{o,opt} = \frac{1}{3}v_w$

The ratio of v_o/v_w determines the C_P value for a specific upstream wind speed. Fig.4.5 shows the power coefficient vs v_o/v_w for a single maximum value of C_P. The maximum value of C_P is 0.59 when v_o/v_w is one-third at optimum condition.

$$C_p = \frac{\left(1+\frac{1}{3}\right)\left[1-\left(\frac{1}{3}\right)^2\right]}{2} = \frac{1.333\times\left(1-\frac{1}{9}\right)}{2}$$

$$= \frac{1.333\times 0.889}{2} = 0.5911 = 59.11\%$$

For maximum mechanical power of the rotor blades is extracted from the wind speed, when the ratio of downstream to upstream wind speed is (1/3). For this condition.

$$P_{max} = 0.295\rho A v_w^3 \tag{4.18}$$

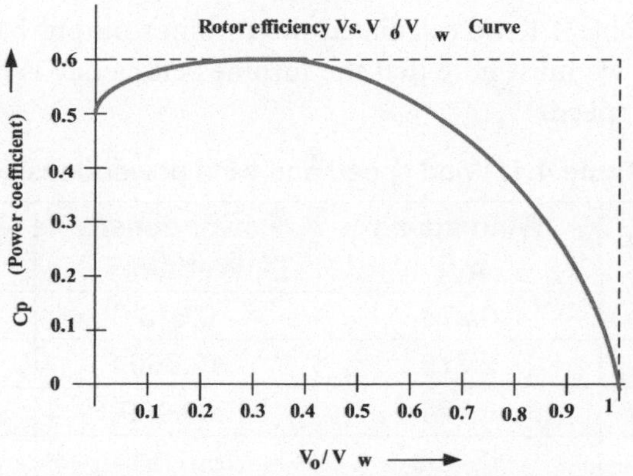

Fig. 4.5: Wind turbine rotor efficiency curve

The theoretical maximum value of C_P is 0.5911. For practical design, the maximum C_P value is less than 0.5 for high-speed, two-blade wind turbines, and between 0.2 and 0.4 for slow-speed wind turbines with more blades.

3.3.3 Energy Production

The main factor of the wind energy extraction from the wind turbine is the wind condition where it is installed. For a specific period, estimating the wind energy production depends on the frequency distribution of the wind speed at the hub height of the wind turbine. Let's say, in a year, the mean wind speed v_{mean} is calculated for a particular location based on n number of observations for the wind speed (v) data using (4.19).

$$v_{mean} = \frac{\sum_{i=1}^{n} v_i}{n} \tag{4.19}$$

The energy production from a wind turbine in a year depends on the average wind speed and wind frequency distribution at that particular site. When the frequency distribution interval is small, the wind is relatively consistent at that point, however, when the frequency distribution interval is large, the wind is highly variable.

3.3.4 Wind Power Density

The wind power produced from the wind turbine per unit swept area is called wind power density (WPD). It is calculated using (4.20).

$$\frac{P_w}{A} = \frac{1}{2}\rho v_w^3 \text{ watt/m}^2 \tag{4.20}$$

The wind power density value depends on the wind speed, wind speed frequency distribution, and air density at any particular location. The unit of WPD is watt per square meter (W/m^2). The monthly WPD is calculated using (4.21), in which v_h = wind speed value at h hour, N = total number of hours, and $\rho =$ air density in kg/m^3.

$$WPD = \frac{\frac{1}{2}\rho\sum_{h=1}^{N} v_h^3}{N} \tag{4.21}$$

In the last column of Table 4.1, we calculated the turbine's output based on the assumption that it is 30% efficient. However, we must note that the turbine's efficiency is dependent on wind speed. It fluctuates according to wind speed.

Table 4.1: Wind speed and wind power density

Wind Speed kmph	Wind speed m/s	Power density Watts/m^2	Turbine output 30% efficiency
1	0.278	0.013	0.004
10	2.778	12.860	3.858
25	6.944	200.939	60.282
50	13.889	1607.510	482.253
75	20.833	5425.347	1627.604
100	27.778	12860.082	3858.025
125	34.722	25117.348	7535.204

Fig.4.6 shows how the wind power density varies with the wind speed. The WPD changes the cubic power of wind speed at air density ρ = 1.225 kg/m3.

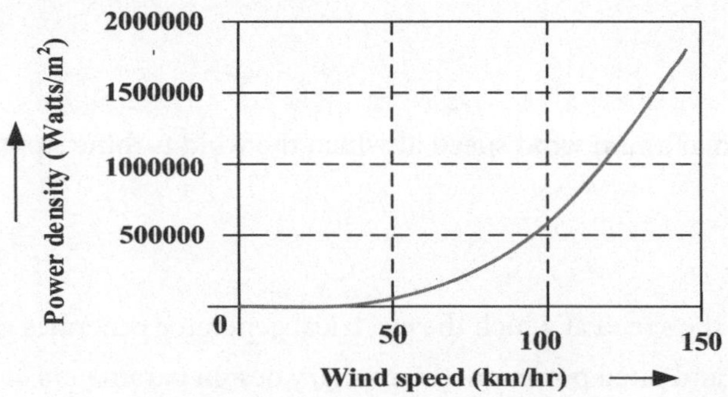

Fig.4.6: Speed vs power density

3.3.5 Relationship Between Energy and Power

Energy is defined as the product of power and time during the period when the power is used. The mathematical representation of the energy is given in (4.22), where, E = energy, P = power, and t = time.

$$E = P \times t \tag{4.22}$$

The watt-hour (Wh) or kilowatt-hour (kWh) is the unit of energy. If a wind turbine gives 100 kW power for 2 hours then the energy produces 200 kWh. If a wind turbine generates 150 kW as average power during a year, then 150×365×24 kWh energy produces per year.

4.4 OPERATING CHARACTERISTICS OF WIND TURBINE

The wind turbine cannot work continuously against the wind speed. It has some operating characteristics and these are explained below. A typical wind turbine power curve is shown in Fig. 4.7.

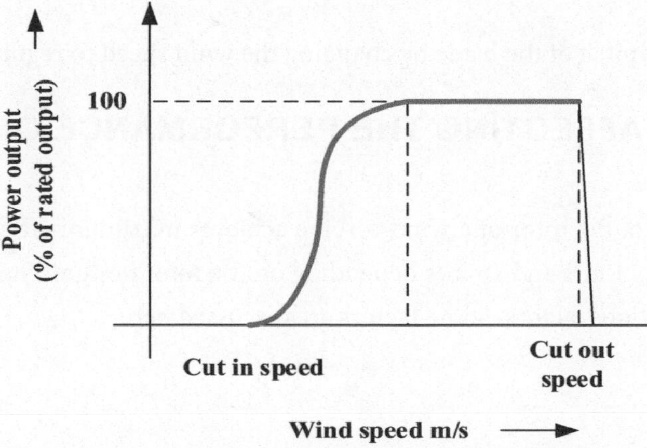

Fig. 4.7: Typical wind turbine power curve

Cut-in Speed

Cut-in speed is the minimum wind speed at which the wind turbine starts operating. This speed is typically 4 m/s.

Cut-out Speed

The cut-out speed is the maximum wind speed at which the wind turbine stops operating. This speed is typically 14 m/s.

Rated Speed

Rated speed is defined as the speed at which the electrical generator generates rated power or maximum power. Rated wind speed and rated power are the primary design parameters of the wind turbine design. The rated speed for most of the machines is in the range of 11 to 16 m/s.

Betz Limit

According to Betz's law, a wind turbine rotor can extract not more than 59.3% of the kinetic energy of the wind. This value is theoretical and is also known as the Betz limit. In practice, the wind turbine rotor efficiency is not more than 59%. More typical efficiency is 35% to 45%.

Pitch Angle (β)

If the wind velocity is below the cut-in speed then the wind turbine is stopped using a brake. Similarly, above the cut-out speed of the wind turbine, it is not operated. The wind turbine blade never keeps perpendicular and parallel to the wind. If the blade is perpendicular to the wind then more stress on the blade and it may be damaged. If the blade is parallel with the wind then the blade is not moving. To reduce stress on the blade, they are tilted at an angle and this angle is called the pitch angle (β).

Pitch Control

It is used to change the pitch of the blade by changing the wind speed to regulate the rotor speed.

4.5 FACTORS AFFECTING THE PERFORMANCE OF WIND TURBINE ROTOR

At the rated wind speed, the rotor of a wind turbine achieves maximum efficiency. Typically, the rated wind speed is between 11 m/s and 16 m/s depending on the rotor design. The performance of the wind turbine depends on various factors. Some factors are discussed here.

(a) Tip speed

(b) Tip speed ratio (TSR)

(c) Aerodynamic efficiency C_P or power efficiency coefficient

(d) Solidity

(a) **Tip Speed:** When the blades of a wind turbine spin, the tip moves faster than the middle, while the root, which is close to the hub, moves at a constant speed. For a modern wind turbine, the blade tip speed is 10 times more than the wind speed. If the wind speed is say 5 m/s, then the speed of the blade tip is 50 m/s. The blade tip speed is directly proportional to the blade length or radius of the wind turbine rotor and RPM. The tip speed is calculated as (4.23).

$$v_{tip} = \frac{2\pi RN}{60}\,\text{m/s} \tag{4.23}$$

Where, N = RPM of the rotor, R = radius of the rotor.

(b) **Tip Speed Ratio (TSR):** TSR is defined as the ratio of the linear speed of the wind turbine rotor's outermost tip speed (tip) to the upstream wind velocity (vo). It is represented by λ and is calculated as follows:

$$\text{Tip speed ratio (TSR), } \lambda = \frac{\text{Blade tip speed } v_{tip}\,(\omega R)}{\text{upstream wind speed, } v_o} \tag{4.24}$$

$$\lambda = \frac{\omega R}{v_o} \tag{4.25}$$

$$v_o = \frac{2\pi NR}{\lambda} \tag{4.26}$$

Where ω = 2πN the angular speed (rad/s) at the blade tip, R = Rotor radius (m), Vo = undisturbed wind speed (m/s). For a specific wind speed, the λ value is increased if the swept area increases. Usually, a higher value of λ is preferred but not the point where the wind turbine produces noise. At a lower value of λ, the torque of the wind turbine rotor is lower and rotates at a slower speed. For a high value of λ, the turbine rotor has low torque but rotates at high shaft speed. For a smooth generation of electric energy, a higher value of λ is suitable. A higher RPM of the rotor provides more noise. Thus, the modern wind power plant has a large rotor diameter and low RPM.

(c) **Aerodynamic Efficiency or Power Efficiency Coefficient (C_p):** Wind energy conversion depends on the CP value of the aerodynamic system. The ratio of actual electrical power produced by the wind turbine to the upstream wind power is defined as CP. The maximum value of CP is 59%. The power coefficient CP depends on the blade pitch angle β and λ and is presented as the CP-λ curve of a wind turbine (Fig.4.8). The aerodynamic analysis of the wind flows around the rotating blade with a pitch angle (β) establishes the relationship between the rotor tip speed ratio (λ) and the wind speed. It is given by (4.27).

$$C_P(\lambda,\beta) = 0.5176\left[\frac{116}{\lambda} - 0.4\beta - 5\right]e^{-21/\lambda} + 0.0068\lambda$$

$$\frac{1}{\lambda_i} = \frac{1}{\lambda + 0.08\beta} - \frac{0.035}{\beta^3 + 1} \qquad 0 \le \beta \le 27^o$$

$$C_P = \frac{\text{Actual power extracted by the rotor}}{\text{Total power available in the upstream wind}} = \frac{P_{actual}}{P_{total}} \tag{4.27}$$

Where $P_{total} = \frac{1}{2}\rho A v^3$

The actual power that a WPP can attain is expressed as (4.28), Where C_p = power coefficient, ρ = air density, A = swept Area, and v = wind speed.

$$P_{actual} = \frac{1}{2}\rho A v^3 C_p \tag{4.28}$$

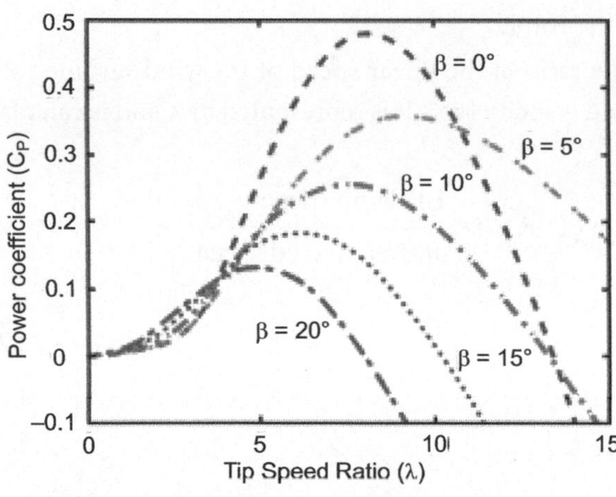

Fig. 4.8: $C_P - \lambda$ curve

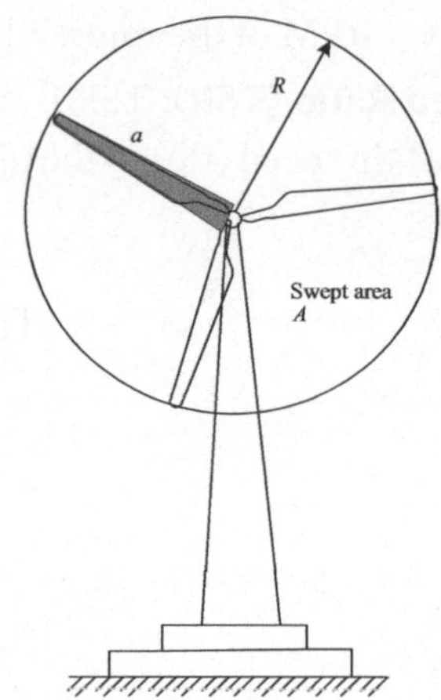

Fig. 4.9: Solidity of wind turbine

(d) **Solidity (σ):** Solidity is defined as the ratio of the overall area of the wind turbine blades to the swept area of the wind turbine rotor. Fig.4.9 shows the various parameters to calculate the solidity. It is calculated using (4.29). in which n = number of blades, R = Radius of the wind turbine rotor, a = projected area of a single blade.

$$\text{Solidity, } \sigma = \frac{\text{Projected blade area}}{\text{Total swept area}} = \frac{na}{2\pi R} \tag{4.29}$$

Maximum power coefficient (C_P) is achieved at a lower tip speed ratio as solidity increases. When a wind turbine has three blades and each blade has *an* area then the total projected blade area is *3a*. The solidity of the wind turbine having three blades is calculated using (4.30).

$$\sigma = \frac{3a}{2\pi R} \tag{4.30}$$

4.6 MAIN COMPONENTS OF A WIND TURBINE

A wind turbine has a tower and a nacelle. The nacelle is made up of several parts, each of which serves a distinct purpose in the process of converting wind energy into electrical energy. Wind turbines have an aerodynamic rotor, transmission system (gearbox), generator, power electronic interfaces, and control system. The picture of the nacelle and rotor of a three-bladed geared wind power plant is shown in Fig.4.10.

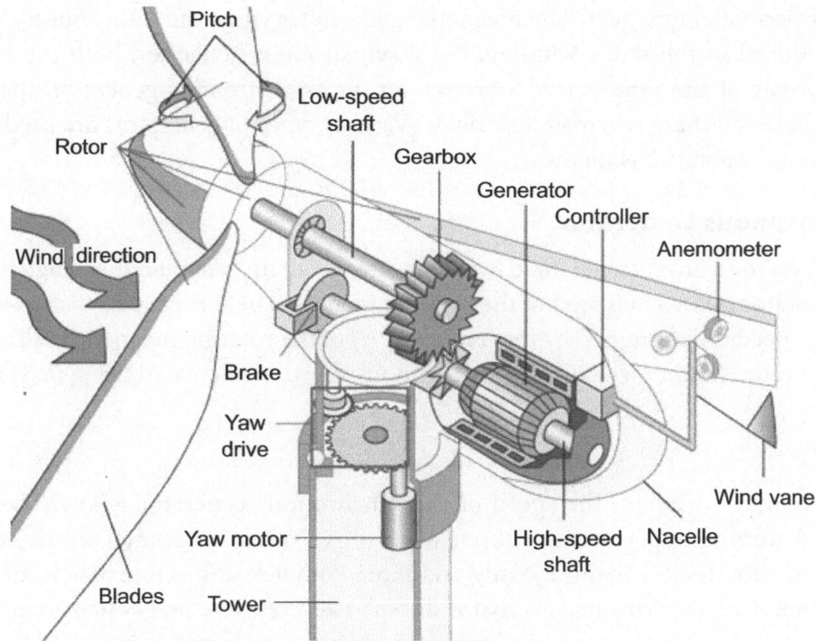

Fig. 4.10: Nacelle and rotor of three-bladed geared wind power plant (Courtesy: electricalacademia.com)

4.6.1 Aerodynamic Rotor

The aerodynamic rotor of the wind turbine is essentially made up of a rotor hub and blades. The blades are connected to the hub, and the hub is connected to the main shaft. The aerodynamic rotor captures the upstream wind power and converts it into mechanical power. The aerodynamic rotor hub is connected to the gearbox through a low-speed shaft. Typically, there are two or three blades on a modern wind turbine.

4.6.2 Transmission System

The actual mechanical power is transmitted to the electrical generator through a transmission system. The transmission system comprises a rotor shaft, gearbox, and brakes. The mechanical brake system is used to stop the wind turbine when the wind speed is below the cut-in speed and above the cut-out speed. The wind velocity is not constant at all times. To match the rated speed of the generator, a gearbox mechanism is required. The gear ratio is usually 1:80, 10:800, etc. Gearboxes are often classified into two types based on their geometrical design. The first one is a pair of gear wheels with parallel axes called a spur and helical gearbox. The second one is a planetary gearbox. It is made up of trains of gear wheels that rotate around each other.

4.6.3 Generator

The generator is an electromechanical component. It converts mechanical power into electrical power. It has a stator and a rotor. The stator is stationary and interconnected to the grid. The rotor is the rotating part of the generator. The rotor comprises the magnetic field system. The magnetic field may be an electromagnet or permanent magnet. The magnetic field rotates when the rotor rotates. When the rotor rotates, emf is induced in the stator winding. For a synchronous generator, both the stator and rotor magnetic fields rotate at the same speed whereas, for an asynchronous generator, there is a relative speed difference between these two magnetic fields. Various types of generators are used in wind power technology. They are explained as follows.

4.6.3.1 Synchronous Generator

Permanent magnets or conventional field winding are used to generate the magnetic field of the synchronous generator (SG). The speed of the rotating magnetic field is called synchronous speed (N_s). The synchronous speed is determined by the frequency (*f*) of the rotating magnetic field and the number of poles (p) of the rotor. Mathematically the synchronous speed is calculated using (4.31).

$$N_s = \frac{120f}{p} \tag{4.31}$$

For a large number of poles, the speed of the synchronous generator is low. The SG is used in direct-drive wind turbine applications without a gearbox. When compared to an equivalent-sized asynchronous generator, the SG is more costly and more complex. It has one major advantage over an asynchronous generator. The advantage is that it doesn't need reactive magnetizing current or reactive power compensation equipment. In the wind turbine industry, two common types of SGs are used. They are named as wound rotor synchronous generators (WRSG), and

Wound Rotor Synchronous Generator (WRSG)

The stator windings of the wound rotor synchronous generator (WRSG) are directly connected to the grid. Direct current (DC) flowing through the field winding creates the magnetic field, which rotates at a synchronous speed.

Permanent Magnet Synchronous Generator (PMSG)

The stator is wound and the rotor has permanent magnet poles. It has high efficiency as its excitation is provided without any energy supply. However, the materials necessary to make permanent magnets are costly and difficult to produce. A full-scale power converter must also be used when using permanent magnets to excite them to convert the frequency and voltage of generation to the frequency and voltage of transmission, respectively.

4.6.3.2 Asynchronous (Induction) Generator

The asynchronous generator's merits are its robustness, mechanical simplicity, and low price. The stator of an asynchronous generator needs a reactive magnetizing current for excitation. It does not have a permanent magnet and is not separately excited. The grid provides the reactive power for the excitation of the asynchronous generator. In the asynchronous generator, the rotor never attains synchronous speed. Hence, an electric field is induced between the rotor and the rotating stator magnetic field by a relative motion called slip (s), which causes a current in the rotor winding. The slip is expressed as (4.32).

$$\text{Slip, } s = N_s - N_r \tag{4.32}$$

Where N_s is the synchronous speed and N_r is the rotor speed. Usually, slip speed is expressed as a fraction of synchronous speed. Normally, it is expressed in percentage (%). The same is given by (4.33).

$$\text{Slip, s} = \frac{N_S - N_r}{N_s} \quad \text{Or Slip, s} = \frac{N_S - N_r}{N_s} \times 100\% \tag{4.33}$$

The speed of the induction motor is always less than the synchronous speed. In the case of an induction generator, the speed of the generator is always greater than the synchronous speed. Thus, it is seen from the above equation that, the slip is positive in the case of the induction motor and negative in the case of the induction generator. A torque acts on the rotor as a result of the interaction between the related magnetic field of the rotor and the stator field. For an asynchronous generator, the rotor is designed as a wound rotor or short-circuit rotor. Short-circuit rotor is also called a squirrel cage rotor and the other is called a wound rotor. Based on the rotor the induction generator is of two types namely **squirrel-cage induction generator (SCIG) and wound rotor induction generator (WRIG).** There is another induction generator called a **doubly fed induction generator (DFIG)**. The details of DFIG will be discussed in section 4.8.

4.6.4 Power Electronic Interface

The mechanical power of the wind turbine is converted into electrical power by the generator and supplied to the power grid via a power electronic interface. As it is installed in between the grid and generator, it should maintain both side's requirements and should be cost-effective. This interface on the generator side makes sure that the turbine's rotational speed is continuously changed to capture the maximum power achievable from the wind. The power electronic interface on the grid side complies with the grid codes like the ability to regulate reactive and active power, voltage, and frequency control irrespective of wind speed.

4.6.5 Control System of Wind Turbine Technologies

A control system is typically part of wind turbine technologies. It is used to operate the wind turbine smoothly under various operational conditions. By passive or active mechanisms, the control system keeps the wind turbine within its typical working range. The passive control mechanism is activated either rotor automatically reduces aerodynamic efficiency or wind speed exceeds a threshold value based on their sensing system. Active controls employ mechanical, electrical, pneumatic, or hydraulic means, as well as transducers to sense the variables that will decide the required control action. Typical variables that are monitored by a control system include the speed of the wind, the speed of the rotor, reactive and active power, voltage, and frequency at the point of integration for the wind turbine. Additionally, if necessary the control system must be capable of stopping the wind turbine.Active control of wind turbines aims to increase power output while decreasing the mechanical components' structural loads, hence extending their useful life and decreasing maintenance costs. The control system is designed in such a way that the wind turbine generates maximum output power even if low wind speeds. If the wind speed becomes more than the rate wind speed, the control system is designed in such a way that the wind power generation should not exceed the rate power value. This is done by reducing the driving force on the rotor blades and reducing the load on the turbine.Currently, there are three ways to control the power output of the wind turbine namely stall, pitch, and active stall control. The key difference between these methods is how the rotor's aerodynamic efficiency is regulated to avoid overloading.

Stall control (passive control): It is the easiest, most reliable, and least expensive way to control power. Here, the blades are attached to the hub and the wind attack angle is fixed. Aerodynamic rotor design leads the rotor to stall "automatically" (losing efficiency) when wind speed exceeds the rated value.

Pitch control (active control): The modern wind turbine's pitch control mechanism is an essential component. To keep the power output constant, the pitch control system must be able to change the pitch angle by a fraction of a degree at a time when the wind speed changes. This is because (1) the pitch control system keeps adjusting the angle of the wind turbine's blades to improve the efficiency of converting wind energy and the stability of power production, (2) it also acts as a safety system in case of high wind speeds or other emergencies.

Active stall control: As the name suggests, this type of wind turbine keeps the blades from stopping by tilting them in the opposite direction of a pitch-controlled wind turbine. This increases the rotor blades' angle of attack for a deeper stall and a larger angle of attack. Active stall control is better than stall control because it can adjust for changes in the density of the air.

4.6.6 Tower

The tower of the wind turbine carries the nacelle and rotor. Wind turbine towers are not only supported structures but also allow their blades to safely clear the ground and access stronger winds found at higher altitudes. The maximum height of the tower is optional, except where area restrictions apply. The cost of larger towers will be weighed against the increase in energy production they provide. Studies have demonstrated that the additional cost of raising tower height is frequently justified by the more energy provided by stronger winds. Large wind turbines are installed on 40-to 70-meter towers. Small wind systems typically use "guyed" designs for their towers. This indicates that three or four sides of the tower are supported by guy wires anchored to the ground. Although these towers are less expensive than free-standing towers, they need a larger area of ground to anchor the guy wires. These guyed towers are sometimes tilted up. This may be done rapidly with a winch and a turbine positioned on the tower. This makes both installation and maintenance simpler. Towers can be made of a tube, a wooden pole, tubes, rods, and angle iron. Depending on the design, large wind turbines can be installed on either lattice towers, tube towers, or guyed tilt-up towers. Towers have to be constructed to be strong enough to support wind turbines and to survive vibration, wind loads, and weather for their entire lifespan.

4.6.7 Yaw System

The yaw system of a wind turbine consists of the yaw drive and yaw bearing. It is situated near the bottom of the mainframe of the nacelle. The wind direction is identified by using a wind vane whereas the speed of the wind is measured using the anemometer. Based on wind vane and anemometer information, an electronic controller commands the yaw drive to orient the wind turbine properly concerning the wind. Each wind turbine usually has at least two yaw drives. The tower's stability is ensured by the moderate rate of yawing, which is necessary to mitigate the effects of enormous forces on the tower.

4.7 CLASSIFICATION OF WIND TURBINE

Wind turbines are categorized based on their turbine generator design, airflow route relative to the turbine rotor, capacity of a wind turbine, generator-driving pattern, power supply method, and turbine installation site.

(a) Horizontal-axis and vertical-axis wind turbines.
(b) Upwind and downwind wind turbines.
(c) Small and large wind turbines.
(d) Direct drive and gear drive wind turbine.
(e) On-grid and off-grid wind turbines.
(f) Offshore and onshore WPP.
(g) Fixed speed and variable speed wind turbine.

4.7.1 Horizontal and Vertical Axis Wind Turbines

Modern wind turbines can be divided into two groups based on how the rotating axis of the rotor blades is set up. They are horizontal-axis wind turbines (HAWT) and vertical-axis wind turbines (VAWT). The majority of wind turbines used for commercial purposes are HAWT. This kind of wind turbine has an axis of rotation that is parallel to the direction that the wind is blowing. Fig.4.11(a) shows a typical HAWT and Fig.4.11 (b) shows the structure of HAWT. These wind turbines have a cheap cost per unit of power production in addition to their high efficiency as turbines, high power density, low wind speeds at which they cut in, and low cut-in speeds. Wind turbines with blades that spin on an axis perpendicular to the ground are said to have a vertical axis. It is independent of wind direction i.e., any direction of the wind is accepted by the vertical axis wind turbine (VAWT). Fig.4.12 shows the structure of a VAWT. Hence, there is no requirement for the Yaw control technique. Since the generator, brake, rotor bearing, gearbox, etc. are installed on the ground. The wind tower design and construction are very simple, hence reducing the cost of the turbine. However, vertical-axis wind turbines must have an external energy source to start.

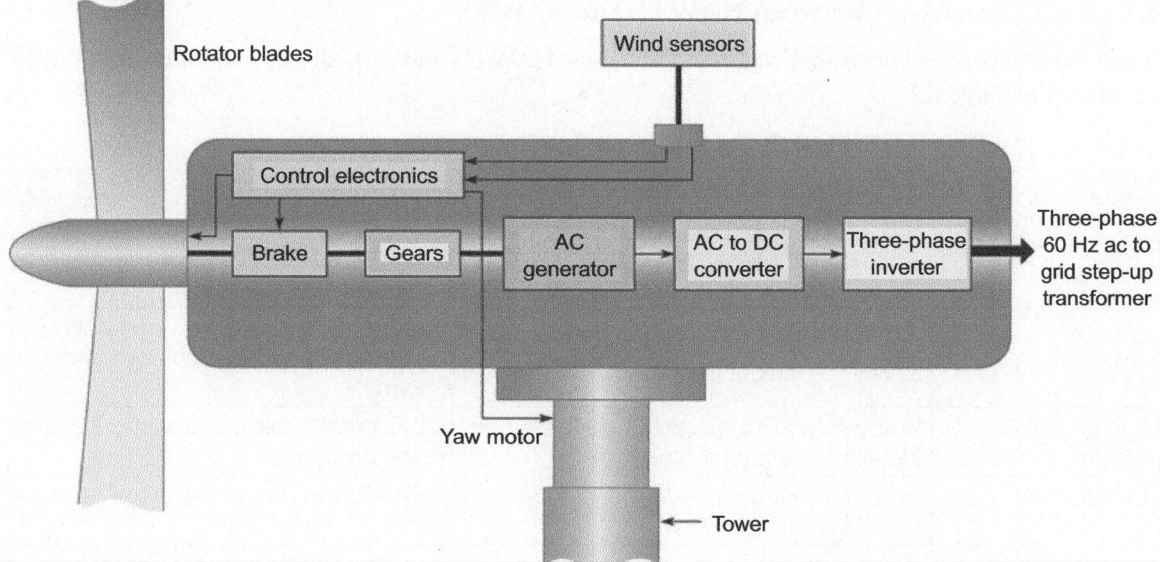

Fig. 4.11: (a) Typical horizontal axis wind turbine (Courtesy: electricalacademia.com)

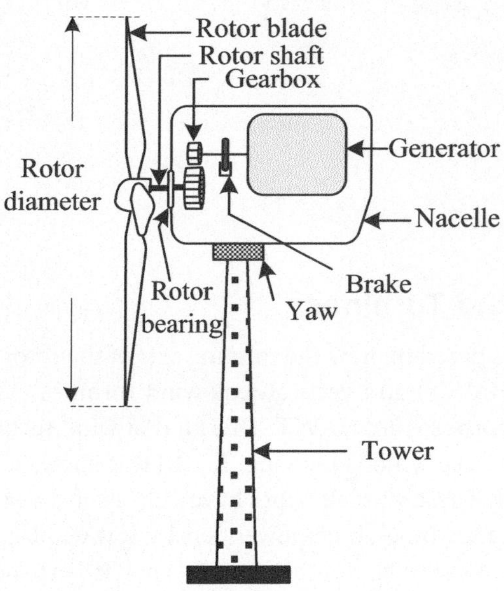

Fig. 4.11: (b) HAWT structure

Fig.4.12: VAWT structure

The maximum possible height of the wind turbine is thus restricted because it only has one end supported at the ground. Vertical-axis wind turbines are rare due to their low efficiency. Vertical axis designs include the Darrieus with curved blades and 35% efficiency, the Giromill with straight blades and 35% efficiency, and the Savonius with scoops and 30% efficiency.

4.7.1.1 Comparison Between HAWTS and VAWTS

A comparison between horizontal axis wind turbines (HAWT)s and vertical axis wind turbines (VAWT) s are listed in Table.4.2

Table 4.2: Comparison between HAWTs and VAWTs

Basis of Difference	Horizontal Axis Wind Turbine (HAWT)	Vertical Axis Wind Turbine (VAWT)
Definition	A HAWT is one whose axis of rotation is horizontal.	A wind turbine is called a VAWT if its axis of rotation is vertical.
Axis of rotation	For the HAWT, the axis of rotation of the turbine is parallel to the wind stream.	For the VAWT, the axis of rotation of the turbine is perpendicular to the wind stream.
Location of electric generator	In the HAWT, the electric generator is installed at the top of the tower.	In the VAWT, the generator is installed on the ground.
Location of gearbox	In HAWT, the gearbox is installed at the top of the turbine tower.	In VAWT, the gearbox is installed at the bottom of the turbine.
Need of yaw mechanism	In the HAWT, the yaw mechanism is required to orient the turbine in the direction of the wind.	The VAWT does not require a yaw mechanism because it receives wind from all directions.

Self-starting	Horizontal axis wind turbine is self-starting.	It is not self-starting; hence a starting mechanism is required to start it from a stationary position.
Design and installation	The design and installation of a HAWT are complex.	The design and installation of a VAWT are comparatively simple.
Operation space of blades	It requires a large space for the blade's operation.	It requires a small space for the blade's operation.
Dependency on wind direction	The operation of HAWT is dependent on wind direction.	The operation of VAWT is independent of the wind direction because it receives wind from all directions.
Height from ground	The height of the HAWT from the ground is large.	It is installed at a comparatively smaller distance from the ground.
Need of nacelle	In the case of HAWTs, a heavy nacelle is installed at the top of the tower.	There is no need for nacelle in the case of VAWTs.
Power coefficient	HAWT has a high-power coefficient.	It has a low power coefficient.
Tip speed ratio (TSR)	It has a high tip-speed ratio.	It has a considerably low tip speed ratio.
Noise produced	The operation of HAWT is noisy.	These turbines produce comparatively less noise.
Efficiency	The ideal efficiency of HAWT is around 50% to 60 %.	The ideal efficiency of VAWT is usually more than 70%.
Hindrance for birds	They cause high obstruction for birds.	They cause less hindrance for birds.
Cost	They are more expensive due to their complex design and installation.	They are less expensive because their design and installation are quite simple.

4.7.1.2 The Advantages and Disadvantages of Horizontal and Vertical Axis Wind Turbines

There are a few advantages and disadvantages of the horizontal axis and vertical axis wind turbines. They are listed in Table.4.3.

Table 4.3: The advantages and disadvantages of horizontal and vertical axis wind turbines

Types	Advantages	Disadvantages
HAWT	Energy conversion efficiency is high. High tower provides access to stronger wind. At high wind speeds, power is regulated through stall and pitch angle control.	Installation costs are higher, and the tower needs to be stronger to hold up the heavy nacelle. Need large cable from tower top to ground. Yaw control technique is necessary.
VAWT	Due to the ground-level gearbox and generator, installation costs are reduced and maintenance is simplified. Operation does not depend on the wind direction. Suitable for rooftops	Wind energy conversion efficiency is low. Changes in torque and mechanical vibrations are common. At high wind speeds, no options for power regulation.

4.7.2 Upwind And Downwind Wind Turbines

Horizontal-axis wind turbines can be further divided into upwind and downwind wind turbines based on how the wind rotor is set up in the direction of the wind. Most horizontal-axis wind turbines in operation right now are upwind turbines. In an upwind wind turbine rotor is facing the wind. Upwind designs avoid flow field distortion when the wind goes through the tower and nacelle. When the wind blows through a downwind turbine, it first passes through the nacelle and the tower before reaching the rotor blades. Without taking tower strike into account, this setup makes it possible to give the rotor blades more flexibility. Downwind turbine output changes drastically because the waves behind the tower and nacelle are distorted and unstable. In addition, an unstable flow field can increase aerodynamic losses and turbine fatigue stresses. A downwind wind turbine's blades may make impulsive or pounding noise.

4.7.3 Small And Large Wind Turbines

Wind turbines are categorized by their rated capabilities namely small, medium, and large wind turbines. Typically, wind turbines with an output power of under 100 kW are referred to as small wind turbines (SWTs). In rural areas, SWTs have been widely employed at homes, farms, and other remote individual applications like water pumping stations, telecom sites, etc. Distributed small wind turbines can enhance local electricity supplies while postponing or avoiding the need to expand transmission line capacity. The majority of wind turbines are medium-sized and have power outputs between 100 kW and 1 MW. This type of wind turbine can be used for village power, distributed power, hybrid systems, wind power plants, etc., both on-grid and off-grid.

Large wind turbines are those with a power output of 10 MW or more. Large-scale wind turbines that can generate multiple megawatts have recently become the norm in the global wind power market. Currently, megawatt wind turbines are used in the majority of wind farms, particularly offshore ones. Wind turbines having a capacity greater than 10 MW are considered ultra-large. Research and development for this sort of wind turbine are still in their early phases.

4.7.4 Direct and Geared Drive Wind Turbine

The drivetrain configuration of a wind generating system determines whether a wind turbine is a direct drive or geared drive group. In geared drive turbine has a gearbox. This gearbox may be multi-stage or single-stage depending on the requirements. The wind turbine rotor is connected to the generator via a gearbox. The low-speed wind turbine rotor shaft achieves the generator-rated speed via the gearbox. Geared generator systems have the benefits of being less expensive, smaller, and lighter. However, using a gearbox can reduce the reliability of wind turbines, as well as raise noise levels and mechanical losses. In a direct-drive wind turbine generator system, the gearbox is not necessary. A wind turbine rotor is directly coupled with the generator. Therefore, direct drive is more efficient, reliable, and simple in design.

4.7.5 On-Grid and Off-Grid Wind Turbines

Both on-grid and off-grid applications are possible for wind turbines. Almost all big and nearly all medium-sized wind turbines are used in grid-connected applications. There is no energy storage issue with on-grid wind turbine systems, which is one of the most obvious benefits.A small wind turbine is mostly off-grid for homes, telecom, farms, and other applications. Wind power generated by off-grid wind turbines, on the other hand, is an intermittent power source that can fluctuate substantially in a short period with little warning. Off-grid wind turbines are often utilized with batteries, diesel engines, and solar systems to stabilize the wind power supply.

4.7.6 Onshore and Offshore Wind Turbines

Onshore turbines: The history of the development of onshore wind turbines is extensive. Onshore turbines have lower foundation costs, better integration with the electrical grid, lower tower and turbine installation costs, and easier operation and maintenance access. Since the 1990s, offshore wind turbines have grown faster than onshore ones. This is because offshore wind is stronger and more consistent than onshore wind. A wind turbine situated offshore can produce more electricity and run for more hours per year than the same turbine installed onshore. Environmental regulations are laxer offshore than onshore. For example, offshore wind turbines no longer have a problem with noise.

Offshore and on-land wind turbines: Large wind farms are built on land for easy construction, cheap maintenance costs, and access to transmission lines. Offshore wind farms, on the other hand, can be profitable. The absence of sufficient land-based wind resources is one of the primary reasons for the development of offshore wind farms. This is especially true in heavily populated locations, such as certain European countries. Another crucial reason is that offshore wind speeds are often substantially greater and more consistent than on land. Wind turbines capture more energy offshore because energy is related to the cube of wind speed. In offshore applications, noise and visual impact are limited. These reasons are driving offshore wind technologies.

4.7.7 Fixed and Variable Speed Wind Turbines

Additionally, wind turbines can be categorized as either fixed-speed or variable-speed turbines. The fixed-speed wind turbine generator operates at a constant speed. The speed of the generator depends on the grid frequency, the number of poles, and the gearbox ratio. Maximum energy conversion efficiency is obtained at a specified wind speed. If the speed changes, efficiency will decrease. Aerodynamic control schemes for the blades are used to protect the wind turbine from high wind gusts. The output power of the fixed-speed turbine is not constant, hence the power supply to the grid fluctuates, causing disturbance to the grid. Therefore, this type of wind turbine needs a robust mechanical design to track high mechanical stresses. On the other hand, variable-speed wind turbines can achieve the highest possible efficiency of energy conversion irrespective of the wind speed at which the turbines are operating. The wind turbine speed is continuously adjusted according to the wind speed. In doing so, the TSR can be kept at an optimal value to achieve maximum power conversion efficiency at different wind speeds.

A power converter system is typically used to connect the wind turbine generator to the utility grid, allowing for variable turbine speed. The converter system controls the speed of the generator, which is mechanically attached to the wind turbine's rotor (blades). The advantages and disadvantages of fixed and variable speed wind turbines are tabulated in Table.4.4

Table 4.4: Advantages and disadvantages of fixed and variable speed wind turbines

Mode of speed	Advantages	Disadvantages
Fixed speed	Simple, sturdy, and reliable Low maintenance and low cost	Energy conversion efficiency is low Mechanical stress is very high More power function occurs in the grid.
Variable speed	Energy conversion efficiency is very high Power quality is improved Mechanical stress is reduced	Additional cost and losses due to the use of converters More complex control system

Manufacturing costs and power losses owing to power converters are the main disadvantages. However, the increased energy production compensates for the additional expense and power loss. In addition, the smoother operation provided by the regulated generator minimizes mechanical stress on the turbine, drive train, and supporting structure. This has allowed manufacturers to produce more affordable, larger wind turbines. Because of the above, variable-speed turbines are the most popular on the market right now.

4.8 LAYOUT OF HORIZONTAL AXIS LARGE WIND POWER PLANT

The main components of the horizontal axis large wind turbine are given below.

(a) Rotor blade,
(b) Rotor hub
(c) Pitch and Yaw control
(d) Amenometer and wind vane
(e) Low and high-speed shaft
(f) Gearbox
(g) Generators (Synchronous and Asynchronous Generator)
(h) Frequency, voltage, active and reactive power control
(i) Power electronics devices
(j) Capacitor banks
(k) Power output AC

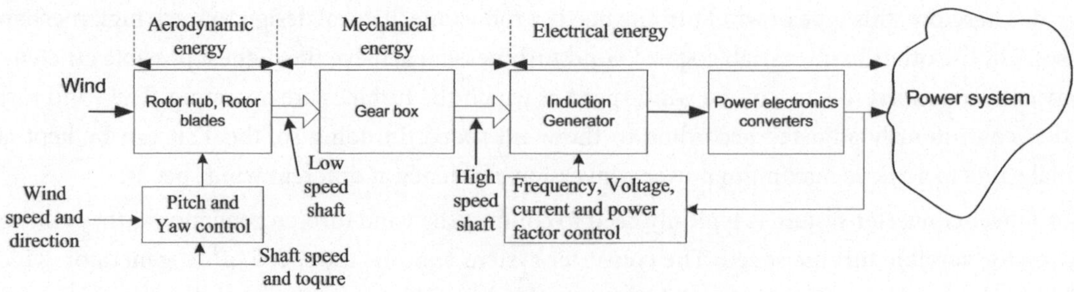

Fig. 4.13: Layout of the HAWT system

Fig.4.13 shows the layout diagram of the horizontal axis wind turbine generator system. The wind turbine consists of blades, a rotor hub, a pitch, and a yaw control mechanism. The blades are attached to the rotor hub. The pitch control mechanism is used to regulate the angle at which the rotor blades are tilted. Anemometer is a measuring instrument that is used to measure wind speed. Also, a wind vane is used to identify the wind direction. The yaw control mechanism depends on the wind vane data. Yaw drive turns the nacelle. The wind turbine rotor is coupled with generators via a gearbox. The low-speed wind turbine rotor shaft is converted into a high speed or rated speed of the generator via a gearbox. A generator is an electro-mechanical machine that converts mechanical energy into electrical energy. The generator is connected to the grid through power electronic devices. A capacitor bank is used to compensate for the reactive power requirement of the induction generator.

4.9 LAYOUT OF GEARED WIND POWER PLANT

Typical components of the geared wind power plant are given below.

(a) Wind turbine rotor
(b) Blades
(c) Shaft
(d) Gearbox
(e) Pitch and Yaw control
(f) Asynchronous generator
(g) Power electronics converter
(h) Capacitor bank

The layout diagram of a geared wind power plant is shown in Fig.4.14. The wind turbine comprises blades, a turbine rotor hub, and different aerodynamic control mechanisms such as pitch and yaw control. Pitch control reduces the mechanical stress on the rotor blades. The turbine rotor is coupled with an induction generator via a gearbox. Two shafts namely low and high-speed shafts are used to achieve the generator-rated speed. The induction generator is integrated with the grid through power electronics switching devices. Power electronic switching devices are used for smooth integration of the generator and grid. The capacitor bank supplies the reactive power to the system when required.

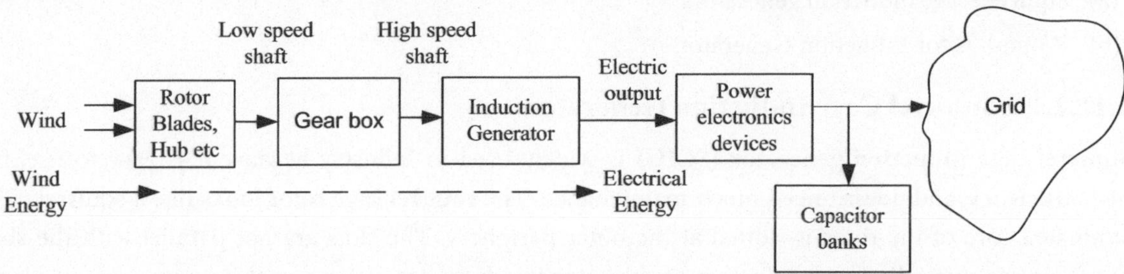

Fig. 4.14: Layout of geared wind turbine induction generator system

4.10 LAYOUT OF DIRECT DRIVE WIND POWER PLANT

Fig.4.15 shows the layout of the direct drive wind turbine system block diagram. The main components of this wind turbine technology are as follows:

(a) Wind turbine rotor
(b) Turbine Blades
(c) Shaft
(d) Synchronous generators such as PMSG and WRSG
(e) Power electronic converters

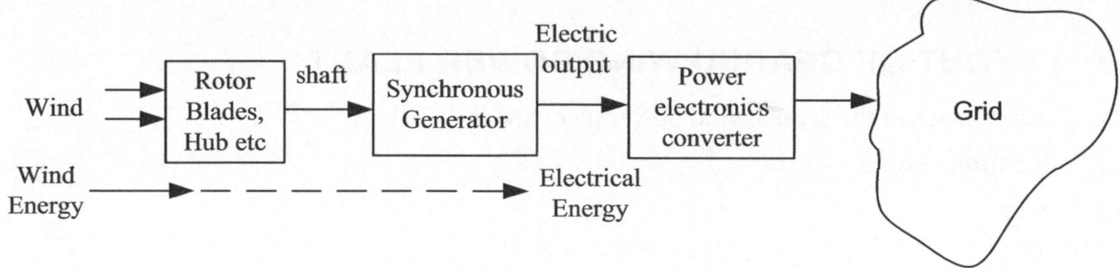

Fig. 4.15: Layout of the direct drive wind turbine system

As compared with the previous plant, this plant has no gearbox. A turbine rotor is directly coupled with a synchronous generator through the shaft. The wind turbine rotor rotates when the turbine blades are moved, accordingly, the generator rotor rotates. The generator converts mechanical energy into electric energy. The output power of the generator is fed into the grid through a power electronics converter.

4.11 ELECTRIC GENERATORS USED IN WIND POWER PLANTS

4.11.1 Constant Speed Electric Generators

There are two types of constant-speed electric generators used in wind energy conversion systems. They are

(a) Squirrel-cage induction generators
(b) Wound Rotor Induction Generator

4.11.1.1 Squirrel Cage Induction Generators

Squirrel-cage induction generator (SCIG) is widely used in industry because it is easy to use, has high efficiency, and doesn't need much maintenance. The squirrel cage rotor looks like a squirrel. The laminated core of the rotor is slotted at the outer periphery. The slots are not parallel with the shaft but these are skewed. The conductors of the rotor windings are copper or aluminum and are placed on the slots. The conductors or the bars are short-circuited at both ends by end rings. Fig.4.16 (a) and

Fig.4.16(b) show a picture of a squirrel cage induction generator and a squirrel cage rotor respectively. The stator is a cylindrical structure inner periphery that is slotted to receive the stator winding. The stator winding is a three-phase winding connected either in star or delta.

Fig. 4.16: (a) Induction generator
(Courtesy: www.alternative-energy-tutorials.com)

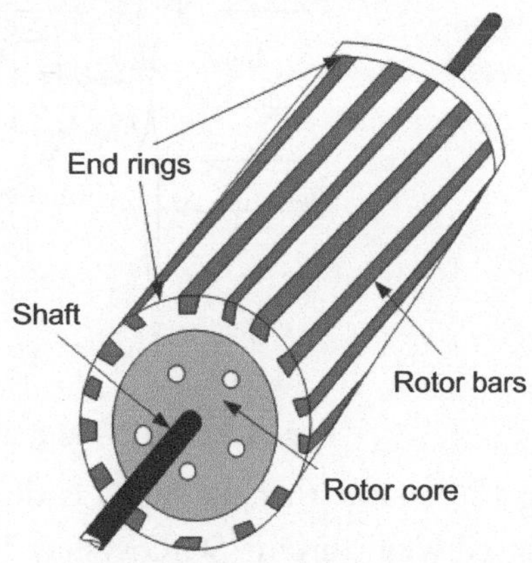

Fig. 4.16: (b) Squirrel case rotor

The stator of a SCIG and a star-connected winding are shown in Fig.4.16(c) and Fig.4.16(d) respectively. SCIG is a very strong and stable generator. When the wind speed changes, the slip changes by a few percent. Thus, the speed of SCIG doesn't change much. In wind turbine technology, a soft starter, and reactive power compensation devices are used. Soft-starter is used to control the inrush current of the SCIG. As the torque-speed characteristics of the SCIG are very sharp, hence the small variation of wind power directly affects the grid. A capacitor bank is used for reactive power compensation. The multiple-stage gearbox and SCIG are used in the fixed-speed wind turbine architecture to transform the mechanical energy from the wind into electrical energy. Many wind turbine manufacturers used this design in the 1980s and 1990s.

Fig. 4.16: (c) Squirrel Induction generator stator
(Courtesy: Internet source)

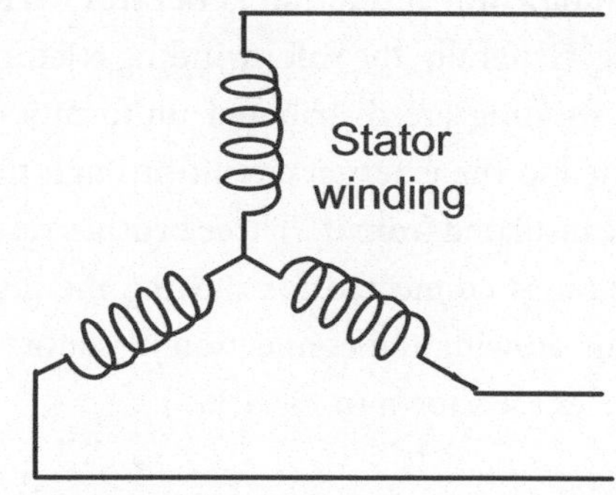

Fig. 4.16: (d) Star-connected stator winding

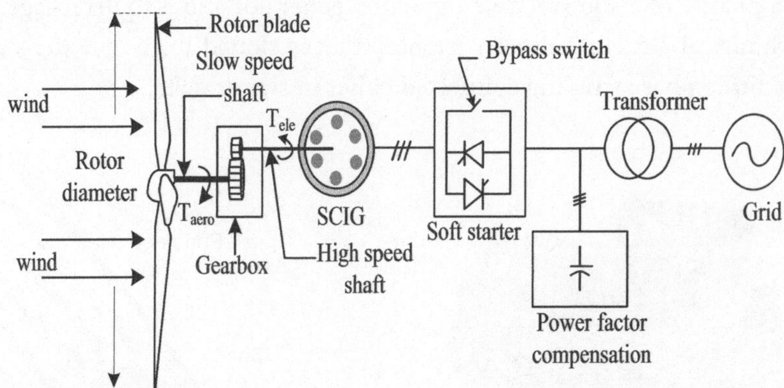

Fig. 4.17: SCIG is connected to a wind turbine and grid system

Fig.4.17 shows, that the SCIG is directly connected to the grid via a transformer in this setup. Fixed-speed wind turbine SCIG system has a soft starter. It is used to control inrush current during the integration of the SCIG into the grid. Also, capacitor banks are used to compensate for the reactive power. Since SCIG operates within a narrow band near the synchronous speed, this turbine operates at a speed that is almost constant irrespective of the wind speed. This approach is popular due to its low cost, simplicity, and durability. The fixed-speed wind turbine idea converts wind speed fluctuations into mechanical and then electrical power fluctuations, causing considerable fatigue and mechanical stress. It also has limited control over the power quality, no control over how much reactive power it uses, and no speed control to make it as aerodynamically efficient as possible. To maximize power output, a pole-changeable SCIG configuration that can accommodate two different rotation rates has been implemented in some commercial wind turbines. Especially, a generator winding set that normally has 8 poles for low wind speeds, and another that typically has 4 or 6 poles for medium and high wind speeds.

4.11.1.2 Wound Rotor Induction Generator

In a **wound rotor induction generator (WRIG)**, the outer periphery of the rotor is slotted to receive a winding. Generally, the rotor winding is a three-phase star-connected winding. The insulated conductors of this winding are distributed uniformly on the stots. The three terminals of the star winding are connected to the external circuit through three slip rings. The slip rings are mounted on the shaft and they are insulated from it. Three brushes rest on the slip rings from which an external circuit comprising of resistors is connected for starting the purpose. The picture of a wound rotor is shown in Fig.4.18. A circuit showing the connection of stators winding, rotor winding along with slip rings, and starting resistances are shown in Fig.4.19.

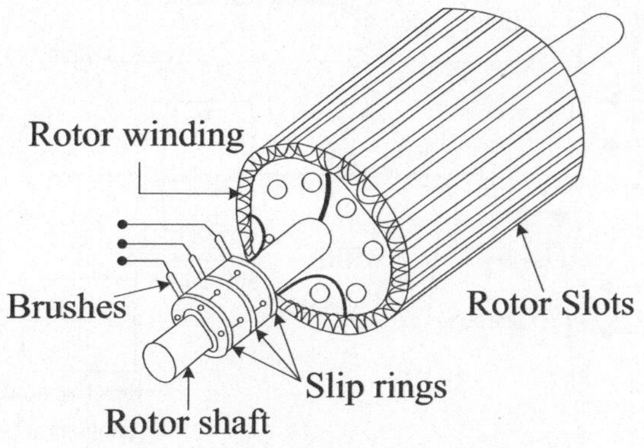

Fig. 4.18: Wound rotor with slip rings

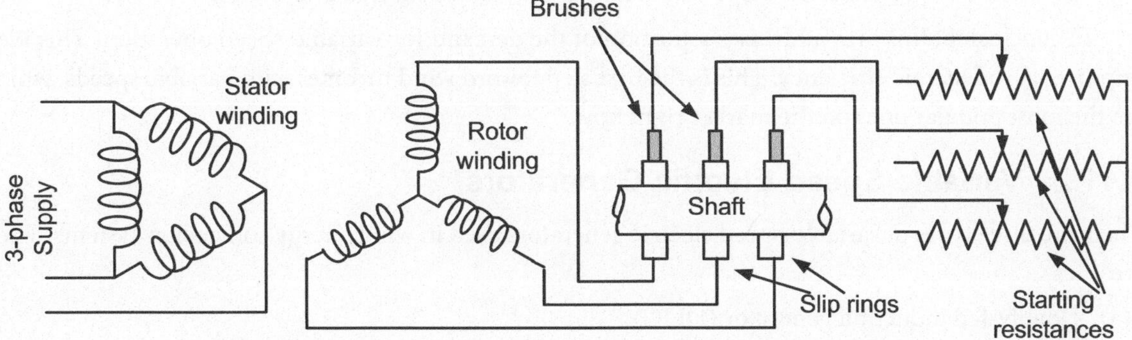

Fig. 4.19: Three-phase wound rotor induction generator (WRIG)

Fig. 2.20 shows the configuration of the limited variable speed wind turbine with WRIG. The WRIG is directly connected to the grid through a soft starter and transformer. Variable resistance is connected in series with the rotor of the WRIG and is adjusted dynamically by a power electronic controller. By changing the additional resistance of the rotor, the wind turbine speed can be modified. Hence, a variable speed operation can be attained by adjusting the energy extracted from the WRIG rotor. The variable speed range depends on the size of the external resistance. Typically the speed range from 0% to 10%, which is a very narrow range. Therefore, this is called limited variable speed or is sometimes called constant speed. However, a portion of the energy of the adjustable resistance is lost as heat. The soft starter is utilized to mitigate the inrush current of the WRIG. A reactive power compensator or capacitor bank is used to provide reactive power for the magnetization of the WRIG. When compared to SCIG, this design features a simpler circuit topology that does not require the use of slip rings, as well as an improved working speed range. To some extent, this model can reduce gust-caused mechanical stresses and variation of power. Some drawbacks include a small speed range that is based on the additional resistance's magnitude, power losses that occur in the variable resistance, and ineffective control over reactive and active power.

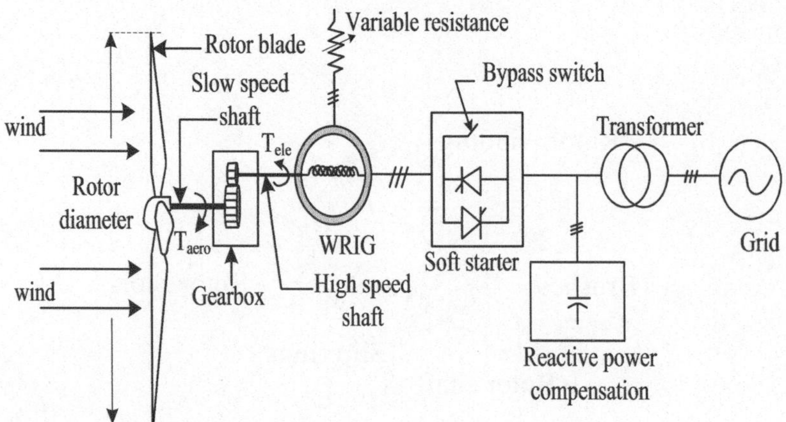

Fig. 2.20: WRIG is connected to a wind turbine and grid system

In conclusion, this idea addresses a portion of the demand for variable-speed operation. This idea improves aerodynamic efficiency. This is the first step toward wind turbines with variable speeds, which are the most popular ones on the market right now.

4.11.2 Variable Speed Electric Generators

There are three types of variable-speed electric generators used in wind energy conversion systems. They are

(a) Doubly-fed induction generator (DFIG)

(b) Wound rotor synchronous generator (WRSG)

(c) Permanent Magnet Synchronous Generator (PMSG)

4.11.2.1 Doubly-fed Induction Generators

A doubly fed induction generator (DFIG) wind turbine system is used for variable-speed wind turbines. Here, the slip ring wound rotor induction machine is used as a generator. The stator of the generator is directly connected to the grid. The rotor slip rings are connected to the grid via power electronics converters. The converters are designed based on a certain speed range. The power converters are not full-scale converters. Typically, 30% -70% of the speed range can be utilized. The speed range is chosen in such a way as to maximize efficiency and reduce investment expenses. As a result, an increase in the speed range around the synchronous speed will increase the cost of the converter. DFIG controls both active power and reactive power separately. One problem with the DFIG is that it always needs slip rings. Fig.4.21 shows a DFIG-based wind energy conversion system.

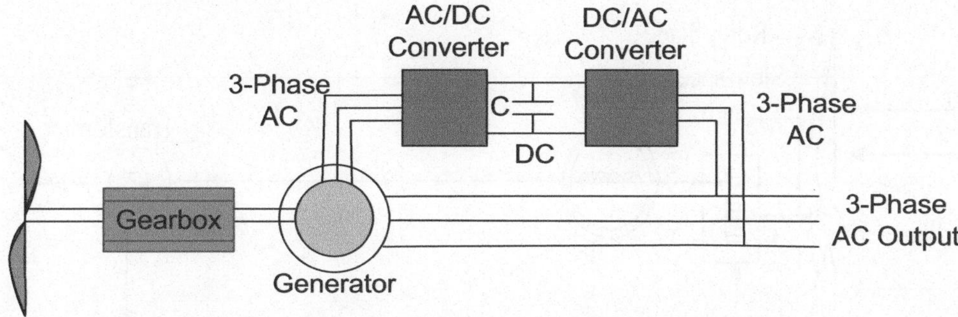

Fig. 4.21: DFIG-based wind energy conversion system

In the SCIG wind turbine system, the rotor circuit is not accessible. If the rotor of the induction generator is wound type then it can be accessed through the slip ring. The variable speed of the induction generator can be achieved by controlling the rotor circuit. The rotor circuit is connected to controllable back-to-back converters. The back-to-back converter comprises rotor and grid side converters sharing the same dc link. By introducing a variable-frequency current into the rotor circuit, the relative speed (frequency) differential between the grid and rotor may be adjusted. As a result, the converters may be controlled to maintain a consistent output under both normal and abnormal operating situations. Excitation of a DFIG can take place through the rotor windings instead of the stator windings. The reactive power is needed for excitation. If needed, the grid-side converter provides the reactive power for the excitation of the stator winding. Thus, a wind turbine equipped with DFIG can be regulated the grid voltage. The stator always supplies real/active power to the grid, whereas real power in the rotor circuit might flow in either direction (from the rotor to the grid or the grid to the rotor), depending on operational conditions. Ignoring losses, rotor circuit power is given by (4.34).

$$P_{rotor} = -sP_{stator} \tag{4.34}$$

where s is the slip, real power feds to the grid is given by (4.35).

$$\begin{aligned} P_{grid} &= P_{rotor} + P_{stator} \\ &= (1-s)P_{stator} \end{aligned} \tag{4.35}$$

Since the stator circuit supplies the main power to the grid whereas the power processing by the rotor circuit can be reduced to approximately 30% of nominal generator power. This implies that the enormous benefit of a wide variety of speeds may be obtained at a minimal cost. Fig.4.22 shows the configuration of the DFIG. A variable-speed wind turbine system is used to generate electric energy by using DFIG via a multi-stage gearbox. The basic operating concept is identical to that of the SCIG-based systems, but in the DFIG, the power electronics converters regulate the rotor active power to achieve a speed range ± 30% of synchronous speed. The rotor converter's rated power is chosen based on cost and speed range. In addition, the converter compensates for reactive power and provides a smooth connection to the grid. A DFIG has a reasonable speed range and other benefits, but it's more sensitive to voltage fluctuations, particularly voltage sags. Large voltage disturbance on the rotor is commonly caused by a sudden decrease in the terminal voltage, which can cause the rotor current to become unmanageable and can even damage the rotor-side converter (RSC). This method reduces machine reliability and gear life due to electromagnetic torque oscillation. To enhance the low-voltage ride-through (LVRT) capability of DFIG, several schemes have been available in the literature. The rotor crow-circuit is usually used to protect the RSC.

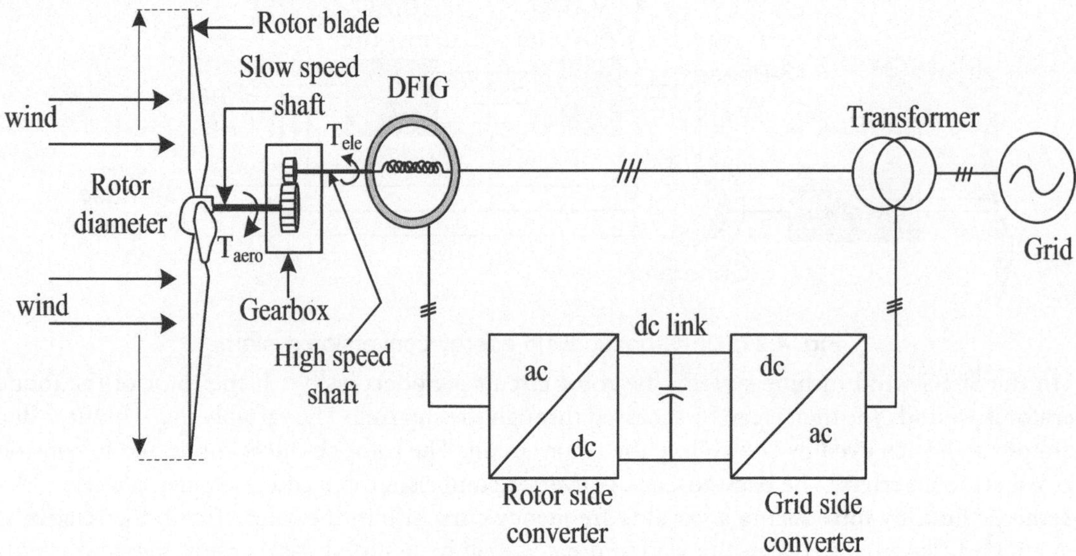

Fig. 4.22: DFIG connected to wind turbine and grid system

4.11.2.2 Wound Rotor Synchronous Generator

The wound rotor synchronous generator (WRSG) is nothing but a synchronous generator. The rotor of WRSG house a field winding. The field winding is excited with DC. Thus magnetic poles are created in the rotor. The stator core of the synchronous generator is of a hollow cylindrical structure. The inner periphery of the stator core is slotted to receive a three-phase stator winding. The rotor of the synchronous machine is rotated with the help of a prime mover at synchronous speed. The stator conductors links with the changing magnetic field and hence as per faradays law of electromagnetic induction e.m.f is induced in the stator conductor. In the case of wind power applications, the prime mover is the wind turbine. A picture of a synchronous machine rotor is shown in Fig.4.23(a) and a star-connected stator winding is shown in Fig.4.23(b).

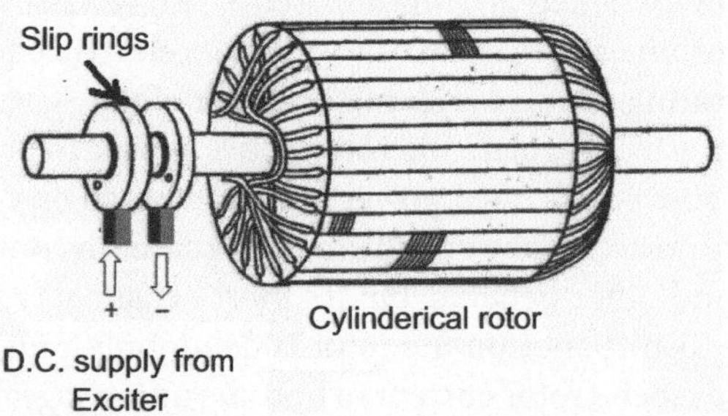

Fig. 4.23: (a) A cylindrical rotor of WRSG

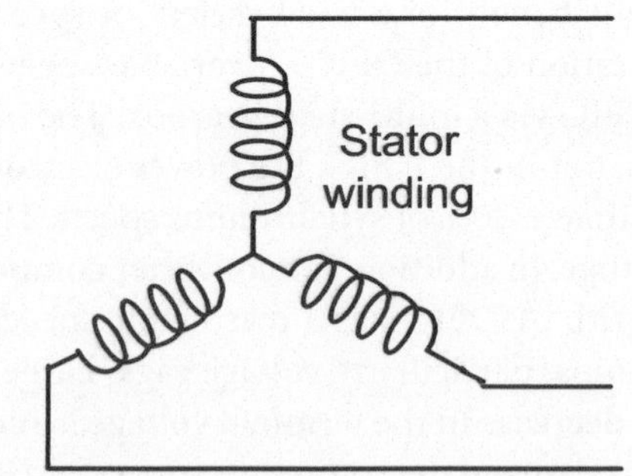

Fig. 4.23: (b) Stator winding of WRSG

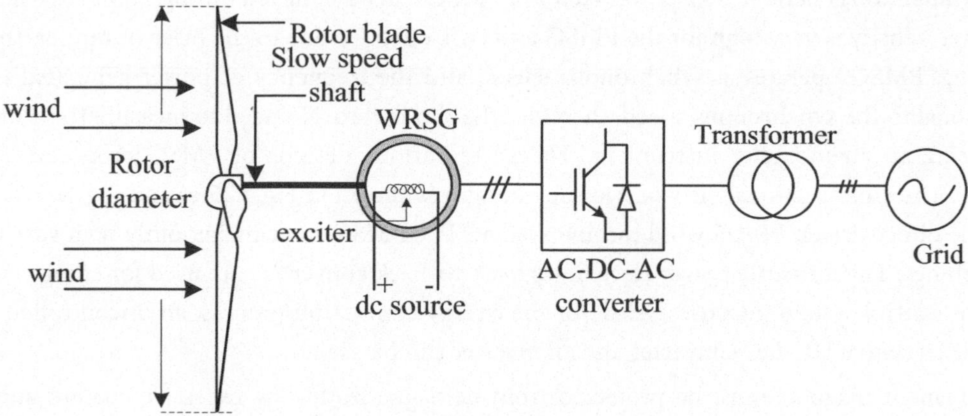

Fig. 4.24: WRSG with the wind turbine system

The wound rotor synchronous generator (WRSG) with a wind turbine system is shown in Fig.4.24. The synchronous speed of a synchronous generator speed depends on the number of poles and frequency. For constant frequency, the number of poles is decided by the synchronous speed of the synchronous generator. To obtain a low-speed synchronous generator like WRSG and PMSG needs a multipole design. In a direct-drive wind power system, the gearbox is eliminated. The turbine rotor is directly connected to WRSG. The rotor speed of a WRSG is fundamentally locked and synchronized with the magnetic field of the revolving stator. The generator terminal voltage and frequency are fluctuated with changing wind speeds. If the grid voltage and frequency do not match with the generator terminal voltage and frequency, then regulate both quantities by adjusting the power electronic converter. Using voltage control of the WRSG can be regulated the magnetizing level of the WRSG, i.e., the voltage of the generator becomes high when the magnetizing level is high also it generates more reactive power and is fed into the grid. In other words, the WRSG can be able to export and import reactive power at a wide range of grid voltage fluctuation by controlling the magnetizing level of the WRSG. The grid parameters like voltage, frequency, and power factor are continuously monitored in the direct-driven WRSG wind turbine power plant technology. The direct-driven WRSG automatically supplies reactive power to the grid with the support of a power electronic converter when the grid's power factor drops below a certain threshold. For direct-driven wind turbine generators, capacitor banks are not necessary to compensate for the grid reactive power.Recent changes have made it possible for WRSGs to have limited fault-ride-through capabilities, which means that they can stay connected to the grid even when there are problems with the grid. This is a feature that grid operators need very much. WRSGs are also used to control the power ramp. However, because power electronic converters are used in the connections between the stator and the grid, this kind of generator is unable to make a significant contribution to the inertia of the system.

4.11.2.3 Permanent Magnet Synchronous Generator (PMSG)

A permanent magnet is used as a rotor in a PMSG to provide the magnetic field required for electricity generation. Hence, no external power supply is required for excitation, and no rotor circuit is required. The maintenance cost is reduced due to its simplest structure. The efficiency of the PMSGs is higher than the induction generator. The power factor of PMSG can be achieved through unity or even leading. The power density is very high for the PMSG and cost-effective due to the price of rare-earth magnets decreasing. PMSG operates at synchronous speed, and the frequency of power generated is directly proportional to the synchronous speed, therefore the slip is zero. No need to measure the wind turbine speed using an anemometer instrument. There are various designs of PMSG proposed by various literature. The cross-sectional view of two such designs is shown in Fig.4.25(a) and Fig.4.25(b). Fig.4.26 shows the direct-driven PMSG wind turbine system. The PMSG can run smoothly with variable-speed wind turbines. The full-scale power electronics back-to-back converters are used for energy conversion and plant control system purposes. Also, for the energy conversion process, an uncontrolled cascaded type rectifier with a DC-DC converter and an inverter can be used.

Permanent magnets must be protected from demagnetization by excessive current and/or heat. Whenever using permanent magnets, it is important to take precautions against demagnetization from excessive currents and/or excessive temperatures.

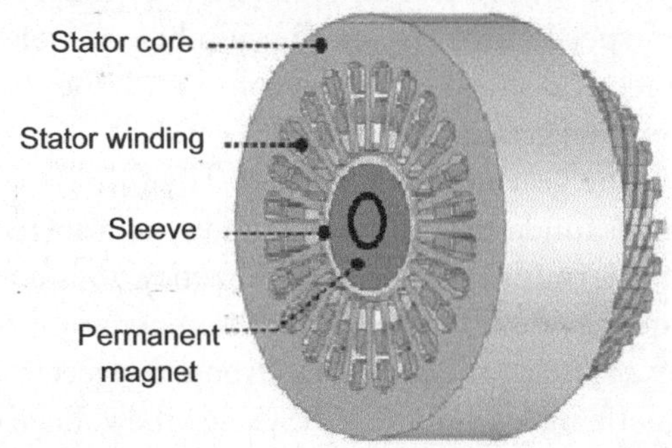

Fig. 4.25: (a) Cross-sectional view of PMSG

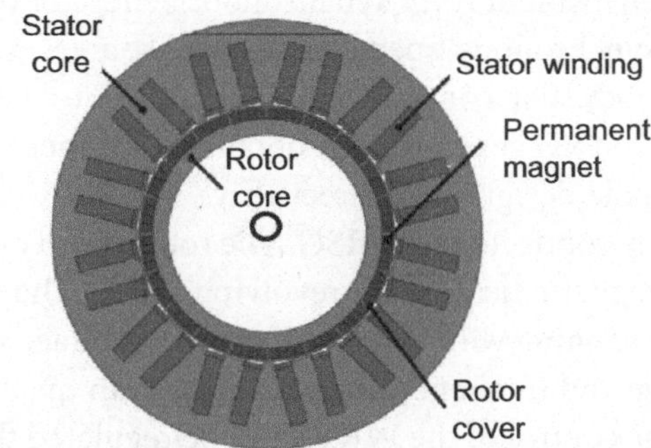

Fig. 4.25: (b) Cross-sectional view of PMSG

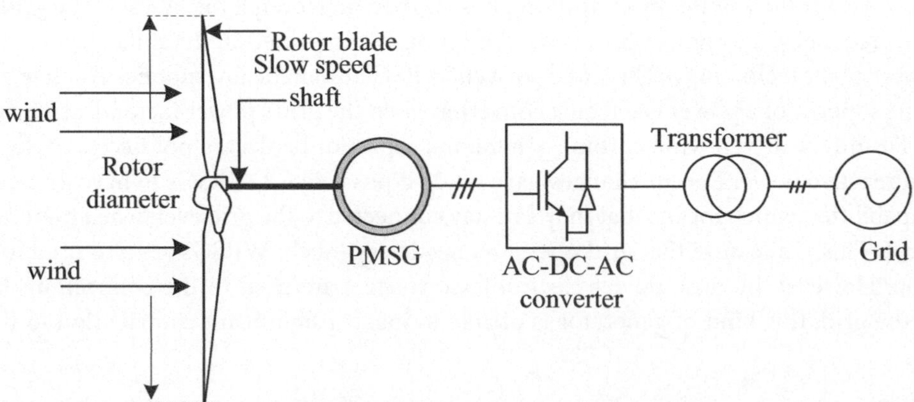

Fig. 4.26: PMSG with the wind turbine system

UNIT SUMMARY

The moving air is called wind. The wind is freely available in nature. Wind power plants emit zero CO_2. Wind energy has the lowest life cycle emissions among all the sources. The site of the wind power plant should be such that the wind contains maximum energy. The various components of wind power plants and their working have been discussed. The various components of wind power plants are works on a few principles. There are many factors such as aerodynamic efficiency, tip speed, tip speed ratio, solidity, etc. that affect wind turbine performance. A wind power plant can be aerodynamically controlled by stall control, pitch control, and active stall control technologies. The layout of different wind power plants has been discussed. The wind power plant may be categorized as constant speed and variable speed type and accordingly various types of electrical generators are used. There are two types of constant-speed electrical generators namely squirrel-cage induction generators, and wound rotor induction generator. There are three types of variable speed type generators namely doubly fed induction generator (DFIG), wound rotor synchronous generator (WRSG), and permanent magnet synchronous generator (PMSG). The working of such variable and constant speed plants has been discussed.

EXERCISES

Example 4.1

At a certain location, the wind speed is 6.1 m/s at a height of 60 m above ground level, and 6.5 m/s at a height of 80 m. Find the power law index, and then extrapolate the wind speed at 100 m above ground level at that specific location.

Solution:

From equation (4.2)

$$\alpha = \frac{\log_{10}\left(\frac{v_2}{v_1}\right)}{\log_{10}\left(\frac{h_2}{h_1}\right)} = \frac{\log_{10} 6.5 - \log_{10} 6.1}{\log_{10} 80 - \log_{10} 60} = 0.221$$

When h_2 becomes 100m, then the corresponding v_2 will be

From eq. ()

$$\frac{v_2}{v_1} = \left(\frac{h_2}{h_1}\right)^{\alpha} \Rightarrow \frac{v_2}{6.1} = \left(\frac{100}{60}\right)^{0.221} \Rightarrow v_2 = 6.83\ m/s$$

So, at 100 m height, the wind speed will be 6.83 m/s.

Example. 4.2

Determine the total upstream wind power in a specific location if the wind speed is 6 m/s and the turbine rotor diameter is 60m considering the air density of 1.225kg/m³ at 25°C.

Solution:

Given data,

wind velocity, v = 6 m/s, rotor diameter, D = 60m, radius, R = D/2 = 30 m, air density, ρ = 1.225 kg/m³

$$\text{Wind power, } P_{wind} = \frac{1}{2}\rho A v^3 = \frac{1}{2}\rho\left(\pi R^2\right)v^3 = \frac{0.5\times1.225\times\left(\pi\times30^2\right)6^3}{1000} = 373.88kW$$

Example. 4.3

In a particular area, the wind speed is 4 m/s for a specific period. Find the total wind power in that specific area. Also, determine the wind power when the wind speed becomes two times of initial speed. Assuming air density at nominal temperature is 1.225 kg/m³ and rotor diameter = 60 m.

Solution:

Given data, wind velocity, v = 4 m/s, rotor diameter, D = 60m, radius, R = D/2 = 30 m, air density, ρ = 1.225 kg/m³

$$\text{Wind power, } P_{wind} = \frac{1}{2}\rho A v^3 = \frac{1}{2}\rho\left(\pi R^2\right)v^3 = \frac{0.5\times1.225\times\left(\pi\times30^2\right)4^3}{1000} \approx 110kW$$

When wind speed, v = 8 m/s,

Wind power,

$$P_{wind} = 0.5\rho\left(\pi R^2\right)v^3 \text{ W}$$
$$= \frac{0.6125\times\pi\times30^2\times8^3}{1000} \text{ kW}$$
$$= 886 \text{ kW}$$

Example. 4.4

The air density at a particular location is 1.162. The value of for a particular month of 31 days for a 10-minute interval. Find the wind power density (WPD).

Solution:

Given, the air density factor, σ = 1.162,

$$\sum_{i=1}^{N} v_h^3 = 1604001 \text{ m}^3/s^3$$

N = 31 × 24 × 60/10 = 4464

$$\therefore \text{WPD} = \frac{\frac{1}{2}\sigma\sum_{i=1}^{N} v_h^3}{4464}$$
$$= \frac{0.5x1.162x1604001}{4464}$$
$$= 208.76 \text{ Watt/m}^2$$

Example. 4.5

For a specific zone, the wind speed is found at 6 m/s. Determine the total upstream wind power extraction by the wind turbine from that wind speed if the wind turbine rotor diameter is 50m considering air density of 1.225 kg/m³ at 25°C. Also, determine the total wind energy generated for twelve days.

Solution:

Given data, wind velocity, v = 6 m/s, rotor diameter, D = 50m, radius, R = D/2 = 25 m, air density, ρ = 1.225 kg/m^3

Wind power,

$$P_{wind} = \frac{0.6125 \times (\pi R^2) \times 6^3}{1000}$$
$$= \frac{0.6125 \times (\pi \times 25^2) \times 6^3}{1000}$$
$$= 259.64\ kW$$

Total energy for 12 days (i.e. 288 hrs) = P_{wind} × 288 kWh

= **74.776 MWh**

Multiple Choice Questions

1. Determine the turbulence intensity for the mean wind speed of 7.5 m/s with a standard deviation of 3.0 m/s.
   (a) 0.40 (b) 0.45
   (c) 5.0 (d) 5.5
2. Determine the total wind power (kW) in an area where the average wind speed is 5 m/s, using a WPP with an 80 m rotor diameter. Assume the air temperature is 25°C with a density of 1.335 kg/m^3.
   (a) 414.24 (b) 378.13
   (c) 366.24 (d) 419.40
3. Calculate the wind power density (WPD) for a given air density of 1.264 and $\sum_{i=1}^{N} v_h^3 = 1604004$ m^3/s^3 for the month of October for a ten-minute interval.
   (a) 229.38 (b) 200.36
   (c) 227.09 (d) 220.12
4. If the wind speed at a site is 6 m/s for half of the year and 8 m/s for the rest of the year and the density of 1.2255 kg/m^3. Find the value of energy content (kWh/m^2) in a year.
   (a) 3906.08 (b) 3608.02
   (c) 3812.22 (d) 3406.22
5. Which of the following is NOT an example of an energy substitute as a measure for energy conservation?
   (a) Replacement of electric heaters with steam heaters
   (b) Replacement of wind power with thermal power
   (c) Replacement of steam-based hot water by solar systems
   (d) Replacement of coal with coconut shells, rice husk, etc.
6. What is the average wind velocity observed on Earth?
   (a) 14 m/sec (b) 4 m/sec
   (c) 1 m/sec (d) 9 m/sec

7. The region at which the turbine starts producing power. Below this speed, it is not worthwhile, nor efficient, to turn the turbine on is called as
   (a) The cut-in speed region (b) The cut-off speed region
   (c) Still higher wind speeds (d) The constant maximum region
8. A nacelle is a large box that houses the power converter, shaft, gearbox, generator, cable, and yawing drive in a wind power plant. Where is it located?
   (a) It is located at the base of the tower. (b) It is located in the lower half of the tower.
   (c) It is located on the tower. (d) It is located in the middle of the tower.
9. Which of the following is a true statement for a fixed-speed system for wind power when compared to a variable system?
   (a) Higher reliability (b) Inexpensive gearbox
   (c) Higher rotor efficiency (d) Low transient torque
10. Which of the following is the basic component of the wind power system?
    (a) Stator with two or three blades (b) Shaft without mechanical gear
    (c) Yoke mechanism (d) Electrical motor
11. Which of the following component is connected to the gearbox in a horizontal-type wind turbine?
    (a) Low-speed shaft (b) High-speed shaft
    (c) Controller (d) Accelerometer
12. Which of the following are the three ways to control the speed of wind turbines?
    (a) Adjusting yaw and pitch
    (b) Allowing the turbine to run at any speed bound with ratings
    (c) Controlling of generators frequency output for double feed
    (d) All the above
13. Which of the following is the function of HAWTs in the gearbox of a horizontal wind turbine?
    (a) Speeds up the rotation of blades (b) Slows down the rotation of blades
    (c) Maintains the speed of blades (d) None of the above
14. What is the height of the HAWT tower?
    (a) 40 to 100 meters (b) 50 meters
    (c) 110 meters (d) 30 meters
15. Which of the following country have a "Jaisalmer-based Wind Park"?
    (a) India (b) China
    (c) US (c) Romania
16. Which of the following defined is as the speed of rotation of the blade and speed of
    (a) Tip-based speed ratio (b) Generator speed
    (c) Transmission ratio (d) None of the above
17. What happens to the speed of wind-type turbines if there is an increase in tip-based speed ratio is large?
    (a) Fastens (b) Slows down
    (c) Come to rest (d) None of the above

18. Which of the following components of a wind turbine system is arranged in the order in which energy is being converted?
   (a) Blades - rotor - electric generator - shaft
   (b) Blades - rotor - shaft - electric generator
   (c) Shaft - blades - rotor - electric generator
   (d) Electric generator - blades - rotor — shaft

19. Which of the following are commonly used commercial wind turbines?
   (a) Vertical and DFIG
   (b) Horizontal and SCIG
   (c) Horizontal and vertical
   (d) DFIG and SCIG

20. What are horizontal wind turbines?
   (a) Wind turbines rotate about an axis perpendicular to the plane of the ground
   (b) Wind turbines rotate about an axis diagonal to the plane of the ground
   (c) Wind turbines rotate about an axis 30 degrees to the plane of the ground
   (d) Wind turbines rotate about an axis parallel to the plane of wind streamlines

21. What is the main function of the tower in a wind turbine system?
   (a) Acts as a support to all other components used in the wind turbine system
   (b) Acts as an antenna for wireless radio communications
   (c) Acts as an electric pole for power transportation
   (d) Destabilizes the wind turbine system

22. Which of the following towers is used for small wind turbines?
   (a) Hybrid tower
   (b) Guyed pole tower
   (c) Electric pole
   (d) Wooden pole

ANSWERS															
1.	(a)	2.	(d)	3.	(c)	4.	(a)	5.	(b)	6.	(d)	7.	(a)	8.	(c)
9.	(a)	10.	(b)	11.	(a)	12.	(d)	13.	(a)	14.	(a)	15.	(a)	16.	(a)
17.	(a)	18.	(b)	19.	(c)	20.	(d)	21.	(a)	22.	(b)				

QUESTIONS AND PROBLEMS

Short and Long Answer Type Questions

1. Differentiate between weather and climate.
2. Which is the largest wind energy in India?
3. What is the relationship between lift and drag?
4. How are lift and drag generated?
5. What are the different forces acting on airplanes or birds?
6. How does an airplane or a bird maintain a constant speed?
7. How does an airplane or a bird rises, slows down, and accelerate?
8. Differentiate the terms weather and climate.
9. Explain the phenomenon of the creation of wind.

10. Differentiate the relation between wind profile and surface roughness.
11. The wind power out of a wind power plant increases to eight times when the wind velocity becomes double. Explain.
12. Describe the impact of slopes and hills on the wind.
13. Why HAWT power plant is more popular than the VAWT power plant?
14. Classify wind turbine power plant.
15. Explain each component of a large wind power plant.
16. What is the function of the gearbox?
17. What are the electrical generators used in wind power plants?
18. Describe the working of a constant-speed SCIG-based wind power plant with the necessary diagram.
19. Describe the working of a constant speed WRIG-based wind power plant with the necessary diagram.
20. What are the schemes for variable-speed wind turbine power plants?
21. Explain the working of DFIG based wind power plant. Provide the necessary diagram.
22. Describe the working of WRSG based wind power plant. Provide the necessary diagram.
23. Explain the PMSG-based wind power plant.
24. Briefly explain the vertical axis and horizontal axis wind turbine generator.
25. Distinguish between the vertical axis and horizontal axis wind turbine.

Numerical problems

1. The output of a wind power plant is 3MW at a wind speed of 8m/s. What will be the output power at a wind speed of 16m/s?
2. The output of a wind power plant is 3MW at a rated wind speed of 8m/s at atmospheric pressure and 25^{0}C. Find the change in output power of the plant if the wind speed is 10m/s.
3. The air density factor and air temperature at a particular location are 1.225 kg/m^2 and 25^{0}C respectively. The average wind speed is 7m/s. Find the total wind power obtained using a wind power plant with a 450m rotor diameter.
4. Calculate wind power out at a location using a wind firm of rotor diameter 50m at a wind speed of 6m/s. The air density factor is 1.225kg/m^3 at 25^{0}C.
5. A three-bladed horizontal axis wind turbine rotor diameter is 30m and the generator rotates 1200 rpm when the upstream wind velocity is 16 m/s at atmospheric temperature 25°C having an air density of 1.225 kg/m^3. Find the blade tip speed in m/s and the rotational speed of the turbine at TSR of 4. Also, determine the gearbox ratio. (Hint: TSR = Blade tip-speed/wind speed, turbine rotor speed = $60\times\omega/2\pi$ rpm, $\omega = \lambda v_o/R$ rad/s, gear ratio = N_{gen}/N_{rot}).
6. Find the size of a wind turbine rotor (diameter in m) that will generate 100 kW of electrical power in a steady wind (hub height) of 7.5 m/s. Assume that the air density is 1.225 kg/m^3, $C_P = 0.59$, $\eta = 1$.

PRACTICALS

Experiment No.1

Title: Identify the routine maintenance parts of the large wind power plant after watching a video program

Aim: To identify the parts of a Large wind power plant

Apparatus/software required: Watch the video at,

(a) https://www.youtube.com/watch?v=y4D_YJKCtgA

(b) https://www.youtube.com/watch?v=vfxX4HMBj6o

(c) https://www.youtube.com/watch?v=P9SyZvHrJvc

Theory: A wind power plant (WPP) is a plant that converts the kinetic energy of wind into Electrical energy. The parts of the Wind power plant are shown in Fig.4.27(a) and (b). In a large WPP, there are almost 8000 components. Every WPP has the following components.

1. Rotor
2. Nacelle
3. Tower
4. Electric substation
5. Foundation

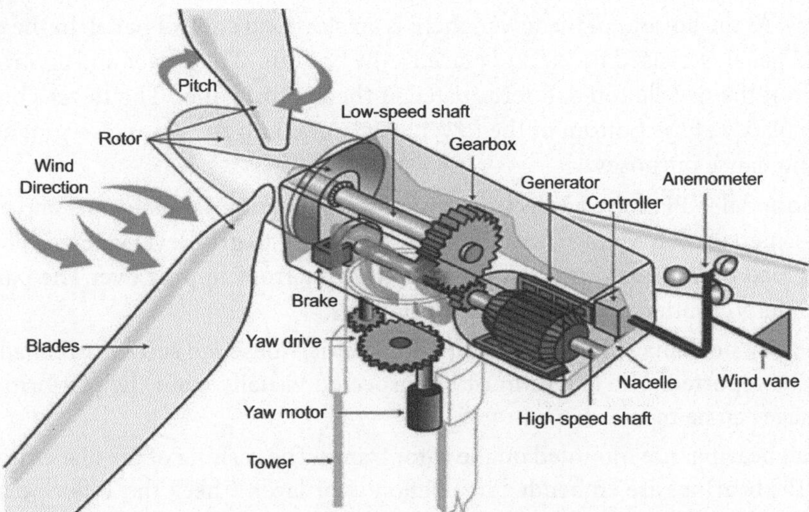

Fig. 4.27: (a) Parts of wind power plant (Curtesy: researchgate.com)

Under each major component, there are many components.

Rotor: The rotor comprises a hub with two or three blades attached to the nacelle. The hub also holds the tip brake control system (in case of a stall control wind turbine) or pitching system (in case of an aerodynamic control wind turbine). The weight of the rotor is carried by the nacelle bearings.

Nacelle: The function of the Nacelle is to hold together all the components of the WPP. The nacelle holds the following components.

Main shaft and high-speed shaft (b) Gearbox, (c) Couplings, (d) Disc brake, (e) Hydraulic system, (f) electric generator, (g) Cooling systems, (h) Electronic controller, (i) Sensors, (j) Electric hoist, (k) Jaw system, (l) Nacelle mainframe (bedplate), (m) Electric and electronic control cables

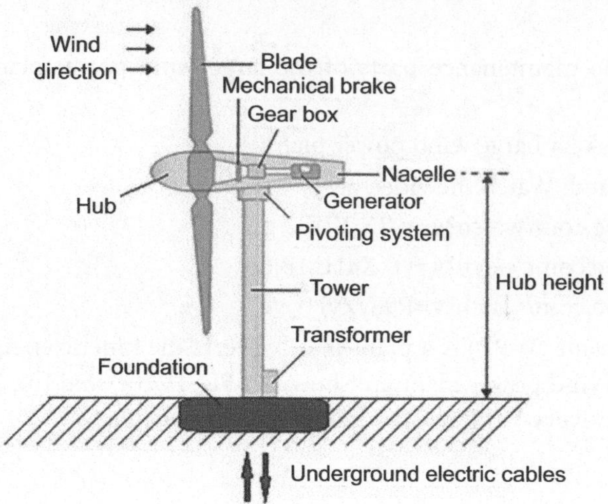

Fig. 4.27: (b) Parts of wind power plant (Curtesy: researchgate.com)

Tower: The main function of a tower is to hold the nacelle high above the ground safely. There are various types of towers, namely lattice towers, steel conical tubular towers, guyed towers, concrete towers, and hybrid towers. At the bottom of the tower, there is an electrical control panel. In the case of a tubular tower, the control panel is housed inside and placed a the bottom. The power and control cables are also brought down from the nacelle top and terminated at the control panel. The tower's bottom electronic controller is also placed at the bottom of the tower. A tower climb system is also provided in the tower to climb for maintenance purposes.

Electric substation: All WPPs have an electric substation comprising a transformer and other switchgear. Using the transformer, the low voltage (say 690V) is stepped up to grid-level voltage. Foundation: It has to bear the dead load of WPP and prevent the wind turbine from tipping over.The parts of the plants which need to undergo routine maintenance are as follows.

1. The blades may be damaged and cracked, and whether these are serious or small surface cracks, they must be reported. The blades must be inspected visually from the platform and the ladder. Small damage can be repaired.
2. The flat shaft bearings are mounted on the rotor frame. The cashing of the blades is mounted on the flat shaft. The bearings are embedded in a Teflon wear layer. Check the Teflon wear layer for scale or corrosion. If found, the V-seal and cell rubber should be replaced.
3. The blade pitching must be checked. If the movement of the blade pitching runs smoothly, the lubrication, as well as the bearings are good. If not, the bearing is damaged and needs replacement.
4. The oil level of the gearbox must be checked, and not a sufficient level to fill the oil as required. The bearings and seal of the gearbox must be checked for wear. The coupling of the gearbox and the generator must be checked for possible damage to the rubber cousins. The RPM sensor must also be checked if not cleaned it is required to clean the same. The backstop must also be checked.
5. Check the lubrication of all the bearings and greased them if required.

6. The yaw unit must be checked for its function.
7. All electrical cables must be checked on conduct and eroding and repair if necessary.
8. All electrical connections must be checked and tighten the bolts if not tightened.
9. Check the climbing cable on the tower and if found damaged, replace the damaged part.
10. Check the welded joints of the flange of the tower.
11. The control panel must be checked for any visual damage and bad connections. Also, check the capacitors.
12. Survey the tower foundation.

Discussion: After completion of this experiment, the students can identify the parts of the large wind power plant and also be able to know the routine maintenance of the parts.

Experiment No.2

Title: Assemble a horizontal axis small wind turbine to produce electric power

Aim: To assemble the parts of a horizontal axis small wind turbine.

Apparatus/software required: Watch the video at,

(a) https://www.youtube.com/watch?v=-HljEywnEf0

(b) https://www.youtube.com/watch?v=65k2Nh8YHFI

(c) https://www.youtube.com/watch?v=yVTJqQfgG_I

Theory: Small wind turbines are small machines used to generate electrical power from wind energy. It is a direct-drive wind power plant in which there is no gearbox. However, in some plant gearbox is also used. This wind turbine has a passive yaw system. The typical output power is 500W to 10kW. Nowadays this range is extended up to 300kW. Small wind turbine power plants are used for residential or industrial purposes. These are used when constant stream and direction of the wind are available in a particular location. Small wind turbines may be horizontal axis wind turbines (HAWTs) or vertical axis wind turbines (VAWTs). In a horizontal-axis wind turbine, the axis of the drive is parallel to the ground. The parts of the horizontal axis of small wind turbines are given below.

1. Rotor
2. Electric generator/alternator
3. Tail vane or yaw system
4. Tower
5. Control and protection systems
6. Gearbox in some small wind power plant

Rotor: It may be of the two-bladed or three-bladed or multibladed turbine. The blads are designed to rotate in a clockwise direction to harness wind energy. The blades are generally fixed to the hub at the appropriate angle. Blades are usually made of glass fiber.

Electric generator/alternator: An alternator produces alternating current (AC) power. Various types of generators are used. In general, a permanent magnet synchronous generator (PMSG) is used in small wind turbine generators. In some plants, a DC generator is used and that can be directly used for battery charging and small power applications. When a high-speed squirrel cage induction generator (SCIG) is used, the SCIG is connected through a gearbox. The gearbox converts low speed to high speed.

Tail vane or yaw system: A simple tail vane is fitted at the back of the nacelle so that the turbine rotor keeps facing the wind. When a tail vane is not available a forced yaw system keeps the rotor facing the wind.

Tower: It could be a tubular type or lattice type. They could be free-standing or guy wired. The standard length of the tower is 20m and 30m. As a general rule, tower hub heights should be 10m above anything around 100m of the tower.

Control and protection system: It is generally situated at the bottom of the tower. The variable output of the alternator is converted to stabilized constant output power using a control system. The type of control system varies depending on the type of application.

Gearbox: The gearbox converts the relatively slow rotation of the rotor to match the rpm of the generator. It is placed between the rotor and the generator. In SWT when SCIG is used gearbox is required otherwise, an SWT gearbox is not required for small rating SWT.The procedure to assemble a horizontal axis small wind turbine is as follows.

1. **Installation of wind turbine tower:** The steel section of the tower can be fabricated off-site at a factory. In general, the parts of the tower are assembled on the site. The bolts are tightened together. After assembling all the parts of the tower, the tower is lifted by a crane and fixed on the foundation.
2. **Installation of the nacelle:** The main shaft, yaw system, generator, and pitch control assembly are assembled in the factory and mounted on the base. The nacelle is bolted to the equipment. The whole assembly is lifted to the top of the tower and secured on it.
3. **Installation of the turbine blades:** The turbine blades are bolted to the hub on the site.
4. **Installation of Electronic controller:** The electronic controller is installed along with the nacelle. Necessary connections are made.
5. **Installation of Electrical power cables:** The terminals of the generator are connected to the power cables and the other ends are connected to the control panel situated at the bottom of the tower.

Discussion: After completion of this experiment, the students can assemble all the parts of a horizontal axis wind turbine.

Experiment No. 3

Title: Dismantle a horizontal axis small wind turbine

Aim: To dismantle the parts of a horizontal axis small wind turbine.

Apparatus/software required: Tools as required to dismantle

Theory: Small wind turbines are small machines used to generate electrical power from wind energy. It is a direct-drive wind power plant in which there is no gearbox. However, in some plant gearbox is also used. This wind turbine has a passive yaw system. The power typical output power is 500W to 10kW. Small wind turbine power plants are used for residential or industrial purposes. These are used when constant stream and direction of the wind are available in a particular location. Small wind turbines may be horizontal axis wind turbines (HAWTs) or vertical axis wind turbines (VAWTs). In a horizontal-axis wind turbine, the axis of the drive is parallel to the ground. The parts of the horizontal axis of small wind turbines are given below.

1. Rotor
2. Electric generator/alternator

3. Tail vane or yaw system
4. Tower
5. Control and protection systems
6. Gearbox in some small wind power plant

Rotor: It may be of the two-bladed or three-bladed or multibladed turbine. The blads are designed to rotate in a clockwise direction to harness wind energy. The blades are generally fixed to the hub at the appropriate angle. Blades are usually made of glass fiber.

Electric generator/alternator: An alternator produces alternating current (AC) power. Various types of generators are used. In general, a permanent magnet synchronous generator (PMSG) is used in small wind turbine generators. In some plants, a DC generator is used and that can be directly used for battery charging and small power applications. When a high-speed squirrel cage induction generator (SCIG) is used, the SCIG is connected through a gearbox.

Tail vane or yaw system: A simple tail vane is fitted at the back of the nacelle so that the turbine rotor keeps facing the wind. When the tail vane is not available a forced yaw system keeps the r rotor facing the wind.

Tower: It could be a tubular type or lattice type. They could be free-standing or guy-wire.

Control and protection system: It is generally situated at the bottom of the tower. The variable output of the alternator is converted to stabilized constant output power using a control system. The type of control system varies depending on the type of application.

Gearbox: The gearbox converts the relatively slow rotation of the rotor to match the rpm of the generator. It is placed between the rotor and the generator.

The procedure to dismantle a horizontal axis small wind turbine is as follows.

1. Switch off all the load and the generator.
2. Brake the wind turbine.
3. Loosen the bolts from the hub which fixes the blades
4. Remove the blades

Discussion: After completion of this experiment, the students can dismantle all the parts of a horizontal axis wind turbine.

Experiment No. 4

Title: Assemble a vertical axis small wind turbine to produce electric power and then dismantle it.

Aim: To assemble and dismantle a small vertical-axis wind turbine

Apparatus/software required: Watch the video at,

(a) https://www.youtube.com/watch?v=2VDVDTIPdg0
(b) https://www.youtube.com/watch?v=ldt405jIR0E
(c) https://www.youtube.com/watch?v=EM-gCvhQhPU

Theory: Small wind turbines are small machines used to generate electrical power from wind energy. It is a direct-drive wind power plant in which there is no gearbox. However, in some plant gearbox is also used. This wind turbine has a passive yaw system. The power typical output power is 500W to 10kW. Nowadays this range is extended up to 300kW. Small wind turbine power plants are used for residential or industrial purposes. These are used when constant stream and direction of the wind are available in a particular location. Small wind turbines may be horizontal axis wind turbines (HAWTs) or vertical axis wind turbines (VAWTs). In a VAWT, the axis of the drive is perpendicular to the ground. The small VAWT will rotate from whatever direction the wind blows. Hence no yaw mechanism is required. The VAWT is beneficial in areas where there is turbulent wind flow. The investment incurred in small VAWT is very low and can be installed on telecommunication towers. It is suitable for low-power applications. The parts of the vertical axis of small wind turbines are give

1. Rotor
2. Electric generator/alternator
3. Tower
4. Control and protection systems
5. Gearbox in some small wind power plant

Rotor: It may be of the two-bladed or three-bladed or multibladed turbine. The blads are designed to rotate in a clockwise direction to harness wind energy. The blades are generally fixed to the hub at the appropriate angle. Blades are usually made of glass fibre.

Electric generator/alternator: An alternator produces alternating current (AC) power. Various types of generators are used. In general, a permanent magnet synchronous generator (PMSG) is used in small wind turbine generators. In some plants, a DC generator is used and that can be directly used for battery charging and small power applications. When a high-speed squirrel cage induction generator (SCIG) is used, the SCIG is connected through a gearbox.

Tower: It could be a tubular type or lattice type. They could be free-standing or guy wired.

Control and protection system: It is generally situated at the bottom of the tower. The variable output of the alternator is converted to stabilized constant output power using a control system. The type of control system varies depending on the type of application.

Gearbox: The gearbox converts the relatively slow rotation of the rotor to match the rpm of the generator. It is placed between the rotor and the generator.

The procedure to assemble a horizontal axis small wind turbine is as follows.

1. **Installation of wind turbine tower:** The steel section of the tower can be fabricated off-site at a factory. In general, the parts of the tower are assembled on the site. The bolts are tightened together. After assembling all the parts of the tower, the tower is lifted by a crane and fixed on the foundation.
2. **Installation of the nacelle:** The main shaft, yaw system, generator, and pitch control assembly are assembled in the factory and mounted on the base. The nacelle is bolted to the equipment. The whole assembly is lifted to the top of the tower and secured on it.
3. **Installation of the turbine blades:** The turbine blades are bolted to the hub on the site.
4. **Installation of Electronic controller:** The electronic controller is installed along with the nacelle. Necessary connections are made.
5. **Installation of Electrical power cables:** The terminals of the generator are connected to the power cables and the other ends are connected to the control panel situated at the bottom of the tower.

The procedure to dismantle a horizontal axis small wind turbine is as follows.

1. Switch off all the load and the generator.

2. Brake the wind turbine.
3. Loosen the bolts from the hub which fixes the blades
4. Remove the blades

Conclusion: After completion of this experiment, the students can assemble and dismantle all the parts of a vertical-axis wind turbine.

Experiment No. 5

Title: Identify the routine maintenance parts of the horizontal axis small wind turbine after watching a video program

Aim: Identify the routine maintenance parts of the horizontal axis small wind turbine

Apparatus/software required: Watch the video at,

(a) https://www.youtube.com/watch?v=JCr90dK18Lk
(b) https://www.youtube.com/watch?v=65k2Nh8YHFI
(c) https://www.youtube.com/watch?v=5JJ5x-CYOP0&t=380s
(d) https://www.youtube.com/watch?v=2VDVDTIPdg0

Theory: Small wind turbines are small machines used to generate electrical power from wind energy. It is a direct-drive wind power plant in which there is no gearbox. However, in some plant gearbox is also used. This wind turbine has a passive yaw system. The typical output power is 500W to 10kW. Nowadays this range is extended up to 300kW. Small wind turbine power plants are used for residential or industrial purposes. These are used when constant stream and direction of the wind are available in a particular location. Small wind turbines may be horizontal axis wind turbines (HAWTs) or vertical axis wind turbines (VAWTs). In a horizontal-axis wind turbine, the axis of the drive is parallel to the ground. The parts of the horizontal axis of small wind turbines are given below.

1. Rotor
2. Electric generator/alternator
3. Tail vane or yaw system
4. Tower
5. Control and protection systems
6. Gearbox in some small wind power plant

Rotor: It may be of the two-bladed or three-bladed or multibladed turbine. The blads are designed to rotate in a clockwise direction to harness wind energy. The blades are generally fixed to the hub at the appropriate angle. Blades are usually made of glass fibre.

Electric generator/alternator: An alternator produces alternating current (AC) power. Various types of generators are used. In general, a permanent magnet synchronous generator (PMSG) is used in small wind turbine generators. In some plants, a DC generator is used and that can be directly used for battery charging and small power applications. When a high-speed squirrel cage induction generator (SCIG) is used, the SCIG is connected through a gearbox.

Tail vane or yaw system: A simple tail vane is fitted at the back of the nacelle so that the turbine rotor keeps facing the wind. When the tail vane is not available a forced yaw system keeps the r rotor facing the wind.

Tower: It could be a tubular type or lattice type. They could be free-standing or guy wired.

Control and protection system: It is generally situated at the bottom of the tower. The variable output of the alternator is converted to stabilized constant output power using a control system. The type of control system varies depending on the type of application.

Gearbox: The gearbox converts the relatively slow rotation of the rotor to match the rpm of the generator. It is placed between the rotor and the generator.

Following routine maintenance must be carried out for horizontal axis small wind turbine

1. Checking and tightening bolts and electrical connections as necessary
2. Checking machines for corrosion and the guy wires for proper tension
3. Checking for and replacing any worn leading edge tape on the turbine blades, if appropriate
4. Replacing components such as turbine blades and/or bearings as needed.

Conclusion: After completion of this experiment, the student will be able to identify the routine maintenance parts of the horizontal axis small wind turbine.

Experiment No. 6

Title: Identify the routine maintenance parts of the vertical axis small wind turbine after watching a video program.

Aim: To identify the routine maintenance parts of the vertical axis small wind turbine

Apparatus/software required: Watch the video at,

(a) https://www.youtube.com/watch?v=2VDVDTIPdg0

(b) https://www.youtube.com/watch?v=ldt405jIR0E

(c) https://www.youtube.com/watch?v=EM-gCvhQhPU

Theory: Small wind turbines are small machines used to generate electrical power from wind energy. It is a direct-drive wind power plant in which there is no gearbox. However, in some plant gearbox is also used. This wind turbine has a passive yaw system. The power typical output power is 500W to 10kW. Nowadays this range is extended up to 300kW. Small wind turbine power plants are used for residential or industrial purposes. These are used when constant stream and direction of the wind are available in a particular location. In a VAWT, the axis of the drive is perpendicular to the ground. The small VAWT will rotate from whatever direction the wind blows. Hence no yaw mechanism is required. The VAWT is beneficial in areas where there is turbulent wind flow. The investment incurred in small VAWT is very low and can be installed on telecommunication towers. It is suitable for low-power applications. The parts of the vertical axis of small wind turbines are give

1. Rotor
2. Electric generator/alternator
3. Tower
4. Control and protection systems
5. Gearbox in some small wind power plant

Rotor: It may be of the two-bladed or three-bladed or multibladed turbine. The blads are designed to rotate in a clockwise direction to harness wind energy. The blades are generally fixed to the hub at the appropriate angle. Blades are usually made of glass fibre.

Electric generator/alternator: An alternator produces alternating current (AC) power. Various types of generators are used. In general, a permanent magnet synchronous generator (PMSG) is used in small wind turbine generators. In some plants, a DC generator is used and that can be directly used for battery charging and small power applications. When a high-speed squirrel cage induction generator (SCIG) is used, the SCIG is connected through a gearbox.

Tower: It could be a tubular type or lattice type. They could be free-standing or guy wired.

Control and protection system: It is generally situated at the bottom of the tower. The variable output of the alternator is converted to stabilized constant output power using a control system. The type of control system varies depending on the type of application.

Gearbox: The gearbox converts the relatively slow rotation of the rotor to match the rpm of the generator. It is placed between the rotor and the generator.

Following routine maintenance must be carried out for small wind turbine plant

1. Checking and tightening bolts and electrical connections as necessary.
2. Checking machines for corrosion and the guy wires for proper tension.
3. Checking for and replacing any worn leading edge tape on the turbine blades if appropriate.
4. Replacing components such as turbine blades and/or bearings as needed.

Conclusion: After completion of this experiment, the students can identify the routine maintenance parts of the vertical axis small wind turbine

KNOW MORE

1. The development of wind power production in India started in 1952. India's installed capacity for wind power production is 4th in the world's total installed capacity. As on 31st July 2022, the total installed capacity of wind power is 40.894 GW. Andhra Pradesh has the highest installed wind power capacity.
2. The first known wind turbine was created in 1988 for Electricity production in the U.S. The world's first multi-megawatt (2MW) wind turbine was constructed in 1972.
3. Jaisalmer Wind Park is the largest wind firm in India. The capacity of this wind firm is 600MW. The firm is developed by Suzlon Energy, the project features a group of wind farms located in the Jaisalmer district of Rajasthan, India.
4. Electronics and power electronics are integral parts of wind energy conversion. The output power from renewable sources is not of constant voltage and constant frequency. Constant voltage and frequency are essential requirements for grid integration and it is done by using electronic devices.
5. Grid integration is an important issue in wind power technology. It is defined as the technical and economical ability of wind power plants and wind firms to connect and operate within an electric power supply network that is compatible with the day-to-day operation and short-term security of the electric supply system.
6. Power quality issue is an important issue in wind energy technology.

REFERENCES AND SUGGESTED READINGS

1. Gupta, B.R., Generation of Electrical Energy, S. Chand& Co. New Delhi.
2. Rachel, Sthuthi; Earnest, Joshua - Wind Power Technologies, PHI Learning, New Delhi, ISBN: 978-93 88028-49- 3; E-book 978-93-88028-50-9
3. Hoon-Ki Lee, Tae-Kyoung Bang, Jeong-In Lee, Kyung-Hun Shin, and Jang-Young Choi1, " Characteristics analysis of a high-speed permanent magnet synchronous generator considering magnetic reactance derived from short circuit analysis", AIP Advances, Vol. 9. No.12, (2019), DOI: https://doi.org/10.1063/1.5129997
4. D.P.Kothari, I.J.Nagrath, "Electrical machines", Fifth Edition, Mc Graw Hill Education.
5. Trevor M. Letcher, Wind Energy Engineering. A handbook for Onshore and Offshore wind turbines. Academic Press, Elsevier. ISBN: 978-0-12-809451-8.
6. Wei Tong, Wind power generation and wind turbine design. WITpress Southampton, Boston, ISBN: 978-1-84564-205-1.
7. Bin Wu, Yongqiang Lang, Navid Zargari, Samir Kouro, Power Conversion and Control of Wind Energy Systems. IEEE Press, John WILEY & Sons. The USA. ISBN: 978-1-118-02900-8.
8. Alatalo M. Permanent magnet machines with air gap windings and integrated teeth windings, technical report 288. Sweden: Chalmers University of Technology; 1996.
9. Muller S, Deicke M, De Doncker RW. Doubly fed induction generator systems for wind turbines. IEEE Ind Appl Mag 2002;8:26_33.
10. https://mnre.gov.in/wind/current status/#:~:text=The%20expansion%20of%20the%20wind,39.25%20GW%20(as%20on 203
11. https://en.wikipedia.org/wiki/Wind_power_in_India
12. https://www.studocu.com › wind-energy-technology-ii
13. https://www.academia.edu/28724752/Problem_Solutions_B_1_Problem_Solving
14. https://byjus.com/wind-energy-formula/

❑❑

5 Economics of Power Generation and Interconnected Power System

UNIT SPECIFICS

Through this unit we have discussed the following aspects:

- Basic terms related to economic power generation and interconnected power systems;
- Base load plant and peak load plants;
- Choice of size and number of generating units;
- Combine operation of power plants;
- Causes of grid faults;
- Blackouts and brownouts;
- Major blackouts at the national and international levels;
- Solution of numerical problems.

The concept of various terms and their definitions related to the economics of power generation are presented. A brief description of the cost of units generated is also discussed. The combined operation of power plants and the advantages of the same are also presented in this unit. The causes of grid faults are discussed. The major blackouts at the national and international levels are presented in brief. Further curiosity and creativity as well as improving the problem-solving capacity of the students are dealt with some numerical examples.

Besides giving a large number of multiple-choice questions as well as questions of short and long answer types marked in two categories following the lower and higher order of Bloom's taxonomy, assignments through several numerical problems, a list of references, and suggested readings are given in this unit so that one can go through them for practice.

Based on the content, there is a "Know More" section appended. This section has been designed to supplement additional information and higher learning skills on the topic.

RATIONALE

This unit on the economics of power generation and interconnected power system will help the students to get a fundamental idea behind the power plants' economics and interconnected power system. The concept of base load and peak loads plants are discussed. The methods of calculation of depreciation are also presented. The cost of power generation and tariff are also discussed. The causes of grid faults are also presented. Furthermore, the major blackouts at national and international levels are presented

Some related problems are pointed out with their solutions which can help further for getting a clear idea of the concern topics on the economics of power generation.

PRE-REQUISITES

Fundamentals of Electrical & Electronics Engineering (ES104)

UNIT OUTCOMES

After completion of Unit-5 students will be able to:

U5-O1: Define various terms related to power plant economics and interconnected power systems.

U5-O2: Analyze the problems related to power plant economics.

U5-O3: Explain the combined operation of power plants and the advantages of the combined operation.

U5-O4: Discuss the causes of grid faults and the sample blackouts at national and international levels.

Unit-5 Outcome	EXPECTED MAPPING WITH COURSE OUTCOMES (1 - Weak Correlation; 2 - Medium Correlation; 3 - Strong Correlation)				
	CO-1	CO-2	CO-3	CO-4	CO-5
U5-O1	-	-	-	3	-
U5-O2	-	-	-	-	3
U5-O3	-	3	-	-	-
U5-O4	-	-	-	3	3

5.1 INTRODUCTION

Energy is a basic requirement for the advancement of civilization. The amount of energy used is the representation of a Nation's development. With the increase in population, the requirement for energy also increases. The size of the energy supply system also depends upon the amount of energy required. When energy requirement increases, the size of the power system that supplies the energy also increases. Several power plants are connected in parallel to meet the customer's energy requirements. Thus power plants are interconnected. There are various types of power plants in interconnected power systems and all plants must be run economically. The economics of power generation includes studies on how one can find the cost of generation, and how optimally the power plants are scheduled to generate electricity at minimum cost considering all the constraints of power generation. In this unit, the terms related to the economics of power generation, power plant economics, grid faults, and interconnected systems are discussed and analyzed.

5.2 RELATED TERMS

5.2.1 Load

The term "load" is most commonly used in power systems. Electrical appliances use electrical energy for their operation. The appliances are connected to the electrical supply system to receive the electrical energy. Thus, one can say that load is imposed on the supply system. In general, the term "load" is used to represent the following.

(a) It indicates a device or an appliance or a group of appliances that consume electrical energy.
(b) It indicates the power consumed by the appliances from the electrical supply system.
(c) It indicates the current drawn by the appliance.

Generally, the load is nothing but the power consumed by an appliance or a group of appliances. It may be also expressed in terms of a current drawn by an appliance or a group of appliances.

5.2.2 Connected Load

The sum of continuous ratings of all the loads i.e appliances connected to the supply system or part of the supply system is called the connected load. For example, if there are 4 ceiling fans of 75W each, 4 tube lights of 40W each, and 1 refrigerator of 200W in a house of four rooms of a customer, then the connected load of the house is calculated as follows.

$$\text{Ceiling fan load} = 4 \times 75\text{ W} = 300\text{W}$$

$$\text{Tube light load} = 4 \times 40\text{W} = 160\text{W}$$

$$\text{Refrigerator load} = 1 \times 200\text{W} = 200\text{ W}$$

$$\text{Total load of the house} = (300+160+200)\text{W} = 660\text{W}.$$

Thus, the connected load of the customer for the house is 660W. In this way, the connected load of all the customers of a locality is supplied by a supply company. The connected load of the locality is calculated by adding the connected load of all the customers of that locality. In this way, the connected load of a utility can be calculated.

5.2.3 Demand

It is the load drawn by an installation i.e appliances of that customer or group of customers from the source of electrical supply averaged over an appropriate and specified time interval. The unit of demand or load may be in kW (kilowatt), kVA (kilovolt amperes), kVARs (kilo vars), or A (amperes).

5.2.4 Demand Interval

It is a period over which load is averaged. The demand interval may be the order of 15 minutes or even more.

5.2.5 Maximum Demand or Peak Load

The greatest among all is the load or demand in a specified period of a system or an installation is called peak load or maximum demand (MD). The specified time interval may be a day, a week, a month, or a year. The installed capacity of a power station can be found, if the peak load is known. A power station must be able to supply the peak load. The cost of the power plant increases when the peak load increases.

5.2.6 Base Load and Peak Load Plants

The load on the power system is not constant at all times because the demands of customers are uncertain. Though customers' demands are uncertain, it is required to supply the same whenever they need it. Thus, loads change with time. The loads on the power system are considered as two parts as follows.

(a) Base load
(b) Peak load

The base load part is the unvarying part of the load and is almost constant throughout the day. On the other hand, the peak load part is the variable part and it is not constant throughout the day. The base load and peak loads are shown in Fig.5.1. The power plants which supply the base load are called baseload power plants. These plants are continuously running. The plants that supply the peak loads are called peak load plants. The peak load plants are in operation at the occurring peak loads only.

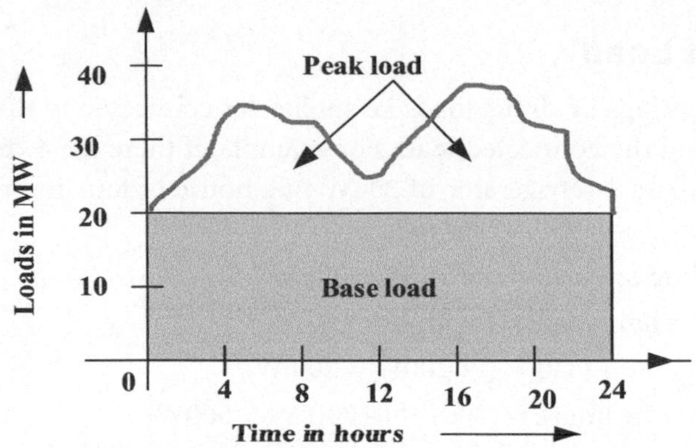

Fig. 5.1: Base load and peak load

5.2.7 Load Curve

The graphical representation of load and time is called the load curve (LC). The loads are in general kW or MW. The load is located on the y-axis and time is in proper sequence on the x-axis. If time is for a day, the curve is called the daily load curve. If the curve represents the load for a month, the curve is called the monthly LC. If the curve represents load variation for a year, it is called the yearly LC. A daily load curve is shown in Fig.5.2. It is also called the chronological load curve.

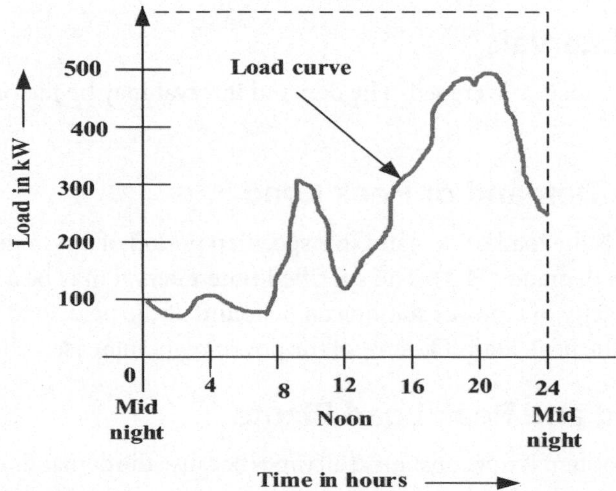

Fig. 5.2: Load curve

The load curve provides the following information.

(a) Variation of load during the hours of the day.

(b) The maximum demand can be obtained from the peak of the load curve.

(c) Total energy generated in a considered period = Area under load curve for the considered period.

(d) Average load $= \dfrac{\text{Area under load curve}}{\text{Total numbers of hours}}$

(e) Load factor $= \dfrac{\text{Area under load curve}}{\text{Total area of rectangle in which the load curve contained}}$

With the help of the above information, the following useful data can be obtained.

(a) Installed capacity of the power system can be decided.

(b) Most economical sizes of various generating units can be decided.

(c) The generating cost can be estimated.

(d) The sequence in which units will run can be determined.

5.2.8 Load Duration Curve

The load duration curve is a curve showing the relationship between loads in descending magnitude and the duration of the load. Thus, the load duration curve shows the greatest load at the extreme left and lesser loads towards the right. The load duration curve can be drawn from the same data from the load curve.

Procedure for plotting load duration curve

(a) From the available data, determine the maximum load (ML) and the duration (TM) for which it occurs.

(b) From the available data, for the next lower load (L1) and find the time (T1) for which it occurred.

(c) In the same way, find the subsequent loads (say L2, L3, L4) and the duration (Say T2, T3, T4) for which they occur.

(d) Plot the load and duration.

Fig. 5.3 shows the load duration curve obtained from the above procedure. Fig. 5.4 shows a load curve or chronological load curve, and Fig. 5.5 shows the load duration curve corresponding to the chronological load curve of Fig. 5.4.

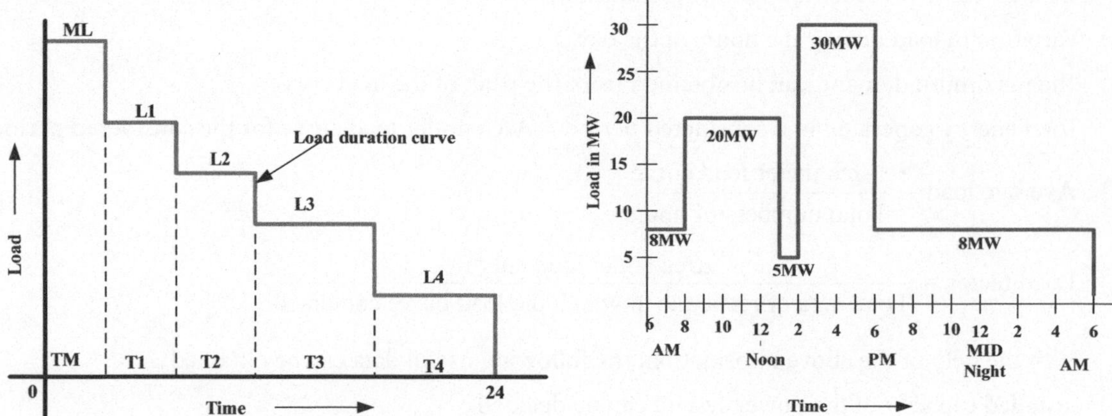

Fig. 5.3: Load duration curve to show the procedure for plotting

Fig. 5.4: Load curve for a day

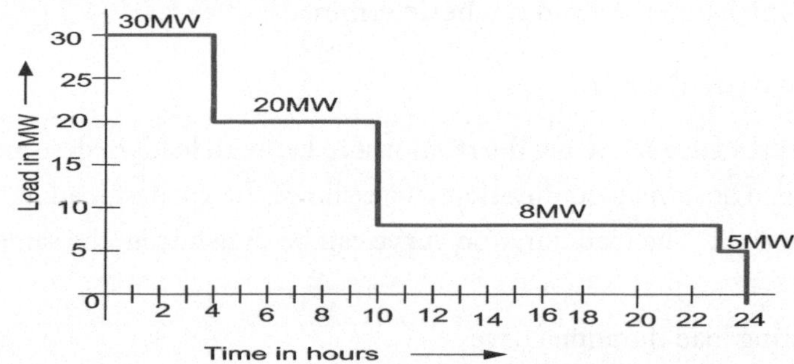

Fig. 5.5: Load duration curve corresponding to load curve of Fig.5.4

The followings are the information received from the load duration curve (LDC).

(a) Provides minimum load present throughout the given period.

(b) Enables the selection of base load and peak load plants.

(c) Area under the LDC represents the associated energy during the considered period.

(d) Average load can be obtained as follows. $\text{Average load} = \dfrac{\text{Area under load duration curve}}{\text{Base of the load duration curve}}$

(e) Any point on the LDC gives the total duration in hours for the corresponding load and all loads of greater value.

5.2.9 Integrated Load Duration Curve

The integrated load duration curve shows the total energy generated (in kWh) for a given load. The ordinate represents load in kW or MW and the abscissa represents energy (units generated in kWh). An integrated load duration curve is obtained from the load duration curve. The abscissa corresponds to each ordinate equal to the area of the duration curve up to the value of the ordinate. The integrated load duration curve corresponding to the load duration curve of Fig.5.4 is shown in Fig.5.6.

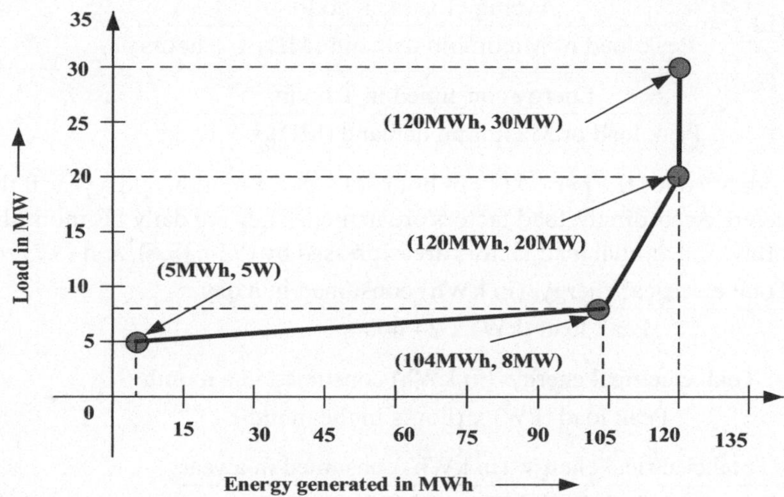

Fig. 5.6: Integrated load duration curve

5.2.10 Demand Factor

It is the ratio between maximum demand and the total connected load of the system. Mathematically it is expressed as (5.1).

$$\text{Demand factor (DF)} = \frac{\text{Maximum demand (MD)}}{\text{Total connected load}} \tag{5.1}$$

The demand factor can be for a part of the system like the system of loads of an industrial or commercial customer instead of the total system. Practically customers do not use all the appliances simultaneously and hence maximum demand is less than the connected load. Thus, the demand factor is generally less than unity.

5.2.11 Average Load

The average load or average demand is the energy consumed in a specified period of hour Mathematically, it is expressed by (5.2).

$$\text{Average load} = \frac{\text{Energy consumed in a specified time period (in hours)}}{\text{Hours in the specified time period}} \tag{5.2}$$

5.2.12 Load Factor

The ratio between the average load and maximum demand of a system over a specified period is called the load factor (LF). It can also be expressed in terms of energy consumed in a specified period (T). Mathematically, the load factor is expressed as (5.3) or (5.4).

$$\text{Load factor (LF)} = \frac{\text{Average load}}{\text{Peak load or Maximum demand (MD)}} \tag{5.3}$$

$$\text{Load factor (LF)} = \frac{\text{Average load x T hours}}{\text{Peak load or Maximum demand (MD) x T hours}}$$

$$= \frac{\text{Energy consumed in T hours}}{\text{Peak load or Maximum demand (MD) x T hours}} \tag{5.4}$$

The LF can be defined for the period (T) in hours of a day, a month, and a year if the hours of these periods are considered. Accordingly, load factors are named. They are daily LF, monthly LF, and annual LF. The daily, monthly, and annual load factors are expressed by (5.5), (5.6), and (5.7) respectively.

$$\text{Daily LF} = \frac{\text{Total electrical energy (in kWh) consumed in a day}}{\text{Peak load (kW) x 24 hours}} \tag{5.5}$$

$$\text{Monthly LF} = \frac{\text{Total electrical energy (in kWh) consumed in a month}}{\text{Peak load (kW) x (hours in the month)}} \tag{5.6}$$

$$\text{Annual LF} = \frac{\text{Total electrical energy (in kWh) consumed in a year}}{\text{Peak load (kW) x (8760 hours)}} \tag{5.7}$$

The cost of energy generation per unit (kWh) depends on the LF. It is seen that for the same value of peak load, the cost of generation is less for a higher value of load factor. The load factor of a specified power plant is called the plant load factor.

5.2.13 Units Generated Per Annum

The unit of electrical energy is expressed in kWh. One unit of energy means 1kWh. The number of units generated per annum can be obtained from the annual load factor and given by (5.7).

$$\text{Unit geneated/annum} = \text{Maximum demand (in kW) x L.F x hours in a year (=8760)} \tag{5.8}$$

5.2.14 Installed Capacity

The installed capacity of a power plant is the total capacity of all available units in the power plant to supply the system load. It is the total capacity of committed units and the reserve units. Committed units are the units that are supplying the load and are in operation. The reserve units are standby units and ready to supply load.

5.2.15 Firm Capacity or Firm Power

The firm capacity of a power plant is the power that is always available to meet the demand even under emergency conditions.

5.2.16 Cold Reserve

The cold reserve of a power plant is the reserve generating power capacity that is available in service but not in operation and ready for immediate supply to the load.

5.2.17 Hot Reserve

The hot capacity is nothing but a margin. The hot capacity of a plant is the capacity that is kept hot and ready to supply the demand. It is usually referred to as boiler excess capacity ready to supply demand.

5.2.18 Operating Reserve

The operating reserve is referred to the capacity of the power plant in service over peak load.

5.2.19 Spinning Reserve

It is the generating capacity connected to the grid and ready to take the load. The units for the spinning reserve are mechanically connected to the turbine but electrically not connected to the load.

5.2.20 Plant Capacity Factor or Plant Factor

The plant capacity factor or capacity factor is defined as the ratio between the average load to the rated capacity of the plant. The rated capacity of the plant is the installed capacity. The plant capacity is expressed mathematically by (5.9).

$$\text{Capacity factor or plant capacity factor} = \frac{\text{Average load}}{\text{Rated capacity of the plant}} \tag{5.9}$$

The capacity factor or plant capacity factor can also be defined as the ratio of actual units generated in a specified period to the maximum possible units that can be generated by the plant in that specified period. It is given by (5.10).

$$\text{Capacity factor} = \frac{\text{Units (in kWh) generated in a specified time period}}{\text{Rated capacity (in kW) x hours in that period}} \tag{5.10}$$

The capacity factor can also express in terms of maximum demand, load factor, and rated capacity as given by (5.11).

$$\text{Capacity factor or plant capacity factor} = \frac{\text{Maximum demand}}{\text{Rated capacity of the plant}} \text{x Load factor} \tag{5.11}$$

5.2.21 Plant Use Factor

The plant use factor is defined as the ratio of units (kWh) generated to the product of plant capacity and hours for which the plant is in operation. It is expressed by (5.12).

$$\text{Plant use factor} = \frac{\text{Units generated (kWh) by the plant}}{\text{Plant capacity x hours of use}} \tag{5.12}$$

5.2.22 Diversity Factor

The time of occurrence of maximum demand of all the customers of a group is not likely to be the same. Maximum demand for some customers of the group is coincident. and that of others do not occur simultaneously. Hence, there is diversity in the occurrence of loads. Due to this diverse nature, it is not required to supply power to all the connected loads to their full capacity at the same time. The ratio of the sum of individual maximum demand (irrespective of the time of occurrence) of various groups or subdivisions of a system to the coincident maximum demand of the whole system. Mathematically, it is expressed by (5.13a) or (5.13b), or (5.13c).

$$\text{Diversity factor, } F_D = \frac{\text{(sum of individual maximum demands)}}{\text{(coinsident maximum demand of the whole susyem)}} \tag{5.13a}$$

Or

$$F_D = \frac{D_1 + D_2 + D_3 + ... + D_n}{D_g(= D_{(1+2+3+...+n)})} \tag{5.13b}$$

Or

$$F_D = \frac{\sum_{i=1}^{n} D_i}{D_g} \tag{5.13c}$$

where D_i = maximum demand of load i, irrespective of the time of occurrence, D_g = Coincident maximum demand of a group of n loads.

5.3 COST OF GENERATION

5.3.1 Introduction

The electric supply company needs to supply electrical power to a large number of custome₹ Efforts are made by the supply company during the design of the power plant and related systems to achieve the overall economy. The cost of generation per unit (kWh) must be lowest as possible so that the electrical can be supplied to the customers at a reasonable rate. While deciding this care must be taken so that reliability of the system must be maintained.

5.3.2 Classification of Costs

Generally, the cost of electrical energy is divided into three. They are as follows.

(a) Fixed cost
(b) Semi-fixed cost
(c) Running or operating cost

(a) **Fixed cost:** Fixed cost is independent of the maximum demand and energy output of the plant. It includes the interest in capital invested in land, the annual cost of the central organization, and the salaries of high officials. The salaries of high-class officials are fixed. It does not matter whether the plant has high or low maximum demand, or it generates less or more. The cost of land is fixed and hence interest on the capital borrowed from the bank is also fixed.

(b) **Semi-fixed cost:** Semi-fixed cost is independent of energy output but dependent on the maximum demand. The size of the plant and installation cost depends on maximum demand. Semi-fixed cost includes annual interest and depreciation on the capital cost plant, transmission system, buildings, distribution system, all types of taxes and insurance, yearly compensation to be given to the workers, and salaries of clerks, and managers.

(c) **Operating cost or running cost:** The operating cost means the expenditure for operation or units (kWh) generated. This cost depends on the number of units (kWh) generated in the plant. The cost of fuel, lubricating oil, maintenance, repairing of equipment, water, wages and salaries of operational and maintenance staff, salaries of supervisors, etc. The more the number of units generated more the operating cost.

The fixed and semi-fixed costs are independent of the units generated. These two are also called "standing costs".

5.3.3 Expression for Total Annual Cost

The total annual cost of generation in a power plant can be expressed in two forms. They are three-part forms and two-part forms. In the three-part form the fixed, semi-fixed, and running costs are shown separately whereas, in the two-part form, fixed cost is merged into a fixed sum per kW maximum demand and added to running cost.

Three-part form: The expression for an overall annual cost of generation is expressed as (5.14).

The total cost of generation = Fixed cost + semi-fixed cost+ operating cost

Or Total cost of generation = ₹(A + B kW + C kWh) (5.14)

where A, B, and C are constants. A is independent of maximum demand and units generated and is expressed in rupees, B is dependent on maximum demand and independent of units generated and expressed in rupees/kW of maximum demand, and C is dependent on unit generated and expressed in rupees/kWh output. The unit of cost here is Indian rupees. It may be other units like USD etc.

Two-part form: It is a simplified version of the three-part form. Here, the total cost is divided into two parts. A fixed sum per kW and a fixed sum per kWh. The fixed part "A" of the three-part form is merged in the fixed sum per kW maximum demand. In two-part form, the total annual cost of generation is expressed as (5.15),

The total annual cost of generation = ₹(A kW + B kWh) (5.15)

Where A is a constant expressed in rupees/kW, and B is a constant expressed in rupees/kWh.

5.3.4 Methods of Determining Depreciation

The value of the equipment is reduced due to constant use. An amount is charged for this reduction and is called a depreciation charge. A suitable amount is set aside every year so that after some time the same equipment can be replaced at a cost equal to the accumulated depreciation charge in this period. There are three commonly used methods for finding depreciation. The methods are given below.

(a) Straight line method.

(b) Diminishing value method.

(c) Sinking fund method.

(a) Straight line method: Here, a constant depreciation charge is made every year. The depreciation charge is calculated using (5.16), where P is the initial cost, S is the scrap value after useful life, and, n is the useful life in year.

$$\text{Annual depreciation} = \frac{\text{Total depreciation}}{\text{Useful life}} = \frac{\text{P-S}}{\text{n}} \tag{5.16}$$

The useful life is the period for which the equipment, building, etc. are in operation after which the same can be replaced. The value of the equipment, building after its useful life is called scrap value.

(b) **Diminishing value method:** In this method, the depreciation charge is made at a fixed rate on the diminished value. Mathematically it is expressed by (5.17) in which x is the annual depreciation, n is the useful life in years, S is the scrap value, and P is the initial investment.

$$\text{Annual depreciation, } x = 1 - \left(\frac{S}{P}\right)^{1/n} \tag{5.17}$$

(c) **Sinking fund method:** In this method, a fixed depreciation is charged each year, and interest is compounded annually. If the annual rate of interest in decimal is r, the scrap value is S, the initial investment is P, and n is the useful life, the sinking fund q is given by (5.18).

$$\text{Sinking fund, q} = (P-S)\left[\frac{r}{(1+r)^n - 1}\right] = (P-S)x \text{ Sinking fund factor} \tag{5.18}$$

The value of q gives the uniform annual depreciation charge. The sinking fund factor is given by (5.19).

$$\text{Sinking fund factor} = \left[\frac{r}{(1+r)^n - 1}\right] \tag{5.19}$$

5.4 TARIFF

The tariff is the rate at which electrical energy is supplied to a customer. The tariff includes the total cost of generating and supplying electrical energy along with a profit. The tariff is not the same for all types of customers because the cost of generation of electrical energy is dependent on the magnitude of electrical energy consumed by that customer and their types of load.

5.4.1 Objectives of Tariff

Like other commodities, electrical energy is also sold to the customer at a rate that includes the return of the cost as well as a reasonable profit. Thus the objectives of the tariff are

(a) To recover the cost of generation at the power plant.
(b) To recover the cost of transmission and distribution.
(c) To recover the cost of operation and maintenance.
(d) To get a reasonable profit on the capital investment.

5.4.2 Types of Tariffs

The tariff is broadly classified as follows.

(a) Simple or uniform tariff
(b) Flate rate tariff
(c) Step rate tariff
(d) Block rate tariff
(e) Two-part tariff
(f) Maximum demand tariff
(g) Power factor tariff

(h) Three-part tariff

A brief description of each type of tariff is given below.

(a) **Simple or Uniform tariff:** In this type of tariff, the per unit cost of energy consumed is charged at a fixed rate. This rate is constant for all types of consumer It does not vary with an increase or decrease of energy consumed.

(b) **Flate rate tariff:** In this type of tariff, the customers are grouped into different groups and each group of consumers is charged at a different uniform rate. The group may be grouped as lighting loads and power loads etc, the tariff of the lighting load is slightly more than the power load because the power load is much more than the lighting load. The use of power load improves the load factor to a great extent.The disadvantages of flat rate are (a) separate meters are required for various types of load such as lighting load, power load, etc. which makes the system complicated, (b) a particular group is charged at a uniform rate irrespective of the amount of energy used.

(c) **Step rate tariff:** It is a group of flat-rate tariffs of decreasing unit chares for a higher range of consumption. Example, ₹5.00 per unit if consumption does not exceed 50kWh, ₹4.50 per unit if consumption exceed 50kWh but does not exceed 200kWh, ₹4.00 per unit if consumption exceed 200kWh

(d) **Block rate tariff:** In this type of tariff, a specified block of energy is charged at a specific rate, and succeeding blocks of energy are charged at progressively reduced rates.

The advantage of a block rate tariff is that the customer gets an incentive to consume more electrical energy. This will increase the load factor and hence cost of generation is reduced.

(e) **Two-part tariff:** In this type of tariff, the rate of charge of electrical energy is divided into two parts. They are fixed charges and running charges. The fixed charges depend on maximum demand and are independent of units consumed. The running charges depend on the unit consumed. The fixed charge is made at a certain amount per kW of maximum demand. In the two-part tariff, the total energy charges is expressed as (5.20),

$$\text{The total energy charges} = ₹A \times kW + ₹B \times kWh \tag{5.20}$$

where ₹ A is the charge per kW of maximum demand and ₹B is the charge per kWh of energy consumed. This type of tariff is mostly applicable to medium-industrial consumer. The drawback of this type of tariff from the point of view of the consumer is that the consumer has to pay fixed charges irrespective of consumption.

(f) **Maximum demand tariff:** This type of tariff is similar to that of a two-part tariff except that in this case maximum demand is actually measured by a maximum demand indicator instead of merely assessing it on the basis of rateable value. The drawback of a two-part tariff is eliminated by adopting a maximum demand tariff structure. The maximum demand tariff is mostly applicable to bulk supplies and large industrial consumers, who have control over their maximum demand.

(g) **Power factor tariff:** In a power factor tariff, the power factor of the consumer load is taken into account. A low power factor increases the rating of the power plant equipment and line losses. The consumer whose load has a low power factor is penalized. There are mainly three types of power factor tariffs. They are given below.

1. **kVA maximum demand tariff:** It is a modified form of a two-part tariff. In this case, the fixed charges are made on the basis of maximum demand in kVA, not in kW. As kVA is inversely proportional to the power factor, a consumer having a low power factor load needs to contribute more towards the fixed charges. The advantage of kVA maximum demand is that it encourages consumers to operate the appliances at a high power factor.

2. **Sliding rate tariff:** It is also known as the average power factor tariff. In sliding rate tariff, an average power factor (say 0.8 lagging) is considered as a reference. If the power factor of the load is below this reference, additional is imposed. On the other hand, if the power factor of the load is more than this reference power factor, a discount is allowed for the customer.
3. **kW and kVAR tariff:** In this type, both active (kW) and reactive power (kVAR) are charged separately. A consumer having a low power factor draws more reactive power and hence shall have to pay more charges.

(h) **Three-part tariff:** In a three-part tariff, the total charges made to the consumers are split into three parts, namely a fixed charge, a semi-fixed charge, and a variable charge. Mathematically, it is given by (5.21),

$$\text{Total charge} = ₹(A + B \times kW + C \times kWh) \tag{5.21}$$

where, A is the fixed charge made during each billing period which includes interest, cost of depreciation on secondary distribution, and labor cost of collecting revenues, B is the charge per kW of maximum demand, and C is the charge per kWh of energy consumed. This type of system of tariff is applicable to bulk consumers.

5.5 CHOICE OF SIZE AND NUMBER OF GENERATOR UNITS

The economics of power generation and the working of power stations depends upon the selection of generating units and their size. The number of generating units and their sizes are determined from the knowledge of the load curve. The following are the factors that are considered for determining the size and number of generating units.

(a) The total generating capacity of the generating units should be able to meet the peak demand of the power plant.
(b) The number of units must be selected in such a way that all the machines run at maximum efficiency.
(c) There must be a spare generating unit of capacity nearly the same as that of the largest unit of the power station. Keeping spare capacity unit increase supply reliability.
(d) There may be an increase in demand in the future. While deciding the size and number of units this aspect also should be kept in mind.
(e) The generating capacity of the power station should be decided by keeping 15 or 20% additional capacity to meet the expected maximum demand.

A minimum number of generating units are chosen in such a that the total capacity of this number of generating units is equal to the maximum demand. From the economics point of view, larger size units are selected because of lower capital cost per kW generation, require less floor area, and less operational labor. The selection of a single generating unit for meeting maximum demand has a few drawbacks such as

(a) to meet the variable nature of loads units may not be run at their maximum efficiency which in turn increases the cost per unit generated,
(b) if the generating units fail or are under maintenance, there will be a complete failure of supply to the consumer.

The above drawbacks can be overcome by installing another generating unit of equal capacity to the single generating unit already available. This will increase the reliability of supply. However, there will be an increase in initial investment. There is an alternative way of selecting numbers and the size of generating units. The selection should be such that it fits the load curve as closely as possible. The generating units should operate at their maximum efficiency all the time when it runs. The reserve capacity unit is only one unit of the largest size chosen and would be much smaller than the maximum reserve capacity. If the capacities of all the units are equal and identical in operation, the initial investment, space required, and spare parts would be less. The appearance would be identical and look good.

The drawback and difficulties in the selection of large numbers of smaller units are:

(a) The floor area required is more.

(b) Increase in maintenance and operation cost of labor.

Thus, it is observed from the above, the numbers of generating units should neither be very small nor very large. The size should be such that it should be compatible with the total capacity of the plant.

5.6 THE COMBINED OPERATION OF A POWER STATION

5.6.1 Introduction

There are various types of power plants in a country. They may be hydroelectric, coal-based thermal (steam), nuclear, gas turbine, and diesel power plants. Power plants are located at a place best suitable for each type. For example, hydroelectric power plants are located at a site where a huge quantity of water is available with sufficient head and facility to store water by constructing the dam. On the other hand steam, nuclear, diesel, and gas plants can be located at or near load centres. To meet the large, variable, ever-increasing power demands, most economic operations, and optimum utilization of the resources in a country or a particular region, it is necessary to integrate all the types of power plants. To do the same the power plants need to interconnect and such a power system is called an interconnected power system or combined operation of power plants. The interconnected system is supervised and controlled centrally.

The combined operation of power plants leads to considerable savings when compared with the independent operation of supplying the same load.

5.6.2 Advantages of Combined Operation of Power Plants

There are many benefits of the combined operation of different types of power plants. They are as follows.

(a) **Flexibility in operation:** The power demand varies at different seasons. Also, the demand is not the same at all times of the day. The plants which have minimum operating costs are in operation for maximum time. The plants with higher operating costs are run only when required by the load demand, and the plants with maximum operating costs are kept in reserve and operated in case of emergency. The starting time of a steam power plant is more than other power plants. It is also required to keep the boiler hot throughout the day and night to keep the stresses and strains caused by temperature variations to a minimum. Thus there is a considerable loss of energy. The operating cost is also very high. Hydroelectric plants can be started, and synchronized quickly. The operating cost is very low. Such plants can meet sudden load changes. Thus this plant is suitable for supplying peak and base loads. Nuclear plants are not suitable for supplying variable loads because nuclear reactors can not be easily controlled to supply variable loads demand. It is mostly suitable for base load plants. Gas turbine plants have low initial costs and low starting times. It is mainly suitable for s supplying peak loads. Diesel plants have uneconomical operating costs. It is operated when necessary in emergency conditions. Thus, if various types of power plants are operated in combination, the operation will be flexible.

(b) **Reliability of supply:** All the plants are not suitable for operation at all times of the year. Steam plants depend on the availability of coal. Hydro plants depend on stream flow. In a combined operation of power plants, there are diverse power plants. Thus, combined operation is more reliable to supply loads.

(c) **Reserve capacity:** The power system has some reserve capacity to meet unforeseen demand, take care of the outages of generating units, and schedule maintenance of generating units. There are large numbers of generating plants in combined operation. Thus the reserve capacity will be reduced. This leads to considerable savings.

(d) **Better utilization of hydro-power:** Hydro-power can be better utilized in combined operations. During the heavy run-off period, the hydro plant can be used to supply the base load. This leads to considerable savings in fossil fuels used in other plants. During the draught period, hydropower plants can be used as peak load plants and steam plants can be used as base load plants.

5.6.3 Selection of Power Plants

In the selection of a power plant, firstly, the size (capacity) of the plant is decided, and secondly, the type of plant is decided.

Selection of size or capacity

The size of the generating plant depends on the purpose for which it is used. Following are the purposes for which power plants are used.

(a) Private industry supply.
(b) Emergency supply or standby supply.
(c) Regional supply.
(d) Grid supply

Private industry supply: The size of the plant for private industry is decided based on the power requirement of different sections of the industry plus additional capacity reserve for future demand.

Emergency supply or standby supply: If the power plant is meant for emergency supply or standby supply, the capacity is decided based on the power requirement that needs to be supplied in the event of failure of grid supply.

Regional supply: In this case, the size is decided based on the present demand of the particular area or region plus some additional capacity reserved for future demand.

Grid supply: The generating plant for grid supply is decided based on the present load supplied by the grid in a particular area plus additional capacity for the load likely to increase in the next 10-20 years. Larger-sized plants have many advantages like economical because some of the costs are hardly affected by the size of the plant. The cost of office space, shops, etc. can spread over more capacity. The operating cost of coal handling plants, cooling facilities, etc. is less per kWh of energy generated in a larger plant. After taking a suitable decision about the capacity of the generating plant to be installed for a particular purpose as mentioned above, the type of power plant is decided. The type of power plant may be coal-fired thermal, hydropower, gas turbine, diesel, and nuclear power plant. The factors that are to be considered for the selection of sites for hydro, and coal power plants are already discussed in the previous units. The selection plants among diesel, natural gas, and nuclear plants are based on the availability of fuel oil, gas, and nuclear fuel.

5.6.4 Coordination of Base Load and Peak Load Plants

The loads on power plants are not constant. The unvarying portion of the loads on a power plant that occur throughout the day is called base load and the varying portion of the loads above the base load whose time of occurrence is unknown is called peak load. The base load needs to supply by the plant continuously throughout the day. The peak load needs to be supplied at the time of occurrence only. Hence, the most economical plant can be chosen for the base load, and the plant which is can be started quickly and is not so economical is normally used to supply the peak loads. If both base load and peak load are to be supplied by only a single plant, the installed capacity of the plant should be equal to or more than the peak load. The case of supplying power by a single unit is uneconomical because the peak load occurs for a short period of the year and most of the time it remains idle. Thus loads on a power system should not b supplied by a single unit. There should be some plants that supply base load and others (maybe different types) supply peak load. Hence, coordination among different power plants is important in the power system. The power plants that are selected for base load supply should have low operating costs, continuous running capability, few operating personnel, and economical maintenance. The power plants that are selected for peak load supply should have the capability of quick start and synchronization, and quick response to load variations. Hydroelectric power plants are economical, with the capability of a quick start and quick response to load change. It is suitable for both base and peak loads. Coal-based thermal plants give the minimum cost of generation per kWh when used as base load plants. To save fossil fuel, it may be preferred for peak load plants. The nuclear plant is preferred for base load plants. The diesel plants are uneconomical and preferred for peak load and emergency plants. The load allocation for various plants is shown in Fig.5.7.

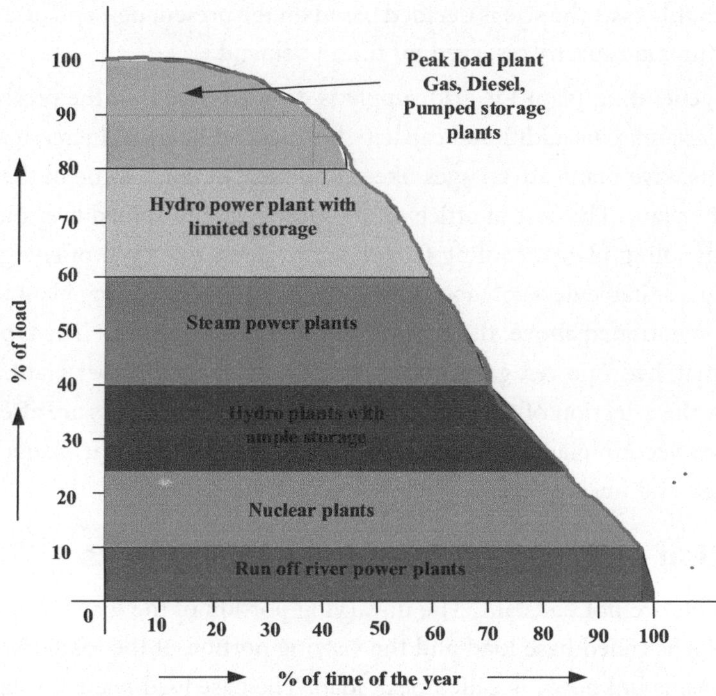

Fig. 5.7: Load allocation to various power plants

5.6.5 Power Plants Interconnections

Several generating plants are connected to form an interconnected grid system. There are many advantages of the interconnected grid system. They are given below.

(a) The amount of reserve plant capacity in the system as a whole was reduced. Load factor and Efficiency of operation improve.

(b) Reliability of supply increased.

(c) The diversity factor is of the whole system improved.

(d) Interconnection of hydro and thermal power plants is economical.

(e) Generators of larger size can be employed resulting in reduce cost/ kWh

5.7 CAUSES AND IMPACT, AND REASONS OF GRID SYSTEM FAULT: STATE GRID, NATIONAL GRID

Electrical power Grids (EPGs) are one of the most critical infrastructures in the globe. This study analyzes new threats to EPGs, their various effects, and various strategies that can be used to prevent or lessen such effects, thereby enhancing EPG resilience. Electrical power systems must increasingly be able to withstand such occurrences; hence, it is critical to comprehend the causes and effects of faults. Electrical power systems must increasingly be able to withstand such occurrences; hence, it is critical to comprehend the causes and effects of faults. This study shows several fault types and their corresponding causes, demonstrating which ones are more frequently discussed in the literature. The severity of the cause will affect the specific effects of the originating fault. If a small cause arises, it will lead to a minor fault that only affects a few residential homes and will be simple to fix, maybe taking just a few hours to complete. A large-scale fault, such as a blackout or a cascade failure, can instead be caused by a large-scale cause, such as a hurricane or terrorist attack, which could affect a wide area and take days or weeks to recover from. Large-scale disruptions have major economic and social repercussions for consumer When opposed to a non-robust system, a robust system is expected to recover from a large outage and be able to return to its pre-outage state. Three key cause clusters are listed in the entry: **Natural Causes**: A variety of natural events, including hurricanes, floods, flooding, earthquakes, tornadoes, heat waves, and solar flares, could cause a fault in the EPG; **Errors**: mistakes made by people or technical problems with equipment; **Attacks**: can be either cyber-attacks, like denial of service, or attacks by people, like terrorism.

Table 5.1

Causes	Faults
Natural Causes	Blackout, Cascading fault, Collapse of transmission towers, Damage and faults on substations, Downed wires or Lines disconnected, Fault currents, Fault of distribution and transmission lines, Fault of transformers, Faults and damage to the overhead transmission and distribution lines, Flashover of transmission lines, Increased current, Line faults, and Power loss, Line overloads, Localized blackouts and momentary interruptions, Short circuits, Stability limits exceeded, Substation flood, Thermal overloads, Transfer capability limited, Transformer slippage on the foundation and fall or complete collapse of the foundation, Underground cable loads affected, and Voltage and frequency instabilities.
Errors	Blackouts, Cascading outages, Fault currents, Fault of transformers, Frequency deviation, Hidden faults of protection, Line faults, Line overloads, Voltage and frequency instabilities
Attacks	Blackout and Cascading failures and Control infrastructures of smart grids affected, Delay, blockage or corruption, Downed wires, Economic and social disruptions, Line faults, Localized blackouts, momentary interruptions, Power loss, and Widespread damage

These factors, when they occur, can result in a wide range of EPG problems. Different EPG faults are shown in Table 1 and are divided into three clusters for each cause of the faults. First, there are natural factors, which take into account extraordinary occurrences like hurricanes, storms, or flooding. Second, there are faults, which can be caused by human or equipment failure, and third, there are attacks, which can be either cyber or physical in nature. The pictorial view of different faults is portrayed in Fig.5.8. Blue squares represent causes, and green triangles represent faults. The squares and triangles are sized by how frequently they are mentioned in the surveyed literature. The frequency of electrical transmission in India is 49–50 Hz. Transmission lines are at risk of failing when the frequency hits its minimum or maximum level. Power grid failure, then, refers to the failure of transmission lines as a result of over or under-frequency. The task of the load dispatch center is to keep the frequency within the range of 48.5 to 50.2 Hz. The Overdraw performed by states is also kept up to date by the National Load Dispatch Center. Due to an excessive load on the transmission lines, states that overdraw electricity over their limits also become the cause of grid failure. Extreme heat has pushed power demand in New Delhi to hit record levels in the summer of 2012, leading to coal shortages across the country. (Because the government rations fossil fuel supplies and imports them from abroad.) Due to the monsoons' delayed arrival, agricultural areas in Punjab and Haryana used more electricity from the grid (Farmers using energy-intensive water pumps for irrigation). Due to the late monsoon, hydropower facilities produced less energy than usual, increasing the load on thermal power plants to meet the need for power. The unauthorized use of electricity is another significant factor in power grid failure.

5.8 BROWNOUT AND BLACKOUT

A ***blackout*** is the complete loss of electricity service in a specific location. In more severe situations, blackouts can last anywhere from a few minutes to weeks. Typically, blackouts are caused by equipment/system breakdowns or weather-related issues. A rolling blackout is a series of controlled disruptions in electrical power service. A rolling blackout is a load-shedding procedure in which predetermined power demand is withdrawn from the electrical system to assist maintain system integrity. While a rolling blackout is usually a scheduled outage, there is usually little to no early notice. Rolling blackouts are a last-resort method used to avert a total blackout of an electrical power system. Rolling blackouts may be implemented in response to a situation in which the electricity demand exceeds the network's power supply capability. In most cases, rolling blackouts are caused by insufficient generation capacity (high-load demand) or insufficient transmission infrastructure.

A ***brownout*** is a brief interruption in power service. A brownout only causes a drop in system voltage; the electrical power source is never completely disrupted. Brownouts are typically planned, controlled incidents that serve to keep a system from failing.

5.8.1 What's the Difference Between a Blackout and a Brownout?

A brownout is caused by high electricity demand that is close to or exceeds a utility's production capacity. When this happens, the utility may decrease the flow of electricity to specific locations to avert a blackout. A blackout is a large-scale service outage caused by extreme weather or power plant equipment failure.

5.8.2 What Causes a Brownout?

The generation of power is a balancing act. Electricity demand is constantly changing, and electrical utilities employ their network of generators, substations, and transformers to ensure that they are producing and distributing electricity in the appropriate amounts. A brownout happens when the utility purposefully reduces the delivery of electricity in some regions when demand is close to or beyond its maximum production capability. During a brownout, energy continues to flow to your home, but at a lower voltage than usual. The dimming of incandescent light bulbs, which happens frequently during brownouts, gives the phenomenon its name. The duration of these planned blackouts might range from a few minutes to many hours, after which the utility should be able to resume full power levels as the demand for electricity should have subsided. Brownouts can also happen spontaneously as a result of damage or malfunction to the grid or a local power plant, however, this is much less often.

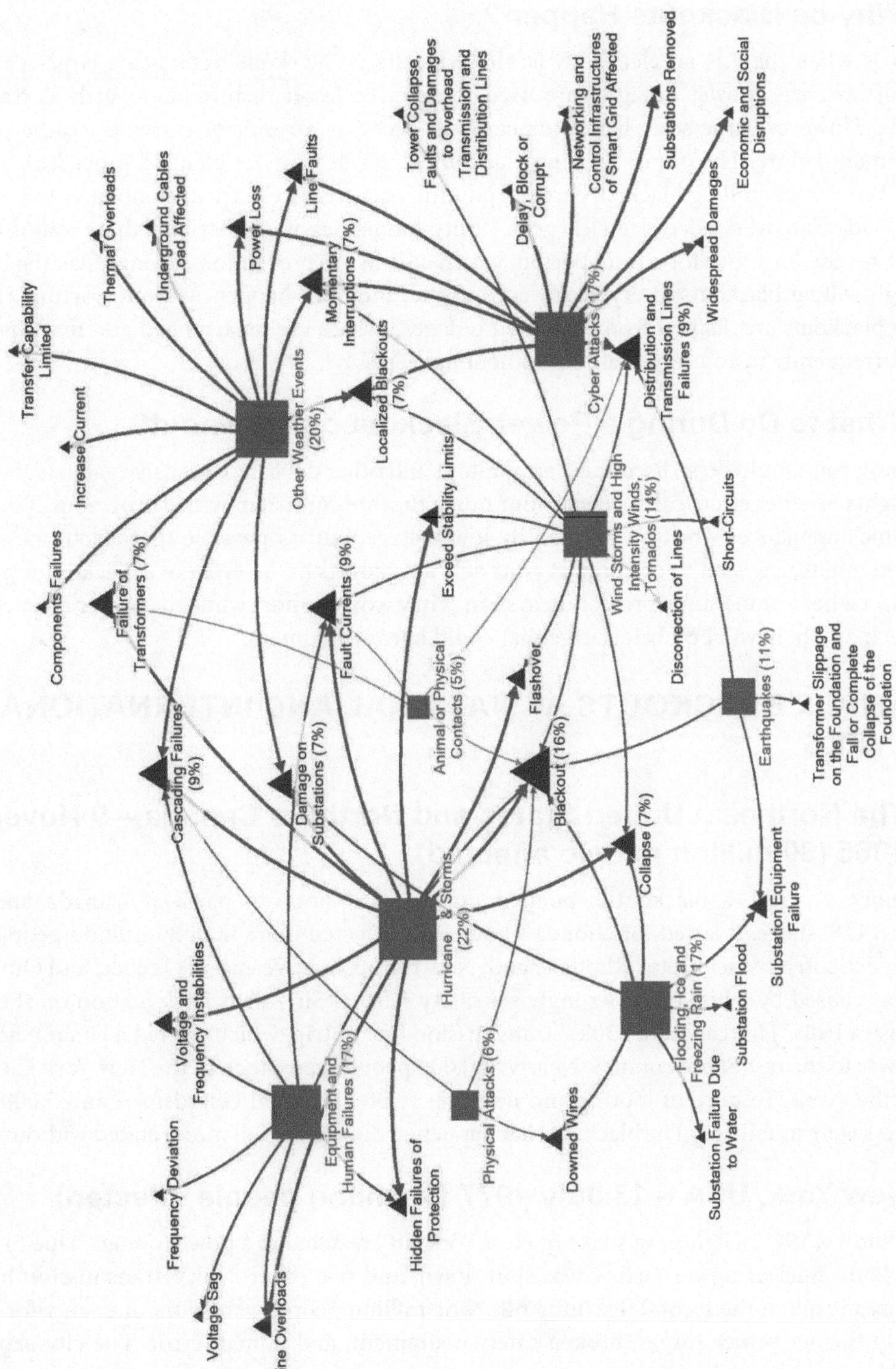

Fig. 5.8: Graphical relationship of EPG faults and causes.

5.8.3 Why do Blackouts Happen?

A blackout is when there is no electricity at all. Typically, a "blackout" refers to a large-scale service interruption, whereas "power outages" are used to describe lesser disturbances, such as transformer breakdowns. However, large-scale blackouts can still occur as a result of extreme weather or power plant equipment failure. The phrase "rolling blackout" describes a more planned procedure. Similar to intentional brownouts, rolling blackouts are purposefully caused by electrical companies to temporarily reduce the load on an overloaded electrical grid. Utility companies often distribute these rolling blackouts throughout several locations for a brief period, which aids in the prevention of longer-lasting blackouts. Even though rolling blackouts are typically announced, they can happen without warning. Blackouts and rolling blackouts are distinct from "planned outages," which are prearranged and made public well in advance, frequently to accommodate equipment upkeep.

5.8.4 What to Do During a Power Blackout or Brownout?

The first thing you should do is disconnect any laptops and other delicate, expensive gadgets if you detect dimming lights or other electrical effects in your home that are consistent with a brownout. The majority of your home's appliances won't be harmed by low voltage, but it's possible that electronics could be harmed. You might also want to disconnect your delicate gadgets in the event of a blackout if your home doesn't have a whole-home surge protection system. They won't be hurt while the power is out, but when it comes back on, there will be a brief surge that could harm equipment.

5.9 SAMPLE BLACKOUTS AT NATIONAL AND INTERNATIONAL LEVELS

5.9.1 The Northeast United States and Northern Canada – 9 November 1965 (30 million people affected)

On November 9, 1965, a blackout happened during rush hour in parts of Canada and several northeastern U.S. states. It lasted for about 13 hours and affected more than 30 million people in New Jersey, Connecticut, Massachusetts, Rhode Island, New Hampshire, Vermont, Quebec, and Ontario. The blackout was caused by a broken or wrongly set safety relay at Sir Adam Beck Station on the Ontario side of Niagara Falls. This caused a 230kV transmission line to trip, which started a chain reaction that shut off power to the rest of the country. Nearly 800,000 people were stuck in the New York City subway because of the event. To prevent looting and damage, 10,000 National Guardsmen and 5,000 off-duty police officers were mobilized. The blackout that happened during the full moon ended without incident.

5.9.2 New York, USA – 13 July 1977 (9 million people affected)

On July 13 and 14, 1977, a lightning strike in New York City resulted in a power outage. Due to tripping, the Indian Point nuclear power facility was shut down, and two other 345kV transmission lines were shut down as a result of the second lightning hit. Nine million people were without energy for about 24 hours due to further power surges, broken safety equipment, and human error. The city experienced widespread looting as a result of the power outage, with rioters destroying some 1,600 stores and arsonists starting 1,000 fires. A total of 3,776 persons were arrested in the city's largest mass arrest ever as a result.

5.9.3 Quebec, Canada – 13 March 1989 (6 million people affected)

On March 13, 1989, the whole province of Quebec in Canada experienced a 12-hour blackout. Six million people experienced a blackout as a result of Hydro-electrical Québec's transmission system collapsing due to a solar geomagnetic storm. The earth's magnetic field changed as a result of the geomagnetic storm, tripping the Hydro-Québec power grid. During the blackout, the Montreal Metro and Dorval Airport were forced to temporarily cease operations, while schools and businesses were closed.

5.9.4 Southern Brazil – 11 March 1999 (97 million people affected)

Following a lightning strike on an energy substation in Sao Paulo in March 1999, 97 million people in southern and southeastern Brazil were left without power. One of the largest hydroelectric power facilities in the world, Itaipu, was shut down as a result of a series of events brought on by the catastrophe. Two of the largest cities in Brazil, Sao Paulo and Rio de Janeiro, were rendered inoperable by the five-hour blackout. In Rio's subway system, some 60,000 people were stranded. 1,200 military police troops were stationed in Rio and the city tunnels in So Paulo were shut down to stop looting and attacks.

5.9.5 India – January 2, 2001 (230 million people affected)

On January 2, 2001, India experienced a news blackout as a result of the failure of the Northern grid, which had 230 million northern Indians relying on the second-largest interconnected network in the nation. The fall was caused by a substation failure in the state of Uttar Pradesh, and inadequate transmission equipment was partly to blame. In addition to the region's more than 80 stranded trains, other operations and services were also suspended. It took 16 to 20 hours to restore the grid, costing as much as INR 5 billion.

5.9.6 The Northeast United States and Canada – 14-15 August 2003 (50 million people affected)

A blackout that occurred in August 2003 had an estimated 50 million people in southeast Canada and eight northeastern U.S. states affected. The worst blackout in North American history, which cost $6 billion in damages and lasted for two days in some areas, occurred during this time. Due to contact with overgrown trees in Northern Ohio, a high-voltage electricity line was shut down, causing the blackout. Three more lines were shut down as a result of FirstEnergy Corporation's malfunctioning alarm system failing to warn the operator A combined task force between the United States and Canada was established after the incident to stop further blackouts.

5.9.7 Italy – 28 September 2003 (57 million people affected)

On September 28, 2003, there was a blackout in Italy as a result of a storm-damaged power line that brought electricity to the country from Switzerland. Nearly all of Italy's 57 million people were affected by the catastrophe, which happened at around 3 AM. Additionally, it stopped 110 trains in Italy carrying more than 30,000 passengers, and trains were halted at the Swiss border for more than 3.5 hour Rome was hardest hit because the interruption happened during Nuit Blanche, an all-night art celebration, while the Geneva Canton region of Switzerland endured a three-hour blackout. Even while some areas were without power for up to 18 hours, about 90% of it was restored after eight hour

5.9.8 Java and Bali, Indonesia – 18 August 2005 (120 million people affected)

In August 2005, there was a power outage that affected 120 million people, or about half of the nation, in the Indonesian islands of Java and Bali. Parts of West Java, Central Java, and East Java also experienced blackouts, in addition to the nation's capital Jakarta and the nearby province of Banten. The collapse of the 19,615 MW Java-Bali power system was caused by a 500 kV transmission line breakdown between Cilegon and Saguling in West Java. The interruption caused transportation services to be disrupted and caused several domestic and international flights to be delayed or canceled. However, it only took 24 hours to fully restore the grid system.

5.9.9 Brazil and Paraguay – 10 November 2009 (67 million people affected)

On November 10, 2009, three transformers on a high-voltage transmission line short-circuited due to severe winds and heavy rain, leaving 67 million people without power for two to four hours across major portions of Brazil and the whole country of Paraguay. Six states in central and southern Brazil, including the metropolis of Rio de Janeiro and Sao Paulo, experienced blackouts; as a result, the Itaipu hydroelectric dam had to be shut down after the lines supplying the facility failed. Both Paraguay and Brazil were affected when the dam, which is located near their shared border, ceased producing 18,000 MW of energy. Due to a lack of street lighting, several car accidents were also reported during the blackout.

5.9.10 India – July 30-31, 2012 (700 million people affected)

In July 2012, northern India saw the worst blackout ever on two consecutive days. On July 30, the Northern grid experienced its first blackout, affecting 300 million people across nine states, including New Delhi, the nation's capital. The new grid, which included the Northern, Western, Eastern, and North-Eastern grids, experienced a larger blackout the following day after the Northern grid was restored and synchronized with it. In over 20 Indian states, 700 million people were impacted. The blackout was attributed to the overuse of electricity by some states and inadequate inter-regional power transmission channels. The occurrences led to several traffic bottlenecks by causing trains to break down and traffic lights to stop functioning. In the country's northern area, mining and building work were suspended and surgeries were postponed.

UNIT SUMMARY

1. A consumer's connected load is calculated by adding the continuous ratings of all the appliances and outlets in his home.
2. A consumer's maximum demand is the amount of electricity that his circuit is expected to use at any one time.
3. The connected load to maximum demand ratio represents the consumer's demand factor.
4. The ratio of the total of individual maximum demands to the maximum demand of the group is known as the group diversity factor. Always more than 1 exists.

5. The peak diversity factor is the proportion of a consumer group's maximum demand to its demand at the system's peak demand. Always more than 1 exists.
6. A chronological load curve depicts the changes in demand over the course of 24 hour Its shape varies according to the type of consumer, including home, commercial, industrial, agricultural, and traction. The system's chronological load curve depicts the changes in system load over the course of 24 hours. The amount of energy used (in kWh or MWh) throughout the course of a day is indicated by the area under a chronological load curve.
7. The load duration curve is a reordering of the load components of a chronological curve in descending order. Thus, it displays the total number of hours that a certain load lasts during the course of the day.
8. The energy load curve displays the energy between various degrees of demand.
9. Between energy and time lies a mass curve.
10. The ratio of average load to peak load is known as the load factor.
11. The capacity factor is the ratio of the average annual load to the rated plant capacity.
12. The utilization factor is the ratio of the highest load to rated plant capacity.
13. The capacity factor is equal to the product of the load factor and the utilization factor.
14. Base load and peak load zones can be distinguished on the chronological load curve.
15. Generally, the cost of electrical energy is divided into three. They are fixed cost, semi-fixed cost, and running or operating cost
16. The tariff includes the total cost of generating and supplying electrical energy along with a profit.
17. A system requires both long-term load forecasting and short-term load forecasting for optimal planning and operation.

EXERCISES

Example 5.1

A consumer is connected to the following loads:

1. 15 lamps each of 60 W
2. 3 heaters each of 1500 W
3. Maximum demand 1750 W

On average, she utilizes 10 lamps for 7 hours/day, each heater for 2 hours/day. Find (a) average load, (b) monthly energy consumption, and (c) load factor.

Solution:

$$\text{Average load} = \frac{\text{actual energy consumed}}{\text{time duration}} = \frac{(10\times60\times7)+(3\times1500\times2)}{24} = 550\text{ W}$$

$$\text{Monthly average consumption} = \left[(10\times60\times7)+(3\times1500\times2)\right]\times30\text{ Wh} = 396\text{ kWh}$$

$$\text{Load factor} = \frac{\text{average load}}{\text{maximum demand}} = \frac{550}{1750} = 0.314$$

Example 5.2

A power-generating plant can handle a maximum demand of 3000 kW. if the number of units (kWh) produced/year is 60 x10⁴ units (in kWh) produced per year. Find out the plant's annual load factor.

Solution:

$$\text{Average load} = \frac{\text{units generated per annum}}{\text{total hour in a year}} = \frac{60\times 10^4}{365\times 24} = \frac{600000}{8760} = 68.49 \text{ kW}$$

$$\text{Load factor (annual)} = \frac{68.49}{3000} = 1.28\%$$

Example 5.3

Find the maximum value for a load with daily consumption of 800 kWh and a load factor of 0.35. Calculate the energy consumption in kWh, if the consumer increases the load factor to 0.55 without changing the maximum demand.

Solution:

$$\text{Load factor} = \frac{\text{energy consumed in 24 h}}{\text{maximum demand}\times 24}$$

$$0.35 = \frac{800}{\text{maximum demand}\times 24}$$

$$\text{Maximum demand} = \frac{800}{24\times 0.35} = 95.24 \text{ kW}$$

In the second case, the load factor is 0.55,

Energy consumed in 24 h = (load factor) × maximum demand × 24

= 0.55 × 95.24 × 24 = 1257.16 kWh

Example 5.4

A generating station may generate up to 63.8×10^6 MW annually, with a maximum demand of 30 MW and a connected load of 46 MW. Determine the load factor and the demand factor.

Solution:

$$\text{Demand factor} = \frac{\text{Maximum demand}}{\text{Connected load}} = \frac{30}{46} = 0.652$$

$$\text{Average demand} = \frac{\text{Generation per annum}}{\text{total hours in a year}} = \frac{63.8\times 10^6}{8760} = 7283 \text{ kW}$$

$$\text{Load factor} = \frac{\text{Average demand}}{\text{Maximum demand}} = \frac{7283}{30\times 10^3} = 0.242 \text{ or } 24.2\%$$

Example 5.5

A 120 MW power plant delivers 110 MW for two hours, 60 MW for six hours, and then shuts down for the remainder of the day. Additionally, it is shut down for 35 days each year for maintenance. Determine the annual load factor.

Solution:

The energy supplied in each working day = (110 × 2) + (60 × 6) = 580 MWh

Plant operates for = 365-35 = 330 days in a year

Hence energy supplied/year = 580 × 330 × 191,400 MWh

Annual load factor =

$$\frac{\text{energy supplied per annum}}{\text{maximum demand}\times\text{working period(hours)}}\times 100 = \frac{191400}{(120)\times(330\times 24)}\times 100 = 20.13\%$$

Example 5.6

A power plant has a maximum demand of 34 MW, a load factor of 67%, a plant capacity factor of 58%, and a plant use factor of 76%. Find the plant's (1) reserve capacity, (2) daily energy production, and (3) maximum daily energy that could be produced if the plant were completely loaded and operating according to schedule.

Solution:

$$\text{Load factor} = \frac{\text{Average demand}}{\text{Maximum demand}}$$

$$0.67 = \frac{\text{Average demand}}{34}$$

$$\text{So average demand} = 34 \times 0.67 \times 22.78 \text{ MW}$$

$$\text{As Plant Capacity factor} = \frac{\text{Average demand}}{\text{Plant Capacity}}$$

$$\text{So plant capacity} = \frac{22.78}{0.58} = 39.27 \text{ MW}$$

Therefore reserve capacity of plant = Plant capacity – maximum demand

= 39.27 – 34 = 5.27 MW

Daily energy production/generation = Average demand × 24

= 22.78 × 24 = 546.72 MWh

The maximum energy that could be produced =

$$\frac{\text{Daily energy produced}}{\text{plant use factor}} = \frac{546.72}{0.76} = 719.36 \text{ MWh/day}$$

Example 5.7

A diesel station offers the following loads to diverse customers:

Industrial consumer = 1650 kW;

Commercial establishment = 620 kW;

Domestic power = 90 kW;

Domestic light = 375 kW;

If the maximum demand on the station is 2400 kW and the number of kWh generated per year is 43×10^5, determine (i) the diversity factor and (ii) the annual load factor.

Solution:

$$\text{Diversity factor} = \frac{1650 + 620 + 90 + 375}{2400} = 1.14$$

$$\text{Average demand} = \frac{\text{kWh generated per year}}{\text{total hours in a year}} = \frac{43 \times 10^5}{365 \times 24} = 490.86 \text{ kW}$$

$$\text{Load factor} = \frac{\text{Average demand}}{\text{Maximum demand}} = \frac{490.86}{2400} = 0.204 = 20.4\%$$

Example 5.8

A power plant's maximum demand is 12,250 kW. The plant capacity factor is 45%, while the annual load factor is 55%. Find out the plant's reserve capacity.

Solution:

The energy produced per annum

$$= \text{Maximum demand} \times \text{annual load factor} \times \text{Total hours in a year}$$

$$= 12250 \times 0.55 \times 8760$$

$$= 59020500 \text{ Wh}$$

$$\text{Plant capacity factor} = \frac{\text{Units generated per annum}}{\text{plant capacity} \times \text{total hours in a year}}$$

$$\text{Plant capacity} = \frac{59020500}{0.45 \times 8760} = 14{,}972.22 \text{ kW}$$

$$\text{Reserve capacity} = \text{Plant capacity} - \text{Maximum demand} = 2722.22 \text{ kW}$$

Example 5.9

A power plant has the following daily load curve:

Time (Hours)	6 - 8	8 - 12	12 - 16	16 - 20	20 - 24	24 - 6
Load (MW)	10	20	30	10	25	10

Plot the load curve and load duration curve. Also, calculate the energy generated per day.

Solution:

Fig. 5.9 shows the daily load curve, Fig.5.10 shows the daily load duration curve. It is easy to see that the area under the load curves is the same. It should be noted that the load duration curve is drawn by arranging the loads in declining magnitude order.

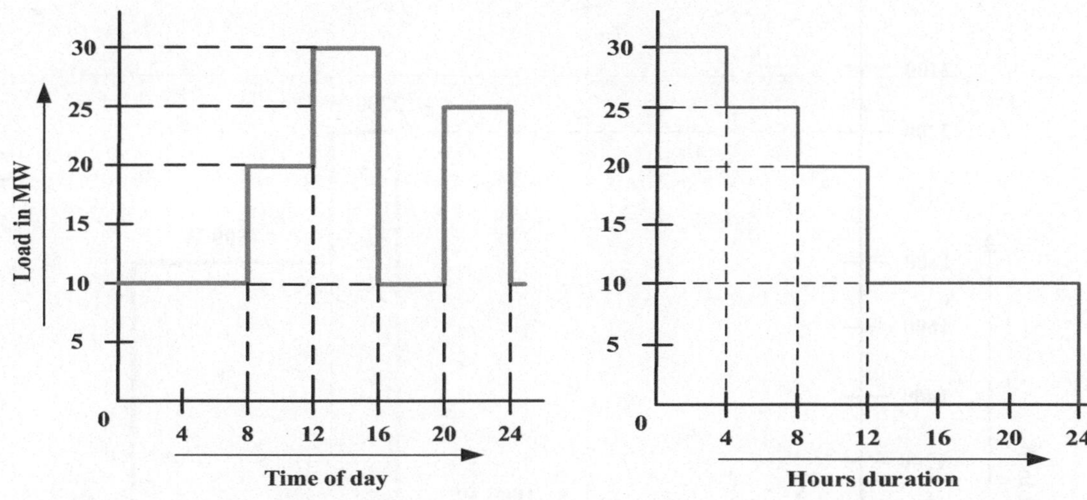

Fig. 5.9: Load Curve for Example 5.9

Fig. 5.10: Load duration curve for Example 5.9

Case-1

$$\text{Units generated/day} = \text{Area (in kWh) under the } \textbf{daily load curve}$$
$$= 10^3\,[10 \times 8 + 20 \times 4 + 30 \times 4 + 10 \times 4 + 25 \times 4]$$
$$= 420 \times 10^3 \text{ kWh}$$

Case-2

$$\text{Units generated/day} = \text{Area (in kWh) under } \textbf{daily load duration curve}$$
$$= 10^3\,[30 \times 4 + 25 \times 4 + 20 \times 4 + 10 \times 12]$$
$$= 420 \times 10^3 \text{ kWh}$$

Example 5.10

The daily demands of three consumers are given below:

Time	Consumer-1	Consumer-2	Consumer-3
12 midnight to 8 A.M.	No load	400 W	200 W
8 A.M. to 2 P.M.	400 W	200 W	400 W
2 P.M. to 4 P.M.	200 W	800 W	1200 W
4 P.M. to 10 P.M.	800 W	1000 W	No load
10 P.M. to 12 midnight	No load	No load	200 W

Plot the load curve and find (i) the maximum demand of individual consumers, (ii) the load factor of individual consumers, (iii) the diversity factor, and (iv) the load factor of the station.

Solution

Fig.5.11 shows the load curve

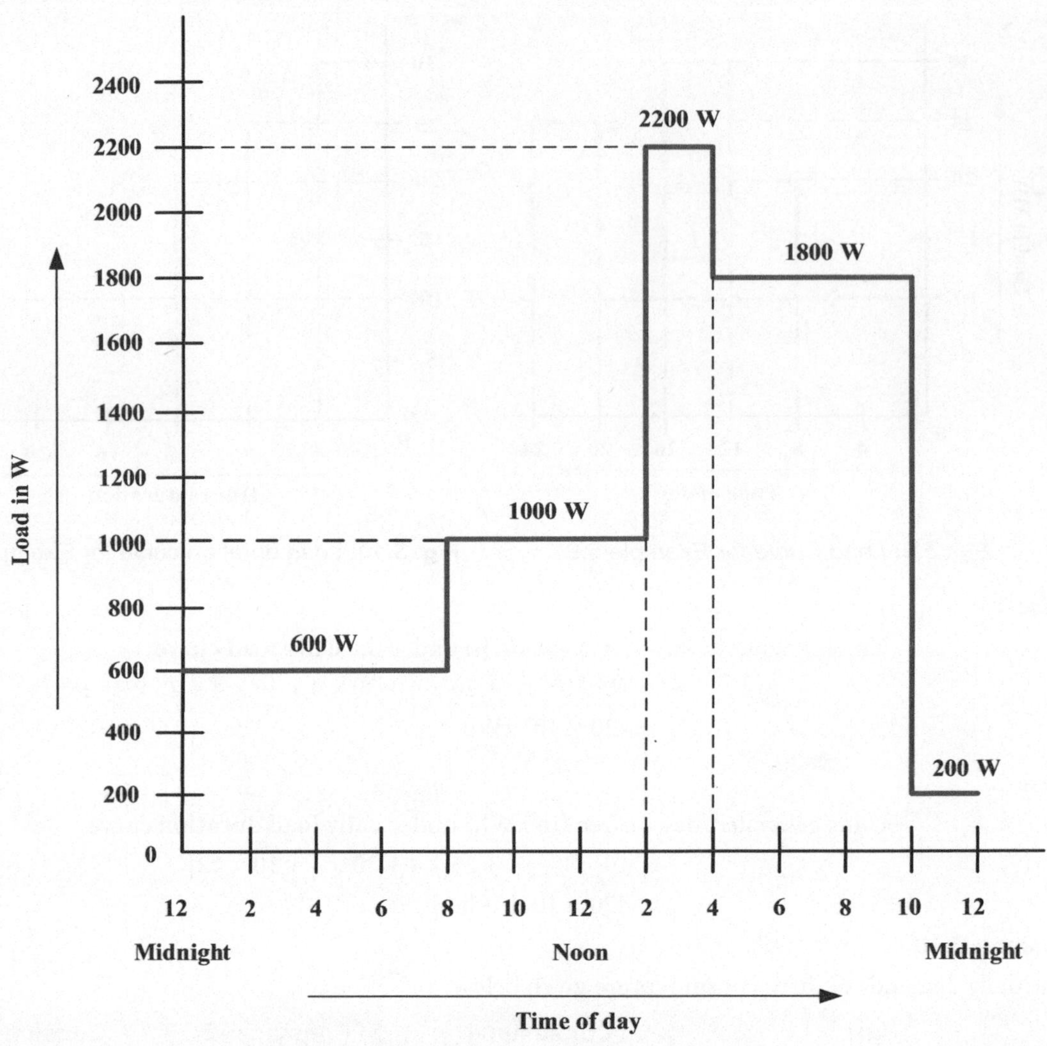

Fig. 5.11: Load curve for Example 5.10

Maximum demand of consumer 1 = 800 W, Maximum demand of consumer 2 = 1000 W, Maximum demand of consumer 3 = 1200 W.

$$\text{Load factor of consumer 1} = \frac{\text{Energy consumed per day}}{\text{maximum demand} \times \text{total hours in a day}} \times 100$$

$$\text{Load factor of consumer 1} = \frac{400 \times 4 + 200 \times 2 + 800 \times 6}{800 \times 24} = \frac{6800}{19200} \times 100 = 35.41\%$$

$$\text{Load factor of consumer 2} = \frac{400 \times 8 + 200 \times 6 + 800 \times 2 + 1000 \times 6}{1000 \times 24} \times 100 = 50\ \%$$

$$\text{Load factor of consumer 3} = \frac{200 \times 8 + 400 \times 6 + 1200 \times 2 + 200 \times 2}{1200 \times 24} \times 100 = 23.61\ \%$$

$$\text{Diversity factor} = \frac{800 + 1000 + 1200}{2200} = 1.36$$

$$\text{Station load factor} = \frac{\text{total energy consumed / day}}{\text{simultaneous maximum demand} \times 24} \times 100 = \frac{6800 + 12000 + 6800}{2200 \times 24}$$

$$= 48.48\ \%$$

Example 5.11

An existing distribution system will be used to electrify a brand-new residential/shopping complex. There will be 500 apartments there, each with a 4 kW connected load. In addition to having 25 general-purpose stores with connected loads of 1 kW apiece and a demand factor of 0.75, the retail center will also offer the following services:

Service	Connected load	Demand factor
1 Flour mill	8 kW	0.75
1 sawmill	4 kW	0.7
1 laundry	15 kW	0.6
1 Cinema Hall	75 kW	0.45

The street lighting for the complex will consist of 250 tube lights of 36 watts each. Assumptions of 0.45 for the residential load demand factor, 2.85 for the group diversity factor, and 1.15 for the peak diversity factor can be made. For the commercial load, the group and peak diversity factors can be taken as 1.5 and 1.7. It is possible to treat as unity the street light demand, group diversity factors, and peak diversity factor Determine the increase in system peak demand caused by this complex.

Solution:

Maximum demand for each apartment = 4 × 0.45 × 1.8 kW

$$\text{Maximum demand of 500 apartments} = \frac{500 \times 1.8}{2.85} = 315.78 \text{ kW}$$

$$\text{The demand for 500 apartments at the time of the system peak} = \frac{315.78}{1.15} = 274.59 \text{ kW}$$

Maximum demand for a total commercial complex

$$= \frac{25 \times 1 \times 0.75 + 8 \times 0.75 + 4 \times 0.7 + 15 \times 0.6 + 75 \times 0.45}{1.5}$$

$$= \frac{18.75 + 6 + 2.8 + 9 + 33.75}{1.5} = \frac{70.3}{1.5} = 46.87 \text{ kW}$$

$$\text{The demand of the commercial load at the time of the system peak} = \frac{46.87}{1.7} = 27.57 \text{ kW}$$

$$\text{The demand for street lighting at the time of the system peak} = \frac{250 \times 36}{1000} \quad 9 \text{ kW}$$

Increase in system peak demand = 274.59 + 27.57 + 9 = 311.16 kW

Example 5.12

On a typical day, a power plant's load is as follows:

Time	12-5 a.m.	5-9 a.m.	9-6 p.m.	6-10 p.m.	10-12 a.m.
Load (MW)	25	45	85	110	25

Plot the chronological load curve and load duration curve. Find the load factor of the plant and the energy supplied by the plant in 24 hours.

Solution:

The chronological load curve is plotted in Fig.5.12. The duration of loads is as under:

Load (MW)	110	85 and above	45 and above	25 and above
Duration (Hours)	4	13	17	24

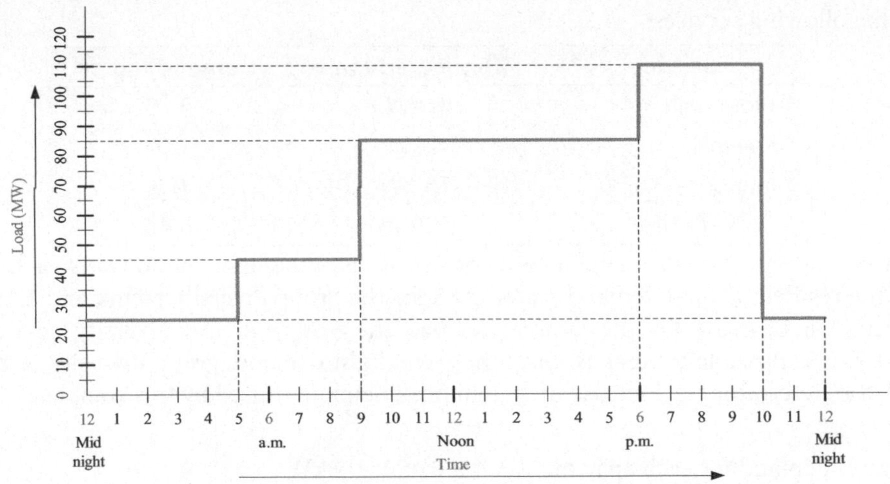

Fig. 5.12: Chronological Load Curve for Example.5.12

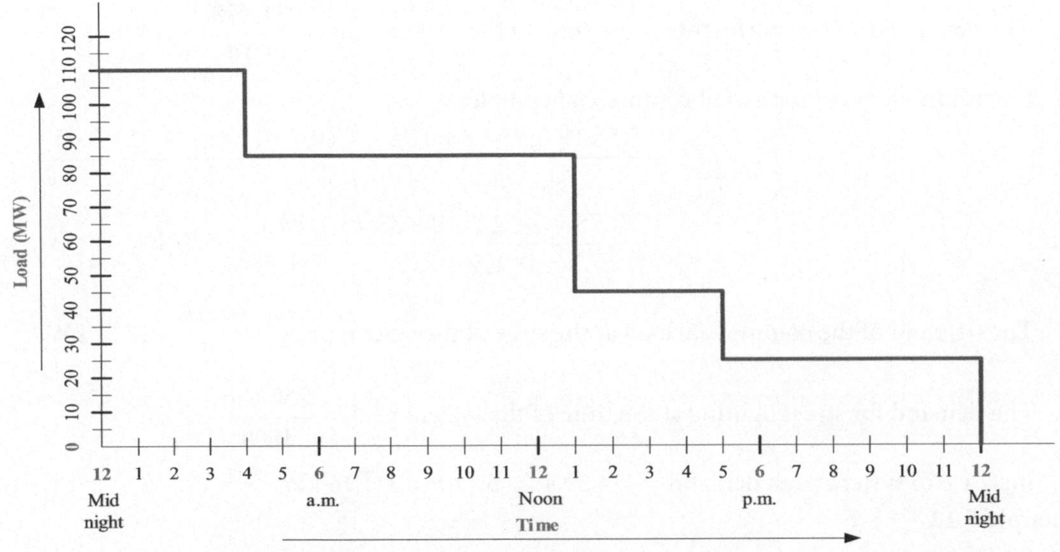

Fig. 5.13: Load duration curve for Example 5.12

The load duration curve is plotted in Fig.5.13. The energy produced by the plant in 24 hours is given as

$$= 110 \times 4 + 85 \times (13 - 4) + 45 \times (17 - 13) + 25 \times (24 - 17)$$

$$= 1560 \text{ MWh}$$

$$\text{Load factor} = \frac{1560}{110 \times 24} = 0.5909 \text{ or } 59.09\%$$

Example 5.13

The power plant of the abovementioned Example 1.12 is having an installed capacity of 130 MW. Determine the capacity factor and the utilization factor.

Solution:

$$\text{Capacity factor} = \frac{\text{Maximum Load}}{\text{Plant Capacity}} \times \text{Load Factor} = \frac{110}{130} \times 0.5909 = 0.499$$

$$\text{Utilization factor} = \frac{\text{Maximum Load}}{\text{Rated Plant Capacity}} = \frac{110}{130} = 0.846$$

Example 5.14

The maximum demand for a given power plant is 45 MW. The capacity factor is 0.57 and the utilization factor is 0.77. Determine (*a*) load factor, (*b*) plant capacity, (c) reserve capacity, and (*d*) yearly energy generation.

Solution:

$$\text{Load factor} = \frac{\text{Capacity factor}}{\text{Utilisation factor}} = \frac{0.57}{0.77} = 0.7402$$

$$\text{Plant capacity} = \frac{\text{Maximum demand}}{\text{Utilisation factor}} = \frac{45}{0.77} = 58.44 \text{ MW}$$

$$\text{Reserve capacity} = 58.44 - 45 = 13.44 \text{ MW}$$

$$\text{Yearly energy generation} = 45 \times 0.7402 \times 8760 = 291786.84 \text{ MWh}$$

Example 5.15

The yearly load duration curve of a small hydroelectric power plant depicts 445 × 10^4 kWh of energy in a year. It is a peak load plant having a 19% annual load factor. If the plant is having a capacity factor of 17%, determine plant capacity. Determine the reserve capacity of the given plant.

Solution:

$$\text{Annual load factor} = \frac{\text{Energy generated during in a particular year}}{\text{Maximum load} \times 8760}$$

$$0.19 = \frac{445 \times 10^4}{\text{Maximum load} \times 8760},$$

So $\text{Maximum load} = 2673.63 \text{ kW} = 2.67 \text{ MW}$

$$\text{Capacity factor} = 0.17 = \frac{\text{Maximum load}}{\text{plant capacity}} \times \text{load factor} = \frac{\text{Maximum load}}{\text{plant capacity}} \times 0.19$$

$$\frac{\text{Maximum load}}{\text{plant capacity}} = \frac{0.17}{0.19} = 0.8947,$$

$$\text{Plant capacity} = \frac{\text{Maximum load}}{0.8947}$$

$$= \frac{2.67}{0.8947} = 2.984 \text{ MW}$$

$$\text{Reserve capacity} = 2.984 - 2.67 = 0.314 \text{ MW.}$$

Example 5.16

The daily load curve data for a system is as follows:

Weekdays

Time	12-6 a.m.	-8 a.m.	-12 noon	- 1 p.m.	-5 p.m.	-9 p.m.	-12 midnight
Load (MW)	50	100	200	150	200	400	100

Saturday and Sunday

Time	12-6 a.m.	–5 p.m.	–9 p.m.	–12 midnight
Load (MW)	150	250	450	200

Draw the load duration curve of one week for the abovementioned system. Determine the weekly load factor.

Solution:

From the above-given data, the consumption duration of each load in the entire week ($24 \times 7 = 168$ hours) is given as:

Load (MW)	Duration
450	4(*hours*) × 2(*days*) = **8** hours
400	**8** + 4 × 5 = **28** hours
250	**28** + 11 × 2 = **50** hours
200	**50** + 8 × 5 + 3 × 2 = **96** hours
150	**96** + 1 × 5 + 6 × 2 = **113** hours
100	**113** + 5 × 5 = **138** hours
50	**138** + 6 × 5 = **168** hours

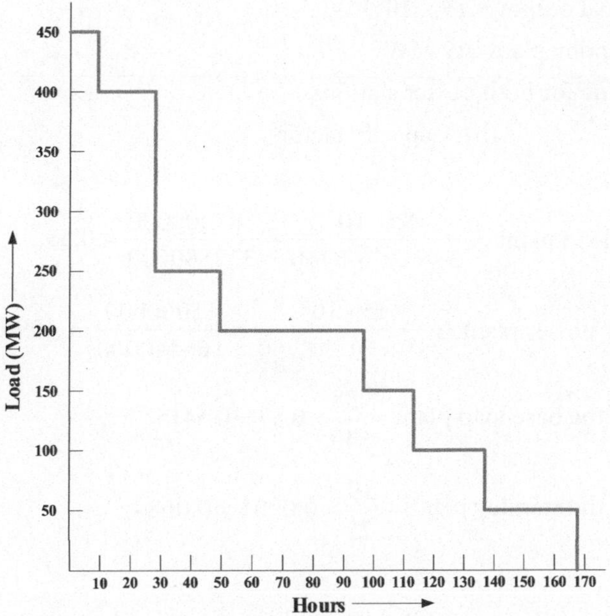

Fig. 5.14: Load duration curve (Weekly) for Example 5.16

The load duration curve is shown in Fig.5.14

The total area within the load duration curve is given below:

$$(450\times 8=3600)+(400\times 20=8000)+(250\times 22=5500)+(200\times 46=9200)+(150\times 17=2550)$$
$$+(100\times 25=2500)+(50\times 30=1500)$$

So the energy consumption in one week is given as

3600 + 8000 + 5500 + 9200 + 2550 + 2500 + 1500 = 65700

$$\text{Load factor} = \frac{65700}{450\times 24\times 7}\times 100 = \frac{65700}{75600}\times 100 = 0.869 \text{ or } 86.9\%$$

Example 5.17

Determine the annual load factor if the average daily load factor is 0.765, the ratio of average daily peak load to monthly peak load is 0.82 and the ratio of average monthly peak load to annual peak load is 0.74.

Solution:

The annual load factor = 0.765 × 0.82 × 0.74 = 0.4642

Example 5.18

A base load plant and peak load plant share a common load as given below:

Base load plant annual output = 185×10^6 kWh

Base load plant capacity = 40 MW

Maximum demand on base load plant = 38 MW

Standby plant capacity = 25 MW

Standby plant annual output = 15 × 10⁶ kWh

Maximum load on standby plant= 19 MW

Determine the following for both power stations

(a) Load factor (b) Capacity factor

Solution:

$$\text{Load factor of base load plant} = \frac{185\times10^6}{38\times10^3\times8760} = \frac{185000000}{332880000} = 0.55$$

$$\text{Load factor of standby power plant} = \frac{15\times10^6}{19\times10^3\times8760} = \frac{15000000}{166440000} = 0.0901$$

$$\text{The capacity factor of the base load plant} = \frac{38}{40}\times0.57 = 0.5415$$

$$\text{The capacity factor of the standby plant} = \frac{19}{25}\times0.0901 = 0.0684$$

Example 5.19

A power station has a rated capacity of 408 MW and the peak load on the plant is 369 MW. Some consumer groups having maximum demand of 123 MW, 108 MW, 84 MW, and 72 MW are connected to the station. If annual load factor is 0.83, determine (*a*) average load (*b*) capacity factor (*c*) energy per year (d) demand factor (*e*) diversity factor.

Solution:

Average load = peak load load factor = 369 × 0.83 = 306.27 MW

$$\text{Capacity factor} = \frac{369}{408}\times0.83 = 0.7506,$$

Energy per year = 306.27 × 8760 = 26,82,925.2 MWh

$$\text{Demand factor} = \frac{369}{387} = 0.953$$

$$\text{Diversity factor} = \frac{123+108+84+72}{369} = \frac{387}{369} = 1.04$$

Example 5.20

A power plant has a maximum demand of 28 MW, a load factor of 63%, and a capacity factor of 58%. Determine (*a*) average demand (*b*) plant capacity (*c*) reserve capacity (d) daily energy generated.

Solution:

Average demand = maximum demand × load factor = 28 × 0.63 = 17.64 MW

$$\text{Plant capacity} = \frac{28\times0.63}{0.58} = 30.41\text{ MW}$$

Reserve Capacity = 30.41 – 28 = 2.41MW,

Daily energy produced = 17.64 × 24 = 423.36 MWh

Example 5.21

The equipment in a power plant costs Rs 15,80,000 and has a salvage value of Rs 79,000 after 22 year Determine the depreciated value of the equipment after 15 years by the following methods:

(a) Straight line method
(b) Diminishing value method
(c) Sinking fund method at 6% compound interest annually

Solution:

Initial cost of equipment (P) = ₹15,80,000
Salvage value of the equipment (S) = ₹79,000
Useful life (n) = 22 Years

(a) *Straight line method*

$$\text{Annual depreciation} = \frac{P-S}{n} = \frac{15,80,000-79,000}{22} = 68227.27$$

Value of equipment after 15 years = P – Annual depreciation × 15
= 15,80,000 – 68227.27 × 15 = ₹5,56,590.95

(b) *Diminishing value method*

$$\text{Annual unit depreciation } (x) = 1-(S/P)^{1/n} = 1-\left(\frac{79,000}{15,80,000}\right)^{1/22} = 1-0.8738 = 0.1262$$

$$\text{Value of equipment after 15 years} = P(1-x)^{15} = 15,80,000\times(1-0.1262)^{15} = 2,08,560$$

(c) Sinking fund method

Rate of interest (r) = 6% = 0.06

$$\text{Annual deposit in the sinking fund is} = q = (P-S)\left[\frac{r}{(1+r)^n-1}\right]$$

$$q = (15,80,000-79,000)\left[\frac{0.06}{(1+0.06)^{22}-1}\right] = \text{Rs } 34,523$$

Therefore sinking fund at the end of 15 years can be given as shown below, i.e.,

$$= q\cdot\frac{(1+r)^{15}-1}{r} = 34,523\cdot\frac{(1+0.06)^{15}-1}{0.06} = \text{Rs } 7,99,794.34$$

Value of plant after 15 years = ₹(15,80,000 – 7,99,794.34)
= Rs 7,80,205.66

Example 5.22

A generating plant has a maximum demand of 48,500 KW. Calculate the cost/unit generated from the following data where, Capital cost = ₹ 93 × 10^6, Annual load factor = 38%, Annual cost of fuel and oil = ₹7.5 × 10^6, Taxes, wages and salaries etc. = ₹ 6 × 10^6 and Interest and depreciation = 10%.

Solution:

$$\text{Units generated per annum} = \text{Maximum demand} \times \text{Load Factor} \times \text{Total hours in a year}$$
$$= 48{,}500 \times 0.38 \times 8760 = 16{,}14{,}46{,}800 \text{ kWh}$$

Annual fixed charges

Annual interest and depreciation=10% of capital cost $= 0.10 \times 93 \times 10^6 = 9.3 \times 10^6$

Annual running charges

$$\text{Total annual running charges} = \text{Annual cost of fuel and oil} + \text{Taxes, wages, etc.}$$
$$= 7.5 \times 10^6 + 6 \times 10^6 = 13.5 \times 10^6$$
$$\text{Total annual charges} = 13.5 \times 10^6 + 9.3 \times 10^6 = 22.8 \times 10^6$$
$$\text{So the } \textit{cost per unit} \text{ is} = \frac{22.8 \times 10^6}{16{,}14{,}46{,}800} = 0.14 = 14 \text{ paise}$$

Example 5.23

A generating plant has an installed capacity of 45,000 kW and delivers 200×10^6 units per annum. If the annual fixed charges are ₹145 per kW installed capacity and running charges are 3 paise per kWh, find the cost per unit generated.

Solution:

$$\text{Annual fixed charges} = 145 \times \text{plant capacity} = 145 \times 45{,}000 = ₹65{,}25{,}000$$
$$\text{Annual running charges} = 0.03 \times 200 \times 10^6 = 80 \times 10^5$$
$$\text{Total annual charges} = 65{,}25{,}000 + 80 \times 10^5 = ₹1{,}45{,}25{,}000$$
$$\text{Cost per unit} = 1{,}45{,}25{,}000 / 200 \times 10^6 = 0.0726 = 7.26 \text{ paise}$$

Example 5.24

A generating station has a maximum capacity of 120 kW and costs Rs 1,80,000. The annual fixed charges are 14% consisting of 7% interest, 7% depreciation, and 3% taxes. Determine the fixed charges per kWh if the load factor is (i) 80% and (ii) 40%.

Solution:

$$\text{Maximum demand} = 120 \text{ kW}$$
$$\text{Annual fixed charges} = 1{,}80{,}000 \times 0.14 = \text{Rs } 25{,}200$$

When the load factor is 80%

$$\text{Units generated/annum} = \text{Maximum demand} \times \text{Load Factor} \times \text{Total hours in a year}$$
$$= 120 \times 0.8 \times 8760 = 8{,}40{,}960 \text{ kWh}$$
$$\text{Fixed charges/kWh} = 25{,}200/8{,}40{,}360 = 0.0299 = 2.99 \text{ paise}$$

When the load factor is 40%

$$\text{Units generated/annum} = \text{Maximum demand} \times \text{Load Factor} \times \text{Total hours in a year}$$
$$= 120 \times 0.4 \times 8760 = 4{,}20{,}480 \text{ kWh}$$
$$\text{Fixed charges/kWh} = 25{,}200/4{,}20{,}480 = 0.0599 = 5.99 \text{ paise}$$

Example 5.25

A generating plant has the following data: installed capacity = 250 MW, capacity factor = 45%, annual load factor = 50%, annual cost of fuel, oil etc. $= 7 \times 10^6$, capital cost $= 10^8$, annual interest and depreciation = 12%. Determine the minimum reserve capacity of the station and the cost per kWh produced.

Solution:

As we know that

$$\text{Load factor} = \frac{\text{Average demand}}{\text{Maximum demand}},\ \text{Capacity factor} = \frac{\text{Average demand}}{\text{Installed capacity}}$$

Then $$\frac{\text{Capacity factor}}{\text{Load factor}} = \frac{\text{Maximum demand}}{\text{installed capacity}}$$

$$\text{Maximum demand} = \text{installed capacity} \times \frac{\text{Capacity factor}}{\text{load factor}} = 250 \times \frac{0.45}{0.5} = 225 \text{ MW}$$

Reserve capacity = 250 – 225 = 25 MW

Units generated/annum = Maximum demand × Load Factor × Total hours in a year

$= 225 \times 10^3 \times 0.5 \times 8760 = 4,20,480$ kWh $= 985.5 \times 10^6$ kWh

Annual fixed charges = Annual interest and depreciation × capital cost

$= 0.12 \times 10^8 = 12 \times 10^6$

Total annual charges = annual running charges + annual fixed charges

$= 7 \times 10^6 + 12 \times 10^6 = 19 \times 10^6$

Cost per kWh = $(19 \times 10^6)/\ 985.5 \times 10^6 = 0.0192 = 1.92$ paise.

Example 5.26

The maximum demand of a consumer is 300kW at 40% load factor. The tariff is ₹110 per kW of maximum demand plus 20 paise per kWh. Find the overall cost per kWh.

Solution:

Units generated/annum = Maximum demand × Load Factor × Total hours in a year

$= (300) \times (0.4) \times (8760) =$ ₹1051200 kWh

Annual charges = Annual maximum demad charges + Annual energy charges

= ₹$(110 \times 300 + 0.2 \times 1051200)$ = ₹243240.00

Hence overall cost/kWh = ₹$\frac{243240.00}{1051200}$ = **₹23.14**

Example 5.27

The total energy consuption of a customer is 8760 kWh. If the energy is charged at ₹0.20 per unit for a period of 500 hours use of maximum demand per year plus ₹0.10 per unit for additional units. The load is 20A terminal at 220V. Assuming load factor and power factor unity, calculate (a) annual bill, (b) equivalent flate rate.

Solution:

Average Load in kW = (220) x 20 x 1/1000 = 4.4kW

$$\text{Maximum demand} = \frac{\text{Average load}}{\text{Maximum load}} = 4.4/1 = 4.4 \text{ kW}$$

Unit consumed in 500 hours = 4.4 × 500 = 2200kW

The charge for 2200kWh = ₹0.2 x 2200 = ₹440.00

$$\text{Remaining units} = 8760 - 2200 = 6560\text{kWh}$$

$$\text{The charge for 6560 units} = ₹0.1 \times 6560 = ₹656.00$$

$$\therefore \quad \text{Total annual bill} = ₹(440.00+656) = ₹1096.00$$

$$\text{Equivalent flat rate} = ₹\frac{1096}{8760} = ₹0.125 = 12.5 \text{ paise.}$$

Multiple Choice Questions

1. Demand factor is defined as
   (a) average load/maximum load
   (b) maximum demand/connected load
   (c) connected load/maximum demand
   (d) average load x maximum load
2. A load curve indicates
   (a) average power used during the period
   (b) averagekWh kW energy consumption during the period
   (c) either of the above
   (d) none of the above
3. Which plant can never have 100 percent load factor?
   (a) Peak load plant
   (b) Base load plant
   (c) Nuclear power plant
   (d) Hydroelectric plant
4. The area under a load curve gives
   (a) average demand
   (b) energy consumed
   (c) maximum demand
   (d) none of the above
5. Diversity factor has direct effect on the
   (a) fixed cost of unit generated
   (b) running cost of unit generated
   (c) both (a) and (b)
   (d) neither a nor b
6. Following power plant has instant starting
   (a) nuclear power plant
   (b) hydro power plant
   (c) diesel power plant
   (d) both (b) and (c)
7. Which of the following component, in a steam power plant, needs maximum maintenance attention?
   (a) Steam turbine
   (b) Condenser
   (c) Water treatment plant
   (d) Boiler
8. A synchronous condenser is virtually which of the following?
   (a) Induction motor
   (b) Under excited synchronous motor
   (c) Over excited synchronous motor
   (d) D.C. generator
9. Which of the following is the essential requirement of peak load plant?
   (a) It should run at high speed
   (b) It should produce high voltage
   (c) It should be small in size
   (d) It should be capable of starting quickly

10. In a power plant if the maximum demand on the plant is equal to the plant capacity, then
(a) Plant reserve capacity will be zero
(b) Diversity factor will be unity
(c) Load factor will be unity
(d) Load factor will be nearly 60%

11. Approximate estimation of power demand can be made by
(a) Load survey method
(b) Statistical methods
(c) Mathematical method
(d) All of the above

12. Utilization factor of a power station is the ratio of:
(a) Maximum demand of a power station to the sum of individual maximum demands
(b) Average demand to the rated capacity of the power station
(c) Sum of individual maximum demands to maximum dema of a power station
(d) Maximum demand on the power station to the rated capacity of the power station

13. High load factor indicates
(a) cost of generation per unit power is increased
(b) total plant capacity is utilized for most of the time
(c) total plant capacity is not properly utilized for most of the time
(d) none of the above

14. A consumer consumes 700 kWh per day at a load factor of 0.4. Without increasing the maximum demand, if the consumer increases the load factor to 0.70, the consumption of energy in kWh would be:
(a) 1225
(b) 1620
(c) 1455
(d) 1275

15. What is the reserve capacity, if the maximum demand of generation of power is 60 MW, the load factor of the plant is 50% and the plant capacity factor is 40%?
(a) 15 MW
(b) 12 MW
(c) 20 MW
(d) 7.5 MW

16. What will be the daily energy product in a thermal power station at a load factor of 0.4 when the maximum demand of the station is 60 MW?
(a) 576 MWh
(b) 876 MWh
(c) 720 MWh
(d) 400 MWh

17. A power station has 5 consumers with their maximum demand as 45 MW, 25 MW, 20 MW, 50 MW and 60 MW. The maximum demand of the station is 300 MW. The diversity factor of the plant is
(a) 0.75
(b) 1.55
(c) 1.50
(d) 0.50

18. A generating station produces 61.5 Mega Units per annum. It is connected to a load of 40 MW and its maximum demand of 30 MW. Calculate the demand factor of the station.
(a) 0.50
(b) 0.75
(c) 0.65
(d) 0.55

19. An Industrial consumer has a daily load pattern of 5000kVAat 0.7 lag for 10 hrs and 2000 kVAat unity power factor for 16 hrs. Calculate the daily load factor.
(a) 0.95
(b) 0.79
(c) 0.75
(d) 0.54

20. Determine the annual bill of a consumer whose maximum demand is 60kW, p.f. 0.80 lagging and load factor is 50%. The tariff used is ₹ 40 per kVA per annum of maximum demand plus 12 paise per kWh consumed.
   (a) ₹ 34, 536 (b) ₹ 44,550
   (c) ₹ 35,366 (d) ₹ 40,250

ANSWERS															
1.	(b)	2.	(b)	3.	(a)	4.	(b)	5.	(a)	6.	(d)	7.	(d)	8.	(c)
9.	(d)	10.	(a)	11.	(d)	12.	(d)	13.	(b)	14.	(a)	15.	(a)	16.	(a)
17.	(c)	18.	(b)	19.	(b)	20.	(a)								

State whether the following are True or False

1. The demand factor may be more than one.
2. Group diversity factor cannot be less than 1.
3. The maximum demand of the consumer multiplied by the group diversity factor equals his effective demand at the distribution transformer.
4. The maximum diversity factor is always less than one.
5. Demand factor for residential loads is roughly 0.6.
6. Consumers in the residential sector had a lower group diversity factor than those in the industrial sector.
7. Peak demand for domestic loads often happens between 6 PM and 10 PM.
8. In industrial facilities with a single shift, demand is essentially consistent during the course of the shift.
9. A chronological load curve shows how demand varies throughout the day.
10. The time of day is the abscissa of the daily load duration curve.
11. The area under a chronological load curve is equivalent to the daily energy consumption.
12. The regions under a daily load duration curve and a chronological load curve might or might not be equal.
13. Power demand is the ordinate in the energy load curve.
14. The abscissa of a mass curve represents time in hour
15. Compared to base load plants, peak load plants have a lower load factor.

ANSWERS															
1.	F	2.	T	3.	F	4.	F	5.	T	6.	F	7.	T	8.	T
9.	T	10.	F	11.	T	12.	F	13.	T	14.	T	15.	T		

QUESTIONS AND PROBLEMS

Short and Long Answer Type Questions

1. Define the terms listed below: Maximum demand, connected load, demand factor, and load factor. How does the load factor affect the cost of generation?

2. What is a diversity factor? Show how raising the variety factor improves a power system's load factor.
3. Discuss the role of load diversity in power system economics.
4. Explain why?
5. A group of consumers' combined maximum demand is never more than the sum of their individual maximum demands.
6. Two systems' load duration curves might not match even though their maximum demand and load factors are equal.
7. A plant's utilization factor may be more than 1.
8. Define cold reserve, hot reserve, operating reserve, and spinning reserve.
9. Describe the meanings of plant capacity factor and plant use factor as well as the significance of each in an electrical power system.
10. Discuss the importance of the load curve and load duration curve.
11. Differentiate between
    (a) Capacity factor and utilization factor.
    (b) Load curve and load duration curve.
    (c) Base load and peak load.
    (d) Base load plant and peak load plant
    (e) Fixed cost and operating cost
    (f) Straight line depreciation and sinking fund depreciation.
    (g) Brownout, and Blackout
    (h) Integrated load duration curve and load duration curve.
    (i) Installed capacity and firm capacity.
12. What is depreciation?
13. Which type of plant has the highest capital cost? Why?
14. How can you classify the cost of generation? Explain each.
15. Why should interest rate affect annual sinking fund depreciation reserve?
16. What does the effect of the load factor on unit generation cost?
17. What are the components of operating costs?
18. What Causes a Brownout?
19. Why do blackouts happen?
20. What to Do During a Power Blackout or Brownout?
21. Explain the past blackouts that occur in India.
22. Explain the blackouts that occurred in U.S and Canada in the past.
23. Explain the details about the blackouts that occurred in Italy, Brazil, and Indonesia.
24. What are the causes of grid faults in the regional and national grid?
25. What are the impacts of grid faults in the regional and national grid?
26. Explain each advantage of the combined operation of power plants.
27. How can you select power plants for combined operation?

Numerical Problems

1. A power plant's maximum demand is 100 kW. The utilization factor is 0.8 and the capacity factor is 0.6. Determine the following: load factor, plant capacity, reserve capacity, and yearly energy production.
2. A power plant can handle a maximum demand of 200 MW. Determine the total amount of energy produced annually if the yearly load factor is 0.55.
3. The maximum demand for a producing station is 450 MW, and it has a connected had of 600 MW. The annual energy production is 2×10^9 kWh. Determine the load factor and demand factor.
4. A power plant's annual load duration curve runs in a straight line from 50 MW to 10 MW. To accommodate the demand, three 20 MW each alternator are erected. Determine the installed capacity, plant factor, maximum demand, load factor, and utilization factor.
5. The load curve of a power plant is linear with the following values at different times:

Time	12	2	5	8	5	6	9	12
Load MW	25	15	15	60	55	100	100	20

   (a) Plot the chronological load curve and load duration curve for the system.
   (b) Plot the energy load curve and mass curve.
   (c) Find the load factor of the system.
   (d) Find the capacity factor and utilization factor if the station capacity is 145 MW.
6. The annual load duration of a power station is a straight line. The maximum load is 45 MW and the minimum load is 25 MW. The capacity of the plant is 38 MW. Find (a) plant capacity factor (b) load factor (c) utilisation factor.
7. The power generation equipment of a power plant cost ₹17,85,000 and has a useful life of 28 years If the salvage value of the equipment is ₹ 83,000 and the annual interest rate is 7%, determine the annual amount to be saved by the straight-line method and sinking fund method.
8. The energy cost of a 150 MW steam station working at 60% load factor comes out to be 12 paise/ kWh of energy generated. What will be the cost of energy generated if the load factor is improved to 70%? The fuel cost of the power station due to increased generation increases the annual generation cost by 8%.
9. The daily load of an industry is as follows. 200kW in first 1 hour, 150Kw for next 7 hours, 50 kW for next 8 hours, and 1 kW for the remaining time. The tariff in force is ₹1000.00 per kW of maximum demand per annum plus ₹2.25 per kWh. Find the expenditure for electricity per year i.e 365 days.
10. A customer need 1 million units/year. The annual load factor is 50%. The tariff is ₹1200.00 per kW plus ₹2.40 per unit. Find the saving in energy cost if his power factor is improves his load factor to 100%.

KNOW MORE

1. The variation of active and reactive power in a power system affects the system frequency and system voltage respectively. The system frequency and system voltage must be maintained constant irrespective of the load change. The power system automatically maintains frequency and voltage constant.

2. Load forecasting is an important issue in power systems. It is divided into long-term and short-term load forecasting. Long-term load forecasting helps the utility for future load demand and prepares for additional infrastructure including additional generating units that will be required in the future. Short-term load forecasting is for monitoring and controlling power system operations.
3. The demand for electrical energy increases day by day but the price of electricity has shown a downward trend. This is because of an increase in generating unit size, reduced plant cost, better plant efficiency, economic operation of the plant, integrated operation of plants, and reduction in transportation loss.
4. There are various types of faults in the power system. They are symmetrical faults and unsymmetrical faults. The fault currents are symmetrical ie. equal in all the phases in the case of symmetrical faults. Three-phase short circuits or three phases short-circuited to the ground are symmetrical faults. On the other hand, when faults currents/ voltages are not the same in all the phases, the fault is called an unsymmetrical fault. An unsymmetrical fault may be a single-line-to-ground fault, double-line-to-ground fault, or double-line short-circuited.

REFERENCES AND SUGGESTED READINGS

1. Gupta, B.R., Generation of Electrical Energy, S. Chand& Co. New Delhi, 2017.
2. Gupta, J.B. A Course in Electrical Power- S. K Kataria and Sons, New Delhi. 2014.
3. Hussain, Ashfaq. Electrical power systems, CBS publications, and distributors, New Delhi, (2007).
4. Wadhwa CL. Electrical power systems. New Age International; 2006.
5. Murty, P. S. R. Electrical power systems. Butterworth-Heinemann, 2017.
6. Bandyopadhyay, M. N. Electrical power systems: theory and practice. PHI Learning Pvt. Ltd., 2006.
7. Rivas, Angel Esteban Labrador, and Taufik Abrao. "Faults in smart grid systems: Monitoring, detection, and classification." Electric Power Systems Research 189 (2020): 106602.
8. https://iea.blob.core.windows.net/assets/68002ee5-537c-4e12-8c40-ee8163cf69d6/Blackouts.pdf.
9. Weedy, Birron Mathew, Brian John Cory, Nick Jenkins, Janaka B. Ekanayake, and Goran Strbac. *Electric power systems*. John Wiley & Sons, 2012.
10. Wadhwa, C. L. *Generation, distribution and utilization of electrical energy*. New Age International, 1989.

APPENDICES

APPENDIX-A

Thermal Plants in Maharashtra

Source: https://cea.nic.in/wp-content/uploads/pdm/2021/06/list_power_stations_2021.pdf

Maharashtra is one of the central Indian states where a considerable amount of electricity is generated, mainly for domestic consumption. Over the years, several thermal power plants have been set up in the state since it receives the supply of crude oil and natural gas in abundance. Besides, these power plants are located mainly on the outskirts, helping different corporations to include heavy power generators and grid overlays. Due to these favorable circumstances, there are many thermal power plants in Maharashtra. The Maharashtrian government has implemented several rules to ensure that these power plants can thrive and continue to provide electricity in the coming years.

List of thermal power plants in Maharashtra

Maharashtra's largest thermal power plant is the Chandrapur Super thermal power station. It has the capacity of producing 2920 MW of power. Five generators of 500 MW capacity and two generators of 210 MW are present at this power plant. Here, water is sourced from Chargaon and Erai dams, while the fuel supply is sourced from the nearest coal mines. Apart from this plant, there are other names too on the long thermal power plants in Maharashtra list, like:

1. Tiroda Power Plant
2. Nashik Thermal Power Station
3. Paras Thermal Power Station
4. Bhusawal Thermal Power Plant
5. Koradi Super Thermal Power Plant
6. Solapur Super Thermal Power Plant
7. Wardha Power Company Ltd
8. Adani Dahanu Thermal Power Station
9. Jindal Thermal Power Plant

APPENDIX- B

Application of Solar thermal plant

Solar Water Heating (SWH) System

Internationally, solar water heating has been identified as one of the most promising decentralized solar applications, having significant potential to reduce electricity consumption and consequent emissions reduction. It is being increasingly recognized as an application tt can help urban areas and industries in reducing their dependence on the grid and reducing diesel/gas consumption. A solar water heater consists of a collector to collect solar energy and an insulated storage tank to store hot water. The solar energy incident on the absorber panel coated with the selected coating transfers the heat to the riser pipes underneath the absorber panel. The water passing through the riser gets heated up and is delivered to the storage tank. The re-circulation of the same water through the absorber panel in the collector raises the temperature to 80^0C (Maximum) on a good sunny day. The total system with solar collectors, storage tanks, and pipelines is called a solar hot water system. Broadly, solar water heating systems are of two categories. They are closed-loop systems and open-loop systems.

In the first one, heat exchangers are installed to protect the system from hard water obtained from borewells or from freezing temperatures in cold regions. In the other type, either thermosyphon or forced circulation system, the water in the system is open to the atmosphere at one point or another. The thermosyphon systems are simple and relatively inexpensive. They are suitable for domestic and small institutional systems, provided the water is treated and potable in quality. The forced circulation systems employ electrical pumps to circulate the water through collectors and storage tanks. The choice of system depends on heat requirements, weather conditions, heat transfer fluid quality, space availability, annual solar radiation, etc. SWH systems are economical, pollution free, and easy to operate in warm countries like ours. Based on the collector system, solar water heaters can be of two types.

1. Flate Plate Collector (FPC) type SWH Systems: In FPC, the fins are made of copper tubes with selective Nickel Chrome plating to which the copper tubes are ultrasonically welded. These fins are covered with toughened glass in an insulated box with an Aluminium frame. In this type of system, the water temperature goes up to 60 to 65° C.
2. Evacuated Tube Collector (ETC) type SWH Systems: Evacuated tubes are the absorber of the solar water heater. They absorb solar energy converting it into heat for use in water heating. Each evacuated tube consists of two glass tubes made from borosilicate glass. The outer tube is transparent allowing light rays to pass through with minimal reflection. The inner tube is coated with a special selective coating (Al-N/Al), which features excellent solar radiation absorption and minimal reflection properties. In this type of system, the water temperature goes up to 85° C.

Normally, for storing water overnight or on cloudy days, a storage tank is needed. A very simple way of doing this, making use of gravity i.e. the thermosyphon system. The principle of the thermosyphon system is that cold water has a higher specific density than warm water, and so being heavier will sink down. Therefore, the collector is always mounted below the water storage tank, so that cold water from the tank reaches the collector via a descending water pipe. If the collector heats up the water, the water rises again and reaches the tank through an ascending water pipe at the upper end of the collector.

Thermosyphon systems operate very economically as domestic water heating systems, and the principle is simple. In contrast to thermosyphon systems, an electrical pump can be used to move water through the system by forced circulation. The collector and storage tank can then be installed independently, and no height difference between the tank and collector is necessary. This type of system is basically used for commercial & industrial applications.

Fuel Savings: A 100 liters capacity SWH can replace an electric geyser for residential use and saves 1500 units of electricity annually.

Avoided utility cost on generation: The use of 1000 SWHs of 100 liters capacity each can contribute to a peak load shaving of 1 MW.

Environmental benefits: An SWH of 100 liters capacity can prevent the emission of 1.5 tonnes of carbon dioxide per year.

Central Financial Assistance: No capital subsidy is available for Solar Water Heating System as per MNRE, GoI letter no.30/31/2012-13/NSM dated on 19th September 2014.

Status/Achievement of our Program: MEDA has received two consecutive awards for maximum installation in the State for the year 2011-12 & 2012-13.

APPENDIX-C

Solar Application

Source: Maharashtra Energy Development Agency (MEDA)

Solar Street Light

The Solar Street Lighting Systems Consists of Solar Photovoltaic (SPV) module, a luminary, storage battery, control electronics, inter-connecting wires/cables, module mounting pole including hardware and battery box. The luminary is based on White Light Emitting Diode(W-LED)/CFL. The luminary is mounted on the pole at a suitable angle to maximize illumination on the ground. The PV module is placed at the top of the pole at an angle facing south so that it receives solar radiation throughout the day, without any shadow falling on it. A battery is placed in a box attached to the pole. Electricity generated by the PV module charges the battery during the day time which powers the luminary from dusk to dawn. The systems lights at dusk and switches off at dawn automatically.

Advantages

1. It is a *standalone system and works even where there is no grid supply*
2. Easy to transport and install anywhere and is suitable for remote areas
3. Provides lighting for 10 – 12 hours daily without running cost.
4. Boon to local bodies as they can save electricity consumption charges
5. No need for manual operation as it has automatic switch "on / off" facility

SPV street lights are being installed by the local bodies – Panchayats, Municipal corporations etc. in large numbers by availing subsidy so as to reduce the recurring power consumption charges. Non-profit organizations can also use them for their campuses.

For technical specification click here http://mnre.gov.in/information/systems-specifications/

Solar Lantern

A Solar Lantern is a portable lighting device consisting of PV module, battery, lamp, and electronics. Battery, lamp, and electronics are placed in a suitable housing, made of metal or plastic or fiber glass. The Solar lantern is suitable for either indoor or outdoor lighting, covering a full range of 360 degrees. PV module converts sun light into electricity, charges the battery which powers the luminaire. Luminaire consists of Compact Fluorescent Lamp (CFL) and an Electronic Circuit.

Advantages

1. It is a pollution free, portable lighting device.
2. It is useful during night hours for doing house hold works and study till late in the night.
3. Solar lantern is a very simple to use and operate.
4. It can provide 3 to 4 hours of continuous light depending upon the model and type of the solar lantern.

For technical specifications click here: http://mnre.gov.in/information/systems-specifications/

Solar Home Light

A solar home lighting system (SHS) provides a comfortable level of illumination in one or more rooms of a house. The SHS consists of a PV module, control electronics, battery, and luminaire(s). There are several SHS models featuring one, two, or four luminaires based on Compact Fluorescent Lamp (CFL). The system could also be used to run a small DC fan or a 12-V DC television along with the CFL. PV module converts sunlight into electricity, which powers the luminaire(s), which consists of Compact Fluorescent Lamp (CFL) and an Electronic Circuit.

Battery Operated Vehicle

Battery Operated Vehicle- Alternate Fuels for Surface Transportation

Battery operated vehicles (BOVs) are run by batteries and are free from noise and air pollution. They are ideally suited for cities are also suitable for use in hospitals, factories, educational institutions, wild life sanctuaries, airports and places of historic importance. BOVs can be operated as public transport vehicles – BOVs are available as passenger cars, 10-seater auto rickshaws and 12-seater vans. MNRE provides subsidy for the same.

1. The battery-operated vehicles (two wheelers) have the following advantages:
2. They have zero emissions and do not pollute the atmosphere.
3. They consume only about 1.5 kWh of electricity to travel 60 km.
4. They can go about 30–50 km on a single charge. This capability meets the needs of average, two-wheeler-riders.
5. Most are used during the day and can be charged late at night, which is advantageous in balancing the electric power load.
6. Electric bikes reduce human exertion. They are structurally simple, convenient to charge, and easy to operate. Users do not need a driver's license to operate them.
7. They are compatible with city roads.
8. They will reduce traffic congestion in the cities.
9. They will help reduce energy consumption. Their annual operating cost is about 15% of that of motorcycles.

Objectives of Programme

- Support for dissemination of all types of Battery-Operated Vehicles (BOVs), Plug Hybrid Vehicles (PHEVs), Hybrid Electric Vehicles (HEVs) and Electric / Exercise-Bike Generator Inverter (E2BI) for their usages by users for surface transportation.
- Support for Research & Development projects on advanced high energy density batteries, ultra-capacitors, control systems and other components for battery operated electric, plug hybrid and hybrid electric vehicles for surface transportation.
- Support for pilot project on technology demonstration for Battery Operated Vehicles, Plug Hybrid Vehicles, Hybrid Electric Vehicles and Electric/Exercise- Bike Generator Inverter (E2B1) for field performance evaluation and leading to commercialization.
- Support for activities related to awareness promotion through education and training, seminars/conferences/symposia in the area of electric vehicles, plug hybrid vehicles and hybrid electric vehicles etc.

Solar Pump

In India, electrical and diesel-powered water pumping systems are widely utilized for irrigation applications. A solar-powered pump is a pump running on the power of the sun. It makes efficient use of solar energy and converts it into electrical energy for pumping water to great heights. A solar-powered pump can be very environment friendly and economical in its operation. This system operates on power generated using solar PV (photovoltaic) system. The photovoltaic array converts the solar energy into electricity, which is used for running the motor pump set. The pumping system draws water from the open well, bore well, pond etc. The water pumping system can be used to irrigate land when the water is to be pumped from a depth of a well or a pond.

Advantages of Solar Water Pumps:

1. It helps in saving Energy.
2. There is no fuel cost - as it uses available free sun light.
3. No electricity required.
4. Can be operated lifelong.
5. It is highly reliable and durable.
6. Easy to operate and maintain
7. It is also useful for clean, drinking water sanitation and also irrigation.
8. It reduces the dependence on rain.
9. It creates wealth for farmers by increasing no of crops.

Types of Solar Pumps -

There are two main types of solar pumps. Surface pumps sit above ground and move water through pipes. These are handy for moving large quantities of water at a slow pace. Surface pumps are commonly found on farms or large irrigation systems where water needs to be moved from a lake or other body to fields or landscaping. There are also submersible solar water pumps. These units are installed underground, but the solar panels are connected above ground. Submersible pumps are used to move water from inside wells to the surface.

For Technical Specification of Solar Pump kindly follow the below link: http://mnre.gov.in/information/systems-specifications/

APPENDIX-D

Grid failure

Source:- Maharashtra Energy Development Agency (MEDA)

Power grid failure

There are five power grid regions in India. they are-

- Northern
- Western
- Southern
- Eastern
- North-Eastern.

Out of all these Regions the NR, ER, WR, and NER are synchronized which is known as NEW Grid. Whereas SR is not synchronized with the rest of the regions with AC lines and hence could run on a slightly different frequency. SR is connected with WR and ER with HVDC links only.

History of major power grid failures throughout the world

Article	Millions of people affected	Location	Date
July 2012 India blackout	670	India	30–31 July 2012
2005 Java-Bali blackout	100	Indonesia	18 Aug. 2005
1999 Southern Brazil blackout	97	Brazil	11 March 1999
2009 Brazil and Paraguay blackout	87	Brazil, Paraguay	10–11 Nov. 2009
Northeast blackout of 2003	55	the United States, Canada	14–15 Aug. 2003
2003 Italy blackout	55	Italy, Switzerland, Austria, Slovenia, Croatia	28 Sep. 2003
Northeast blackout of 1965	30	the United States, Canada	9 Nov. 1965

2012 blackout in India: The **July 2012 India blackout** was the largest power outage in history, occurring as two separate events on 30 and 31 July 2012. The outage affected over 620 million people, about 9% of the world population, or half of India's population, spread across 22 states in Northern, Eastern, and Northeast India. An estimated 32 gigawatts of generating capacity was taken offline in the outage.

- History of electrical infrastructure in India:
- The Indian electrical infrastructure was generally considered unreliable.The Northern grid had previously collapsed in 2001.
- 27% of the power generated was lost in transmission or stolen, while peak supply fell short of demand by an average of 9%. Hence the nation suffered from frequent power outages that could last as long as 10 hours.
- About 25% of the population, about 300 million people, had no electricity at all. The power generating stations are hooked onto an interconnected network of transmission lines and substations. These generating stations supply electricity through these transmission lines.
- The companies responsible for distribution take the power coming through these lines and forward it to the consumers. This is how electricity reaches millions of homes.
- The stability of the grids depends on a delicate equilibrium of the demand-supply chain. The amount of load is directly proportional to the amount of power generated.
- When the equilibrium between power generated and consumed gets
- disturbed and the load becomes more, it leads to tripping of the line.

Reasons for power grid failure

- In the summer of 2012, leading up to the failure, extreme heat had caused power use to reach record levels in New Delhi leading to coal shortages in the country.(as fossil fuel stocks are rationed by the government and are imported offshore.)
- Due to the late arrival of monsoons, agricultural areas in Punjab and Haryana drew increased power from the grid (Farmers using energy-intensive water pumps for irrigation)
- The late monsoon also meant that hydropower plants were generating less than their usual production and hence the load on thermal power plants increased to support the demand of the load.
- Illegal utilization of electricity is also a major reason for power grid failure.
- India's basic energy shortage is compounded by the policy of selling electricity to consumers at politically correct prices i.e. sometimes cheap and even free to voters. Here the government-owned distribution monopolies have failed. This loss estimates up to 1% of the gross domestic product in the country.

States affected by the grid failure

- States on the Northern grid: Delhi, Haryana, Himachal Pradesh, Jammu & Kashmir, Punjab, Rajasthan, Uttar Pradesh, Uttarakhand
- States on the Eastern grid: Bihar, Jharkhand, Orissa, West Bengal
- States on the Northeast grid: Arunachal Pradesh, Assam, Manipur, Meghalaya, Mizoram, Nagaland, Sikkim.
- Lack of information at the base station (33kV sub-station) on the loading and health status of the 11kV/415V transformer and associated feeders is one primary cause of inefficient power distribution.
- Due to the absence of monitoring, overloading occurs, which results in low voltage customer end and increases the risk of frequent breakdowns of transformers and feeders.
- In fact, the transformer breakdown rate in India is as high as around 20%, in contrast to less than 2% in some advanced countries.

APPENDIX-E

Bio Energy

Biogas Power/Thermal (off-grid) Programme

Source:- Maharashtra Energy Development Agency (MEDA)

It is important to encourage decentralized biogas-based projects from organic degradable waste. Encouragement to such kind of projects will benefit to the individual farmers, village industries (e.g., agro/food processing/kitchen waste etc.). Recovery of energy from these wastes is possible through bio methanation process as anaerobic digestion is the most suitable alternative than composting. Methane gas (CH_4) popularly known as biogas is one such alternate sources of energy which has been identified as a useful hydrocarbon with combustible qualities as that of other hydrocarbons. In order to promote biogas based thermal/ power generation projects, specifically in the small capacity range (kW_{eq} to 250 kWeq.), such projects can be taken up at any village-level organization, institution, private entrepreneurs, or individuals etc. in rural areas for generation of electricity as well as for thermal applications. The funds would be released on re-imbursement basis after successful commissioning of the biogas project. The biogas plants should be completed within 18 months from the date of sanction of the project.

APPENDIX-F

Wind Power

Source:- Maharashtra Energy Development Agency (MEDA)

The investor-friendly policy shift by the Government of India and the Government of Maharashtra since 1983-84, has resulted in the effective commercialization of the wind power sector. Out of the total installed capacity of 20492MW renewable power in the country and Wind Power projects share 14156 MW.

That puts India as the fourth largest producer of wind power in the world:

1. Germany (27126 MW)
2. USA (40216 MW)
3. Spain (20674 MW)
4. India (14156 MW)

5. Denmark (3805 MW)
6. China (38280 MW)

Wind Potential Assessment -

The assessed wind power potential in the country is about 49130 MW, while in Maharashtra it is 5439 MW. Sites with Annual Mean Wind Density above 200 W/m2 are considered suitable for wind power projects. 339 such sites have been identified in the country, of which 40 sites are in Maharashtra. Wind speed monitoring is in progress at 211 Sites To instill confidence in the investors, demonstration projects worth 7.34 MW installed capacity was initiated in the state with support from MNRE, installed by MEDA. Also, MEDA with its own funds has set up a 3.75 MW additional demonstration Wind Power Project as a source of revenue generation. Thus, the total capacity of the demonstration Wind Power Project by MEDA is 11.09 MW in Maharashtra. Investor-friendly policies of the Government of Maharashtra and the technical viability of demonstration projects have attracted private investment of more than Rs11895 crore in the wind sector so far. Nearly 2309 MW of private wind power projects have been installed in the State up to March 2011).

Technological Advancement:

The commercial viability of wind power projects is gradually increasing due to technological advancement. Replacement of old 250 kW wind turbines of 30 m height with 1.0 MW single unit size of 50 m has provided an edge for attractive investment. Higher wind power density due to increased height, lower installation cost per MW and less land requirement make a case for choosing higher unit size of wind turbines. Fortunately, wind turbines of 1 MW are being manufactured in the country and still higher capacity units of 1.25 MW and 1.5 MW are under trial at Center for Wind Energy Technology (C-WET), Chennai. The production capacity of domestic wind turbines industry is 500 MW per year, which can go up to 750 MW per year based on demand.

REFERENCES FOR FURTHER LEARNING

10. Nag. P. K. Power Plant Engineering, McGraw Hill, New Delhi, ISBN: 978-9339204044
11. Tanmoy Deb, Electrical Power Generation, Khanna Publishing House, Delhi (Ed. 2018);
12. Soni, Gupta, Bhatnagar, A Course in Electrical Power, Dhanpat Rai and Sons, 2005, ISBN: 9788121924962
13. Solanki Chetan Singh, Renewable energy Technologies; A Practical Guide for Beginners, PHI School Books (2008).
14. Solanki, Chetan Singh, Solar Photovoltaics: Fundamentals, Technologies, and Applications, PHI Learning, New Delhi, ISBN: 9788120351110
15. Gupta, B.R., Generation of Electrical Energy, S. Chand& Co. New Delhi, 2017.
16. Gupta, J.B. A Course in Electrical Power- S. K Kataria and Sons, New Delhi. 2014.
17. Wadhwa C.L. Electrical power systems. New Age International; 2006.
18. Wadhwa, C. L. *Generation, distribution and utilization of electrical energy*. New Age International, 1989.
19. Hussain, Ashfaq. Electrical power systems, CBS publications, and distributors, New Delhi, (2007).
20. Weedy, Birron, Mathew, Brian John Cory, Nick Jenkins, Janaka B. Ekanayake, and Goran Strbac., Electric power systems. John Wiley & Sons, 2012.
21. Murty, P. S. R., Electrical power systems. Butterworth-Heinemann, 2017.
22. Bandyopadhyay, M. N. Electrical power systems: theory and practice. PHI Learning Pvt. Ltd., 2006.
23. Rivas, Angel Esteban Labrador, and Taufik Abrao. "Faults in smart grid systems: Monitoring, detection, and classification." Electric Power Systems Research 189 (2020): 106602.
24. K. Hasan Saeed & D. K. Sharma, Non-conventional Energy Sources, S.K. Kataria & Sons, New Delhi.
25. D. S. Chauhan, S. K. Srivastava, Non-conventional Energy Sources, New Age International publishers, Third Ed, 2012
26. Tiwari, G. N., Solar Energy-Fundamentals, Design, Modelling and Applications, Narosa Publishing House, Fourth reprint 2019.
27. Michael Boxwell, Solar Electricity Handbook; Green stream publishing ltd, UK-2011
28. Dr. H. Naganagouda, Solar Power Hand Book, (2014)
29. D. Mukherjee, Fundamentals of Renewable Energy Systems Paperback, New Age International Publisher; First edition (2011)
30. G.D Rai, Non-conventional Sources of Energy, Khanna Publishers, Delhi, 2012
31. Kothari D.P. and Signal K.C., Renewable Energy Sources and Emerging Technologies, PHI; 2 Edition (2011)
32. Mridula Ramesh, The Climate Solution, Neelkamal publication - 2009

33. Khartchenko, N.V., Green Power: Eco-Friendly Energy Engineering, Tech Books, and New Delhi, 2008.
34. Banerjee B. P., Handbook of energy and environment in India, Oxford University Press, 2005 India
35. Cunningham, W.P, Environmental Science,11th ed., McGraw-Hill, 2010.
36. Report on Material and component specification Dual axis tracked parabolic dish, and Single axis tracked parabolic trough, UNDP-GEF CSHP, Ministry of New and Renewable Energy, Government of India, December 2015.
37. Rachel, Sthuthi; Earnest, Joshua, Wind Power Technologies, PHI Learning, New Delhi, ISBN: 978-93 88028-49- 3; E-book 978-93-88028-50-9
38. Hoon-Ki Lee, Tae-Kyoung Bang, Jeong-In Lee, Kyung-Hun Shin, and Jang-Young Choi1, " Characteristics analysis of a high-speed permanent magnet synchronous generator considering magnetic reactance derived from short circuit analysis", AIP Advances, Vol. 9. No.12, (2019), DOI: https://doi.org/10.1063/1.5129997
39. D.P.Kothari, I.J.Nagrath, Electrical machines, Fifth Edition, Mc Graw Hill Education.
40. Trevor M. Letcher, Wind Energy Engineering. A handbook for Onshore and Offshore wind turbines. Academic Press, Elsevier. ISBN: 978-0-12-809451-8.
41. Wei Tong, Wind power generation and wind turbine design. WIT press Southampton, Boston, ISBN: 978-1-84564-205-1.
42. Bin Wu,Yongqiang Lang, Navid Zargari, Samir Kouro, Power Conversion and Control of Wind Energy Systems, IEEE Press, John WILEY & Sons. The USA. ISBN: 978-1-118-02900-8.
43. Alatalo M. Permanent magnet machines with air gap windings and integrated teeth windings, technical report 288. Sweden: Chalmers University of Technology; 1996.
44. Muller S, Deicke M, De Doncker RW, Doubly fed induction generator systems for wind turbines. IEEE Ind Appl Mag, 2002;8:26_33.
45. https://www.mahaurja.com/meda/en/grid_connected_power/small_hydro
46. https://www.tatapower.com/businesses/hydro.aspx
47. https://en.wikipedia.org/wiki/Koyna_Hydroelectric_Project.
48. http://www.doed.gov.np/storage/listies/December2019/guidelines-for-operation-and-maintenance-of-hydropower-plants.pdf
49. https://cea.nic.in/wp-content/uploads/2020/04/chapter-6.pdf
50. https://www.publications.usace.army.mil/Portals/76/Users/182/86/2486/EC%201130-2-216.pdf?ver=2019-05-30-143437-757
51. https://policy.asiapacificenergy.org/sites/default/files/GUIDELINE%20FOR%20THE%20T%26C%20OF%20SMALL%20HYDRO_2015.pdf
52. https://policy.asiapacificenergy.org/node/3334
53. https://openjicareport.jica.go.jp/pdf/11737046_17.pdf
54. ttps://www.ppa.org.fj/wp-content/uploads/2020/10/Micro-Hydropwer-System-Install-Guideline-V1.pdf

55. National institute of occupational health, "Environment, Health and Safety Issues in Coal Fired Thermal ...http://www.nioh.org › publications › pdf
56. https://electricalshouters.com/thermal-power-plant
57. https://cea.nic.in/wp-content/uploads/pdm/2021/06/list_power_stations_2021.pdf
58. https://cea.nic.in/wp-content/uploads/installed/2022/02/installed_capacity.pdf
59. https://en.wikipedia.org/wiki/Steam_engine
60. https://en.wikipedia.org –internet source for various topics.
61. https://mnre.gov.in/wind/current status/#:~:text=The%20expansion%20of%20the%20wind,39.25%20GW%20(as%20on 203
62. https://en.wikipedia.org/wiki/Wind_power_in_India
63. https://www.studocu.com › wind-energy-technology-ii
64. https://www.academia.edu/28724752/Problem_Solutions_B_1_Problem_Solving
65. https://byjus.com/wind-energy-formula/
66. https://iea.blob.core.windows.net/assets/68002ee5-537c-4e12-8c40-ee8163cf69d6/Blackouts.pdf.
67. https://www.google.com/url?sa=t&source=web&rct=j&url=https://cea.nic.in/wp-content/uploads/pdm/2021/06/list_power_stations_2021.pdf&ved=2ahUKEwiTnf7SqtH7AhWr-zgGHaB4AjcQFnoECBQQAQ&usg=AOvVaw2YFiBm9MGnEiefEroZ5L2a

CO AND PO ATTAINMENT TABLE
(TO BE INCORPORATED BY AUTHOR)

Course outcomes (COs) for this course can be mapped with the programme outcomes (POs) after the completion of the course and a correlation can be made for the attainment of POs to analyze the gap. After proper analysis of the gap in the attainment of POs necessary measures can be taken to overcome the gaps.

Table for CO and PO attainment

Course Outcomes	Expected Mapping with Programme Outcomes (1- Weak Correlation; 2- Medium correlation; 3- Strong Correlation)											
	PO-1	PO-2	PO-3	PO-4	PO-5	PO-6	PO-7	PO-8	PO-9	PO-10	PO-11	PO-12
CO-1	3	1	3	3	-	-	-	-	-	-	-	-
CO-2	3	3	3	3	-	-	-	-	-	-	-	-
CO-3	3	1	3	1	-	-	-	-	-	-	-	-
CO-4	3	2	3	1	1	-	-	-	-	-	-	-
CO-5	3	3	2	3	1	-	-	-	-	-	-	-

The data filled in the above table can be used for gap analysis.

INDEX

D

E

F

G

H

I

❑❑